D0638637

THE TRUE 'INTREPID'

Sir William Stephenson
and the Unknown Agents

Bill Macdonald

**THE TRUE
'INTREPID'**
Sir William Stephenson
and the Unknown Agents

Canadian Cataloguing in Publication Data

Macdonald, Bill (William James), 1956-
    The True Intrepid: Sir William Stephenson
    And the unknown agents

Includes bibliographical references and index.
ISBN 1-894254-01-5

1. Stephenson, William Samuel, Sir 1896-
2. World War. 1939-1945--Secret service--Great Britain. I. Title.

D810.S8 1998   940.54'8641'092
C98-920154-6

First edition

Editor: Allan Safarik
Designer: N J Sawatsky

With thanks to:
Dolores Reimer
Arn Smith

Printed in Canada by Friesens Book Division

Publisher: Tim Lawson
TIMBERHOLME BOOKS LTD
159-19567 Fraser Highway
Surrey, British Columbia
Canada V3S 6K7

To the memory of William S Stephenson,
to the people who worked for him and for
the family he left behind
—Bill Macdonald

VITAL STATISTICS, MANITOBA.

Schedule A.—For Registration of a Birth by Parents, Guardians, Occupants, Medical Practitioners and Nurses.

Municipality *Winnipeg*

When born.	23ʳᵈ January 1897
Where born.	Winnipeg
Name.	William Samuel Clouston
Sex, Male or Female.	Male
Name and Surname of Father.	William Hunter Stanger
Name and Maiden Surname of Mother.	Sarah Goodina Johnston
Occupation or calling of Father.	Laborer
Name of Doctor in attendance, or of Midwife or other person if no doctor.	Dr Balderson
Signature, Description and Residence of Informant.	Wᵐ H. Stanger
When Registered.	
Name of Clerk.	
REMARKS.	

JUN 1 2 1990

I CERTIFY THAT THE WITHIN IS A TRUE COPY OF THE INSTRUMENT OF WHICH IT PURPORTS TO BE A COPY.

DIRECTOR OF VITAL STATISTICS

After being filled up this slip is to be sent to the clerk of the municipality in which the birth occurred. It will be transmitted postage free if the envelope is left unsealed, and has marked on the upper right hand corner, above the address, the words, "Vital Statistics Returns—."

EXTRACTS FROM THE LAW.

Persons residing in an unorganized district may effect registration of births with the clerk of any municipality contiguous to the district in which they reside.

The father of any child born in this Province, or in case of his death, inability, or absence, the mother, or in case of the death or inability of both parents, any person standing in place of the parents, or if none such there be, then the occupant of the house or tenement in which the child was born, or the medical practitioner or nurse present at the birth, shall, within thirty days from the date of such birth, give notice thereof to the clerk of the municipality in which such child was born, giving as far as possible the particulars required in Schedule A * * * which particulars shall be entered by the municipal clerk on the forms supplied him for that purpose. In registering the birth of an illegitimate child, it shall not be lawful for the name of any person to be entered, as the father, unless at the joint request, in writing, of the mother and of the person acknowledging himself to be the father; and in all cases of the registration of the birth of illegitimate children, the municipal clerk shall write the word "Illegitimate" in the column set apart for the name of the child, and immediately under the name, if any.

If any person herein required to report or record facts relating to births * * * refuses or neglects to do so within the time named such person shall be liable to a fine of not less than five dollars nor more than twenty-five dollars and costs.

5000-98-2-96

Contents

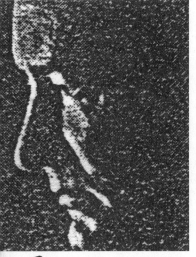

"You know what you must do at once. We have discussed it most fully, and there is a complete fusion of minds between us. You are to be my personal representative in the United States. I will ensure that you have the full support of all the resources at my command. I know that you will have success, and the good Lord will guide your efforts as He will ours. This may be our last farewell. Au revoir and good luck!"

—Stephenson recalling Churchill's instructions on leaving for New York

Rockefeller Center, headquarters of British Security Coordination

CRITISH SECURITY CO-ORDINATION

Section II
The Unknown Agents

Section III End Notes

Publisher's Foreword

"Just call me Bill."

I had the amazing good fortune to meet Sir William Stephenson in March 1985, at his home in Bermuda, when I was 31 years old. Due to his close relationship with my father, Colonel Tom Lawson of London, Ontario, he treated me like a grandson. Sir William was the most brilliant man I have ever met and at the same time warm, thoughtful, humorous and a great inspiration to me.

My mother Miggsie and my dad first met Sir William in the 1970's. In 1938 they spent their honeymoon in Bermuda and in later years returned for anniversaries. My grandfather, who had known Sir William briefly during WWII, suggested to my dad that he pay his respects. It was the beginning of a lasting friendship, for the two veterans found much in common. They had both fought for freedom and were especially concerned for the future of the free world, given the Communist threat of the times. They exchanged telexes and letters on a regular basis in addition to the yearly visits by my parents.

My father shared some of his correspondence with 'Intrepid' in his weekly family letters, and talked of him with great admiration. Dad attended the 1983 presentation ceremonies of the Donovan Award to 'Intrepid' in New York and later represented Sir William at the dedication of a monument to 'Camp X' at Whitby, Ontario in 1985. In September 1985, my father had the honour of presenting Manitoba's highest award, 'Chief Hunter' in 'The Order of the Buffalo Hunt,' to 'Intrepid' in Bermuda.

My dad asked for my input to create a banner for Sir William's 89th birthday in January 1985, to be hung on the outside of a small truck— we came up with, "Loads of Best Wishes from your friends." My father

7

suggested to me that if I wanted to take advantage of the opportunity to meet the most famous Canadian alive, and perhaps the greatest Canadian ever, he could arrange an introduction. I had read the international bestseller, *A Man Called Intrepid,* and was enthused to follow his advice. It changed my life.

In 1985 I had the honour of visiting with Sir William where he received me in the living room of his modest-sized home, overlooking the Atlantic Ocean. He was comfortable in a special 'vibrating' chair (my father got an identical one soon afterward due to a sore back), and I hung on to every word 'Intrepid' spoke. His daughter Elizabeth, who did driving, filing, and telexing duties, served us both small glasses of white wine during our dialogues. He had an impressive library of wartime memoirs and intelligence books. His speech was sometimes difficult to follow, but his mind razor-sharp and full of creative ideas.

Our conversations embraced an astounding number of topics, and we talked about many of the current political and military struggles that were taking place in many diverse parts of the globe. He told me how he was active with visits from US and Canadian political figures virtually on a daily basis. As an elder statesman, Sir William was a vibrant man who conducted a busy life that included sending and receiving many communiques. In November 1985, he was honoured when the new CSIS college was officially opened and named: 'The Sir William Stephenson Academy.'

'Intrepid' shared with me his thoughts on propaganda, referring to the Nazi, Goebbels, who said, "the bigger the lie, the more often repeated, the more effective it is." Sir William felt that anti-propaganda services from wartime, like OWI (Office of War Information) and Radio Free Europe (started by the Carnegie Foundation), should be re-activated. He agreed with me that modern music and musicians could help play a role due to their influence on young people (i.e. *We Are the World* concert, 45 major acts broadcast worldwide). He also thought if sloganeering could be modified by peace groups to call for 'disarmament with verification' (behind the Iron Curtain), that the threat of nuclear war could be reduced.

We had lunch twice during my visits, at a local restaurant and the Bermuda Yacht Club. The guests who accompanied us, including his good friend Tom Childs and Glynnis Stevenson, treated him with warm respect, as did the Bermudians we met. He was well liked by all.

'Intrepid' made time for me which I felt I could not possibly deserve, with all of the commitments and appointments he had with renowned visitors, like Ernest Cuneo. With the characteristic twinkle in his eyes, he said, "just call me Bill," but I replied that, out of respect, I had to address him as "Sir William." My son is named in his honour (Bryan Peter William). He gave me the codename 'Timex,' and I feel his spirit urging me onward every day.

I returned to the passion of my life, music and song writing, and was inspired to write the song, *The Quiet Canadian*. It became the title of my first album, which I dedicated to Sir William, my mom and dad, and their generation.

Sir William's passion was his service to others. I discovered a desire in myself, to want to contribute and in some way carry on the work to which he dedicated his life. Even at his advanced age, in frail health and after a full lifetime of work, his first and dominating thoughts each day were the future of the world and the welfare of all mankind. He was a pioneer in thinking of the world as a 'global village.'

In 1997, I was asked to make an address at the opening of The Sir William Stephenson Library in Winnipeg, by Syd Davy, President of the Intrepid Society of Winnipeg (dedicated to preserving and spreading the story of Sir William). It was on this occasion I met Bill Macdonald and I was deeply impressed by his intellect and his knowledge of Sir William's life. He told me of his manuscript and about the research he had undertaken to bring the true story of Sir William to light.

I kept in touch with Bill and sometime later I had the privilege of reading his work. *The True Intrepid: Sir William Stephenson and the Unknown Agents* tells the story of a remarkable man and sets the record straight on many issues that critics and professional espionage writers have argued about for decades. For the first time we learn about the Unknown Agents, many of them Canadians from every walk of life, who staffed BSC during the war years. There are many interviews with the BSC staff in Section II. It is appropriate that the work and achievements of communications genius Benjamin de Forest Bayly are discussed in depth for the first time in this volume.

'Intrepid' once said to me, "young men need pressure to perform." I believe this 'pressure' comes from within. The desire we all have to share the positive things in life with each other is a natural part of being human, and working together we can surely make this world a better place for all. Each of us can make a difference.

Sir William's sentiments were that the common enemies of mankind should no longer be each other but "poverty, disease, and ignorance."

Since meeting Bill Macdonald, I founded Timberholme Books Ltd., the vehicle for placing this astounding work is in your hands. (Thanks to my wonderful wife Karola for her support and patience, and to our super team—John Channer, Wendy Craig, Chris Churney, Tom Finkelstein, and especially to editor Allan Safarik, Dolores Reimer and designer Neil Sawatsky.) It is the documented story of a great man whose life is an inspiration to us all.

Lastly, a favourite saying from Sir William, taken from a telex to my father at the beginning of 1989, "A merry heart maketh good medicine."

Tim Lawson
September 1998
Langley, BC

Preface

This book retraces the life of World War II spymaster William Stephenson and the organization he created, British Security Coordination. Yet it didn't start out that way, and its course was predicated by a number of twists, some unique to the world of espionage.

Stephenson, known widely as 'A Man Called Intrepid,' died in Bermuda January 31, 1989. His war efforts were celebrated in his lifetime in two major books, but subsequently, some observers questioned certain aspects of his career, others attempted to discredit his reputation or reduce his role in history. He died relatively forgotten. Stephenson's obituaries said he was a Canadian, born in Winnipeg in 1896, a graduate of Argyle High School, and the son of a lumber mill owner. An interesting life come to a close. Rest in peace.

However, there were no lumber owners named Stephenson in Winnipeg at the turn of the century. No one with his parents' names lived in the city then. Manitoba Vital Statistics have no record of the ex-spychief's birth. There was no Argyle High School. So began the difficult task of trying to learn about the life of Bill Stephenson.

Basic facts about Stephenson's life were incorrect, but his biographic puzzle pieced together gradually, helped blaze a trail elsewhere. As this project evolved, curiosity about the real details of Stephenson's life and career also led to questions about why the wrong information appeared in the first place, and why it remained the recorded history.

Obviously a partial answer to the mystery around Stephenson's background was his occupation. In espionage lingo a 'legend' is a fake biography of a spy used to provide him or her with a cover. Stephenson, an important clandestine agent during a world war, was in a position where relatives, business associates, and friends could be possible targets for blackmail, kidnapping, or reprisals. They could provide clues to the agent's whereabouts, motives, modus operandi, and how to stop him. Stewart Menzies, Winston Churchill's World War II, MI6 chief, is said to have destroyed his personal papers when it appeared Britain could be invaded. Stephenson did more than that—essentially, becoming a man without a factual background. Untraceable. A perfect spy. A larger, perhaps unanswerable question is why the misinformation was continued long after the war, and in two biographies.[1]

Accurately following Stephenson's life on the Canadian prairie through to his undercover activities in the Second World War was a daunting challenge. It was possible to get answers from the two major books written on Stephenson and his career, but some reservations remained. Both authors seem to have had some 'cloak and dagger' experience, and both British-born writers knew Bill Stephenson prior to writing about him. Harford Montgomery Hyde, who wrote the first book, *The Quiet Canadian* (1962), worked for British Intelligence during the war. Obviously he had to deal with certain restraints in Britain's Official Secrets Act. William Stevenson, who wrote *A Man Called Intrepid* (1976) and *Intrepid's Last Case* (1983), admits to having some experience in 'operational intelligence.'[2] Both Hyde and Stevenson depict a fictitious life in Canada for Stephenson. Since these volumes are obviously flawed in coming to terms with Stephenson's early life it is difficult for a neutral observer to determine where, in the respective books, accuracy stops and fiction begins.

The books left a rather strange wake. The events leading to their publication, and the controversy they stirred up, are of interest in themselves. For example, Stephenson wanted Hyde's book published, and then he stifled it. He didn't want a second edition published and he quashed attempts to dramatize his story in film. Stevenson's *A Man Called Intrepid* portrays the ex-Winnipegger as a behind-the-scenes influence on many of the war's events and a confidant of Roosevelt and Churchill. Yet Stephenson and his organization are not mentioned in many, perhaps most, general histories of the war. One reviewer labeled the book, "from start to finish utterly worthless." At least one critic said Churchill didn't know Stephenson, his North American intelligence man.

The aftermath of the books, especially the Stevenson tomes, was not only recognition for Stephenson, but confusion about his career. Close associates, former employees, and some writers have found the life and work of William Stephenson somewhat baffling. The American author and historian Joseph Lash, who published the Churchill—Roosevelt correspondence wrote, "It is impossible on the basis of material available to American scholars to establish what is true, inflated, or deliberately distorted in William Stevenson's *A Man Called Intrepid.*"[3] Following Stephenson's death, his friend for more than thirty years Derek Bedson still wanted to know, "What was it he was appointed to, exactly, in New York?" Former wartime personnel of Stephenson's also have trouble distilling his story. "It's a murky world isn't it? It's hard to separate truth from fiction," said Patsy Sullivan, who was employed in Stephenson's inner office. Another BSC employee, the writer Roald Dahl, thought any author would have trouble retracing Stephenson's life and should face the fact that his ex-boss was an enigma. "And it had nothing to do with the Secret Service. It was the man himself."

The organization Stephenson headed used deception to conceal and influence, and in many instances the truth was never recorded, or will not be released. Information at the intelligence agency was on a need-to-know basis, and staff seldom knew what was transpiring in the next room. Another potential roadblock to a spy biographer is obtaining an unbiased overview, given the suspicious nature of some books in the espionage genre. If intelligence work is 'secret service,' it is somewhat incongruous that there are books that reveal the inside stories of secret service agencies.

These literary oxymorons are often written by people with some inside knowledge of the operation of an intelligence organization—either previous employees, or those who have had access to informers of the agencies. Many are written by people using pseudonyms and contain pages of non-footnoted information. Virtually all of the major books on diplomacy, the history of war, and politics are footnoted and well-annotated with extensive indexes. Books in the espionage genre, which for the most part have been written by people with academic credentials, often appear without much, if any supporting material.

A retired KGB Colonel, Mikhail Lyubimov, wrote that there was widespread belief in the former Soviet Union that such books were orchestrated by intelligence agencies.[4] The writer Bradley F Smith has expressed similar conclusions about certain books. In 1968 Stephenson called Kim Philby's Cold War memoirs *My Silent War*, "just another piece of Soviet propaganda designed to denigrate and ridicule the intelligence services of the western powers."[5] Any reviewer of the genre who attempts to use such books as background information should maintain a certain amount of skepticism and keep in mind many files are closed, and a primary objective of some operations is to misinform.

Unfortunately in Stephenson's case, facts verified in available documents may not be true—Stephenson himself is quoted as saying, "Nothing deceives like a document."[6]

There is some information relating to Stephenson and BSC in various American archives. There were a few Canadian documentaries done decades after the war in which some of the participants touched on Stephenson's activities. The Central Intelligence Agency's former staff historian published a new history in 1996 which includes information about Stephenson. The British are not as forthcoming. During the course of my research they withdrew material relevant to Stephenson's career. The previously available files of Montgomery Hyde were closed to the public by the British government after his death, partially reopened and closed again after this author went through the heavily weeded remains (see Appendix D). For Britain's Foreign Office it seems the less known about Sir William Stephenson, the man Churchill said was, "dear to his heart," the better.

BSC's papers were destroyed at the conclusion of the war, but a summary of some of the organization's undertakings was complied in Canada and completed in 1945. Still considered 'Top Secret,' sections of this elusive document, nicknamed the 'Bible,' were made available to this author by a person who wishes to remain anonymous.

Although espionage sources can sometimes be suspect, some basic information proved helpful during this project:

- There is an old spy adage: Espionage is a combination of information and disinformation. Loyalty and betrayal. Believe nothing. But remember everything.
- In certain academic modern history courses, some of the

reference books on reading lists related to spying are fiction. It is said a few books of fiction portray espionage more accurately than any text book. The author John Le Carré (former intelligence officer David Cornwell), for example, for years submitted his work to the British government for vetting.[7]

• During the course of this research, it became apparent that at least one ancient Chinese manuscript was still used for reference by military and defence organizations, sometimes word for word. Sun Tsz's, *The Art of War*, from approximately the sixth century, says: "Let your plans be dark and impenetrable as night, and when you move, fall like a thunderbolt." Tu Yu quotes a saying of T'ai Kung which has passed into a proverb: "You cannot shut your ears to the thunder or your eyes to the lightning—so rapid are they. Likewise, an attack should be made so quickly that it cannot be parried."

The German word 'Blitzkrieg,' used to describe their rapid attack, means lightning war.

The most important source of information about Stephenson and his career proved to be the people around him during the war. They made additional material available and the attempt to retrace the path of Stephenson unexpectedly led to new information about the war. The conclusion of this undertaking revealed that there were actually four jurisdictions contributing to the western Allies' behind-the-scenes maneuvering during the conflict: Britain, the United States, Canada, and the Stephenson organization.

Although they were called British Security Coordination, the Stephenson group were very much a law to themselves. They made many deals with other countries separately, and distributed information amongst the three western Allies. They controlled many of the secrets of the three countries, including ULTRA and MAGIC, and also had communication influence in the South Pacific and Asia. There were a number of British appointments at BSC, but essentially, Stephenson contacted his friends, put them to work, and had them find staff. They recruited thousands, mostly Canadians. Stephenson worked for no salary and financed many of the undertakings himself. The important work these people accomplished during the war has never been fully explored.

The approach for this book is first a chronicle of Stephenson's life, with an attempt to verify the factual. The second section details stories of people who worked with him at the time of crisis, what they did, and what they had to say. For the most part they have never before discussed their war work. From the totality of their stories one can surmise the enormity of Stephenson's undertaking and his accomplishments. What began as research into the house location of a Canadian prairie spymaster became a strange journey back to what has been called the greatest event in human history, the Second World War.

Bill Macdonald
Winnipeg, 1998

Introduction

Churchill's Spymaster: A Search for the Real 'James Bond'

Although Stephenson was from my hometown, Winnipeg, Manitoba, I knew little of the WW II spychief. I read Sir William's obituaries in the local paper and in the Canadian magazine *Maclean's*, with passing interest, but there seemed to be next to nothing in other media. It was Stephenson's death notice in the British *Manchester Guardian Weekly* that eventually set wheels in motion. The headline read: "Churchill's Spymaster—A Model For Bond."

> "Sir William Stephenson, the wartime spymaster whom Churchill called INTREPID has died (January 31, 1989) in the home he retired to in Bermuda, aged 93.
>
> ... Fleet Street had almost forgotten this remarkable figure until the publication of a biography (*A Man Called Intrepid*) in 1976, when (intelligence writer) Chapman Pincher was moved to call him "the nearest thing to James Bond, Callan, and 'M' rolled into one." In fact the Anglo-American show Stephenson ran in New York, the British Security Co-ordination has been described by another historian of the spy trade as 'the largest integrated intelligence network enterprise in history.'
>
> ...Ian Fleming was one to serve under him, and there's not much doubt that elements in Bond's make-up were derived from Stephenson, not least his love for fancy gadgetry."[1]

The obituary went on to say Stephenson was a decorated pilot of the First World War, the winner of a King's Cup air race, and a one time European lightweight boxing champion. He was notorious for his martinis served in huge glasses. The obituary concluded: "born Winnipeg, 1896, son of a lumber mill owner."

With this information I decided to write a freelance piece on the former Manitoban's childhood house and neighbourhood. I set off to do some research for an article but it turned out to be not quite that simple an undertaking.

Two Stephenson biographies, *The Quiet Canadian* (titled *Room 3603* in the United States), by Harford Montgomery Hyde (1962), and *A Man Called Intrepid* by William Stevenson (1976) were consulted. The foreword to *Room 3603*, written by Ian Fleming, played up the James Bond theme. Bond was a, "highly romanticized version of the true spy," Fleming wrote, Bill Stephenson was "the real thing." Neither of the books list a Canadian address for Stephenson, and they display an ignorance of Winnipeg, where Stephenson spent the first decades of his life. They state that Stephenson was from Point Douglas, "just outside Winnipeg," and "near Winnipeg." Actually Point Douglas is regarded as 'inner city' about ten blocks from the geographic centre of Winnipeg.

The books give Stephenson's birth date as January 11, 1896. Microfiche from the major newspaper of the time, the daily *Manitoba Free Press,* had no birth announcement within months of this date. Of course, not everyone put birth announcements in newspapers. Tracing the date through Manitoba's Department of Vital Statistics turned up no record of a William S Stephenson born January 11, 1896. However, government records might not be complete.

Although *A Man Called Intrepid* said the day Stephenson was born, January 11, 1896 was, "the coldest day in recorded history in that bleak part of the American continent,"[2] according to the paper's weather report, it was a typical winter day in Winnipeg.

Both books and Stephenson's obituaries say the former spychief's father was a descendent of Scottish settlers and a lumber mill owner. His mother, *A Man Called Intrepid* says, was of Norwegian ancestry. Winnipeg's *Henderson's* directories of streets, families, and businesses of the late 1800's indicate there were no lumber mill owners named Stephenson in Winnipeg at that time. According to the residential street index, no couple with Stephenson's parents' names: William Victor, and Christine Stephenson, lived in the city. The directories seldom listed the children of the house, so there was no sign of a young William S Stephenson living in Winnipeg around the turn of the century.

Stevenson's *A Man Called Intrepid* includes excerpts from

Stephenson's high school report card and quotes one of Stephenson's school teachers. Records from the time were sparse, so there was little chance of finding a class list or a report from Stephenson's alma mater, Argyle High School. This led to discovery there was no Argyle High School. At the time an Argyle Elementary School existed, but it was strictly for younger students, and didn't go higher than grade eight.

Hyde's *The Quiet Canadian* indicates Stephenson returned to Winnipeg for a short time from Europe after the First World War. The *Henderson's* directories revealed that there was a Wm S Stephenson living at 175 Syndicate Street in 1920. He worked for the Franco British Supply Company. Syndicate Street is in Point Douglas.

The woman living at 175 Syndicate Street had been at that address for about forty years, and she didn't know anything about William Stephenson or the history of her house. She recalled that two elderly women she didn't know had visited her place, and told her the house had been the home of a prominent relative. On another occasion, many years before, a woman in a local historical society told her she lived in the house of a famous person. Eventually the amateur historian was located.

"He wasn't a Stephenson," Elly Heber said. "They just took him in."

Heber said Bill Stephenson was born into another family, and was raised by the Stephensons, after his natural family could no longer afford to care for him. She learned about the Stephenson family from a now-deceased elderly Point Douglas resident she interviewed. She also recalled once meeting an elderly man named Gislasson who knew the Stephenson family.

When he was located Ragnar Gislasson said his father was a friend of Stephenson's adoptive father, Vigfus. Gislasson visited the Syndicate Street house during, and following, the First World War with his father and he frequently met Bill Stephenson. The former Sergeant-of-Arms at the Manitoba legislature recalled once seeing a picture of the young Stephenson returning to the European conflict in a Winnipeg newspaper in about May of 1918. Every page of every edition of the May, 1918, *Manitoba Free Press* was consulted. Finally a picture of Stephenson was found headlined: "Wins Military Cross." The picture was the same as a photo in *The Quiet Canadian*. The newspaper photo and caption underneath proved where Stephenson lived, and that his parents' names were different than recorded in his biographies.[3]

The Manitoba Legislature has information files on prominent Manitobans. The Stephenson file consists of a few local newspaper clippings which indicate Stephenson covertly visited Winnipeg in the summer of 1980, and was escorted around his old neighbourhood by Derek Bedson, a Winnipeg friend. When contacted, Bedson said he met Bill Stephenson in the 1950's in New York, when he was working for Canada's External Affairs Department. He knew very little about Stephenson's war career, and although he showed him around town he knew nothing of Stephenson's Winnipeg background. But once, he met someone who seemed to know a lot about Stephenson's early life— Manitoba's then Lieutenant-Governor, George Johnson. Why would he know?

"Do you know his racial background?" Bedson asked.

"It sounds quite WASPish."

But Johnson wasn't a WASP.

"He's pure Icelandic. That's the secret of them," Bedson said.

"That's the secret of the Icelanders. They suddenly get you. You think you've got another WASP, and you've got an Icelander."[4]

Johnson knew of the Stephenson family because of the close ties of Manitoba's Icelandic Canadian community. William Stephenson's parents were not Scottish immigrants or from Norway; they were Icelandic Canadians.

George Johnson, then the Queen's representative in Manitoba, was a retired doctor, and his father was a doctor. Stephenson's relatives were patients of his father, he said, and he knew some of Stephenson's relatives. Christine Stefansson, of Selkirk, Manitoba, was the sister of Stephenson's adoptive mother, Kristin. She saved a newspaper clipping from a small Icelandic paper that named Stephenson's natural parents, and gave a conflicting year of birth.

Eventually the provincial Department of Vital Statistics located a copy of the birth certificate of William Samuel Clouston Stanger, born January 23, 1897. Stanger later became better known as William Samuel Stephenson.

William Stephenson's unlikely Canadian roots: Ethnic background—

wrong. Parents names—wrong. Parent occupation—wrong. Birth date, day and year—wrong. Birth name—wrong. School—didn't exist.

Obviously a number of questions came up during this stage of research. Two popular biographies had been written, and most of the information on the first twenty years of the subject's life—his formative years—was bogus. Stephenson's relatives indicated they mysteriously stopped hearing from him in the 1930's when he was in England, and for the most part, never heard from him again. There hadn't been a 'falling out' or arguments in the family.

With the Winnipeg research more or less completed, a former wartime employee was found. Molly Phair was the only Winnipegger who worked for Stephenson's top-secret World War II spy organization, British Security Coordination, who still lived in the city. Phair was still somewhat reluctant to talk of her war work, but said she worked in BSC's Japanese Section, relaying coded messages. Such a department is not mentioned in the books on Stephenson.

Records of who worked for Stephenson's BSC were destroyed following the war. Former employees who attempted to have seniority recognized were told there was no record of them ever working there. Phair said that a few years previously, a meeting of former employees took place. There was a 'spy reunion' in Toronto in 1986, organized completely through word of mouth and mutual friends. The BSC alumni in Toronto helped point the way to people in other Canadian cities, and to contacts in Europe and the United States. Although they were sworn to secrecy, they were all eager to learn more about the life of William Stephenson.

The world of espionage and spymasters often does not lend itself to conventional biography. Stewart Menzies's biographer said his character was such that it would baffle anyone who tried to take his measure—especially the enemy. William Shirer said of the Abwehr's Wilhelm Canaris, "he was so shadowy a figure that no two writers agree as to what kind of man he was or what he believed in." Stephenson fit a similar mold.

It soon became evident there were many people who had strong views about Bill Stephenson one way or the other. Books about him have been called unreliable. As a result of these books, small details of his career, such as the dates he may have met certain people for dinner, came into question decades later.

Verbatim accounts often help circumvent author interpretations and disagreements about trivial details. Most of the employees in Section II of this volume have never previously talked in detail about their wartime experiences. Their opinions and contributions deserve an airing. BSC's records were destroyed so their recollections are unique. The section contains a lot of oral history. For the most part, I have attempted to step back and leave the facts as I found them.

SECTION I

The Life of William Stephenson

"The truth is incontrovertible. Panic may resent it; ignorance may deride it; malice may distort it, but there it is"
—*Winston S Churchill*

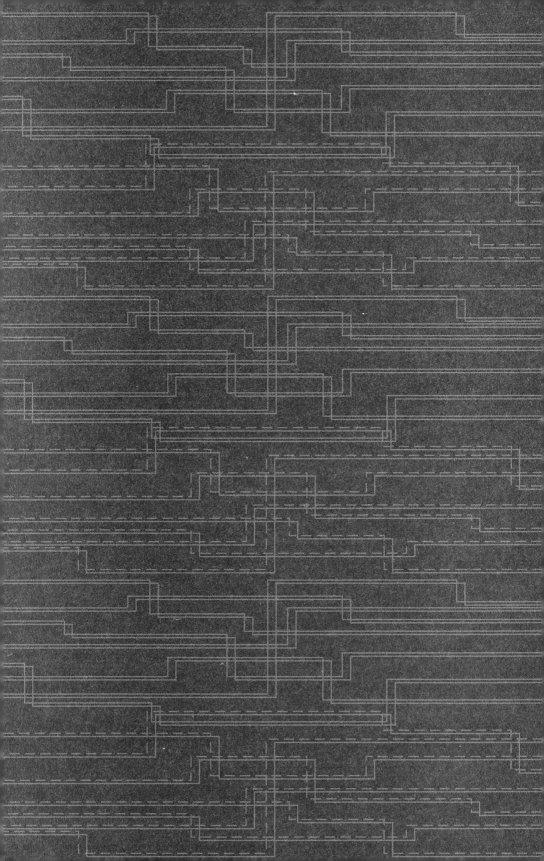

"I'm a Winnipegger."

Sir William Stephenson

The Globe and Mail (Toronto)

May 20, 1982

Where do spymasters come from?

During the Second World War a prominent Allied trio rose to power and established a symbiotic relationship which helped smooth the road to victory. Stewart Menzies (b. 1890) was born in London, raised in Scotland, where his family owned Europe's second largest distillery. His family controlled Hallyburton castle and estate, with the surrounding twelve farms, near the Royal Grounds at Balmoral. Menzies was raised an English gentleman: Ludgrove, Eton, the Life Guards, the Beaufort Hunt, and White's Club.

William 'Wild Bill' Donovan (b. 1883) was born in Buffalo, New York, the son of Irish immigrants. Donovan attended Catholic schools and his education was partially financed by a local Bishop. He attended university in Niagara Falls and at Columbia, and became a successful and prominent Wall Street lawyer.

And then there was Bill Stephenson from Winnipeg, Canada.

Winnipeg, the capital and largest city of Manitoba, lies midway between the Atlantic and Pacific Oceans in the heart of Canada. The town sprang up around the junction of the Red and Assiniboine Rivers, about a hundred kilometers north of the American border. To the west and south stretch thousands of miles of prairie. To the east and north is the rocky, lake-studded wilderness of the Canadian Shield.

The Inuit, Dene, Cree, and Assiniboine people have inhabited Manitoba for about 5000 years. The first Europeans established an outpost on the Hudson Bay coast in 1682. Eventually French traders arrived inland to the south from the east, and farmers from Scotland and Ireland began to settle the plains in the early 1800's.

The first immigrants from Iceland arrived in Manitoba in 1875. Many of the settlers fled the island nation because of a series of ravaging volcanic eruptions and severe winters.

In 1883, among the Icelandic immigrants were Karitas Gudmundsdottir and her family. Karitas, widowed twice in Iceland, emigrated to Canada with her adult children: three sons, Thorarinn Gudlaugsson, Gudmundur Gudlaugsson, Kristjan Gudmundsson, and two daughters Gudrun Gudmundsdottir, and Kristin Gudlaugsdottir. They sailed for North America, visited relatives in North Dakota, and then moved north to Manitoba. Kristin (b. 1858) was pregnant, and came to Canada with her new husband, Vigfus Stephenson (b. 1857).

By 1886 Vigfus and Kristin Stephenson were living in Winnipeg. Kristin's brothers and Vigfus worked in a Point Douglas lumber yard, Brown and Rutherford. The brothers later farmed in rural Manitoba near Rosser, and moved to Lundar in the Interlake area north of Winnipeg. Vigfus, Kristin, and young daughter Johinna and son Gudlauger ('Lou' b. 1883) Stephenson, continued to live in Winnipeg on the banks of the Red River, in the Point Douglas area, with a half dozen other families. Vigfus worked at a variety of labour jobs, and by 1893 the family saved enough for a house in Point Douglas on Syndicate Street.

There were many other Icelandic immigrants in the neighbourhood, and Kristin became good friends with Sarah Johnston. Sarah was also born in Iceland, and was the widowed daughter of John and Sarah Johnston. On April 7, 1894, at the age of 25, Sarah remarried to William Hunter Stanger, who was 39. Stanger was born in the Orkney Islands, but had been in Canada since 1869. Supply vessels of the Hudson Bay Company often stopped at the Orkney Islands on their way to Canada to pick up workers. It is likely Stanger was previously employed by the Hudson Bay Company at Fort Garry. At the time of his marriage to Sarah Johnston, Stanger worked at Ogilvie Flour Mills as a labourer, fireman, and carter.

Around the turn of the century, much of Winnipeg had a high infant mortality rate. Typhoid and small pox were rampant, and there were many medical complications caused from drinking the muddy water of the Red River. The Stanger's first child, Gloria Elizabeth Stanger, died at the age of eleven months in December of 1895, from peristalsis.[1] Their second child, a son, survived. On January 23, 1897, William Samuel Clouston Stanger was born. The Stangers later had a daughter Mary Isabella, in 1899, and a son, Andrew James Christie, in the summer of 1901. The young couple moved frequently in the Point Douglas area of Winnipeg, from 195 Gomez in 1895, to Higgins Street in 1896, to 180 Stephens Street two years later, and finally to 136 Angus. In 1899, William Stanger began suffering from a muscle disorder, likely brought on by a lifetime of labouring. On November 26, 1901, he died of progressive muscular atrophy.

The Stangers were not wealthy, and Sarah Stanger was left on her own with an infant, a two year old, and a four year old. For a time she worked as a char lady for Dr Charles Jamieson on Pacific Street, but it soon became evident she didn't have the financial resources to raise three children on her own. She approached her friend Kristin Stephenson, who once lived a street behind her, about what to do. It was decided she would give her son Bill to the Stephenson family to care for. The young William Samuel Clouston Stanger eventually became William Samuel Stephenson.

"His mother was a very special friend of my aunt's," remembers Bina Ingimundson, William Stephenson's cousin. "When her husband died, she had three children. There was no way she could support them. So she gave Bill to my aunt."

Point Douglas historian Elly Heber says when the young Bill Stanger became the young Bill Stephenson, the process was not similar to modern adoptions. "It was not straightforward at all," Heber said. "There was nothing done about adopting him."[2] It is not known what happened to Sarah Stanger and her children. By 1903 they had left the house on Stephen Street and there is no indication from Winnipeg street directories that they remained in the city. Relatives of the Stephenson family believe that she and her other two children may have moved to Chicago.

One of Vigfus Stephenson's friends, Hjalmar Gislasson, immigrated to Winnipeg from Iceland in 1900, and he also started work at the Ogilvie flour mill in Point Douglas. Hjalmar and his son Ragnar frequently walked across the Louise Bridge from Newton Street to Syndicate Street to visit the Stephensons. Point Douglas was an area full of new immigrants, Ragnar remembers, and they frequently socialized and helped each other out. "All the Icelanders were together there. They gathered in the same places," he said. The Red River was only meters from the Stephenson's Syndicate Street house. Park area, with trails through the woods worthy of a young boy or girl's explorations, surrounded the river. Gislasson, born in 1906, remembers Kristin Stephenson was generous and kind, and she filled him full of cookies and milk whenever he went over. He often visited with Bill who was nine years older than he, but the youngest in the Stephenson family. "He wasn't a big guy," Gislasson remembers. "He was a good looking kid."

Stephenson was a very quiet child who kept to himself when he was little, Elly Heber remembers being told. He was studious and a bit of a loner. "I don't think he ever bragged. He kept things to himself," Heber says. Irv Stefansson, a second cousin remembers hearing his relatives say Bill Stephenson had a photographic memory. He could walk into a room, walk out, and when questioned afterward, he could remember every object that was in it.

Vigfus Stephenson's place of work

The Stephenson family spent many summer holidays on the Breckman farm near Lundar, and Bill helped in the store and learned to ride a horse.[3] He became close friends with Harold Stephenson, his brother Lou's son. Harold was an excellent athlete and both he and Bill Stephenson liked watching boxing. Following a night of boxing at Winnipeg's amphitheater, Stephenson nicknamed Harold 'Bun' after one of the boxers.[4]

Stephenson's adoptive father Vigfus worked as a labourer in the nearby Brown and Rutherford lumber yard. [Vigfus was not a common name at the time. Enumerators for *Henderson's* directories had a few problems with the spelling, listing him as Wigfus (1896, 1898), William (1900), Vadfus (1901, 1902), Vegfos (1913), Vegos (1914, 1916), Vitfus (1919, 1920), and Vikfus (1918).] Kristin stayed at home and raised the children. Gudlauger and Gudmindur ('Mindy' b. 1891) became successful plumbers. Julianna (b.1894) was a secretary. Johinna (Jennie b.1884) married Bill Hodgkins and raised a family in Winnipeg.

Bill Stephenson attended the nearby Argyle Elementary School which was built in 1895 at the cost of $30,000, and was considered very contemporary. The school incorporated many features considered up-to-date including slate blackboards, cloak rooms running the width of classrooms, and "new fangled electric bells."

Children were not legally required to attend school in Manitoba until the Compulsory Attendance Act was passed in 1916. Argyle was a grade one to eight school, not a high school, and Stephenson completed grade six. Stephenson's foster brother Lou Stephenson is quoted as saying young Bill's six-year scholastic career was "undistinguished," but "he was a tiger-cat for debate."[5]

After completing grade six, Bill Stephenson left school, perhaps out of economic necessity, and started to work for the Sprague Lumber Yard. Later he worked as a telegram delivery boy for the Great North West Telegraph Company on Main Street. After a few years with the firm he eventually did some 'keying.' "People didn't have a chance to get an education all the time," says Bina Ingimundson, "and I don't think Uncle Vigfus and Auntie Steena really had the money. Julianna was a private secretary, and Mindy and Lou both learned their plumbing, what you call apprentices, somewhere. In later years, Lou and Mindy were successful plumbers, but the Stephensons weren't well off. He delivered telegrams for the telegraph company. That's what he did for a long time."

It is difficult to hypothesize if any events in Bill Stephenson's early life helped prepare him for a career in espionage. Many years later Stephenson said his only prerequisite experience was reporting on German military industrial build-up during the 1930's. He did not undergo extensive formal training, or work his way up Britain's SIS hierarchy. However, some events in pre-war Winnipeg may have remained with an impressionable youth endowed with photographic memory.

The Stephenson's residential district went into decline as he grew up. When it was first established, Point Douglas, encircled by river on three sides, was a desirable residential area, and many of the founders of the city had homes there.[6] But in the 1880's, Canadian Pacific's main rail line bisected the neighborhood and the area began to transform. Factories and saw mills gradually moved in, to be close to the train, and the area became a less desirable housing district. Montreal-based Ogilvie Milling Company, where William Stanger and many Icelandic immigrants worked, finished their large flour mill on Higgins Street in 1882, just up the street from where Stephenson was born. A typhoid epidemic swept the area in 1904 and 1905, and there were frequent cases of small pox. Numerous health problems occurred due to contaminated drinking water until 1919, when an aqueduct piped in fresh water to Winnipeg, from Shoal Lake, near the Ontario border. To compound the problems of the neighbourhood, Point Douglas became Winnipeg's 'red light' district.

Tagging along with Winnipeg's fast growth and prosperity, came social problems and vice. When the city was incorporated in 1874, the new city council quickly received complaints calling for the removal of "houses of ill fame." In 1883, an association of church ministers and citizens petitioned City Hall about the houses of ill repute. The city responded by creating segregated areas for prostitution, and instituting regular police patrols in those areas. Unfortunately for the Stephensons, prostitution was sequestered into two small streets, Rachel (renamed Annabella) and McFarlane in Point Douglas, the streets next to Syndicate Street and only meters away from where the Stephensons were bringing up their family. By 1909, there were a hundred bawdy houses in Winnipeg.[7] In the spring and summer of 1910, living on the west side of Syndicate was similar to having a seat at an outdoor peep show. On McFarlane, blinds were seldom drawn and the business of the houses sometimes spilled out into the backyards, and could be easily viewed from Syndicate.[8] Syndicate Street residents protested to City Hall.

"It was the red light district," remembered Ragnar Gislasson. "On Annabella street there were prostitutes in all the houses. It was considered a pretty tough area." Syndicate Street had become the proverbial 'wrong side of the tracks'.

Similar social problems were occurring all over North America, and American groups such as the National Vigilance Committee, and the Alliance for the Suppression and Prevention of the White Slave Traffic expanded to Canada. A lobby group, the Moral and Social Reform

League, formed in Winnipeg in 1907, consisted of a number of community and religious groups, including the Icelandic Lutheran Synod. The League started a campaign to rid the city of the prostitution in Point Douglas, and produced a report entitled: *The Problem of Social Vice in Winnipeg*, penned by a prominent clergyman, Rev. Dr F DuVal. The paper emphasized that there was tacit approval of prostitution and segregated vice from the city's police and elected politicians, and it chastised the shirking of their duties.

Winnipeg politicians ignored the clergyman's report and groups such as the Board of Trade stayed out of the issue completely, in effect lending silent approval to the status quo.[9] But in November of 1910 the situation changed, when the Toronto paper *The Globe & Mail* interviewed the head of the Moral and Social Reform League, Rev. Dr JG Shearer, and publicized the problems in Winnipeg. Eastern headlines read: "Social Evil Runs Riot in Winnipeg, Vice District Growing, Every Den an Illicit Liquor Dive."[10] The Toronto reports fueled the topic in Winnipeg, and Point Douglas vice became an issue in the next civic election. *The Manitoba Free Press* reported that Winnipeg City Council thought the Toronto stories were simply part of the election campaign of reform-backed mayoralty candidate ED Martin.[11] Eventually the vice issue became more obscure, and the focus was diverted from social problems in Point Douglas, to a defence of Winnipeg's reputation. The incumbent mayor, Sanford Evans, did not comment publicly on remarks to the eastern press, but editorials in the Winnipeg newspaper *The Telegram*, owned by Evans, labeled Rev. Shearer a "monomaniac" and a "liar, and a slanderer."[12] With the vocal and strongly partisan support of *The Telegram,* and the less active support of the *Free Press*, the mayor succeeded in pushing the issue of the large residential red light district into background, and replaced it with the issue of defending Winnipeg's 'good name.'[13] The reformers were even forced to defend their integrity. At one meeting, the Reform League-backed candidate Martin had to defend himself against charges that he was a candidate of foreign agitators.[14]

Evans won the election and the status quo prevailed. Brothels on Annabella and McFarlane streets operated for another thirty years. The Stephensons didn't stay around to watch. Following World War I, they moved out of the neighbourhood to Winnipeg's west end, and rented out their Syndicate Street home.

■

There was an incident in young Bill Stephenson's life which must have stayed with him over the years; he became embroiled in the manhunt and capture of a bizarre and infamous Manitoba criminal of the time.

Tranquillity in the rural village of Plum Coulee, Manitoba, had been shattered the afternoon of December 3, 1913, when the local bank manager HM Arnold was shot and killed during a robbery by a disguised man. A twenty-one jewel watch later found in a get-away car was traced through a Winnipeg pawn shop's records as belonging to John Krafchenko. Krafchenko had a lengthy criminal record, and was rumoured to have been seen in the vicinity of the bank. "He has a genius for robberies requiring desperate action," *The Manitoba Free Press* reported.[15]

At the time Krafchenko was 33 years old, and recently released from Stony Mountain Penitentiary, north of Winnipeg. His criminal activity began when he robbed a bank manager transporting funds between Plum Coulee and Winkler in southern Manitoba. Krafchenko escaped across the American border on a bicycle, and he was later traced to Romania, southern Europe, South America, Montana, and Prince Albert, Saskatchewan, where he was captured, and sentenced to two years in prison. Krafchenko escaped and fled to Winnipeg. He was eventually recaptured, and after his release from prison, he worked as a machinist under an assumed name in the St. Vital area of the city. Krafchenko was said to have worked as a civil engineer and locksmith, and was supposed to have had a working knowledge of fifteen different trades, and speak five languages. He also toured different parts of Canada as a wrestler named Pearl Smith. He was described as, "One of the most cultured men imaginable. He knows more about police work than most of the force." Krafchenko reportedly idolized as his hero William Miner, a renowned bank and train robber, known as the Gentleman Bandit, or the Gray Fox.[16] Following the Plum Coulee murder-robbery, photographs and descriptions of Krafchenko were sent across Canada and the northern

United States. Posses were organized and sent out to scour the surrounding rural districts for him.

Less than two weeks later, the manhunt was successful. "Krafchenko, Desperado, Captured by Police in Winnipeg House," screamed a headline of the December 11, 1913, *Manitoba Free Press*. The accused was holed up in a rooming house on College Avenue, with two loaded revolvers, and blood-stained Bank of Montreal money. Reportedly he was planning to leave Winnipeg disguised as a woman. Krafchenko was first sighted in Winnipeg on William Avenue, where he had moved into a rooming house posing as a doctor named Fairchild. The landlord there said Dr Fairchild frequently talked about his medical cases, and the operations he had performed, and even treated one of the lodgers for a toothache. A witness later said Krafchenko moved from the William Avenue house to College Street because he was afraid that he was 'spotted.' Precise details of Krafchenko's identification and apprehension were not released.

According to Bina Ingimundson, young Bill Stephenson was instrumental in Krafchenko's capture. His delivery job for Great North West Telegraph took him all over the city, and he identified the fugitive master of disguise. "He was delivering on a bicycle, and he saw him. He notified the police," Ingimundson says.

Because of the mystique surrounding Krafchenko in the community, secrecy was used as a shield for informers. Newspaper reports said police, "seemed unwilling … to give out the exact details of how they found Krafchenko." They said that certain persons had to be covered, or some of Krafchenko's friends were liable to cause the 'stool pigeons' to go missing some morning and another mystery might be added to the annals of Winnipeg police history.[17]

Winnipeggers excitedly crowded the court house to get a glimpse of Krafchenko, and later, near the police station where he was held, at least 300 people filled the street. But the accused thief and murderer treated his preliminary hearing with a bored annoyance. "Oh get through this thing so I can go rabbit shooting in the spring," he said in court.

The court was told that when Krafchenko was captured, amongst his possessions was a fountain pen, that was possibly filled with explosive nitroglycerin. When this was announced, "it caused every man in the audience to sit bolt upright with ears strained forward to catch this latest and remarkable phase of Krafchenko's craftiness." After his arrest, Krafchenko asked for his possessions, and notified police about his pen. He advised that the fountain pen be emptied into a nearby sink. Police slowly drained the liquid into a full basin of water. The police officer who emptied the pen said the nitroglycerin looked a lot like ordinary ink, but nevertheless he was in a hurry to get rid of it, and Krafchenko looked relieved when the pen was emptied. He said it was a load off his mind. "If one of the officers had let it drop, it would have blown them all to pieces."[18]

Following the preliminary hearing, on January 9, 1914, Krafchenko was committed to trial on murder and robbery charges. The next morning he escaped from his third floor prison cell. Police said Krafchenko was provided with a revolver, a skeleton key, and rope to break out from a window, about thirty feet above ground. Newspapers speculated about accomplices, "under the spell of his fascinating personality," and called him the most dramatic and magnetic character in the history of Manitoba crime. There were even some indications Manitobans were actually rooting for the charismatic criminal. "Desperado's Sensational Escape Appeals Strongly to Women of Winnipeg," said a headline in *The Winnipeg Telegram*. This brought letters of protest and condemnation from many local women, including Nellie McClung, the famous Canadian suffragette. McClung called such comments, "idiotic driveling that discredited women as a class." A Royal Commission was created by the provincial government to investigate the escape, and editorial cartoons portrayed Krafchenko in a forest, hunting rabbits.[19]

One person likely not enthused with Krafchenko's breakout, and the accused's popularity, was young Bill Stephenson, a possible 'stool pigeon.' Ingimundson remembers, "He was just a kid on a bicycle."

The Royal Commission investigating the escape met in secrecy, and there was a prevailing sense of shock, urgency, and tension surrounding the proceedings. Even police constables appeared edgy. Some were reluctant to be identified publicly after they testified, and others used false names when questioned by newspaper reporters. A mysterious eavesdropper was detained for covertly listening to the proceedings through a partition door.[20]

On January 18, 1914, Krafchenko was recaptured in a Winnipeg block. Within twenty-four hours, five other men were taken into custody for aiding his escape, including his attorney, a legal clerk, a former building trade official, and a prison guard. Krafchenko was eventually found guilty of robbery and murder. He was hanged in Winnipeg in the summer of 1914.

The observant young man on the bicycle who turned in a desperate criminal and was labeled a 'stool pigeon' by a sensational press became anonymous. Secrecy and discretion entered William Stephenson's life at a young age. One wonders if Stephenson remembered the charismatic, athletic, and cultured Krafchenko in future discussions with his friend and neighbour in Jamaica, Ian Fleming.

2 World War I

When World War I started in 1914, Stephenson was working for the Great North West Telegraph company on Winnipeg's Main Street, but by the winter of 1916 he decided he wanted to contribute to the Great War. He enlisted in the 101st Battalion, Winnipeg Light Infantry, on January 12, 1916.[1] Stephenson's incorrect birth date, January 11, 1896 appears in his enlistment papers,[2] and his occupation is listed as telegrapher. His medical description at the time said that Stephenson had brown eyes, dark hair, and a dark complexion. He was 5' 5" tall with a 32" expanded girth. The medical officer who examined the young recruit wrote, "passed as bugler," under cause for unfitness. He was then sent to train at unluxurious, frigid facilities near Winnipeg. Stephenson complained about his lot in a post card to his friend Harold (Bun).

> *Dear Harold*
> *We arrived in this forsaken dump and had to sleep in the cold with nothing on the first night because the blankets were held up. I was sorry I didn't see you again Saturday—It was because the car I was in got a blow-out. Give my regards to everyone.*
> *Bill*
> *I'll be in town soon I think.*

Back at a family gathering in Winnipeg Stephenson became irritated when he found out that his cousin Bina Ingimundson's foster brother, Joe Breckman, joined an army group that was used for recruiting and wasn't going overseas. "I remember when Joe joined the 108th battalion, Bill was very upset," recalled Ingimundson. "He said Joe should never have joined that battalion. Joe never went overseas but he became quite a good trombone player."

Stephenson sailed to Britain on the SS Olympic, landing on July 6, 1916. Upon arrival he sent Harold an army issue, pretyped generic post card to say he was there safely. For security reasons, it revealed no details.

Somewhere in England.
Safe at port of disembarkment.
Nothing unusual to relate, and daily drill, physical exercises, games and music all added to the pleasures of the journey.
Will send letter on arrival at headquarters.
Bill
Cpl. W Stephenson
No. 700758
101st Overseas Battalion (WLI)
Canadian Expeditionary Forces
c/o Army Post Office, London

Soon after arriving in England, Stephenson was transferred to the 17th battalion and he likely was sent to France in mid July, 1916. He was wounded and gassed less than a week later and returned to England to convalesce at Sherncliffe, and train near Oxford and at Exeter College. It took him about a year to recover. During that time he took courses in the theory of flight, internal combustion engines, communications and navigation.[3] While at the school of aeronautics the former telegraph operator set a speed record for wireless communication.[4] He also canoed, trained with various weaponry, and did some instruction.

It is conceivable that during this time Stephenson met for the first time, William Donovan, the future head of the America's Office of Strategic Services (OSS). *A Man Called Intrepid* tells of a meeting between Stephenson and Donovan during the First World War, but it has also been written that Donovan didn't remember meeting Stephenson before 1940. However according to a biographer of Donovan, he wrote in a letter to his wife Ruth that he met an unidentified Canadian in London during the war and they dined together.[5]

Stephenson was promoted to acting Sergeant in September of 1916, and later became a full Sergeant. In April of 1917, he joined the Cadet Wing of the Royal Flying Corps for flight instruction.[6] Stephenson trained near Denham, and received his wings at an RFC field at South Carlton, Lincolnshire. In February of 1918 he went to France with the RAF.[7] When he reported for duty with the 73rd Squadron the orderly officer was another Canadian, Thomas Drew-Brook. As a result of the gas attack, Drew-Brook said later, "Stephenson still looked pale and rather delicate." He took one look at the novice pilot and, "with my usual perspicacity," privately advised his flight commander that, "we should let A Flight have him." It was to no avail. They were stuck with the diminutive Canadian flyer. Tommy Drew-Brook later became Bill Stephenson's best friend.[8]

During the war Stephenson began to box competitively and participate in service competitions as a featherweight. In France, he made friends with a burly American heavyweight, Gene Tunney. "He was an excellent boxer and won the featherweight championship of the Inter Allied Games (at Amiens)," Tunney said in a 1960's radio documentary. "Everybody admired him. He was quick as a dash of lightning. He was a fast, clever featherweight … he was a fearless and quick thinker."[9] Two decades after meeting Tunney, Stephenson counted on his friendship to covertly open doors in the United States.

Stephenson was evasive about his boxing weight in later years. He cabled William Stevenson in 1974 during the writing of *A Man Called Intrepid*, to say that he boxed in a heavier division.

ANY REFERENCE BOXING IT IS LIGHTWEIGHT NOT REPT NOT BANTAM BUT NOT TOO IMPORTANT ONE WAY OR OTHER STOP.[10]

In the beginning, according to Drew-Brook, Stephenson did nothing spectacular in 73rd Squadron but he was where he should have been. This changed during March of 1918, when Stephenson's Sopwith Camel was attacked by two enemy aircraft and severely damaged. He landed out of control and was nearly killed. Stephenson emerged from his plane, "as mad as hops," Tommy Drew-Brook remembered in a letter to Montgomery Hyde. "He immediately got into another machine and the first thing we knew there was a report that he shot down two Germans. He never stopped going from then on, until his career was ended by a Frenchman."[11]

Stephenson was awarded the Military Cross in April 1918, and the Distinguished Flying Cross in August 1918. There has been some controversy about exactly how many enemy aircraft were shot down by Stephenson. According to an authority at Cross & Cockade International, a World War I Aviation Society, Stephenson shot down a total of twelve aircraft. The French paper *Avion* reported following his disappearance in 1918, when Stephenson was a prisoner of war, that he had previously shot down eighteen aircraft and two kite balloons.[12] It is not known how many he shot down the day he was taken prisoner. Other reports say he shot down as many as twenty-six aircraft. In any event he became a highly regarded fighter pilot. The French paper *Avion* mourned his disappearance.

When Captain WS Stephenson M.C., D.F.C. C. de G. was reported "missing," it wrote:

"The brief notice printed above is from the French casualty list and brings a sorrowful message to Aviators on every Allied Aerodrome. France too has good reason to cherish the memory of this brilliant young Canadian pilot and to pray that he descended alive.

It appears that on the afternoon of July 28th, Captain Stephenson decided to make a lone patrol of the line. Regular Scout patrols had been canceled for the day owing to stormy weather.

About four miles within the Bosche Lines, just over F——, one of our reconnaissance machines was being attacked by seven Fokker Biplanes which had been hiding in the dense clouds a few hundred meters above. According to American balloon observers, a British machine of the pattern Stephenson flew (which later proved to be Stephenson) suddenly dove out of the clouds and without hesitation attacked the leader of the enemy formation, shooting him down in flames. There followed a terrific battle in which the daring captain made excellent strategic use of the clouds and succeeded in shooting down another German machine, while a third went spinning to the ground out of control. The others then disappeared in the clouds and Stephenson was seen turning sharply toward the French reconnaissance machine and rapidly overtaking it. When just alongside the French machine the British scout suddenly sideslipped and dropped in a series of nosedives and stalls as if the pilot was unconscious or the controls had been shot through. The observers then lost sight of the scout and nothing further has been heard of the courageous and dashing pilot.

'Icelandic Flyer' is the caption for this item about Stephenson in Votgorold, *May 11, 1918, an Icelandic language newspaper of the time*

Previous to this engagement, Captain Stephenson had destroyed two enemy kite balloons and eighteen aeroplanes. It was said of him, that at the battle of Chateau-Theirry he, 'lived in the air,' over the River Mairn and helped in great measure, with thousands of well placed machine gun bullets, to prevent enemy engineers from rigging their pontoons. A Canadian Tommy who knew the horrors of the Front Line remarked, 'You can always know when Steve is over. He comes right down to say hello and never forgets the boys on the ground when things are hot.'

His pilots are searching keenly for the remains of his machine. They will be pleased to learn—as will all of France— that Captain Stephenson, a pilot of superlative skill and courage, a sound flight commander and good sportsman, has now been awarded the Croix de Guirre avec Palme by the President of the French Republic. It is sincerely hoped that this gallant Canadian is unhurt and, at worst, a prisoner."[13]

Tommy Drew-Brook, in a letter to Montgomery Hyde, recalled the end of his friend's fighter pilot career. "The unfortunate French observer saw this machine out of the corner of his eye, spun his gun and fired a burst into Bill which killed his engine and put one bullet through his leg. He landed just in front of the German front line, crawled out of his machine, and headed for our lines, but unfortunately a German gunner hit him again in the same leg and that stopped him and resulted in him being captured. Bill did not bail out over German territory. We didn't have parachutes."[14] Back in Winnipeg following the war, Ragnar Gislasson remembers Stephenson describing a somewhat less exotic capture. "He remembered the plane hitting the ground and then he lost consciousness."

Stephenson was taken prisoner and interned at Holzminden. He found confinement very boring and to keep busy he started stealing small items from the guards. A fellow Winnipeg prisoner, John Huggard, didn't like Stephenson's tactics, as he even stole from a deceased officer. Later Drew-Brook also became a prisoner of war and he was hospitalized at Holzminden. One day an excited Bill Stephenson came to visit him and he furtively showed him a tin opener he had stolen from a guarded room, where canned goods were stockpiled. "He was full of delight at the success of his theft, but then when I failed to see any significance beyond this, he showed me the can opener had been patented in 1915, which meant that the Germans had been unable to patent it in any other country than Germany, Austria, and Turkey." Stephenson told Drew-Brook he planned to escape from the camp as soon as possible, and he was going to take the can opener with him, and patent it in every other country in the world. "He did escape and took the can opener with him, and I think he did patent it and I believe was successful in making considerable money out of it. I think Bill is still a little sensitive about this story."[15]

Stephenson was more than a little sensitive about it. He later called the story apocryphal.[16] An editorial missive from Stephenson, cited in a June 23, 1962, letter from Dick Ellis to Hyde said, "All references nonexistent tin opener must be eliminated."[17] There is no reference to the can opener in either *The Quiet Canadian* or *A Man Called Intrepid*.

Stephenson escaped the prisoner of war camp—there are no recorded details—shortly before the end of the war, and by 1919 he was back living in Winnipeg with his parents on Syndicate Street. The young veteran couldn't forget his European experience. He kept a stolen picture of the POW camp commander for years. He joined the Aero club of Manitoba, and he often talked of desperate situations of the war to his family and friends. He didn't however, talk about himself or of his heroics in winning medals. Ragnar Gislasson, a frequent visitor to the Stephenson home, remembers quite clearly Stephenson's stories of the war, but didn't know he had won any medals.

He still had his can opener. Stephenson set his sights on the business world. He and a friend, Charles Wilfrid Russell, started a company called Franco-British Supply. The company became the patentees and manufacturers of the can opener, which they called the Kleen Kut. The can opener Stephenson took from the German camp was a twin handled, clamp-style manual can opener still used today. When it opens a can, it leaves a smooth edge. Before the Kleen Kut, can openers were quite primitive and lids of cans were basically hacked off, leaving a jagged surface. The firm were also agents for hardware, stainless cutlery, the Duntley Magneto Break Timer and automotive accessories. Working out of a seventh floor office on Winnipeg's Main Street, the duo hired staff, advertised all over North America, and the sky seemed the limit.

Irvin Stefansson, a second cousin of Stephenson's, remembers being told his relative was an energetic businessman who had an active mind, and was very inventive. Around this time Stephenson devised a new type of mouse trap, and took samples out to Lundar to convince the Breckman brothers to sell it in their store.

Bina Ingimundson recalls her cousin Bill was seldom idle. "He was always busy at something. He had a wonderful convertible. He always seemed to have money because he delivered telegrams for a long time." Ingimundson remembers as a confirmation gift from her parents in 1919, she was given a trip to Winnipeg, and she stayed with the Stephensons on Syndicate Street. Cousin Bill acted as the perfect host and showed the fourteen-year old and her sister the town. "I'll never forget Bill had a convertible car. He took my sister and I for a drive all over City Park and Winnipeg, showing us the city, and just entertaining us. It was marvelous. He was so nice to us, and it was the same in the home. Always treated us like, well ... like cousins."

In some accounts it is reported Stephenson lectured following the First War at the University of Manitoba. The University has no record of him being on staff, and none of Stephenson's living relatives believe this to be the case, or can recall that Stephenson had any special educational expertise. "He was selling pots and can openers," his cousin Bina says. "I don't think so. As far as I know, he quit school in grade six. Started to work, delivering telegrams at first on bicycle. All his education is what he's picked up on his own."

Bill Stephenson moved out of the troubled Point Douglas district later in 1919, and into a rented house at 988 Ingersoll Street, in Winnipeg's West End. The Stephenson family moved in with him shortly afterward, and they rented out their Syndicate Street house. In the 1920's the Stephenson family moved to the Verona apartments on Victor Street, close to their Church, First Lutheran at 580 Victor. The Stephensons rented out the Point Douglas house until 1931, when Vigfus sold it to his son-in-law, Bill Hodgkins.

In September of 1919, Stephenson took part in Winnipeg's social event of the year, and he was officially decorated with the Distinguished Flying Cross by a man who would have a direct influence on his later activities, the Prince of Wales. Stephenson and over 160 others were awarded their war decorations by the future King Edward VIII, later the Duke of Windsor, at a large presentation at the University Campus, and a reception followed at the new Provincial Legislature building. The City of Winnipeg dressed up for the function, spending a thousand dollars on flags and bunting. The mayor appealed to the citizens of Winnipeg to decorate their own premises in a manner befitting the "unique event" in civic history. British flags were flown on all light standards on Portage Avenue and Main Street to greet the Royals and double streamers stretched across the streets at various intersections. The Canadian Pacific Railroad decorated the train station and the Royal Alexandra Hotel, "creating a blaze of color and illumination." A large stage, displaying Royal standards bearing the Prince's Coat of Arms was constructed in front of Winnipeg's City Hall. Carpeting was extended from the stage to the curb, surrounded by palms and others plants supplied by the city's parks board. Electric lights were strung all over Winnipeg's City Hall to spell out: 'The Prince. God Bless Him.' [18]

Stephenson's association with the Duke two decades later was covert and less formal.

Stephenson attended a reception and dance at Government House for the Duke with Margaret Farquhar. "I don't think that he was any particular boyfriend, but it was a big event, and they all attended, and she went with him," says Margaret Jamieson, Margaret Farquhar's daughter. Stephenson's date came from a family of ten, and he was a good friend of one of Margaret's brothers, Charlie Farquhar.

Stephenson and Russell formalized their business relationship in January 1921, and filed incorporation papers. The company moved to 57 Victoria Street and the young entrepreneurs went about raising more capital. According to Ragnar Gislasson, Vigfus Stephenson contributed a large amount, and he became one of his son's company's shareholders. Bill Stephenson also canvassed many in the Icelandic Canadian community, and other relatives for loans.

The new company, Stephenson-Russell Limited, was incorporated February 2, 1921, "to carry on the business of Manufacturers Agents, Exporters and Importers of hardware goods, cutlery, auto accessories, groceries, timber, and goods, wares and merchandise of every description." It was also created to apply for patents and trademarks, and to sell stock. William Samuel Stephenson and Charles Wilfred Russell were the corporation agents. James Francis Pike, a broker, and Clive Jeffrey Macleod, and John Campbell Broadfoot, two Winnipeg lawyers, were the other directors of the new company. The amount of capital stock was to be $30,000 divided into three hundred shares of one hundred dollars each, and the directors each took one free share.

The two businessmen bought a couple of vehicles, and Russell spent a lot of time on the road trying to market company goods through stores in rural communities. Stephenson-Russell made contact with some of the pioneers of radio such as Radio Distributing, and Radio Technology Laboratories of Newark, New Jersey, and Haynes Radio of New York. Stephenson took a lot of merchandise to his relatives in Lundar, and he and GK Breckman tried to set up a hardware store. Breckman eventually became a shareholder in Stephenson-Russell. John Huggard, who was in the same prisoner-of-war camp as Stephenson, also became a shareholder. Stephenson's attempt to set up a new hardware store in Lundar using his stock, was unsuccessful. "That didn't work out. The town was too small for a hardware store there," his cousin remembers.

Unfortunately very little worked out for Stephenson-Russell. Although Stephenson's poached can opener was an evolutionary product, he and Russell had trouble selling them in western Canada. The entire region had suffered from a recession since the beginning of the First World War. Freight rates increased and commodity prices plummeted, stifling the agriculture sector. The opening of the Panama Canal in

1914 compounded the local recession, as Winnipeg's role as a transportation centre began to slowly decrease. Economic problems and social strife cumulated in the Winnipeg General Strike of May, 1919. It was a tough time to start a new business in Winnipeg.

The company fell behind on their taxes and couldn't pay their rent. On August 13, 1922, a little more than a year after incorporating, Stephenson-Russell filed for bankruptcy. "All I heard about that company was they lost their shirts," Ragnar Gislasson remembers. Ninety-seven creditors all over North America were owed money. By August of 1924, when the final company disbursements occurred, only eleven were reimbursed money they were owed. Eighty-six other suppliers, companies, and individuals were paid only four and a half cents on their dollar.

According to the Stephenson-Russell bankruptcy papers, Wilf Russell, one of the company owners, was paid for selling his corporation stock. He was the only shareholder to be compensated at the demise of the company. According to Margaret Jamieson, an unfortunate fire consumed the struggling business's effects, when Wilf Russell was away and Bill Stephenson was in charge. "My father described a mysterious fire that took place one time, when Wilf was out on the road. The business failed after that, and the partnership split up," Jamieson remembers. "But Wilf and Bill Stephenson seemed to get together again."

Bill Stephenson became a difficult person to find following the bankruptcy. Winnipeg's *Henderson's* directories list him as living with his parents, in a Victor Street apartment in 1923. But legal bankruptcy papers of August, 1924 still have his official residence as 988 Ingersoll Street. However, in reality, Stephenson didn't linger long in Winnipeg to field inquiries from creditors. He left town—quickly—and headed for England. An article of August 28, 1923 in *The Manitoba Free Press* said Stephenson arrived in Britain, "just over a year ago," which corresponds with the bankruptcy date of Stephenson-Russell. There was no formal farewell. "He left in a rather bad odour," said Joan Morrison, Bun Stephenson's daughter."He got money from many people in the Icelandic community, and didn't pay it back. Then he left town in the dark of the night."

Margaret Jamieson remembers hearing that Stephenson's business activities not only sped his departure from the city; they delayed his return. "My father said he didn't think that William Stephenson would ever come back to Winnipeg, because he thought that there might be a warrant out for his arrest. I think that he lived by his wits, and had to learn to do so early in his life, and I just think that he was a con man, as we would call it today."

The fiscally-challenged entrepreneur's wits served him well in England. Incredibly, by the end of 1922, Bill Stephenson, the unsuccessful Winnipeg can opener salesman, was being hailed as a "brilliant scientist," by the *London Daily Mail*. By mid-1923, there were more accolades for him in the British Press:

"This young man has come to his Mother country from the far Canadian west and in a remarkably short space of time has established himself as a brilliant scientist and as a leader of industry. A rare combination."[19]

Conversations

Bina Ingimundson, Stephenson's cousin

Ingimundson last saw Stephenson in the early 1920's, when he stayed with her family in Lundar and helped her relatives set up a hardware store in the town with some of his merchandise:

"They went broke. That's when he went back to England. And shortly after that, he invented the wireless photography."

"I don't know how much they saved out of the business when they closed it."

"I remember hearing he made a lot of money in the radio business. Evidently he must have been successful at it."

Why do you think Sir William's biographies say he was the son of a lumber mill owner?

"That's a stupid mistake, because Vigfus was ... he was never well off. He was, well he wouldn't have been living on that house on Syndicate, if he had been. If you'd ever seen it. You know. The bathroom was in the basement and through a trap door, when I used to visit there."

Ragnar Gislasson, Stephenson family friend

Gislasson had not seen Hyde's book, *The Quiet Canadian* before. He replied to excerpts about Stephenson's life in Winnipeg:

"And it was at Point Douglas that the elder Stephenson, who was descended from one of the early Scottish settlers, had his lumber mill, and that his son spent his boyhood."

"Ha!"

"Outside of the classroom his tastes ran to boxing and he was a creditable light-weight performer in the school boxing ring."

"Well, I don't know anything about his boxing, but I don't imagine that—maybe they were different at Argyle School—but I never heard of them having boxing as part of the physical education, in those days. My school never did."

Rosalind 'Robbie' Hyde, Author Montgomery Hyde's widow

The Quiet Canadian 'tells a false version' of Stephenson's early life in Canada. Montgomery Hyde died in 1990. His widow Rosalind was amazed that her husband's biography was so inaccurate:

"My husband was a historian," she said. "There's no money in it. Everything is checked and rechecked. One of the few joys is pointing out mistakes in another's work. What you're saying is incredible!"

William Stevenson, Stephenson biographer

Stevenson's *A Man Called Intrepid* describes the subject's fictitious life in Canada. It quotes an Argyle High School teacher of Stephenson's and cites a passage from his high school report.

"He was restless and inquisitive," recalled an Argyle teacher Jean Moffat. *"A bookworm, we always thought, except he loved boxing. A wee fellow, but a real one for a fight. Of course, y'see, he was the man o' the house since the time he was a toddler..."* (p. 4)

This is rather surprising as Stephenson didn't complete junior high or high school, and there was no Argyle High School. He grew up with two brothers, and none of the relatives remember Stephenson boxing as a child. I was able to reach the author by phone in Bangkok, Thailand, where he was living in a hotel. Stevenson, a naturalized Canadian, still speaks with a noticeable English accent.

"There's not a great deal I can help you with," he said, "because I just accepted his account of his life. I said in the book he was adopted (the book doesn't say that), and I gave the names of the parents he described as his, and I had no reason to question he was telling me the truth."

"How about this teacher you interviewed, Moffat?"

"In the book?"

"Yeah."

"I don't know. I don't recall the details in the book at this point."

"Because you quoted some teacher."

"In the book?"

"Yeah."

"I really honestly don't recall."

"And what she says isn't really true. Or doesn't jive with what I found anyway."

"Did you speak with her?"

"No. I'm wondering if she exists. Because she talks ..."

"I think the teacher I do recall was one who came down to Bermuda and was introduced by him to me."

"Oh. Because she mentions he was the only boy of the house and he wasn't. He had two brothers."

"Uh, huh."

"And stuff like this."

"Look you've caught me (in the middle of things). I'm actually late for an appointment."

3 Britain

Bill Stephenson set off for Britain in mid-1922 and travelled quickly, stopping in Toronto to see Tommy Drew-Brook for only about half an hour. One of the first people Stephenson looked up in England was his friend Charles Farquhar, a Winnipegger who stayed in London following the Great War. Although Stephenson-Russell was bankrupt in Winnipeg, surprisingly Bill Stephenson seemed to have money. The company also apparently regained some life, as a Stephenson-Russell surfaced in 1922 at 28 South Audley Street in London.

Through his Winnipeg company, Stephenson gained some knowledge of the manufacture and distribution of radios and this is an area he decided to pursue. He invested in the General Radio Company and Cox Cavendish Electrical Company Limited. These firms were early manufacturers and distributors of radio sets in Britain and were also involved in research. Through those investments he met and worked with phototelegraphy expert T Thorne Baker. Baker was well known for an apparatus used to send photos over telephone lines, and he was working on wireless photography for the *London Daily Mail*.

It appears Bill Stephenson, although he had no formal educational background in electronics, was somehow able to assist Baker. The *Daily Mail* had been conducting research into wireless photography since 1908. Previously the element selenium provided some success in converting light into electric currents, but it was a slow process. Stephenson devised what he later described to Hyde, as a 'light sensitive device' which increased the rate of transmission. He realized that if the process was sped up even further, moving pictures could be transmitted—television.

The August 28, 1923, *Manitoba Free Press*, citing British Press reports, lauded his overseas achievements:

"Due partly to his efforts and a tremendous advertising campaign, broadcasting was established in England on a highly efficient and comprehensive scale within a few short months and his companies were the first in England to produce a complete range of broadcasting equipment suitable for public use."

By August of 1923, Stephenson was the managing director of the General Radio Company and the Cox Cavendish Electrical Company. These companies manufactured radios at Twyford Abbey Works on Acton Lane in Harlesdon, and had showrooms at 105 Great Portland Street for their wireless, X-ray and electro-medical supplies.

PATENT SPECIFICATION 218

Application Date: April 18, 1923. No. 10,572/23.
Complete Left: Feb. 18, 1924.
Complete Accepted: July 17, 1924.

PROVISIONAL SPECIFICATION.

Improvements relating to Apparatus for Transmitting Electrically Scenes or Representations to a Distance

We, WILLIAM SAMUEL STEPHENSON and GEORGE WILLIAM WALTON, both British subjects, of Twyford Abbey Works, Acton Lane, Harlesden, N.W. 10, in the County of London, do hereby declare the nature of this invention to be as follows:—
This invention relates to apparatus for transmitting pictures, photographs or other representations to a distance electrically and to apparatus for dealing with the problem known as television. The present invention is particularly concerned with methods for quickly causing an illuminated spot to traverse a picture or object to be transmitted or to be viewed at a distance, and with apparatus for this purpose as light as possible in order to eliminate vibration and of as small bulk and as cheap as possible.
According to the present invention, a narrow slit is caused to move in one direction across the picture or object to be viewed and another horizontal slit is caused to move more quickly in a direction at right angles to the first. The result is that the small opening resulting at the intersection of the slits appears to travel across the picture and then back across the picture in the opposite direction ...

The *Free Press* report continued, "Stephenson also devoted himself to solving the problem of the wireless transmission of photographs and television (seeking by wireless) (sic). He has gone a long way toward the solution of these problems and has been successful in transmitting photographs by wireless suitable for newspaper reproduction."[1]

At the time, the *Daily Mail* was run successfully by Lord Northcliffe, but in the early twenties he received stiff competition from Maxwell Aitken, Lord Beaverbrook. The plucky Canadian publisher bought the low circulation *Express* in 1917 and quickly turned it into a money earner. The circulation of Beaverbrook's paper took off and eventually the *Express* achieved the largest circulation of any newspaper in the world. Rivalry between the London dailies escalated in the 1920's, and for a time both papers gave subscribers gifts, such as free accident insurance policies. During the newspaper battles of early 1920's Beaverbrook likely met the young Bill Stephenson. The press baron's subscription promotions involved unusual giveaways. "Bewildered readers," of Beaverbrook's paper's, "found themselves offered everything from free can openers to free radios."[2] This bewildering combination was very familiar to Bill Stephenson.

In the late summer of 1923, Stephenson returned to Canada aboard the SS Montcalm for a short visit and promotional trip. He landed in Montreal and then stopped in Toronto and New York. At Toronto's 1923 Canadian National Exhibition, he displayed his company's x-ray apparatus and radio sets.

Wilf Russell and Stephenson returned to England together. It was an eventful crossing for the young entrepreneurs. Stephenson was drawn to one of the passengers, the petite Mary French Simmons. The Simmons family were wealthy tobacco growers from Springfield, Tennessee, and Mary and her sister were sailing from New York to London for business. Russell was attracted to Mary's sister. The two Winnipeggers approached the sisters and began dating them in Britain.

In early 1924, Charlie Farquhar told Stephenson he was going to bring over his sister to England for a visit, and suggested Bill pay to bring over his step-sister Julianna as well. The men sent travel money to Winnipeg, and Julianna Stephenson and Margaret Farquhar headed overland to the east and sailed for England. On the ship across the Atlantic, Margaret realized Julianna was already out of money and paid for her meals. Stephenson sent over ticket money but not spending money. His sister was obviously not prepared for the high cost of world travel and the lengthy transit time. But the sisters received the royal treatment in Britain. The relatively wealthy Winnipeg transplants showed their siblings all over London in a new convertible. Unfortunately on the return journey Julianna was injured aboard ship. Her injuries were not treated properly and she never fully recovered. In the summer of 1928, four years after the trip to see her brother, she died at the age of 33. Apparently there was another repercussion as a result of the English journey. Julianna was very fond of Bill, and became envious of his wealthy American girlfriend and his new opulent lifestyle, a world away from Winnipeg. Bina Ingimundson remembers hearing her relatives say cousin Julianna Stephenson died of a broken heart.

Bill and Mary Simmons fell in love and were married July 22, 1924, in a small ceremony at the South Kensington Presbyterian Church in central London. None of Stephenson's relatives were present at the wedding. Wilf Russell was Stephenson's best man, and Julia French acted as a witness. Bill Stephenson's life was quickly gaining a new prominence. The August 31, 1924, *New York Times* Sunday Pictorial Section ran a picture of doe-eyed Mary Simmons, under the caption: "American Girl Weds Canadian Scientist." Simmons, "was married recently to Captain William Samuel Stephenson, inventor of a device to send photographs by radio," the paper reported.

A certified copy of Bill Stephenson's marriage certificate was obtained by Montgomery Hyde for writing of *The Quiet Canadian* in 1962, and is in his files at Churchill College, Cambridge. There are no signatures on the certificate from the General Register Office in London and the document is full of inaccuracies. It incorrectly lists

Marriage Certificate and newspaper picture of Mary Stephenson

Stephenson's age at the time as 28 years. The groom's father's name is registered as William Stephenson, rather than Vigfus, and his rank or profession is, "of independent means." Perhaps even more unusual is that at the time of the wedding both Stephenson and Mary Simmons are said to be residents of 2 Hanover Terrace WII. But the London directory of postal addresses at the time indicates they did not live there. From 1923 to 1926 it was the residence of an Alfred William Thomas. On this primary document, Stephenson's age is wrong, his father's name is false, his father's occupation is inaccurate, and the couple's address is wrong. It is difficult to hypothesize why this is. Did Stephenson give inaccurate information? Could it have been altered? It is another obtuse piece of the mysterious puzzle that was the life of Bill Stephenson.

For a short time Mary ran a tobacco shop on Upper Street, London. Wilf Russell eventually married Mary's sister and later moved to Tennessee.[3] Bill's business interests continued to have remarkable success. General Radio expanded to stores on Regent Street and Baker

Street. He patented the wireless photography process with George William Walton, and it is said to have made him a millionaire before he was thirty.[4]

Following Stephenson's death there were two articles in London's *Sunday Telegraph*, one by a pseudonym Mandrake, the other, citing the Mandrake editorial, by Hugh Trevor-Roper, questioning Stephenson's achievements. Montgomery Hyde, responding to skepticism that Stephenson did any work on the transmission of pictures, wrote in a letter to the editor (*The Sunday Telegraph*, February 26, 1989) that Stephenson gave him a copy of his patent, "which I still possess," and that the Stephenson material was on deposit at Churchill College, Cambridge. Following Hyde's death, his papers were closed by the British government. When the file was reopened for a short period of time many documents were withdrawn, citing Britain's national security and concerns over Crown copyright. Strangely Stephenson's wireless photography patent, which presumably was in Hyde's file, was one of the items withheld by the British government.

Stephenson seemed to gravitate to Canadians in London and he maintained many business connections back home. He and British Columbia native AJ Taylor formed a holding company called Stephenson Taylor, and in late 1925 they added a third partner Amedee Mercier. By the end of the decade, Stephenson Taylor became British Pacific Trust, with Bill Stephenson as Chairman. The trust company looked for investment opportunities worldwide. In British Columbia the group formed British Pacific Properties with Lord Southborough, Fred Taylor, Charles Hayward and Dominion Bridge Company of Hamilton, Ontario. Land owned by the partnership was north, across the harbour from Vancouver, and not easily accessible. Stephenson brought Guinness family interests into the syndicate to build a bridge to the new residential district. The Lion's Gate Bridge, now a famous Vancouver landmark that towers over the entrance to the harbour, was eventually completed across the First Narrows from Stanley Park to West Vancouver. This gave the developers the right to develop British Properties, an exclusive residential area in West Vancouver.[5]

In 1934 an aircraft built by Stephenson's General Aircraft Limited won the King's Cup air race. He hired Flight Lieutenant HM Schofield to fly the plane, registration number G-ACTS, which won with an average speed of 134.16 miles an hour in poor weather conditions. According to Hyde, the victorious aircraft was a twin-engine monoplane that could fly and climb using only one engine, which was unheard of at the time.[6]

Stephenson travelled all over Europe and throughout the world, and was in touch with leading bankers, financiers, and industrialists. The banker Charles Hambro became a neighbour, backer, and friend.[7] Stephenson controlled Alpha Cement, which was one of the largest cement companies in Britain. In the spring of 1936, Stephenson joined the board of Pressed Steel Company, which made ninety percent of Britain's car bodies.[8]

Stephenson told Thomas Troy he took control of the company earlier in the decade from the Edward G. Budd Company of Philadelphia. He said it was a thirteen million dollar deal that took thirteen minutes. Troy couldn't confirm the transaction.[9]

According to Bill Ross Smith, a later employee, Stephenson interests built Cramner Court in Chelsea, one of the first apartments in Britain with central heating.

In the early thirties, possibly earlier, Stephenson formed Sound City Films.[10] The company established Shepparton Studios and became home to producers such as: Norman Loudon, Wainwright brothers, Embassy Pictures, Argyle Talking Pictures and Fitzpatrick Pictures. In 1934 seven features were shot at Sound City, including Alexander Korda's *Saunders of the River*. In 1935 substantial expansion took place, and by the end of the decade, dozens of films were shot annually at the studios. Shepparton became the largest film studios outside Hollywood. Korda became a good friend of Stephenson's, as did many others in the film industry.

Stephenson helped form Earls Court Limited in 1935. The firm acquired from the London Passenger Transportation Board a ninety-nine year lease on the twenty-one acres of Earls Court Exhibition Grounds. On the site they constructed a large exhibition building. British Pacific Trust sponsored the original stock issue.[11]

Stephenson's numerous undertakings reportedly involved him with many of the great names of the twenties and thirties, such as George

Bernard Shaw, HG Wells, and Greta Garbo. He socialized to an extent with politicians such as Beaverbrook and Winston Churchill. It has also been recorded in British newspapers that Stephenson became an associate of aircraft designer Reginald Mitchell, and encouraged him to complete the Spitfire.[12] It also appears Stephenson's financial or other assistance may have helped Briton Frank Whittle's efforts to produce the jet engine.[13]

The Winnipegger, born to a family so destitute he was given away to a friend, didn't become an elitist, laissez-faire millionaire. He sought out new ideas and ways to improve society. "I believe with Churchill, that 'the destiny of mankind is not settled by material computation,'" he said, many years later, in one of his few documented public appearances. It has been recorded that Stephenson actually met Winston Churchill for the first time through an association with Fabian socialists and trade union leaders.[14] Stephenson became friends with the Nawab of Bhopal and the Aga Khan. With their assistance, he helped underwrite development schemes for poor areas of the Middle East and India, to help raise the standard of living of the people there. "This he regarded from every point of view as the most rewarding field for the investment of capital overseas."[15]

In 1934, Stephenson headed a mission of technical experts to India, prior to the formation of the Africa and Asia development company, to look at ways of developing the sub-continent's local natural resources. He took two Canadians with him, the renowned hydro-electric engineer Henry (Harry) Acres and Colonel Beverly Macdonald, an expert on railway and dock construction. Acres, regarded as an engineering genius, was said to be a gentleman with an intimidating presence. An American geologist, Eugene Dawson, and English chemical engineer Robin Edgeworth-Johnson accompanied the Canadians. The trip concentrated on the two predominantly Muslim states in India, Kashmir and Bhopal. The group also travelled to Afghanistan and Tibet, covering some Himalayan trails on horseback.

Stephenson's many business activities also frequently took him to the continent where he became aware of Nazi philosophy early on, and this cognizance led to his reports back to Britain about the activities of the Reich.

According to Hyde, details of Stephenson's business career were fairly common knowledge at the outbreak of World War II.[16]

Back in Winnipeg, Stephenson's activities were not well known. In the mid-1930's the Stephenson family stopped hearing from Bill, and for the most part they had no contact with him ever again. All they knew is he'd done well in business in England. Stephenson's relatives learned of his life and espionage career from a smattering of later newspaper articles, and from the books that were written about him. There was no 'falling out' in the family. Stephenson's relatives are at a loss to explain why this took place. Vigfus died in 1937. Kristin, unable to support herself, moved in with one of her sons, and died in October, 1940. By the late 1960's Stephenson's brothers and sisters were dead, as was his good friend, his brother's son Bun. Many remaining relatives were saddened by Stephenson's 'disappearance,' and the fact he did not acknowledge his mother's death. By 1940, all aspects of Bill Stephenson's life were completely shrouded. Somehow, the resourceful can opener salesman became involved in espionage at the highest level.

By the mid-thirties, the period when Stephenson broke with his past by severing his family ties, his corporate records are lacking in information. Shepparton Studios has no records of who owned it before the war. A history supplied by the studio quotes from Hyde's *The Quiet Canadian* that Stephenson owned the studio in 1934. The studio has a record of British Lion, run by Alexander Korda, buying most of the facilities from Stephenson in 1946. Earls Court, London's huge exhibition centre, has had an archivist since 1985, but he had no information about directors or owners before 1957. Although the archivist, Victor Bryant, inherited a room full of books and trunks, he could find no records from before the war, other than papers relating to shows that were put on. "We have no record of who built it," said Bryant. "Records are very, very scarce."[17]

At some stage of the 1930's Stephenson became involved in intelligence gathering and other areas of espionage. There has been much conjecture about how and when this exactly took place. According to Hyde Stephenson's formal introduction to Britain's Secret Intelligence Service, and it's wartime head, Stewart Menzies (pronounced Mingiss), was facilitated through Sir Ralph Glyn, a Conservative back bench MP.

Glyn, later Lord Glyn, was a director of British Match Corporation. The company obtained some of their raw materials from Sweden, as did Stephenson's Pressed Steel. Glyn, a friend of Menzies, and one of his 'honourable correspondents,' introduced Stephenson in 1936, according to Menzies's biographer.[18] On the eve of World War II, Menzies was promoted to chief of British Secret Intelligent Service (SIS), known by the initial, 'C.'

Stephenson's connections with British Intelligence appear to surface in the construction and operation of the Earls Court exhibition building. Although the Earls Court archives has no ownership information, there is a record of a bankruptcy in July of 1939. The *Financial Times* of July 7, 1939, lists the directors as, "Sir Ralph Glyn MP, Sir Maurice Bonham Carter, Sir Felix JM Brunner, Mr FR Lewis (managing) and Mr WS Stevenson (sic)."

Glyn had connections with British intelligence. Sir Felix Brunner was prominent in the chemical business (ICI). Bonham Carter and his wife were good friends of Winston Churchill. Lady Violet Bonham Carter wrote a book about the former prime minister in 1965, *Winston Churchill as I knew Him.*

The construction of Earls Court was a huge undertaking, even more remarkable occurring during the depression. The general contractors, Hedgemen Harris, introduced construction methods not yet used in Britain. It was built at the cost of over £1,250,000, and employed up to 3,600 men at a time.[19] The structure, when completed, was the largest reinforced concrete building in Europe. The span of the roof over the central area was 250' by 350', without columns, at a height of 120'. It provided over seven acres of exhibition space, seating for 20,000, and had four restaurants with a capacity of 4,000. "Daylight has been entirely eliminated from the building in order to give control at all seasons of the year over both temperature and light."[20]

Many delays occurred in construction of the mega project. Eight men were injured when scaffolding collapsed and there were nearly thirty work stoppages due to strikes.[21] In May of 1936, residents of the nearby Kensington mansions applied for an injunction to halt construction because of the noise levels, as extensive work was being carried on day and night. Lawyers for Earls Court argued that the company had no control over the people doing the work and denied legal liability. Walter Monckman KC, acted on behalf of one of Earls Court's contractors.[22] Monckman was a close adviser and friend of King Edward the VIII. Following the Duke of Windsor's exile in late 1936, Monckman was used to courier messages to him from Winston Churchill.

Sir Ralph Glyn explained at the Earls Court building's first annual meeting in November, 1936, that the greatest contributing factor to construction delays was a lack of steel. The delivery of steel had been unavoidably held up, "owing to the present campaign for rearmament."[23] Stephenson, a board member with interests in steel, aircraft, and cement industries, would be well aware of supply and demand situations.

Earls Court Grounds Ltd. controlled the fair grounds on which the exhibition building was constructed. Before the facility was built, from the mid-twenties until the mid-thirties, Earls Court offices were in downtown London, at 55 Broadway, Westminster SW 1. The address of Britain's intelligence service MI6 (SIS) was 54 Broadway Street, SW 1.

Only months before war broke out in 1939, Earls Court declared bankruptcy. It was fortunate timing for war preparations. The largest reinforced concrete building in Europe, containing restaurants, and with no light to the outside world, was soon converted into a factory making and testing barrage balloons.[24] It could be operated around the clock, even during blackouts.

Stephenson's business connections and other associations seem to have directed him into the world of espionage. "We were all friends, you see," Stephenson told a reporter in 1982. "Churchill and the rest. We were a group of friends who saw the war coming."[25]

According to Charles (Dick) Ellis, a career intelligence officer, Stephenson began "providing a great deal of information on German rearmament to Mr Churchill, who at that time was not in office, but was playing quite an important role in providing background information. There were members of the House of Commons who were much more concerned about what was happening than the administration seemed to be at that time."[26] Stephenson had few official contacts and his work was all done through his personal relationships with people such as Churchill and Fred Leathers.[27] Ellis was first introduced to Stephenson by

Glyn near the end of 1938, while he was doing some research on German rearmament.[28]

Stephenson's European business links provided him a unique window on the activities of Nazi Germany. He may have witnessed the 'burning of the books' in May 1933.[29] According to Stevenson's book, Stephenson met with German military and aviation officials following his winning of the King's Cup air race in 1934, "while in London, his friends tore up his past." At these meetings he is said to have learned more of Nazi doctrine and of the strategy of blitzkrieg—lightning war. "The real secret is speed—speed of attack, through speed of communications," one German official reportedly told Stephenson.[30]

The meetings seem possible. According to Hyde's *The Quiet Canadian*, Britain's Air Minister at the time, Lord Londonderry, was impressed with an aircraft designed by Stephenson's company. Londonderry, a pilot, purchased one of Stephenson's twin-engined monoplanes and Hyde flew with him in it on many occasions.[31] (Hyde worked for Londonderry, as a private secretary, and was researching a book on the second Marquis of Londonderry, Castlereagh.) Londonderry was also involved in the coal industry, and as a result had many connections on the continent. He was an "uncritical" admirer of Nazi Germany.[32] He met with Nazi leaders in 1935 and 1936 and Ribbentrop came to stay with him. Harold Nicolson, author and British parliamentarian from 1935-1945, referred to him simply as "Hitler's friend."[33] It is possible that Britain's Air Minister's plane came to the attention of German officials on one of his visits, and they arranged to meet the manufacturer.

Toward the end of 1934, Desmond Morton, who supplied information to MI6, was told his first priority should be to find out about Nazi aircraft and aero-engine production.[34] Morton, a neighbour of Winston Churchill, headed the Industrial Intelligence Centre (IIC). Frequently Morton had lunch with the Conservative backbencher, and soon afterward Churchill would release figures of the Nazi rearmament to the House of Commons.[35] Stephenson's first intelligence reports likely went to Morton.

Although forbidden by the Versailles Treaty, the Nazis began an aircraft building program in 1934. On November 28, 1934 Winston

Churchill warned parliament the Nazis were building an air force that could threaten Britain.[36] He found little support for his warnings of an impending Nazi threat, and Britain's rearmament was a very slow process.

FW Winterbotham who worked for MI6, in *The Nazi Connection* (1978), tries to explain the position of the British intelligence community, and why Churchill seemed to be alone in the House of Commons in speaking against Hitler. Churchill, well briefed by Desmond Morton, continually rose in the house to ask questions on German air rearmament. Winterbotham, in a book obviously vetted by the security agencies, places the blame on British Prime Minister Stanley Baldwin, for not heeding the advice of the security agencies. According to Winterbotham, on at least one occasion, Baldwin rose to answer a question, with the latest estimates that MI6 had been asked to send him, "in his pocket, only to reply he had no information on the subject."[37]

In May of 1935 Baldwin began to agree with Churchill's concerns. Eventually the country began to prepare for possible military threat. Baldwin does not credit his experts' advice leading him to that conclusion. He said in the house, referring to estimates of German air strength, "I was completely wrong, we were completely misled on that subject." The second half of Baldwin's remark was, "of course untrue," according to Winterbotham, but Baldwin was determined that, "somebody else should take the blame." Baldwin ordered an enquiry into the whole subject of German air rearmament at Cabinet committee level in July, 1935.[38]

Placing the blame solely on Baldwin ignores many other factors of the time. The *Economist* was attacking Churchill. It stated that German arms were not approaching equality with Britain's, there were no grounds for panic and "there was no immediate menace confronting us or anyone else." It is common knowledge that the *Economist* was well connected to Britain's Foreign Office. (Kim Philby and others, for example, had no trouble securing jobs with the publication.) If Britain's intelligence officialdom was concerned with the rise of Hitler and Baldwin's inactivity, it seems strange the information was not publicized through the media.

In March of 1935, Churchill attacked the German defence estimates which had previously been presented to the house. For example, the British estimated the Nazis were producing a hundred aircraft annually, whereas Germany, according to Churchill, was producing one hundred and twenty-five per month! If Baldwin had proper information, as Winterbotham says, why would he release wrong information? John F Kennedy's *Why England Slept* asks many obvious questions.[39]

"In any discussion of Britain's rearmament efforts, the question always arises—why did the British leaders make these appalling mistakes in regard to Germany's output? Why did Baldwin, for example, make such an error in his calculations in 1934? Why did the British continue to make them in 1935 and 1936? These mistakes were fatal, as the British planned their own production in accordance to what they thought Germany's. Were they misinformed? Were they merely over-confident? Was their attention so concentrated on their immediate domestic concerns that they slept undisturbed by warlike preparation on the continent?"[40]

Blaming Baldwin seems a rather simplistic answer. Baldwin may have been, "looking for somebody to take the blame," but there certainly seemed to be numerous worthy candidates.

Following Baldwin's 1935 confidential enquiry, in which people such as Desmond Morton presented reports, Lord Londonderry was forced to resign as Air Minister. Winterbotham was present at the enquiry, but the former intelligence agent does not mention any specifics that caused Londonderry's removal. Instead Winterbotham raves about the seventh Marquis's ability to throw a party. "Poor Lord Londonderry had been Baldwin's scapegoat. A most delightful man, I'd always felt that he was far too sensitive to be in the hurly-burly of politics in the thirties: he was much more suited to his role of brilliant political host at Londonderry House. Here he and his wife gave glittering parties for diplomats, politicians, writers and artists; he performed to perfection the delicate job of intermingling the various sections of national life."[41] Winterbotham doesn't mention Lord Londonderry's affinity for the Nazis.

Lord Londonderry wrote to Ribbentrop in 1936: "As I told you, I have no great affection for the Jews. It is possible to trace their participation in most of those international disturbances which have created so much havoc in different countries."[42]

It is generally accepted that Bill Stephenson fed German rearmament information to Desmond Morton and Churchill. This was first made public in 1951. *The Quiet Canadian* was released in 1962, when Churchill was alive, and syndicated in newspapers around the world, including the *Sunday Times of London*. Stephenson's activities during the thirties were never questioned. Stephenson's contributions are not mentioned, even in passing, in Winterbotham's book or HH Hinsley's prewar history of Britain's intelligence services.

The Canadian businessman had a myriad of information sources, especially in Scandinavia and Switzerland. As time passed, Stephenson wanted to utilize more than personal contacts to publicize the Nazi buildup, as he was not sure his material was being properly used. He became frustrated at the apathy and haphazard response of Britain to the rise of Hitler. Later he said Bickham Sweet-Escot's book *The Baker Street Irregulars* was a prime example of how "little Englanders had no idea what planet they were orbiting on," and why in some cases, "they had to be hurriedly removed even from lower echelons as stupid misunderstandings comprising largely hot air have tendency to float to higher altitudes." After rereading the book which deals with the thirties and the formation of the organization which eventually became SOE, Stephenson stated, "must congratulate myself on what magnificently icy self control I must have had to exercise on such occasions."[43] Eventually Dick Ellis opened new channels for Stephenson in British Intelligence.[44]

There are indications that Stephenson may have plotted in the late thirties to assassinate Adolf Hitler. Colonel F N Mason-McFarlane, Britain's Military Attaché in Berlin, and Stephenson both offered to shoot Hitler with high powered sporting rifles at a rally, according to Stewart Menzies's biographer.[45] Stephenson, in correspondence to the writer William Stevenson, said there were "suggestions in 1938 for averting the impending calamity," and he believed the most practical plan was put forth by a Calcutta lawyer, Rahman Siddiqui, which involved arming a "young English crackshot with high-powered telescopic sighted rifle."[46] The plans to stop Hitler were vetoed by

Britain's foreign secretary, Lord Halifax, who, "didn't want to use assassination as a substitute for diplomacy."[47]

It has also been documented that Stephenson was involved in a plan to disrupt the transporting of Swedish iron ore to Nazi Germany through subversive means.[48] The plan, one of his own suggestions, was okayed by various intelligence authorities in Britain. There was a breach of security however, and some of Stephenson's allies in Sweden became nervous. According to Dick Ellis, the King of Sweden contacted the King in England and asked that any sabotage plans be stopped, as he feared a German invasion. The British Foreign Office which "had some idea of what was going on," feared a Russian invasion of Scandinavia, as they were already at war with Finland. Stephenson returned reluctantly to Britain.[49] In any event, Stephenson's espionage activities attracted the attention of Winston Churchill.

Stephenson's first consequential meeting with Winston Churchill, in early 1938, was brought about by Fred Leathers, the co-founder of Alpha Cement. In a discussion with Leathers about another company, William Cory & Sons, Stephenson related his concerns about German political developments and their effects on fuel, coaling and general shipping. Stephenson told Leathers he thought war was imminent. At the meeting at the Alpha Offices, in the ICI buildings on Embankment, Stephenson said Britain was "woefully unprepared" to meet what he knew to be a mightily prepared German threat. "We were a sitting bird if we did not make a sensible, most urgent, effort to spread our wings," he recalled later. Leathers told Stephenson he was holding forth just as Churchill did. Since he was lunching with Churchill that day at the Cory dining room, he asked Stephenson to join them. "We had a delectable lunch and a most animated discussion, as Winston and I found ourselves to be on the same wavelength sometimes of ultrahigh frequency," Stephenson remembered. "And indeed it remained so to the end, despite some outside efforts to disrupt the unbroken close liaison. Thereafter we met together at every opportunity."[50]

Adolf Hitler came to power in 1933 with plans for a thousand-year Reich. Hitler occupied the Rhineland in March 1936, and the Nazis marched into Austria in March of 1938, the Sudetenland in the autumn of 1938, and the rest of Czechoslovakia in March of 1939. Other areas of the world were in turmoil. Italy annexed Ethiopia. The Soviet Union and Finland were at war. There was a civil war in Spain, and Japan had invaded China. The League of Nations appeared powerless.

There was little public outcry concerning the fascist invasions in British establishment circles, or in western democracies in general. When Hitler marched his troops into the Rhineland in 1936, Britain's future Ambassador to the United States, Lord Lothian, seemed unconcerned. He commented, "After all, they are only going into their own back-garden." According to Winston Churchill, this was the representative British view at the time.[51]

Joachim von Ribbentrop, then the German Ambassador to Britain, justified the invasions by saying nations large and small have the right to colonies and, "Germany must formally reject every form of argument which seeks to dispute this right with her."

The United States Ambassador in England, Joseph Kennedy, seemed to hold similar views. In 1938, after Hitler's troops had occupied the Rhineland, Austria, and Czechoslovakia, Kennedy said in a speech that he thought democracies should learn to live with the Nazis, and not attempt "to widen the divisions now existing between them, by emphasizing their differences."

Fortunately for Britain, American President Roosevelt was concerned about global developments. He saw the fascist invasions as crimes, rather than a 'right to colonies' issue. "It seems to be unfortunately true that the epidemic of world lawlessness is spreading," he said in an October, 1937 speech in Chicago.

In early August of 1939, Albert Einstein, who fled Germany to escape Jewish persecution, wrote to Roosevelt and warned him of the possibility of an atomic bomb. On September 1, 1939, Hitler invaded Poland, triggering the Second World War. Ten days later Roosevelt began corresponding privately with Winston Churchill who had become First Lord of the Admiralty.

In London Joseph Kennedy soon determined the island was a lost cause and he considered aid to Britain fruitless. He consistently warned Franklin Roosevelt "against holding the bag in a war in which the Allies expect to be beaten."[52]

Later, Lord Beaverbrook thought 'fifth column' activity could be used to help convince the United States that Europe's problems were a concern. He wrote to Winston Churchill suggesting Scandinavian Americans be urged to demonstrate, collect money, and protest the German and Russian threats to their homelands. But Beaverbrook didn't think the demonstrations would occur through osmosis.

"... If the Scandinavian demonstrations were successful the movement should extend to the Czech population, and also to the Poles ... the responsibility for the project must not rest with the Foreign Office or any other Government department. If there is any difficulty, there must be complete and absolute repudiation."

He concluded in his letter that, "a competent man should be urged to go the United States."[53]

At the time the United States had no comprehensive intelligence service—there was no Central Intelligence Agency, or National Security Agency. With world instability rising, and possible war looming, Roosevelt asked Churchill for assistance in setting up an American intelligence service. A small clique that advised Churchill on intelligence matters (Desmond Morton and a few others) appointed Bill Stephenson to the job.

"There were three or four people that were Churchill's advisors on intelligence matters, and they were the ones who appointed Stephenson to get the job of educating OSS (Office of Strategic Services)," said Benjamin Deforest (Pat) Bayly, Stephenson's wartime communications head. "Roosevelt had requested this, and Stephenson was appointed for this job. But it wasn't through MI6. So there was always a funny feeling there. Nobody quite knew where his authority came from. Or ended."

Britain's lack of military preparation for the Second World War is well known. The contribution (or lack) of Britain's intelligence services, both MI5 and MI6 to the state of unpreparedness has been subject to somewhat less scrutiny. Beginning in 1979, an official intelligence record, the multi-volume *British Intelligence in the Second War*, edited by Sir Harry Hinsley, was released. This voluminous narrative doesn't really specify why the deep thinkers of British officialdom weren't more suspicious that Adolf Hitler was up to something during the 1930's. It seems non-officials, businessmen such as Bill Stephenson, were supplying intelligence to those wanting to publicize the military buildup of the

Nazis. Why this state of affairs occurred, and the reasons why warnings continually fell on deaf ears has never been fully delineated. When asked in 1964 why the Secret Service had a reputation of having done little or nothing during the war, Stewart Menzies, its wartime head conceded, "I think we were rather badly beaten in the beginning."[54] According to the author RG Grant, Admiral Sir Barry Domville, a former head of British Naval Intelligence, found Hitler "absolutely terrific," and was jailed during the war. The Earl of Cottenham left MI5 as he could not accept a war with Germany, and Frederick Winterbotham, the head of MI6's air section and postwar author, would have preferred Britain and Germany unite against Russia.[55]

There is evidence this was a general feeling of Britain's establishment at the time. Alvin Finkel and Clement Leibovitz's well-documented 1997 book *The Chamberlain-Hitler Collusion* asserts that in 1938 Neville Chamberlain made a deal with Hitler that gave the dictator control of central and eastern Europe in return for assurances western Europe, Britain and the Empire would not be attacked. This would eventually rid the elites of Europe of the Communist threat. The plan fell apart when Hitler decided democracies in Britain and France could not be relied upon to keep pro-Nazi leadership in power in their respective countries. In the words of the authors, "Hitler had more faith in British and French democracy than the rulers of Britain and France themselves."[56]

In any event, it appears MI6 was circumvented somewhat when Roosevelt requested intelligence assistance.

From the diary of permanent undersecretary for Foreign Office, Alexander Cadogan, who was part of the inner machinations of the time, it is possible to obtain a somewhat uncensored view of the desperate situation in England at the start of the war. At the end of the decade, during Britain's greatest crisis, it appears elements of the British Foreign Office and the intelligence services were in a state of confusion and disarray. In fact, it's difficult to tell which side some people were on.

Excerpts from Cadogan's diary:[57]

"Tel from Washington, which seems to give us time on the leaks of the last two years. Fear someone in the office has been compromised. Saw Haskin, Admiral's Vysyo (?) about it. Very unpleasant." –September 4, 1939

"... Report (belated) from SIS that our secret documents were communicated in July and Aug. from the Central Dept. to the German Government! I can trust *no one*. Must look into the whole thing." (The diary does not show the result—Dilks) –January 26, 1940.

"... saw Kleffens with H before cabinet. K in good heart—a nice fellow, and he doesn't look like capitulating. Things never looked blacker."–May 14, 1940

"G. Lloyd at 3.30 with H (Halifax). He agreed to try and overhaul SIS which wants it badly!"–May 25, 1940.

"Tape says Hitler and Musso are meeting to decide on terms. What a nightmare!"–June 17, 1940

"'C' came round with what looks like an indication of Germans being ready for a mass attack on the 5th. But he is a rather nervous babbler."–September 3, 1940

Fortunately for democracy in Europe, the week "things never looked blacker," Winston Churchill became Prime Minister of Britain. Churchill began casting lifelines to North America. He gave a rope to Bill Stephenson.

4 British Security Coordination

The morning of May 18, 1940 as recorded by Randolph Churchill:

"I went up to my father's bedroom. He was standing in front of his basin and was shaving with his old fashioned Valet razor. He had a tough beard, and as usual he was hacking away.

'Sit down, dear boy, and read the papers while I finish shaving.' I did as told. After two or three minutes of hacking away, he half-turned and said: 'I think I see my way through.' He resumed shaving.

I was astounded, and said: 'Do you mean we can avoid defeat (which seemed credible), or beat the bastards (which seemed incredible)?'

He flung his razor into the basin, swung around, and said:—'Of course I mean we can beat them.'

Me: 'Well I'm all for it, but I don't see how you can do it.'

By this time he had dried and sponged his face and turning around to me, said with great intensity: 'I shall drag the United States in.'"[1]

Bill Stephenson began his North American sojourn in the spring of 1940. He contacted Gene Tunney the celebrated American boxer, a friend since WW I. The former heavyweight knew J Edgar Hoover well and he was asked to forward a letter to him. The missive from Stephenson was quite unexpected, Tunney remembered.

"Quite to my surprise I received a confidential letter that was from Billy Stephenson, and he asked me to try to arrange for him to see J Edgar Hoover, the head of the FBI. I found out that his mission was so important that the Ambassador from England could not be in on it, and no one in official government. So Mr Hoover said to me, 'all right, I'll make him my first appointment.'"[2]

Stephenson wanted his meeting with Hoover to be covert. "Sir William did not want to make an official approach through well-placed English or American friends; he wanted to do so quietly with no fanfare," Tunney wrote in 1969, responding to a request for information from CIA historian Thomas Troy, "It was my understanding that the thing went off extremely well."[3]

Tunney in his correspondence doesn't specify why British authorities were not to know of the Stephenson—Hoover encounter. In fact decades later Tunney questioned whether divulging this information would cause trouble to himself and Stephenson. When he responded to Troy, the former boxer sent a copy of his reply to Stephenson in Bermuda. In his letter to Stephenson Tunney wrote "Let's hope that neither of us will lose his head now that the war has been over for twenty-five years."[4]

Stephenson's first meeting in North America with Hoover is thought to have occurred in April of 1940. There is no precise record of what took place, but obviously it dealt with cooperation in intelligence matters. According to Hyde, Hoover told Stephenson that any liaison between the SIS and the FBI could be interpreted as contravening American neutrality laws and he would only contravene the policy if he had a direct order from the White House. Hoover stipulated that if there was to be a corroboration, he wished it to be through Stephenson and himself only, and no other US government office should be informed.[5] It is also recorded that Stephenson revealed to Hoover that communication between Roosevelt and Churchill was turned over to the Germans by a code clerk in the American Embassy in London, the domain of defeatist Ambassador Joseph Kennedy.[6] (It is interesting to note that the FBI later transmitted BSC messages to Britain, so it is likely communications security was discussed at an early stage). Stephenson agreed to Hoover's conditions and went about getting presidential approval.

The intermediary chosen was Ernest Cuneo, a lawyer from New Jersey, and a friend of Stephenson's. Cuneo worked for New York City Mayor Fiorello La Guardia and had expertise in international law. He had also done work for the Democratic National Committee which gave him presidential connections. He eventually became Ambassador Plenipotentiary with direct access to Roosevelt or Churchill day or night.[7] Cuneo later became the president of the large news service, North American Newspaper Alliance (NANA), and editor at large of the *Saturday Evening Post*. Cuneo had numerous contacts in the media and he was a friend of, among others, Walter Winchell.[8] Stephenson later called him the leader of "Franklin's brain trust."[9]

In the spring of 1940, Cuneo met with Roosevelt and reported back that the President wanted, "the closest possible marriage between the FBI and British Intelligence."[10]

Stephenson returned to Britain following the meeting. He was unsure of where and how he should try and help the Allies, or what his role should be during the war. He was offered the position of Passport Control Officer in New York City, which was a cover occupation for the SIS representatives abroad. He would replace Sir John Paget in the United States. Paget reportedly was removed reluctantly by the head of British Secret Intelligence Service, Stewart Menzies ('C'). Winston Churchill was insistent that Stephenson get the job. Stephenson, an independent operator, was reluctant to accept any government posting, especially if it meant answering to what he referred to as, "that gang on Broadway." He consulted many people to help decide his course.

In early May 1940 he attended a gathering at Beaverbrook's Stornoway House with Churchill, Boom Trenchard, Lord Southborough, Duff Cooper, Lord Leathers, Billy Hughes (a former Prime Minister of Australia) and General Maurice Gamelin of France.[12] Following the dinner, his task was decided. Stephenson remembers Churchill, who became Prime Minister May 10, 1940, took him over to a draped window, and said:

"You know what you must do at once. We have discussed it most fully and there is a complete fusion of minds between us. You are to be my personal representative in the United States. I will ensure that you have the full support of all the resources at my command. I know that you will have success, and the good Lord will guide your efforts as He will ours. This may be our last farewell. Au revoir and good luck!"[13]

Stephenson travelled back to the United States in mid to late May. The new Passport Control Officer and Britain's Ambassador Lord Lothian met with Franklin Roosevelt at the White House and according to Stephenson, they discussed, "in most warm and friendly terms all aspects of the oncoming wave of developing horror that was then Nazi moving venomous entrapment."[14]

Stephenson sent word to Britain that Roosevelt wanted a close relationship between the FBI and British intelligence. "The fact that this cooperation was agreed upon is striking evidence of President Roosevelt's clarity of vision. The fact that it has to be kept secret even from the State Department is a measure of the strength of American neutrality. It is an essential first step towards combating enemy operations, but it is insufficient to meet the demands of the situation. The Nazis in America are already well organized and well entrenched. They realize the extent of British dependence on American material aid and so direct their subversive propaganda toward buttressing the wall of traditional isolationism by which the president is encompassed."[15]

Stephenson flew back to Europe and he and his wife prepared for the move to New York. He contacted General Hastings (Pug) Ismay (Churchill's Chief-of-Staff), Colin Gubbins (later head of Special Operations Executive), the banker Charles Hambro, Fred Leathers (Stephenson's business partner, a shipping and transportation expert who joined the British cabinet), Lord Selborne (future Minister of Economic Warfare).

Stephenson saw himself as Churchill's alter ego enmission to the Western Hemisphere to implement "his wishes," and to "establish favourable attitude to assure supplies flowing eastward and any other steps required to keep British ship of state afloat from Dunkirk onwards."[16] His assignment according to the secret BSC history was "To do all that was not being done, and could not be done by overt means, to assure sufficient aid for Britain, and eventually bring America into the war."[17]

5 New York City

Stephenson and his wife Mary flew to Paris and then to Genoa, and from there set sail for New York.[1] On June 15 1940, British Ambassador Lord Lothian heralded the formal arrival of a new Passport Control Officer, in a letter to US Undersecretary of State Sumner Wells.

> "His Majesty's Ambassador presents his compliments to the Secretary of State and has the honour to inform him that Captain Sir James F Paget, has been succeeded as British Passport Control Officer in New York by Mr WS Stephenson, and that the latter is expected to arrive at New York in the SS "Britannic" on or about the 20th of June next. Lord Lothian would be grateful if the authorities of the Port of New York might be requested to accord to Mr Stephenson on his arrival in this country such facilities as be considered appropriate."[2]

Bill and Mary Stephenson arrived in New York June 21, 1940. He gave the Waldorf Astoria hotel as their address and described their length of stay in the US as indefinite.[3] On his admission papers Stephenson said he had been in New York and California previously in 1940.

For many years the British Passport Control Office was located in a small room in the British Consulate at Exchange Place in downtown Manhattan. There was one assistant staff, a clerk, and a secretary. Stephenson took one look at the cramped office, decided it was unsuitable, and set up shop elsewhere. In the early stages, he worked out of an apartment at Hampshire House, overlooking Central Park.[4] He lived not at the Waldorf, but at the St. Regis, which was owned by Roosevelt's friend Vincent Astor. Stephenson had the help of the career intelligence officer, Australian-born Charles (Dick) Ellis, in getting the organization off the ground. Churchill, Ellis recalled decades later, asked Stephenson, "to go to New York, realizing what a task he was faced with, and knowing Stephenson as he did very well, he picked the right man to do this job. Firstly, he was Canadian. Secondly, he had very good American connections ... he had a sort of fox terrier character, and if he undertook something, he would carry it through."[5] Another Australian, Bill Ross Smith and two Britons, John Pepper and Walter Bell, ostensibly with British Passport Control, were also early staff. The new spychief recruited his Canadian friends, AJ Taylor and Tommy Drew-Brook, and the organization grew. Apart from liaison and lobbying of influential Americans, the beginnings of his espionage organization were fairly unproductive. "I started from scratch," Stephenson said later. "I had no experience. I was a business man and in the early days of the job, I got plenty of bangs on the head.[6]

"I needn't enlarge too much upon what my principal concerns were upon arrival in New York," Stephenson told journalist Shaun Herron in a radio interview. "Obviously the establishment of a secret organization to investigate enemy activities ... To institute adequate wartime security measures in the Western Hemisphere, in relation to British interests in a neutral territory, were of importance and the American assistance in achieving this objective was essential."[7] To help implement this they established contacts with foreign language groups. They also made connections with Visiting Nurses, Salvation Army, Traveler's Aid, Greater New York Fund, Maritime Union, and the International Institute. Stephenson also sought to obtain destroyers, aircraft, military supplies and equipment, as the British had left much of their weaponry behind at Dunkirk (May/June 1940).

Obtaining supplies for the embattled island was not a straightforward task for Stephenson as there was a conflicting picture on what was about to transpire on the continent. America's eyes on Europe, the Ambassador to France, William Bullit, and the Ambassador in London, Joseph Kennedy, both thought Britain had little chance of survival and no leadership. Bullit had "no use for Chamberlain and almost none for Churchill," it was reported to Roosevelt. "There are no real leaders, as he sees it, in all England in this time of grave crisis."[8] Former British Prime Minister Neville Chamberlain wrote in his diary in early July 1940: "Saw Joe Kennedy who says everyone in the USA thinks we shall be beaten before the end of the month."[9] Kennedy later cabled Roosevelt to say he was delighted to hear that the President said he was not going to enter the war because, "to enter this war, imagining for a minute that the English had anything to offer in the line of leadership, or productive capacity in industry that could be the slightest value to us, would be a complete misapprehension ... It breaks my heart to draw these conclusions about a people I sincerely hoped might be victorious, but I cannot get myself to the point where I believe they can be of any assistance to the cause in which they are involved"[10]

In the United States there was a general apathy towards Europe's problems, and Japanese expansionism. A policy of nonintervention was an aftermath of WWI. "There was a surge of isolationism, a feeling there was no reason for getting involved in WWI," said Averell Harriman, Roosevelt's roving ambassador years later."We made a mistake and there were a lot of debts owed by European countries. The country went isolationist."[11] Not even Roosevelt could be sure the aid to England would not be wasted under the circumstances.

"The procurement of certain supplies for Britain was high on my priority list," Stephenson recalled, "And it was the burning urgency of this requirement that made me instinctively concentrate on the single individual who could help me. I turned to Bill Donovan."[12]

Donovan

Bill Donovan was a successful lawyer of Irish American background, a decorated soldier from World War I. It is not definite when Stephenson first met Donovan. They may have met in Europe during WWI. The two may have met in the thirties during the deal for Pressed Steel handled by Donovan's New York law firm, Donovan, Leisure, Newton and Irvine. In any event Stephenson usually referred to the Republican lawyer as an old friend, and people who knew them both also believe there was a pre-war relationship.[13]

According to one of Donovan's biographers Stephenson telephoned Donovan upon his landing in New York, in late June 1940, and met with him within the hour.[14] Donovan helped arrange a meeting with Secretary of the Navy Frank Knox, Secretary of War Henry Stimson, and Secretary of State Cordell Hull, where the main topic was Britain's lack of destroyers, and the possibility of finding a formula for transfer, without legal breach of US neutrality, and without affront to American public opinion, of fifty "over-age" destroyers to the Royal Navy.[15] Stephenson suggested that Donovan should visit Britain "with the object of investigating conditions at first hand and assessing for himself the British war efforts, its most urgent requirements, and its potential chances of success."[16] Through Frank Knox, the owner of a Chicago newspaper, who was a good friend of Beaverbrook, Donovan's trip to appraise Britain's chances for survival was organized. Stephenson says he arranged that he be afforded every opportunity to conduct his inquiries in Britain. "I endeavored to marshal my friends in high places to bare their breasts."

There has been some speculation on Stephenson's actual involvement in setting up Donovan's trip, but part of the conjecture may be a reluctance to admit the foreign manipulation of events that occurred in a neutral country. "One wonders whether Donovan felt some indelicacy in detailing Stephenson's pre-COI assistance," concludes CIA historian Troy who conducted what is referred to as 'official research' into that time period.[17] Desmond Morton, a member of Churchill's inner circle at the time, seems to reveal the precariousness of the situation in a September, 1941 letter. Morton wrote "... Another most secret fact of which the Prime Minister is aware, but not the other people concerned, is that to all intents and purposes US Security is being run for them *at the President's request* by the British. A British officer sits in Washington with Mr Edgar Hoover and General Bill Donovan for this purpose and reports regularly to the President. It is of course essential that this fact should not be known in view of the furious uproar it would cause if known to the isolationists."[18]

Dick Ellis said afterward that the planning of Donovan's trip was done by Stephenson. "Stephenson was able through his contacts in Washington, to obtain results on a number of matters that would have been quite impossible at that time done through the embassy. For instance, he persuaded, through Donovan, for Mr Hanniman (sic Harriman) to be sent to London just after Dunkirk. Harriman and Donovan came over to London, Stephenson made all the necessary arrangements through Mr Churchill. They saw, with their own eyes, what the military picture was in England. And when they returned to

Washington and reported that in their opinion this country (Britain) could hold over provided certain equipment was made available, that I think, was the biggest effort that he undertook—and it could be undertaken by a man in his position who was independent. And I think possibly because he was a Canadian. Right throughout the war the more confidential channels of communication between the Prime Minister and President ran through Stephenson's office." [19]

Other indications of Stephenson's role in the trip can be found in OSS records. In 1944 when Donovan read an OSS statement that "Lord Lothian ... arranged for Donovan to see Churchill himself," Donovan struck out Lothian's name and wrote "Bill Stephenson" in the margin.[20]

General Donovan left for Britain by air from Baltimore via Bermuda and Lisbon on July 14, 1940. Stephenson later called the trip one of the most momentous missions ever undertaken by any agent in the history of western civilization.[21] The American Embassy in London was bypassed, and Donovan's itinerary was arranged through other channels. US Ambassador Joseph Kennedy had been wired previously by Secretary of State Cordell Hull about the possibility of a Donovan junket. Kennedy was against the idea."Our staff, I think is getting all the information that possibly can be gathered, and to send a new man here at this time is to me the height of nonsense and a definite blow to good organization." Kennedy later stressed the trip would "simply result in causing confusion and misunderstanding on the part of the British."[22] The Ambassador was ignored. Donovan was in England about two weeks. He saw as many people as he could, and developed ties with influential figures in British public life and, according to Stephenson, representatives of all classes in Britain. He visited industrial areas and military training centres. He met with American foreign correspondent Edgar Mowrer and other journalists. He met with embassy officials, unbeknown to Kennedy, such as Military Attaché Brig. General Raymond Lee. Lee wrote in his diary "He (Donovan) is really over here to gain firsthand knowledge of how the Conscription Law is working and what sort of legislation is required successfully to operate a counter-espionage organization. He expects to be heard by Congress on these two things. He feels we will have conscription soon and, as he phrases it, 'Our attitude toward it will be a test of our soul.'" [23]

Britain lost all of the country's military equipment on the beaches of Dunkirk in the summer of 1940. Their ally France had capitulated. The island, virtually unarmed, faced a triumphant Germany in Europe. Donovan was to say later, "They could not have properly fought off a properly trained battalion." Hitler himself anticipated an easy conquest and the British were measuring their prospects in terms of a last-ditch stand against impossible odds. Donovan established headquarters at Claridges and every effort was made to learn all possible from the British war experience.[24] He and his entourage flew back to the US in early August, 1940. The American lawyer returned to the United States with at least four deep convictions: (1) That the British would fight to the last ditch (2) But they could not hope to hold the last ditch unless they got supplies at least from America. (3) That supplies were of no avail unless they were delivered to the fighting front—in short that protecting the lines of communication was a *sine qua non*. (4) That fifth column activity was an important factor ...

When Donovan returned he wrote a series of articles dealing with German Fifth Column activities which appeared in major newspapers and were broadcast on a nation-wide hookup. It was the first broadcast to the United States by any speaker other than the president. The Secretary of the Navy and Donovan pressed for the Destroyer for Bases deal with the President despite strong opposition from below and procrastination from above.[25]

On August 22, 1940, Stephenson reported to London that the destroyer deal was agreed upon. The agreement for transferring 50 aging American destroyers for the rights to air and naval bases in Bermuda, Newfoundland, the Caribbean, and British Guinea was announced September 3, 1940. The bases were leased for 99 years, and the destroyers were of great value as convoy escorts. Following the destroyers for bases deal, Stephenson thanked Donovan on behalf of His Majesty's government, "whilst thinking that many of my fellow Canadians might be saved from a wetting in the cold North Atlantic as the result ..."[26]

According to Lord Louis Mountbatten, who became the British Chief of Combined Operations, the destroyers were a result of Stephenson's lobbying. "We were told that the man primarily responsible for the loan of the 50 American destroyers to the Royal Navy at a critical moment was Bill Stephenson, that he had managed to persuade the President that this was in the ultimate interests of America and various other loans of that sort were arranged. These destroyers were very important to us. I was at sea at that time, because we were very short of escorts for our convoys against the unrestricted U-boat warfare, and although they were only old destroyers, the main thing was to have combat ships that could actually guard against and attack U-boats. That was absolutely vital until such time as the United States themselves came into the war."[27]

Stephenson said later that the deal would not have happened without the assistance of Donovan, and he described his work with him as covert diplomacy.[28] Other supplies that Stephenson was instrumental in obtaining for Britain, with assistance from his American friends, included a hundred Flying Fortresses for the RAF coastal command, and over a million rifles for the newly formed home guard. Later they were able to obtain kayaks, landing craft, sub chasers for blockade running, wireless equipment, radio valves, parachute outfits, passports, and war material for the Middle East.[29]

"I believe too that he (Stephenson) was the man who persuaded President Roosevelt to declare that the Persian Gulf and the Red Sea were no longer combat areas within the meaning of the American neutrality Act," remembered Mountbatten, "so that it was possible for the Americans to send war material to the British in the Middle East Theater, and the ships the whole way escorted by American ships."[30]

BSC is also said to have set up 24-hour security patrols on rail lines, terminals and docks where goods were being prepared for Britain, supplied weekly figures to London on oil production in occupied Hungary and Romania, passed on production figures of Japanese industry, hired a psychic to make 'controlled' predictions, and fabricated numerous phony documents at Canadian Station M with the assistance of the RCMP.[31]

To achieve this level of success Stephenson quickly set about expanding the New York SIS establishment, and he decided to move to Rockefeller Center on Fifth Avenue. Lord Southbourgh, a co-director of Stephenson's British Pacific Trust, was familiar with the complex, as he had been involved in the development of the Center's British Empire

Building, and discussed the construction with Nelson Rockefeller. Stephenson also contacted John Harris of the construction company Hedgeman Harris, who worked on the complex and on Stephenson's Earls Court, and Harris also recommended that Stephenson set up his headquarters in the building. Nelson Rockefeller was contacted and he approved of the initiative. Rockefeller leased the area inexpensively, as a contribution to the US war program.[32]

Stephenson also began to contact friends. AJ Taylor, one of his first Canadian business associates, helped recruit personnel, and Taylor's daughter Kathleen became one of Stephenson's first secretaries. Stephenson also approached his friend since WWI, Tommy Drew-Brook, who was a stockbroker in Toronto, to help with staffing. They sought out Canadians. Canadian business executives, newspaper people, Canadian Broadcasting Corporation officials, technical experts, and police authorities were approached. Drew-Brook recruited a University of Toronto professor, Benjamin de Forest (Pat) Bayly to handle communications. Herb Rowland, a Toronto investment dealer, did much of the recruiting in Canada.[33] Saskatchewan native Grace Garner, then a journalist in Toronto, eventually became the organization's head secretary. Tom Hill, from Portage La Prairie, Manitoba, who was editing an engineering publication in Toronto, was brought in to write reports and help in the day to day office activities.[34] The general population was recruited as well.

An advertisement was devised and put into a number of Canadian newspapers:

To Work For Britain

A Department of the British Government in New York City requires several reliable young women, fully competent in secretarial work and matriculation or better educational standing. The chief need is for expert file clerks and for typists and stenographers able to take one hundred and twenty-five words per minute. Dependable character and satisfactory background essential. Those selected can expect to serve for the duration of the war. Wages and working conditions are good. Travelling expenses to New York will be paid. Apply in your own handwriting, stating your age, education, and parentage with full details of your business experience and enclosing a recent snapshot. Also give two responsible references. Address your application to Box 1087 Telegram.

Following an interview and a security check by the Royal Canadian Mounted Police, successful candidates became members of Stephenson's organization. Many of the staff were hired through newspaper ads—at least 800 people, mostly women.[35]

Although BSC has been called an important part of Canada's war effort, it is difficult to discern this from the books written about Stephenson by the British-born authors.[36] Hyde, in *The Quiet Canadian*, devotes a half paragraph to the Canadian contribution. (The English writer refers to Stephenson as Bill Donovan's "closest British friend.")[37] *A Man Called Intrepid* mentions a handful of Canadians in passing, and stretches the contributions of the Canadian recruits to about two pages.[38] The *Intrepid* author presents a rather solitary show, with Stephenson darting all over the globe, doing everything for the organization, except serving the coffee and running out for donuts.

BSC's records were destroyed following the war, and there are few references to the Canadian contingent in papers that have surfaced since. Following the war, most press reports about the Stephenson organization refer exclusively to what the "British" were doing in America. Even the American CIA historian Thomas Troy refers to Stephenson as, "one of several very influential but relatively unpublicized Britons," sent to the United States.[39] Five decades later, just exactly what over a thousand Canadians were doing in New York City during the war remains largely unknown. Stephenson, once asked why so little had leaked out from his wartime associates replied, with a twinkle in his eye, "that is because most of them were 'quiet Canadians' too."[40] The organizational secrecy Stephenson sought to establish held firm until after his death.

The Isolationists

"Immediately after the collapse of France, not even the President himself could be assured that aid to Britain would not be wasted in the circumstances," remembered Stephenson. "I need not remind you of the diplomatic dispatches from the United States Ambassadors in London and Paris, that Britain's stand was hopeless and the majority of the cabinet in Washington were inclined to the same conclusion. All of which found vigorous expression in organized isolationism."[41]

British Security Coordination took aim at the isolationists.

American isolationism was organized in groups such as The America First movement, and various German-American Bunds. Prominent individuals such as Charles Lindbergh spoke out against the folly of joining Europe's wars. By the spring of 1941, BSC estimated there were 700 chapters and nearly a million members of American isolationist groups.[42] Britain's Ambassador reported that nine out of every ten Americans were determined to keep America out of the war. Some like the American Nazi party were determined to aid the Axis.[43]

BSC agents were dispatched all over the country to attend meetings, to keep track of members, and design and instigate effective counter-propaganda.[44]

Stephenson declared "political warfare" on Britain's enemies in America and he sought out sympathetic journalists and media moguls. The publisher of the *New York Post*, George Backer, Ralph Ingersoll, the editor of *PM*, Helen Ogden Reid who controlled the *New York Herald Tribune*, Paul Patterson publisher of the *Baltimore Sun*, AH Sutzberger, president of the *New York Times*, Walter Lippmann, Walter Winchell, and several other columnists eventually became important allies.[45]

There were attempts to woo the ownership of hostile papers such as Roy Howard, the president of the Scripps-Howard chain, but if that failed, there was a plan to put anti-British papers out of business. For example it was discovered the Hearst newspaper chain owed a Canadian paper mill over ten million dollars in the form of demand notes which were renewable every six months. Stephenson sought to buy the notes and call for payment, but the British treasury vetoed that idea and refused to provide the money.[46]

A New York-based radio station with a powerful short wave transmitter, WRUL, was subsidized by BSC and became a propaganda vehicle. The Stephenson organization "recruited foreign news editors, translators, and announcers to serve on its staff. It furnished it with news bulletins, with specially prepared scripts for talks and commentaries." [47]

Isolationists groups were monitored, targeted, and harassed. When isolationist Senator Gerald Nye spoke in Boston, in September of 1941, thousands of handbills were handed out attacking him as an appeaser and Nazi lover. Following a speech by Rep. Hamilton Fish, a member of a front group, the Fight For Freedom, delivered him a card which said, 'Der Fuhrer thanks you for your loyalty,' and photographs were taken. An attempt was made to disrupt an America First rally at Madison Square Garden by printing phony tickets.

Americans were approached to join the cause and help report on the isolationists. Soon after Donald Downes joined the Free World Association, a New York-based group organized by statesmen and refugees from a variety of Axis-occupied countries, he was approached by a 'Mr Howard' from British Security Coordination. 'Howard' told Downes, "Our primary directive from the PM (Mr Churchill) is that American participation in the war is the most important single objective for Britain. It is the only way, he feels, to victory over Nazism." 'Howard' told Downes they believed groups such as America First were actually fronts for the Nazis, and asked for Downes' assistance in proving it. The American agreed to help, but his relationship with BSC was to remain covert and nebulous. If Downes were caught, 'Howard' stressed to him, "we have never heard of you!"[48]

In the next four months, through Downes and his contacts alone, BSC gleaned information on German Consulates in Boston and Cleveland, the Italian Consulate in New York, the German Embassy, a number of pro-Axis American politicians, a country town where *Scribner's Commentator* was published, the Bund headquarters in Yorkville, a German biology instructor, a bakery frequented by a German Embassy secretary, a retired American general, and two export officials from General Motors. Downes sought and received assistance from groups such as the Jewish Anti-Defamation League, the CIO, and from US army counter-intelligence.

Downes eventually discovered there was Nazi activity in New York, Washington, Chicago, San Francisco, Cleveland and Boston. In some cases they traced actual transfers of money from the Nazis to the America Firsters.[49] Downes later became an important OSS operative working for William Donovan.

After the Americans joined the war in December 1941, BSC didn't need to focus on swaying American opinion any more. Stephenson remained active within the new parameters. He is regarded as the midwife of Donovan's wartime espionage organizations.

The Coordinator of Information (COI) and Office of Strategic Services (OSS)

Franklin Roosevelt wanted an all-encompassing intelligence service with an international scope that could report on the Nazis and Japanese expansionism. In mid-1940, the situation regarding security and intelligence in the US was in the words of Dick Ellis, "far from satisfactory." There was a great deal of competition between various services such as naval intelligence (ONI), and military intelligence (G-2), and each had limited operations.[50] Following the fall of France, Dunkirk, and the possibility Britain would be invaded, large intelligence-gathering problems loomed for the Americans due to a lack of a coordinating body. Because of inter-service rivalries it seemed unlikely one of the services would assume a leadership role, and the others would offer to subordinate their activities to it. To help prepare for possible war, Roosevelt set up the Coordinator of Information (COI) on July 11, 1941 to help centralize the myriad of intelligence sources and named Donovan its head.[51]

Bill Donovan, an outsider, was put in place by Roosevelt as America's first combined intelligence chief. He had numerous personal attributes (a decorated soldier, lawyer, and public servant) which commanded respect. "He had great power in Washington because he was a friend of the president," remembered Stephenson years after the war. "A close personal friend of the president, and (he) was constantly in contact with him. In addition, there was a practical advantage, from the president's point of view, in keeping Donovan actively engaged upon his side, because he was very close to what might be described as the opposition at the time. He was a Catholic and an Irishman. Republican."[52]

Although Donovan was a worthy choice as an intelligence head, in the early months it was an uphill struggle. He had little to contribute to the intelligence net that would justify his position. It was only a matter of time before he would be squeezed out of existence according to Ellis. Stephenson knew this, and supplied Donovan with product that he could distribute. He gave him "practically everything" in the way of background information. To compliment his own channels, Stephenson made numerous quick trips to London, created a direct link with censorship and security in the Caribbean and established closer relations with

Canada's External Affairs and the RCMP. He gave Donovan almost everything, according to Ellis. He also organized training. "By providing D (Donovan) with training facilities for his officers, S (Stephenson) was able to shorten the time needed for COI to stand on its own feet."[53]

Stephenson helped plan the organization necessary to carry out Donovan's functions as coordinator. He aided the task of consolidating the activities of scattered intelligence units into a single organization, set up the framework of the headquarters and field operations. He made available experienced British officers, and arranged for members of COI staff to receive administrative and field work training at British schools. Hundreds of COI and OSS were trained before and after the American entry into the war.[54]

Much of the training was done at a secret Canadian location. With the assistance of Tommy Drew-Brook, a parcel of farmland outside Toronto at Whitby, Ontario was purchased and converted into North America's first spy school. The exact startup date of the camp is the point of some contention. In the early days Gladstone Murray of the CBC helped disguise the purpose of the property purchase. Later the Canadian Department of External affairs, the RCMP and the FBI provided assistance.[55] At Special Training School 103, known as Camp X, groups of North American agents were versed in self-defence, lock picking, safe blowing, second story entry, map reading, explosives and incendiaries, radios, listening devices, and codes and ciphers. Stephenson's contacts in the film industry were put to use at the camp. Zoltan Korda, the brother of Alexander Korda, was at Camp X, and he supervised the design of mockups of various Nazi locations that were to be approached by parachuting SOE and OSS recruits. Zoltan, according to Stephenson, was an expert in reproducing the various points of entry and exit from plans usually provided by Colin Gubbins.

Alexander Korda and his wife Merle Oberon were part of what Stephenson called his 'private army' who performed as far afield as Hollywood. Stephenson had influence in numerous spheres. As strange as it seems, he apparently arranged to have a Noel Coward tour of South Africa rescheduled, as the actor and author appeared tired and Stephenson thought a postponement would cause less trouble in the long run than if Coward was to break down midway through it.

Stephenson sent Coward on a forced holiday.[56] According to Coward, Stephenson's men met him later in Jamaica and Natal.

The Ontario camp became a communications centre linking Washington, Ottawa, New York and London, organized by Pat Bayly. It also carried messages from further afield and couriers were employed to supplement the system. TD Ingall was a courier between the radio transmitter at Camp X, called HYDRA, and Washington, Ottawa, Toronto, and Montreal. "During that time I became well aware that BSC was a very extensive and worldwide organization," Ingall recalled in a letter.[57]

According to Donovan, Stephenson was responsible for satisfactory cooperation between the COI (and later OSS) and the British Intelligence service. He accompanied him to Britain and established the necessary contacts with the heads of British Naval and Military intelligence and other agencies. In addition, he took the necessary steps to provide Donovan "with a regular flow of secret information from sources available to his own organization, including highly confidential British censorship material not normally circulated outside British Government departments."[58] From August 18, to December 7, 1941, Donovan was in touch with Stephenson on at least 36 occasions.[59]

Stephenson set up a Washington office to keep in touch with COI, and Donovan set up a New York office in Rockefeller Center to keep in touch with BSC. On August 9, 1941, Stephenson indicated to London that the Donovan office was functioning.

On October 24, 1941, Franklin Roosevelt informed Winston Churchill about Donovan's new post and told the Prime Minister he was setting up a London office. FDR's letter to Churchill said the Coordinator of Information had, "the most helpful cooperation from the officers of His Majesty's Government who are charged with direct responsibility for your war effort."[60]

Donovan asked Stephenson for the services of experienced officers to help lay down the framework for his headquarters and to help establish field operations. Ian Fleming, who visited North America with the Director of British Naval Intelligence, Admiral Godfrey, left notes for use of the new organization, but his role in the laying the groundwork for the agency is greatly exaggerated, according to Ellis.[61]

Donovan was totally dependent on BSC until several months after Pearl Harbor, and Stephenson did much of the propping up of Donovan on his own, without the knowledge of intelligence officials in Britain. According to Ellis, there was not hostility towards COI on the part of 'BI' (British Intelligence), but they were skeptical about passing information to the new American service. Ellis says this was because, "There was little knowledge of the US conditions or of the leading personalities in the US scene. Some of the old hands had memories of the last war, and of some aspects of the aftermath, and felt that close cooperation would be difficult to achieve and sustain. (Stephenson) faced this situation by forming his own judgment, as the man on the spot, and took the steps that I have described above. It is quite possible that certain officers of BI would have suffered attacks of apoplexy had they been aware of the extent of collaboration already achieved with the emergent US organization, the passing of information and advice, and frank discussions of technical matters, etc."[62]

The writer Bradley F Smith in *The ULTRA-MAGIC Deals* emphasizes the unique situation with the United States and Britain, along with Canada, sharing decrypts, intercepts and top-secret information. Indications are that Stephenson and possibly others were giving the British information to the Americans anyway without going through formal channels. In October 1941, the US military attaché in London noted a dispatch he was sending to Washington regarding the Russian campaign contained information from the "British Intercept Service," and therefore needed to be kept secret "even from the British mission."[63]

According to Ellis, by June of 1942 the British agencies were accustomed to dealing with their US counterparts. "BSC had evolved the machinery for maintaining liaison, and members of both British and US service had been in personal contact with each other."[64]

Journalist Sydney Morrell reported, "BSC covered every area of intelligence activities, from detecting enemy agents, to counter-intelligence, to protecting British and American installations throughout the Western Hemisphere, as far as I know it was the only case where a great many secret activities, which were functioning in different organizations and under different control in other countries, were under one control in this hemisphere ... where all of his (Stephenson's) efforts were given to not just bringing America in but to helping the Americans gear themselves for the struggle."[65]

Stephenson made numerous trips, perhaps as many as forty-three, to Britain during the war, but few are documented. Even when trips were made public, names were changed. For example, on December 6, 1940, Bill Donovan left on a trip to the continent. Travelling under the name Donald Williams, he was recognized by reporters as William Donovan. It is not known how the reporters were tipped off to Donovan's trip, but the *New York Times* reported that Donovan spoke to two passengers en route, a Mr Desgarges from France, and a Mr O'Connell. According to Donovan biographer Richard Dunlop, 'Mr O'Connell' was William Stephenson.[66]

The Pan-Am Clipper landed in Bermuda and was held up there because of bad weather. CIA historian Thomas Troy says the two men spent eight days in Bermuda and Stephenson showed Donovan the extensive operation on the island where mail, passengers, and goods were checked by British censorship before continuing in transit across the Atlantic. Some of the letters were checked for secret ink and it was at the Bermuda intercept station that the first micro-dot was discovered. The unit was very efficient. Following the war, Nadya Gardner of the Bermuda unit, analyzed and evaluated Nazi documents from Frankfurt station while working for 'TOD' in Washington, and she reported to Stephenson, "it was most gratifying to see that we, in Bermuda, had missed almost nothing."[67]

The intercept work was extensive and tedious. A July 21, 1941 mail intercept report from Jamaica to Montgomery Hyde reported on five days at the beginning of July when 3,727 letters were examined out of 12,320. Of these there were 32 submissions sent to the consulate in New York.

Donovan proceeded to Lisbon and then Britain, where he met with Churchill December 18, 1940. According to some reports, Churchill told Donovan of Hitler's planned attack on the Soviet Union the next spring which was determined from 'ULTRA' decrypts. Donovan proceeded to the continent and to Yugoslavia. The unofficial version of events of Donovan's secret, but publicized trip, is that subsequently documents were stolen from him in Belgrade by German agents that were following him. Donovan's papers were phony and were prepared in New York, according to Dick Ellis.[68] Donovan's conversations with Air Force General Dusan Simovic led to a change of thinking in the Balkans, away from the Nazis, and a revolution followed in late March of 1941. Hitler was outraged at the turn of events and diverted many of his forces away from the eastern front and into Yugoslavia. The official version seems to be that Donovan had no formal position with the American government at the time, so nothing of the sort happened.

In a cable that has never been footnoted, Churchill is said to have written Roosevelt that, "Stephenson and Donovan carried about the single outstanding intelligence coup of the Second World War when they delayed the Nazi invasion of Russia."[69] Through ULTRA decrypts the Allies knew that Hitler was massing an attack on the Soviet Union. For Hitler, according to Churchill, the Yugoslav coup came, "out of the blue," and a blow to Yugoslavia had to be struck with, "unmerciful harshness."[70] Churchill quotes the German general Keitel as saying, "The decision to attack Yugoslavia meant completely upsetting all military movements and arrangements made up to that time. 'Marita' (Greece) had to be completely readjusted. New forces had to be brought through Hungary from the north. All had to be improvised." The Yugoslav diversion delayed the Nazi invasion of Russia by about six weeks. By December of 1941, some German units were suffering 40 percent frostbite casualties, and the temperatures were as low as 38 degrees below zero with strong winds. As a result Hitler's forces were held up and eventually defeated by the Soviet forces and the Russian winter.

Churchill mentions in passing Donovan's trip to Belgrade in his history of the Second World War, but there is no suggestion he had covert plans. However he does leave a possible clue that other factors may have been involved in the turn of events. Oddly enough, at the conclusion of his chapter on Yugoslavia, following the Nazi assault, Churchill mentions that the zoo in Belgrade was damaged during the Nazi bombing and the inhabitants escaped. He refers to the actions of a particular animal. "A bear, dazed and uncomprehending, shuffled through the inferno with a slow awkward gait down towards the Danube. He was not the only bear who did not understand."[71] The bear is the symbol of Berlin.

At least two other Stephenson trips are documented. In June 1942, Donovan, Jim Murphy, and Preston Goodfellow went to New York where they picked up William Stephenson, continued to Montreal and left for Britain the next day. The OSS records also record a Stephenson trip to Europe in August of 1942, with Lettice Silverston and Walter Wren.[72] This is the approximate time (August 19, 1942) of the ill-fated Canadian-British assault at Dieppe.

6 London

It is not known what exactly Stephenson did in Britain during the war. Obviously he met with various department heads of the British war effort and reported on the situation in the Western Hemisphere. Who else he met with, and if he had larger influence will probably remain a mystery. "It is doubtful he had any direct influence over intelligence matters in Europe after 1939, other than through his close connections with Donovan's OSS," concludes the writer Mary Lovell.[1] However, this judgment is quite broad. Donovan's OSS were sending people all over Europe. He is quoted as saying, "Bill Stephenson taught us all we knew about foreign intelligence." Stephenson was also the North American representative of Special Operations Executive which trained foreign nationals, and organized numerous drops into occupied Europe.

Many of the activities of the SOE, the OSS, and resistance forces were of immense importance even before the invasion of Europe. For example in Scandinavia Danish physicist Niels Bohr, a nuclear expert, was slipped out of Europe away from the Nazis to the Manhattan Project. In Norway the trained resistance blew up the heavy water plant at Norvic, and later destroyed the last supplies. It appears Stephenson helped provide equipment for resistance activities. Following the war, the former head of SOE, Colin Gubbins, wrote to William Stevenson and said, "We arranged in Denmark for Niels Bohr to be smuggled out by resistance to Sweden in a fishing boat thence onto the UK. The fast torpedo boats were I believe classified officially as submarine chasers that's what we called them anyway. We also had two from Bill which were used on the Shetland-Norway run putting in and picking up agents. They were an absolute Godsend. Up till their arrival at Scalloway (our Shetland base) we had been working with Norwegian trawlers and crews for years using the methods of stealth and disguise but latterly had unbearably heavy losses—German air activity, fewer and fewer local boats fishing in Norwegian coastal waters and fearful storms — how we and our Norwegian crews blessed 'Little Bill.'"[2]

In the files of William Stevenson is an illustrated paper with a description of the location of a message hidden in a key for Niels Bohr. The note was to be sent to JUSTITBRAADEN, a Danish government department.[3]

Gubbins, in an undated foreword, said Stephenson's activities could be best described as, "a series of brilliant individual coups against Axis powers in the true tradition of secret intelligence with modern embellishments which in fact had an influence on military operation in the main theaters ... We who were in SOE owe a profound debt to Stephenson and to all who worked closely with him in co-operation with him in so many vital aspects of inter-allied achievement."[4]

It seems likely Stephenson at least had a knowledge of major intelligence events taking place in Europe and the planning it entailed. It also appears Stephenson provided valuable assistance to the proceedings.

Since Churchill saw American assistance as Britain's salvation and Stephenson was ostensibly appointed by Churchill, he obviously met with the Prime Minister in London on occasion. In the files of Montgomery Hyde is an account of a meeting between Ernest Cuneo, Stephenson, and Winston Churchill that Stephenson arranged.[5] Cuneo helped coordinate public policy and he was appointed as an Ambassador Plenipotentiary with a priority of direct access to the Prime Minister night or day, which Cuneo says, "on emergency occasion we used."[6] According to Cuneo, "No small part of our conversations dealt with coordinated public policy of our countries, in which both Winchell and Beaverbrook were factors with whose efforts we were enabled to coordinate effectively."[7] Cuneo is also quoted as saying, "Stephenson was the only man who had the unqualified support of both Franklin Roosevelt and Winston Churchill."[8]

Colin Gubbins also indicates that Stephenson played an important intermediary role between the two world leaders. Years after the war, Gubbins, the wartime head of SOE, contacted Dick Ellis, as he heard the former intelligence officer was writing a book on the Donovan/Stephenson collaboration. Gubbins called Stephenson's conduit role vital and, "played in the very highest quarters—at the top level in fact—in the Downing Street/White House 'affaire' which led to such splendid results ... I moved only rarely in the rarefied atmosphere of the top circles where the two Bill's had their stomping ground but Bill Stephenson's slightest wish is to me more that a command."[9]

Any look at Stephenson's possible influence in the European theater should not disregard his business interests. He had a full time secretary, Miss AM Green, in England looking after his affairs. Although he was occupied in North America, his European businesses didn't disappear. As mentioned earlier, Earls Court was converted to the manufacture of barrage balloons. The cement industry (Alpha Cement) was obviously involved with fortifications and airfields. Stephenson was involved with aircraft manufacture, and Pressed Steel was transformed to suit the rearmament program. At the beginning of World War II, his Shepparton Studios were requisitioned by the War Office and the craftsmen were directed towards the war effort. The workshops were used for the manufacture of Wellington bombers and decoys—fake guns, aircraft and landing strips. On the studio's reservoir the Barnes-Wallace bouncing bomb was tested.[10]

In available files there is little pertaining to Stephenson's activities in Europe during the war, but there are indications he had influence there. On June 15, 1942 Montgomery Hyde wrote 'Harrington' a letter from New York. In it he says, "WS has gone to London with Bill Donovan for three weeks. His ('little Bill's') presence is long overdue there."[11]

While Stephenson was away in Europe back in New York it seems his friends continued the wining and dining of American officials. In the files of Montgomery Hyde is a invitation to a dinner party at Stephenson's business partner AJ Taylor's flat at The Moorings in New York. The Canadian invited to the June 1942 gathering John McCloy, the US Assistant Secretary of War, Vilmar Stefansson, the famous Icelandic Canadian Arctic explorer who was working for the US Navy, Hyde, Lawrence Whiting, of the US Army & Navy War Department, and Frank Hopwood, a director of the Asiatic Petroleum Company and the son of Lord Southbourgh.[12]

Hyde also met with Hoover on occasion on behalf of BSC and they exchanged information.[13] According to his book *Secret Intelligence Agent*, Hyde also visited the Bahamas to meet with the Duke of Windsor.

Censorship

British Security Coordination received suspicious mail coming and going from the United States and the Caribbean. The British Censorship Bureau had an office in New York at 15 Broad Street headed by Charles Des Graz. In early October 1941 Des Graz sent Stephenson by safe hand a report of Japanese postal and telegraphic censorship and interception during the First World War. The information flowed both ways. In October 14, 1941, BSC sent Des Graz an MI5 report on the movements of European art treasures that was ascertained through post censorship intercepts.[14]

There were glitches in the flow of information. A major flaw was uncovered by Des Graz 'accidentally' in the autumn of 1941. BSC was supposed to secure ports and watch for saboteurs in the Western Hemisphere, but the organization was no longer receiving the intercepted correspondence of known security risks. October 30, 1941, Des Graz reported to Montgomery Hyde in a letter marked SECRET that Bermuda sent letters to or from persons on the 'General Security Black List' to London unopened. "It seemed to me that this was a very questionable practice as, if the persons in question are in North or South America, their correspondence seems primarily a question for your office." The instructions to forward the letters had come from London in January of 1941. Des Graz assumed the London edict was misinterpreted in Bermuda. He wrote "Bermuda Sorters took this I think wrongly as an instruction to forward them unopened." Des Graz immediately changed the practice and if the "contents might interest your office you can receive early information and a photostat if necessary." On average this amounted to forty letters a week Des Graz reported. Soon afterward Stephenson created a BSC mail intercept capability.

On November 27, 1941, when US negotiations with the Japanese appeared headed nowhere, Stephenson asked the Director General of Postal and Telegraph Censorship Edwin Herbert for general information from Hong Kong and Singapore intercepts to be relayed to the Americans. "We are very anxious to satisfy them at this present time." He expressed interest in German and Japanese activities in the Far East and the Americas and reports on political developments in Japan and China. Stephenson then requested all the intercepts from the Asian colonial city states. "I feel however it would be more satisfactory to have all intercepts from Hong Kong and Singapore as we now have adequate arrangements for dealing with them here."[15]

BSC added censorship to it's various departments. Dorothy Hyde was an expert in mail intercept and forgery, and gave instruction to the FBI. Later she was joined in the department, known as Room 99, by Betty Raymond.

But dealing with intercepted mail involved more than the mechanics of covert opening and closing. To contend with intercepted correspondence, many avenues had to be covered. Not only were they looking for possible spies and saboteurs, BSC had to stem any possible flow of strategic resources and monitor potential supplies. In the wartime files of Montgomery Hyde is a list of books that were ordered, including language dictionaries for Dutch, Portuguese, Chinese, and Japanese. There were dictionaries of engineering and chemical terms; directories of Norway, Italy, and Central Europe, and telegraphic addresses for France and Italy. They ordered a Banker's Almanac that listed the banks of the world, Katzaroff's patent dictionary and books on trade and finance, Imperial Chemical Industries chemical catalogue, and the ICI catalogue of names and uses of chemicals. Various Who's Who directories were ordered, as well as Lloyd's shipping supplements. Subscriptions to *Time, Newsweek, Life,* the *Sunday New York Times* and New York daily papers flowed into the offices.[16] In Hyde's files are overdue notices for some of the above material from New York libraries. (As Pat Bayly said later, "We were breaking every law in the book.")

BSC employed many linguists to translate intercepts, and financial people who understood the flow of capital and resources. Colonel Louis Franck, a descendent of a series of governors of the Belgian Central Bank, was considered a bullion expert.[17] Other business people joined the organization such as Richard Coit, Ingram Fraser, David Ogilvy, Ivor Bryce and Herbert Sichel. British journalists joining the organization included Sydney Morrell and Christopher Wren. Roald Dahl, who became a children's writer during the war, worked for the organization in Washington. Paul Dehn, who later wrote the screenplays for a few early James Bond movies, was an instructor at Camp X. Playwrights Benn Levy, Eric Maschwitz, and Giles Playfair worked for BSC. A number of university dons, such as Gilbert Highet, AJ Ayre, Ken Maidment, and FW Deakin joined the cause.

The Stephenson organization was multi-faceted and criss-crossed many diverse spheres. "BSC was not just an extension of SIS," wrote CIA historian Thomas Troy, "but was in fact a service which integrated SIS, SOE, Censorship, Codes and Ciphers, Security, Communications—in fact nine secret distinct organizations. But in the Western Hemisphere Stephenson ran them all."[18]

Plate 1: Vigfus and Kristin Stephenson, adopted young William Samuel Clouston Stanger (b. 23 January, 1897), and renamed him William Samuel Stephenson (photo 1912)

Plate 2: (Above) Stephenson, age 12, taken at the Breckman farm near Lundar, Manitoba (photo 1909)

Plate 3: (Right) By age 15, WSS had been working for three years as a telegram delivery boy for Great North West Telegraph Co (photo 1912)

Plate 4: Clockwise: Kristin (Breckman) Stephenson, Julianna (Lulu) holding Bill Hodgkins, Johinna Hodgkins, Lillian Stephenson, Vigfus Stephenson, Margaret Hodgkins, Bill Stephenson (in fedora) and Victor Hodgkins (photo 1920)

Military Number, 101st Overseas Batallion (WLI),
Canadian Expeditionary Forces, first revealed to the
author on a post card sent by WSS to his family

Plate 5: Enlistment papers and part of WSS's military record

Plate 6: Captain WS Stephenson, 73rd Squadron, RAF, awarded Military Cross, April 1918 and the Distinguished Flying Cross, August 1918

As a Sopwith Camel pilot, WSS brought down many enemy planes before he was shot down by friendly fire (a French aircraft) and captured by the Germans

SALTER AND ARNOLD LIMITED

301-304 ROYAL BANK BUILDING

WINNIPEG

FINAL DIVIDEND SHEET — STEPHENSON & RUSSELL LIMITED — WINNIPEG.

Creditor   Address   Preferred Claims

PETITION

FOR ISSUE OF LETTERS PATENT
INCORPORATING

STEPHENSON & RUSSELL LIMITED

UNDER

"The Companies Act"

The Willson Stationery Co., Ltd.

STEPHENSON-RUSSELL LTD
WINNIPEG-CANADA.
STEPHENSON-RUSSELL, LIMITED,

THE BANKRUPTCY ACT.

IN THE MATTER OF THE ESTATE OF STEPHENSON & RUSSELL
WINNIPEG MANITOBA.

TAKE NOTICE THAT:

1. A final dividend sheet has been prepared. The
herewith (a) a copy of the dividend sheet with n
the claims objected to and whether any reservati
therefor. (b) an abstract of the receipts and ex
trustee, which abstract indicates what amount o
received by the trustee for moneys in his hands

2. After the expiry of fifteen days from the d
of this notice, dividends on all debts not obje
time of payment will be made.

3. That the undersigned trustee of the propert
apply to the Registrar in Bankruptcy at the Cou
Street, Winnipeg, on the 4th. day of September
twelve o'clock noon, or so soon thereafter as
heard for an order fully discharging it from any
obligations with respect to the above estate and for a release o
the security provided by the undersigned.

Dated this 20th day of August, A.D. 1924.

SALTER AND ARNOLD LIMITED,

Trustee.

301 Royal Bank Bldg., Winnipeg.

(Above) Incorporation of Stephenson-Russell, and its unfortunate end (below) in bankruptcy
Plate 7: (Inset) Wilf Russell, (photo 1938)

Plate 8: The Stephenson family home at 175 Syndicate Street (as seen today), Point Douglas, Winnipeg

Plate 9: Base inscription on the Cairn of Tears monument dedicated to Scottish Heritage, located beside the Red River, ironically claims Sir William Stephenson to be of Scottish ancestry

SIR WILLIAM STEPHENSON
CC., MC., DFC., DSc.(MIL.), LLD.(WPG.), DSC.(MAN.)
THE MAN CALLED "INTREPID" (WWII)
BORN POINT DOUGLAS, WINNIPEG. 1896

Plates 10, 11: It is difficult to find any Winnipeg memorial to William Stephenson. In a Small Point Douglas park behind a 5 metre tall statue of 18th C poet Markian Shashkevitch is a granite marker dedicated to Stephenson. Much of the inscription is incorrect. In winter, the monument is buried in snow. (Above, author Bill Macdonald)

Plate 12: With friends in London: (left to right) Charlie Farquhar, Julianna Stephenson, William Stephenson, Jane Farquhar-Olsen and Margaret Farquhar (photo 1924)

Plate 13: Charlie Farquhar, Julianna Stephenson, William Stephenson, Jane Farquhar-Olsen and Dave Farquhar (photo 1924)

Plate 14: Out for a spin in Stephenson's convertible (photo 1924)

Mary Simmons and William Stephenson married July 22, 1924

AMERICAN GIRL WEDS CANADIAN SCIENTIST: MISS MARY FRENCH SIMMONS of Springfield, Tenn., Who Was Married in London Recently to Captain William Samuel Stephenson,

Plate 15: Stephenson and scientist T Thorne Baker developed a method of sending photos by wireless so that pictures could be transmitted instantly. On December 27, 1922, the first transmitted photo (two skiers) appeared in the Daily Mail

PATENT SPECIFICATION

Application Date: April 18, 1923. No. 10,572/23.   **218,766**

Complete Left: Feb. 18, 1924.

Complete Accepted: July 17, 1924.

PROVISIONAL SPECIFICATION.

Improvements relating to Apparatus for Transmitting Electrically Scenes or Representations to a Distance.

We, WILLIAM SAMUEL STEPHENSON and GEORGE WILLIAM WALTON, both British subjects, of Twyford Abbey Works, Acton Lane, Harlesden, N.W. 10,
5 in the County of London, do hereby declare the nature of this invention to be as follows:—

This invention relates to apparatus for transmitting pictures, photographs or
10 other representations to a distance electrically and to apparatus for dealing with the problem known as television. The present invention is particularly con... ...ably causing

and vibration as any television apparatus, in order to be successful must be free from vibration. If the slits in one disc are all inclined in the same direction to 50 radii of the disc, the opening can be caused to move across the object in the same direction in successive lines: if alternate slits are inclined in opposite directions, the opening can be made to 55 move backwards and forwards in successive lines.

A result exactly equivalent to the intersecting slits can be obtained by means of two revolving mirrors. One 60 ...rror is arranged with a ver-

Plate 16: Film Director Alexander Korda with his wife Merle Oberon. Korda partnered with Stephenson as owners of Shepparton Studios outside London

Plate 17: The Stephenson home during the 1930's on New Cavendish Street in London

Plate 18: August 4, 1941, Franklin D Roosevelt and Winston Churchill met secretly on the battleship Prince of Wales in Placenta Bay, Newfoundland to confer on an Anglo-American alliance which resulted in the Atlantic Charter

7 Washington

BSC created a small Washington office to act as a home base in the American capital and Stephenson was in contact with the British Embassy in Washington. The first Ambassador he dealt with was Lord Lothian, Philip Kerr. Lothian died under somewhat strange circumstances in December, 1940, and he was eventually replaced by Lord Halifax. Stephenson was not a big Halifax fan. "Edward the holier than thou type—a poor choice to follow Lothian but it got him out of Winston's way and into mine dammit."[1]

When the United States was still neutral, Axis and Vichy embassies and foreign missions became unique windows on continental activities. The activities of Jean-Louis Musa, a French Vichy official, were closely monitored. His phone calls were tapped and meeting rooms bugged. According to the BSC history a number of embassies were penetrated.

Elizabeth Thorpe, code named 'Cynthia,' may have obtained valuable Italian Naval ciphers. In the spring of 1941 she also discovered through Italian Admiral Alberto Lais that Italian ships were going to be scuttled in American harbours. Subsequently Lais was asked to leave the United States. Later, in May 1941, she was asked to concentrate on the Vichy Embassy. 'Cynthia' posed as a newspaper woman and became romantically involved with the Vichy press attaché Charles Brousse. Eventually she secured copies of nearly all the telegrams to and from the French Embassy and was instrumental in obtaining the French Naval cipher. Brousse started supplying more and more material, memorizing conversations, and passing on notes he took at briefings. BSC also had two other informants relaying information from the embassy. In the summer of 1941 the SI division of BSC compiled a comprehensive report on the Vichy French in the United States with an appendix of photostated documents and transcripts of recorded telephone conversations. According to the BSC history, Stephenson took it to London in July 1941 and arranged for a copy to be given to Roosevelt. The American President is said to have called it "the most fascinating reading I have had in a long time—the best piece of comprehensive intelligence work I have come across since the last war."[2]

Stephenson leaked parts of the report to the New York *Herald Tribune* and the paper published a series of articles at the end of August and beginning of September 1941 linking the Vichy Embassy in Washington to Nazi interests. "Vichy French Embassy in Washington Shown as Heading Clique of Agents Aiding Nazis," one headline read. The US Secretary of the Treasury Henry Morgenthau congratulated the paper for the journalist feat.

There were also embassies penetrated in Mexico and Columbia. BSC had contacts inside the Japanese Embassy in Washington and Japanese Consulates in New York and San Francisco. There was also some success in direct penetration of the Saburo Kurusu mission that travelled to the United States shortly before the Pearl Harbor attack. BSC was able to obtain information on Spanish intentions and ciphers through the Basques in the United States and around the world. Most Basques remained loyal to President Aguirre, who had been forced to flee after Franco's victory. The janitor at the Spanish Embassy was used to relay information.

According to Hyde's *The Quiet Canadian* and the BSC history, there was reason to believe the Vichy French were tapping the Western Union trans-Atlantic cable, possibly using the French islands of St. Pierre and Miquelon as a base, and passing convoy information to the enemy. BSC agents were sent to the islands off Newfoundland and through surveys found 97 per cent of the population were pro-de Gaulle.[3]

BSC also kept track of a number of international business people and celebrities. In the files of Montgomery Hyde there are a number of clippings on the Swedish industrialist Axel Wenner Gren who was thought to have had pro-Nazi sympathies. Elsa Schiaparalli, a prominent dress designer, was also thought to have worked against the allied interest. BSC believed many people, such as in Schiaparalli's pro-Vichy sentiment, were inspired by avarice and a determination to prosper in the world, irrespective of whether or not it was Nazi-ruled.

Stephenson kept abreast of the scientific developments on both sides, such as the robot bombs, through Charles Lindemann at the British Embassy in Washington. He was the brother of Frederick

Lindemann, Viscount Cherwell, a physicist, who performed a similar function for Churchill. Cherwell's brother was deputied to Stephenson so he "could pass on information of such importance it would warrant informing FDR personally."[4] Stephenson also conferred with atomic scientist Chaim Weizmann and Albert Einstein.[5] Weizmann met dissident German chemist Willstatter in Zurich in 1939 and began to work in London on tracing those who could help the Germans build atomic bombs.[6] Weizmann saw Stephenson early in 1944 and Einstein and Stephenson discussed scientific and political matters during long walks through Central Park. Stephenson says the physicist was escorted by Shaun Herron, who later became a novelist/journalist in Winnipeg. Herron had to accompany Einstein from Princeton to assure that "the lamb entered the train at Princeton Junction bound for New York and not the opposite direction."[7] Stephenson is said to have provided protection in 1940 (John Hart, formerly of the RCMP) for Henry Tizard. The British scientist brought many of the besieged island's scientific secrets to the US for development, such as radar and the jet engine.[8]

■

As BSC expanded, the files they collected became immense. Numerous filing clerks were employed, and a filing expert from Canada's Royal Canadian Mounted Police was loaned to BSC to set up a quick access system. The historian Gilbert Hyatt and his associates constantly added to BSC files. Hyatt, later of Columbia University, thought the advance of history could be studied not only through class movements, or competing nations, but through the progress of individuals and their families. He set up large card files for personalities, German and other, throughout South America which would "enable our office to predict how in such and such an area, a segment of the population or an individual might react as the war took one turn or another." He collected information about individuals, about their right and left hand men, their families, habits, and their backgrounds. After the direct military threat became less crucial in South America, BSC concentrated on the industrial threat, and flows of capital. Hyatt's card system also tried to identify people who could be susceptible to blackmail. "This is really one of the purposes of espionage," he explained later. "Every human being has his weaknesses. In war or in a very tight political struggle both sides try to discover and then play on these weaknesses. If you have cards which indicate weaknesses of that kind reaching so deep into a man's personality structure, you can clearly become aware that the enemy will attempt to play on such weaknesses and take what steps you see fit to counter play."[9]

Problems With the Americans

In early 1941 Stephenson's vocation was officially renamed. A January 21, 1941, letter from His Majesty's Charge D'affaires to the US Secretary of State announced: "Mr W S Stephenson, hitherto British Passport Control Officer in New York, has been appointed to the position of Director of Security Coordination in the US."[10] However his job description was still rather vague and not widely advertised. Stephenson was the representative of MI6 and SOE in the Western Hemisphere, and in late October of 1942 he was made MI5 rep in the Western Hemisphere. According to a coded message sent to the West Indian Colonies this was a result of "greatly increased importance of security measures in Caribbean and West Indian waters and improved coordination with the Americans."[11]

It was impossible for Stephenson's expanding espionage and public relations organization not to draw some attention to itself. To be effective BSC had to deal with a number of American departments and various individuals. But at least when they started, they were a foreign intelligence network working in a neutral country, so they had to be covert. Churchill said that in wartime the truth was so precious it had to be surrounded by a bodyguard of lies. Stephenson had a convoy encircling BSC. He also kept quite silent about the scope of his activities.

Hoover obviously knew Stephenson, but this knowledge didn't extend far down the bureaucratic ladder. A Treasury department report of February 6, 1941 from special agent Bannerman, indicates others in the bureau had little idea what was going on, or were keeping quiet. Bannerman said, "Stephenson is not known to any of the Federal officials or agencies in New York that deal with anti-sabotage, nor have any of the Federal agencies ever heard of him ... Many of the British officers in New York did not know Mr Stephenson and did not know anything about his new position ... As yet Mr Stephenson is not known to either the New York police or the New York office of the FBI," and "Mr Stephenson has so far refused to reveal the exact whereabouts of his office and the entire matter has been handled with the utmost secrecy."[12]

According to a defining memo from the British Embassy, Stephenson's employees were simply watching ships.

"The duties of these (BSC) officers are two-fold:

(a) to enforce security regulations on board British and British-controlled ships coming into port.

(b) to report either to the Director of Security Coordination, Mr Stephenson, or to the local United States authorities with whom Mr Stephenson is in contact, any circumstances which appear to menace the security of the British or British-controlled shipping."[13]

By the spring of 1941, the American State Department was concerned about what appeared to be occurring. A March 31, 1941, letter from Assistant Secretary of State Adolph Berle reported to Sumner Welles that, "the head of the field service appears to be Mr William S Stephenson ... in charge of providing protection for British ships, supplies etc. But in fact a full size secret police and intelligence service is rapidly evolving ... (with) district officers at Boston, New York City, Philadelphia, Baltimore, Charleston, New Orleans, Houston, San Francisco, Portland and probably Seattle." It said Stephenson employed both regular secret agents and a much larger number of informers, and Berle urged his activities be curtailed.[14]

Berle was worried that Stephenson's network was going to cause problems. "I have in mind, of course, that should anything go wrong at any time, the State Department would be called upon to explain why it permitted violation of American laws and was compliant about an obvious breach of diplomatic obligation.... Were this to occur and a Senate investigation should follow, we should be on very dubious ground if we have not taken appropriate steps."

The situation came to a head with the possible implementation of the McKellar Bill in the winter of 1942. People such as Adolf Berle wanted foreign agents expelled, or else registered and kept under tight reins. In a February 5, 1942 lobbying letter from Berle to FDR, he wrote that British espionage and counterespionage was under the misleading title of Security Coordination. He urged the registration of foreign agents and questioned why other country's spies should be in the US. "Logically, why have it?"[15]

In his diary at the time, Berle wrote about the lead-up to the bill's fate. "Security Coordination intervened with the embassy, but the embassy said they could do nothing about it. Thereupon they intervened with Bill Donovan who promptly put in a memorandum to the President asking him to veto the bill which was on his desk. I am impressed with Donovan's courage, though I don't think much of it in terms of national wisdom. Why should anyone have a spy system in the United States? And what will it look like a little later when someone finds out about it?"[16] Berle seemed to think he was up against an organized lobbying clique. He later wrote that "The lend lease boys called me last night."

Stephenson obviously wanted the McKellar Bill to disappear and he lobbied influential people to see that it did. For example, Robert Sherwood, a Roosevelt speech writer and a friend of Stephenson's, wrote the President and said "This bill is a hangover of isolationism" and "would seriously hamper our numerous activities abroad."[17]

The bill was vetoed by Roosevelt February 9, 1942, but Stephenson's public relations problems were far from over. Later that month he reported to London that an anti-British feeling was on the increase in the US, "amounting almost to hostility," outside the strictly military sphere. The cause arose from a desire to put the US in fighting order on a nationalistic basis Stephenson's report concluded.

The day the McKellar Bill was vetoed Stephenson asked his staff for ways to improve Anglo-American relations.

Later in the month Stephenson had more problems. On Feb. 13, 1942, Berle's diary reported that a Mr Tamm of the FBI called, "with a piece of information which is at once amusing, disturbing and irritating." A BSC agent, Dennis Paine, was supposedly trailing Berle and trying to get 'the dirt' on him. However all he discovered out of the ordinary was that Berle had twin tubs in his bathroom. Stephenson was called on the carpet by US government officials, and Paine was expelled from the United States. There is another version to the story. According to former BSC operative Bill Ross Smith, the episode was an FBI public relations exercise. The FBI knew Paine worked for BSC and to help prove their vigilance in the US, they pounced on him.[18]

At the end of the month a meeting took place between Attorney General Francis Biddle, Adolf Berle, J Edgar Hoover, Admiral Wilkinson, and General Raymond Lee "about Stephenson working under the title of Security Coordination." Biddle concluded BSC's existence "may have been arranged by an informal agreement between Churchill and the President before the war." He thought some of the undercover men were "irresponsible" and the informants BSC used were "unscrupulous." "There are at present ninety names registered with the state department and it is believed over 300 agents are working." Biddle was also concerned that several thousand coded messages a month were being sent and received by BSC through the FBI radio in Maryland.[19]

On March 5, 1942 Biddle, the British Ambassador Lord Halifax, a British minister Ronald Campbell, FBI head Hoover, and Adolf Berle met to discuss limiting BSC's activities to liaison only, and Biddle's conclusion that British intelligence "probably needed a different type of man to head it." The British Ambassador, Lord Halifax, told the meeting Stephenson did nothing without the permission of the FBI, and that they exchanged results. When Hoover was called in, he said that didn't correspond to his impression at all. Stephenson sometimes reported afterward what he was doing, and frequently not then. When Hoover was bluntly asked whether he thought Stephenson was the man to head the organization, Mr Hoover responded that, "he had no quarrel with Mr Stevenson (sic) and had pleasant personal relations with him." He did not, however, feel that they were on terms of such confidence with BSC or with Mr Stephenson as to make close relations possible. Specifically they were never sure whether they were getting the whole story, and they knew that in many cases they were not. Certain instances were discussed in which BSC had tapped wires and shanghaied sailors, and the matter was being reported to the Attorney General. Lord Halifax said that his 'mental structure' was altered when he learned that there was not a close working relationship between Hoover and Stephenson.[20]

Five days later Berle wrote with some alarm that FBI radio was sending two or three hundred messages a week, "in secret code for the British Intelligence here to the British Intelligence in London ... *and no one knew anything about it.*" He was told they were secret messages between Roosevelt and Churchill, but Berle decided "Somebody has been doing some tall lying here." He figured it was Stephenson. Berle concluded the Canadian had probably transferred a considerable number of agents in the country to Donovan's payroll, on the excuse that they are to be used in 'recruiting personnel' for some overseas work in which Donovan is engaged.[21]

Years after the war Berle said he admired Stephenson "greatly," according to David Ogilvy who met the American bureaucrat in the 1960's. However Berle thought some of Stephenson's staff took too many risks before Pearl Harbor. Berle, according to Ogilvy, "felt it was his duty to prevent them causing public scandals which would have played into the hands of the Irish Congressmen and other isolationists."[22]

For his part Stephenson explained "Adolf Berle was slightly schoolmasterish for a very brief period due to misinformation," but the former Under Secretary of State "could not have been more helpful when factual situations were clarified to him."[23]

American bureaucratic checks on BSC continued, although they received only limited response.[24] Throughout the war BSC was required to give lists of employees and job descriptions as various US departments tried to keep tabs on their activities.

There seems to have been a few attempts to get rid of the Canadian spymaster. On June 18, 1943 Canadian diplomat Tommy Stone wrote to Stephenson to say he heard from the British High Commission in Ottawa that GC Denham was going to take over BSC. In fact Denham took over MI5 in the United States, but not the whole show. According to Hyde, he only had a hazy conception of what his new duties involved.[25] But Stone knew even if Stephenson was not Britain's representative, he would not be leaving his post. The Canadian representative wanted the details of the "new organization you are going to build up in Washington. Would appreciate a line or two on these matters or would you rather give it to me verbally."[26]

South America

Stephenson sent numerous agents and support personnel through-out Central and South America. According to Dick Ellis, the intelligence establishment in England didn't recommend this, it was brought on by a request from the FBI. "They had no trained officers, they had nobody with any knowledge of languages or of Latin America, and they came ... and they said 'will you help us?'"[27] Stephenson's schemes in South America caused a certain amount of apprehension in London where it was felt Central and South America were American areas. Stephenson operated largely on his own. Some of the contacts were through the British Embassies and trade missions. Others were not. The American diplomat Spruille Braden, in his book *Diplomats and Demagogues*, gives a first-hand account of a Stephenson agent using American resources.

In May 1941 on a train to New York, Braden, the American Ambassador in Columbia, complained to an acquaintance, journalist Ulric Bell, about a lack of intelligence in South America. Bell told Braden about Bill Donovan, and he said Donovan's trips to Europe were to study Nazi Fifth Column activity. Bell worked for Donovan and arranged a meeting. Donovan explained to Braden a theoretical series of subversive operations involving propaganda, sabotage, and espionage, which could occur, and Braden thought similar activities were already taking place in Columbia. Toward the end of their meeting Donovan asked Braden if he wanted to meet, "the head of British Intelligence, a Mr So-and-So." Braden met Bill Stephenson at the Metropolitan Club in New York, and Stephenson told Braden that he was reorganizing his intelligence service in Columbia and would send a man named Stagg down to meet with him. "I'll put him under your orders," Stephenson told the Ambassador. Stagg was instructed by Stephenson to act as a playboy and to report to Braden, who was to use Stagg as his own agent. "Of course Stephenson knew that the British Minister and his legation staff were phlegmatic," Braden recalled."They didn't even know his organization existed."[28]

Stagg and his wife arrived in Bogota from Equador. He played polo and tennis, loved to dance, go to parties, and entertaining. "It was perfectly obvious he was just a frolicsome dilettante." The Ambassador gave Stagg priority when he appeared at the embassy, and his staff could not understand why. However Braden found Stagg very efficient, with a quality organization. On one occasion Braden reported to Stephenson's agent that there was a large meeting at the German Legation and the street was full of cars. Ten minutes later Stagg arrived with one of his men and his wife. The couple walked down the street past the German legation at a normal pace and Stagg's agent memorized the license number of every car—over two dozen altogether. Because of the memory feat they were able to trace that every car owner was tied into the Nazi movement.

One day Stagg brought the Columbian Ambassador a copy of a letter that purported to be from Major Elias Belmonte Pabon, the Bolivian Military Attaché in Berlin, to the German minister in La Paz, telling of a plot to overthrow the government of Bolivian President Penaranda. Stagg told Braden that they had intercepted a transcript of the letter and wanted the original and he asked if the Americans could intercept the diplomatic pouch. The State Department reported back that they would have nothing to do with the interception of diplomatic mail. Weeks later, Braden heard the Bolivian government had received information about a possible coup, and a Major Belmonte was involved. The same letter Braden had seen in his office was read over the radio word for word. The Bolivian government sent the German minister out of the country and broke off diplomatic relations. (Bolivia was a major source of wolfram, used in steel and arms manufacture.) When Braden congratulated Stagg on the interception of the letter, he was surprised to learn BSC had not intercepted the letter, they forged it. Early in 1941, Stephenson received information from J Edgar Hoover that Belmonte was in touch with Nazi elements in Bolivia. He sent Hyde down to Bolivia to survey the situation and cabled people to be on the lookout for a German diplomatic bag. Stephenson took the letter to Hoover, who took it to Hull and then to Roosevelt. The circulated letter was forged, Stagg told Braden, and having forged the letter Stephenson had to devise the appearance of authenticity.[29] In Hyde's *The Quiet Canadian* he writes about his trip to South America and the Bolivian situation, but he says the Belmonte letter was intercepted on an elevator in Buenos Aires.[30] Braden calls Hyde's account "the classic 'amalgam', the combination of truth with falsehood that is of all snarls the hardest to unravel."[31]

According to the BSC history, in August of 1940 the possibility was explored of staging a French coup in Martinique that would help release gold, ships and aircraft. In the files of Montgomery Hyde are a number of South American maps showing, among other things, the location of raw materials, oil refineries and radio stations. There are also wartime New York newspaper clippings of Axis activities in the southern hemisphere. The organization seems to have kept close tabs on the flow of money and smuggling of industrial diamonds, platinum, and wolfram. During the course of the war, Stephenson represented Britain's MI6, MI5, the Political Intelligence Department, Special Operations Executive, the Office of Naval Intelligence, the Security Executive and Special Branch of Scotland Yard. His BSC office was the liaison for similar organizations in the United States and Canada. According to Ernest Cuneo, Stephenson engaged in covert diplomacy, supplied intelligence to Britain, monitored the flow of people, mail, and commodities to and from Europe, conducted intelligence operations from propaganda and political warfare against isolationists, established a hemisphere port security system and ship's observer scheme, built and operated the Camp X training centre, and established a covert communications system.[32] But due to the nature of the activities, the exact extent of BSC's operations will probably never be known. Following the publication of Hyde's *The Quiet Canadian*, Sir Bede Clifford, the governor of Trinidad and Tobago during the war, wrote to Hyde and said he knew of William Stephenson at the time. He recalled taking a Spanish diplomat for a drive on the island and for lunch at Government House "while Stephenson's agents went through his baggage."[33]

1945

As the war progressed and gradually swung in favour of the Allies, Stephenson was given some recognition for his contribution. In 1944 following the D-Day landings he was knighted, and it was publicly proclaimed January 1, 1945. The announcement in *The Times* of London herded him into a list with over forty others ("William Samuel Stephenson employed in a department of the Foreign Office"). At the end of March, 1945 J Edgar Hoover discovered Stephenson had been knighted. "It is certainly one (honour) that is both well-earned and well-deserved," the FBI head wrote. "In years to come you certainly can with great satisfaction look back to the very worthy contribution which you have made, not only to your own country, but to those of its Allies in this world conflict. When the full story can be told, I am quite certain that your contribution will be among the foremost in having brought victory finally to the United Nations' cause."[34]

Soon after D-Day Donovan wrote to President Roosevelt and to the Joint Chiefs of Staff recommending Stephenson be awarded the American Distinguished Service Medal. "The extensive experience of the British Government in the fields of secret intelligence and special operations was made available to this country largely through the efforts of William Samuel Stephenson. Without his help it would not have been possible to establish the instrumentalities for these purposes in time to aid the American war effort. He not only enabled the United States to borrow on British experience, but he helped to secure and train the personnel initially required for this undertaking. At every step in the creation of these instrumentalities, he contributed assistance and counsel of such value that his services may be considered exceptionally meritorious both to the Government of the United States and to the entire Allied cause."

Stephenson wasn't awarded the Medal and received no public recognition from the Americans until the end of 1946. The British held up the presentation of the American award to Stephenson—a key figure in the survival of the British Isles. Over a year after the end of the war, on the letterhead of his law firm, Bill Donovan wrote to Alexander Cadogan to say he was "much perturbed to learn there appears to be some delay by the Foreign Office in returning formal approval" of the Medal of Merit to Stephenson. Donovan explained in the letter that Stephenson had already received the Medal of Merit in a ceremony after the war anyway, without their permission. He wrote that the medal was the highest civilian decoration awarded by the President, and Stephenson's case was unique, as for the first time it was presented to a foreigner. "I felt sure that you personally would be pleased with the implications of the blanket approval of the operations of the British secret organization in the United States during the war (all of which were under Stephenson)."[35]

Donovan and Stephenson were together May 7, 1945 when word reached them Germany had signed for peace. The following day Stephenson wrote to those who worked for him, from senior officials to clerks and thanked them for their service.

8 The BSC History and the Last Case

At the end of the war, the files of British Security Coordination were packed onto semi-trailers and transported to Canada. Stephenson wanted to have some record of the activities of the agency "to provide a record which would be available for reference should future need arise for secret activities and security measures for the kind it describes."[1] That purpose had been "advanced to the point of immediacy ... with the advent of atomic weapons," he wrote in the foreword. The archives were collated, summarized and destroyed at Camp X. BSC's chief secretary Grace Garner got the papers ready, assisted by Eleanor Fleming and filing head Meryl Cameron. Stephenson wanted Garner, a former editor, to try writing the history. "He wanted me to have a stab at it, but I couldn't do it," she remembered. "I made the files quite cross-referenced and the stuff was handed over to them complete."[2] The result was a history of the organization written by Tom Hill, Gilbert Hyatt, Roald Dahl and Montgomery Hyde. Like most of the activities of BSC, the process was conducted in secret. The history was put together at Camp X, and shuttled in army vehicles at night to be printed at an Oshawa, Ontario, print shop. "We had a couple of security people to carry this stuff back and forward to the camp," Hill recalled. "My wife and I lived in the hotel. We were both picked up in the daytime." The final editing was done by Giles Playfair in New York. Hill stayed at the camp and did the final checking and printing. There were 20 copies of the book printed—Hill put ten into a safe in Montreal, and ten went to Stephenson for distribution. "One went to Churchill," Hill remembered, "and one had to go to each of the heads of security intelligence organizations, and SOE, and Lord Beaverbrook, Minister of Aircraft Production during the war, and he probably sent one to Lord Leathers of Transport."[3]

Hill was to be the guardian of the remaining copies. "I put them in a safe, left them for a year, and then Sir William didn't want them anymore," he remembered. "I took them out to my wife's family farm in Quebec and burned them. All ten spare copies." Hill, who worked with

Stephenson following the war, regretted not keeping a copy for himself, as the history of BSC has become an elusive publication. None of the remaining ten copies have ever surfaced publicly for more than a few hours. It is often referred to as the 'the Bible', and it is still classified as 'Top Secret' by Britain's MI6.[4] The account of Stephenson's secret organization has been called "one of the most astonishing documents in history," by the former British MP and intelligence writer Rupert Allason, who writes under the name Nigel West.[5]

Chroniclers of BSC, Montgomery Hyde and William Stevenson were given access to the secret history by Stephenson. "Place Bible in safe keeping of 'Bill,'" Stephenson cabled Stevenson in 1973.[6] Some sections of the BSC history are very similar to Hyde's accounts in *The Quiet Canadian*—almost word for word.

Gouzenko

In early September of 1945, Stephenson was on his way to see Canadian Prime Minister Mackenzie King at the Seignory Club, outside Ottawa. King couldn't make the meeting as he was ill, so Stephenson proceeded to Under Secretary of State in Canada's Department of External Affairs, Norman Robertson's Ottawa house. At Robertson's he heard details about Igor Gouzenko, a Soviet Embassy cipher clerk who was looking for assistance. Gouzenko was 26 at the time and working for the GRU, Soviet Military intelligence. "During my residence in Canada," he wrote after his defection," I have seen how the Canadian people and their government, sincerely wishing to help the Soviet people sent supplies to the Soviet Union, collected money for the welfare of the Russian people, sacrificing the lives of their sons in the delivery of supplies across the ocean—and instead of gratitude for the help rendered, the Soviet government is developing espionage activity in Canada, preparing to deliver a stab in the back to Canada—all this without the knowledge of the Russian people."[7] Reportedly Gouzenko committed a minor breach of security and he and his pregnant wife Svetlana were supposed to return to the Soviet Union. They decided to stay in Canada instead.

Stephenson was amazed to learn Gouzenko was not in safe custody and the young couple were still roaming Ottawa. The Soviet Union was regarded as an ally, and the disgruntled embassy employee soon found no doors were widely opened for him. "Nobody would listen to him," Stephenson said later. "The Prime Minister himself, Mackenzie King, had said that he thought it was too hot a potato ... to interfere in this case." King apparently thought suicide would be a possible recourse for the defector. "If suicide took place, let the city police take charge ... but on no account let us take the initiative," he recorded in his diary.[8] Stephenson got in touch with Tommy Stone who worked for Robertson and was later Canada's Ambassador to the Netherlands, discovered where Gouzenko was and may have even driven to the defector's apartment. Stephenson recommended the RCMP take possession of him as soon as possible, or a least post guards. Gouzenko was taken into protective custody. Later Jean Paul Evans and Peter Dwyer, British-trained BSC employees, were sent to interview him. Eventually Gouzenko was shuttled to Camp X near Toronto, where he and his wife lived in guarded seclusion.

Stephenson controlled the overseas distribution of Gouzenko's revelations and the documents he took with him following his debriefing. The Canadian and British High Commission transmission links had been compromised, so BSC New York provided a secure communications link to Britain.[9]

Gouzenko and the material he took with him revealed a large Soviet espionage network in Canada and the US. His information led to the arrest of the 'atom spies' Klaus Fuchs and Alan Nunn May in Britain. He also implicated American government officials Harry Dexter White and Alger Hiss in the United States. His knowledge of codes and cover names likely aided the decrypting done in the US of VENONA.[10] He is regarded as the most important defector of the era, and his revelations are often regarded as the beginning of the Cold War.

The defection of Gouzenko was not known publically until February 4, 1946, when the American journalist Drew Pearson reported on a large Soviet espionage network operating in North America. The publicity may have been prompted by Stephenson. "It was through Drew Pearson that we forced action lift diplomatic fears likely ensue from the great monster in Gouzenko affair as you will recall," cabled Stephenson.[11]

Following the debriefing of Gouzenko, the Canadian government arrested a dozen suspects and set up a Royal Commission in 1946, headed by Robert Taschereau and R L Kellock, to deal with the charges. The inquiry was closed to the public, and some details were still secret many years later.

Gouzenko was known for being somewhat touchy with journalists and others who he thought defamed him. He disliked the word 'defector' and frequently threatened people with lawsuits. According to Gouzenko lawyers Nelles Starr and Alan Harris, he was trying to protect his reputation. He thought that before the Soviets would try to kill him, they would try to destroy his credibility to the point of ridicule.[12]

After Stephenson's death, Canadian writer and politician John Bryden, in *Best Kept Secret*, questioned whether Stephenson was actually involved in the Gouzenko affair. In the period between his defection and his death in 1982, Gouzenko, living under an assumed identity, made his presence known to many journalists in and around Toronto, including Peter Worthington, and William Stevenson, the author of *A Man Called Intrepid*. Worthington, the only person other than family at Gouzenko's funeral, wrote that Stephenson "probably saved Gouzenko from being returned to the Soviets."[13] From correspondence between Stevenson and the ex-spy master in Bermuda, it appears Gouzenko and his wife had no doubt Stephenson was instrumental in providing a safe haven in Canada. "They asked to be remembered to you," Stevenson wrote Stephenson in 1976, "and said again that they feel they owe their lives and those of their children to you."[14] Stevenson's final book about the former spychief, *Intrepid's Last Case*, dealt loosely with the Gouzenko incident.

9 Postwar

From 1946 to early 1951 Stephenson lived in semi-retirement in Montego Bay, Jamaica, while maintaining a residence in New York on East 52nd Street. His British business was looked after by Miss AM Green in Carshalton, Surrey. Stephenson's financial interests were moving from Europe to the Western Hemisphere. In 1946, he began to wind down his involvement in the film business. Stephenson sold 74% interest of Sound City Films for £380,000 to British Lion, which was controlled by his friend, Sir Alexander Korda, and the studio went through a large expansion and renovation program.

Stephenson and Mary were known for entertaining during the war, and they continued to attract a wide variety of personalities to their various homes. Stephenson's friends Noel Coward, Beaverbrook, and Ian Fleming bought residences in Jamaica. Following the war, among Stephenson's friends were Louis St. Laurent, Brooke Claxton, Dana Wilgress (former Canadian High Commissioner in London), the Aga Khan, Henry R. Luce (Editor-in-Chief of *Time* Inc.) and the British newspaper barons Kemsley, Camrose, and Rothermere. He frequently used the telex machine in his house and looked forward to his regular correspondence with Lord Louis Mountbatten. In his later years Stephenson bought a satellite dish to keep in touch with world events.

Following the death of Brigadier Richard Malone (1985), the former publisher of the Toronto *Globe and Mail*, Stephenson recalled in a letter to the paper a Jamaican dinner at his house in 1946 with Malone, Canadian politicians JL Ralston and CD Howe, 'Max' (Lord Beaverbrook), Beaverbrook's houseguest, Henry Luce, and Stephenson's own house guests, 'Fred' (Lord Leathers, British Minister of War Transport) and 'Pug' (Lord Ismay, Churchill's right hand military man).[1]

According to the journalist McKenzie Porter, Stephenson surprised many famous guests by inviting them to visit a neighbour who turned out to be a local farmer with whom he chatted for hours. He also played host to scores of 'obscure people' he met and liked during his travels. He sometimes hired local people to sing to his friends, and every Christmas he threw a party for between four and five hundred. In Jamaica he provided funds for a new church in the neighbourhood. Following the war Stephenson rose each morning at five, reportedly ate like a bird and lost his taste for French wine. The couple maintained a house in Montreal, often vacationed in Prince Edward Island, read a lot, and collected paintings and books.[2]

In 1951 the Stephensons sold their house, Hillowton, in Jamaica, to the Reynolds Aluminum Company, and began living in New York.[3] The apartment took up an entire floor of the building. The Stephensons' neighbours above were the publisher Henry Luce and his wife, while below them lived the century's most famous recluse, Greta Garbo.

Later in 1951 Stephenson was appointed chairman of the Newfoundland and Labrador Corporation, a Crown company, by the new Canadian province's first premier Joey Smallwood. He helped attract new industries and investment during 1952 to the tenth province, and his success was said to have "kept Joey Smallwood busy for the next three years." In October of 1952, Stephenson resigned as the chairman of the Corporation, because he thought it should have a local head. Newfoundland's Premier accepted the resignation with reluctance and regret. "You achieved a magnificent result in a very short space of time, and I and the Government and people of Newfoundland must ever be grateful to you," Smallwood wrote.[4] He asked that Stephenson continue to act as Newfoundland's representative in the United States.

Stephenson later helped in organizing some of the financing for the huge Churchill Falls hydro development in Labrador, through his business contacts in Britain, notably Edmund de Rothschild.[5]

"He is a great Canadian and has done more than any other man to bring Canada's enormous potential to the notice of international investors," John Pepper was quoted as saying in a magazine story (1952). Pepper, who worked in Stephenson's inner office during the war, became one of first presidents of the British American Canadian corporation, and later Stephenson helped set him up in the Newfoundland pulp and paper business.

Stephenson was one of the originators and mainsprings of the British American Canadian Corporation, which changed its name to the

World Commerce Corporation. The company at 25 Broad Street, New York, tried using barter agreements and dollar guarantees to get around currency restrictions that slowed world trade. They also helped develop poorer countries. The *Christian Science Monitor* quoted an Italian businessman, saying: "If there were a hundred World Commerces there would be no need for the Marshall plan." *Time* magazine reported that long before Truman called for the export of US knowledge and capital to other world nations, "the same idea had occurred to a small forward-looking group of US, British and Canadian capitalists."[6]

The company had its ups and downs. Many of the organizers were formerly in British Security Coordination or the American Office of Strategic Services. "The idea was to take advantage of the organization and international contacts that were set up during the war," Tom Hill remembered. "The goal was to set up various companies mostly in Central and South America." David Ogilvy arranged business in the United States. George Merton, who eventually joined the CIA, organized South America, says Hill. The University of Manitoba graduate, who helped edit a western intelligence bulletin during the war, was the secretary, and believes he was asked to be involved because of his engineering background. Others joined, such as: Sir Charles Hambro (banker, former head of SOE), Russell Forgan, (Glore Forgan group of bankers, successor to David Bruce as head of OSS Europe), Lester Armour (formerly OSS London), Sidney Weinberg, WK Eliscu (former OSS operatives) and Rex Benson (SIS). Nelson Rockefeller, J J McCloy, Richard Mellon, and Sir Victor Sassoon also had interests in the company. Joseph Grew, the ex-US Ambassador to Japan, Trans-America Corporation, and Atlas Corporation were said to be involved.[7]

The company didn't do well. Frank Ryan became World Commerce head, and Stephenson reportedly arranged for him to see Lord Leathers (wartime Transportation Minister), Sir William Rootes (auto manufacturer), Richard Coit (stockbroker, who worked for SOE in North America), Sir Alexander Korda (film producer), Moir Mackenzie (Federation of British Industries), Lord Selborne (Economic Warfare Minister); from the newspaper business Beaverbrook, Ian Fleming (British Naval Intelligence, Foreign Department head at Kemsley Press), Sir Campbell Stuart (director of the *Times*), Sir Ralph Glyn (politician and businessman), Fred Hudd (Canadian High Commissioner), and bankers such as Charles and Olaf Hambro. Later Ryan family interests, which were involved in international textile, sold a controlling interest in the company and about two thirds of the World Commerce staff was let go.[8]

To expand WCC's political influence former US Secretary of State Edward Stettinius joined the company. "He brought with him a few people," Hill remembered, "Donovan was our lawyer, and ultimately the company wasn't doing well, and wasn't making a profit, so they brought in the bankers that put up the money." Hill eventually parted with the company and Stephenson arranged for him to move into the cement business.

Hill thought Stephenson was not too enthusiastic about the switch back to the business world. "He was drinking with Donovan at this point, but was able to rally around when needed."

One of the successes of WCC was to help bring a cement industry to Jamaica. Sir John Huggins, the Governor of Jamaica, approached Stephenson for assistance, and he began a lengthy association with the Jamaican cement industry in the early 1950's. Before his involvement, all of Jamaica's cement was imported. Stephenson became the Chairman-of-the-Board of the Caribbean Cement Co. Limited, and Sir William Wiseman, the British Passport Control Officer during the First World War, served on the board. In a speech Stephenson gave to shareholders, in the spring of 1961, the company declared a profit of over £600,000, and he said that since 1952 the total savings to the country, as a result of domestic production, was over three million pounds.[9] He remained involved with the cement industry for many years.[10]

During the sixties he continued to be an active promoter of the Caribbean. In 1961 the cement plant began a large expansion and the *Kingston Daily Gleaner* headline September 28, 1961 proclaimed, "Sir William Stephenson backs Jamaica." Later that year the paper reported on a Stephenson New York address in which he described the stable political climate in Jamaica following a referendum.[11]

The retired spychief also turned his attention to his home province. One of the main connections was through Derek Bedson, who he met in the fifties. Bedson worked for Canada's Department of External Affairs at the United Nations. He and Stephenson met regularly and Bedson visited Bermuda on numerous occasions. In the fall of 1953 Stephenson helped organize a New York agenda for Ron Turner, Manitoba's Minister of Industry and Commerce, when Turner was on an industrial development tour. Stephenson's assistance enabled Turner to meet with New York's top industrialists and investment people. Turner and the Deputy Minister later travelled with Hill to Britain, where Stephenson made sure doors were opened for them.

Soon afterward Stephenson became the honorary chairman of Manitoba's Economic Advisory Board which helped funnel investment to the province. In December of 1954, his position was formalized as he was named to the province's Economic Advisory Council. Stephenson got two Englishmen to join him on the board, Wiseman and Lord Semphill. Wiseman, formerly New York Passport Control, was the retired president of the investment bankers Kuhn Loeb. Semphill was the former chairman of the London Chamber of Commerce and involved in the British car industry and various technical bodies.[12] The group gave the Manitoba government accelerated access to the highest levels of world finance. "The very fact that he (Stephenson) agreed to have his name used working with the reconstruction period or anything of that kind would be very prestigious," Douglas Campbell, Manitoba's Premier from 1950-1958 said later.[13]

In the early sixties Stephenson suffered a serious stroke. It greatly affected his speech and slowed him down. His Bermuda doctor Maurice Fulton called the stroke "a devastating vascular accident," but with the constant help of his wife, Stephenson "fought back with as much tenacity and bravery as ever shown on the field of battle or the field of international espionage."[14] In the seventies Fulton was quoted as saying, "Sheer willpower has kept him going for the past quarter century."[15] Following the stroke Stephenson and his wife left New York for good and retired to Bermuda for what has been described as 'self imposed exile.'

Roald Dahl saw his former boss in New York before the move to Bermuda and was amazed at the stroke's effects and the deterioration of Stephenson's speech. The writer was impressed with the work of a British neurosurgeon Kenneth Till, who treated Dahl's son following a traffic accident. Dahl recommended he visit Stephenson in Bermuda.

It is not known whether Till's stay in Bermuda improved Stephenson's medical condition, but years later Dahl wrote to Stephenson to tell him the doctor was well. "I believe that somehow his contact with you and the generosity you have shown towards his family has given him a tremendous boost," Dahl wrote.[16]

During the 1970's Stephenson continued to press for the development of tidal power, especially for power generation in the Bay of Fundy.[17]

In the early 1980's, Stephenson donated $100,000 to the University of Winnipeg, and through the auspices of the Winnipeg Foundation the capital is used to provide annual student scholarships. At the time it was the largest amount of money that had ever been donated to the university. Ironically the first person to win a scholarship was a Breckman, a great-great-nephew of Stephenson. In a round-about way Stephenson returned to the community some of the money lent to him that launched his business career nearly six decades before.

■

One of Stephenson's good friends in later life was David Young, Air Canada's head in Bermuda from 1982 to 1986. Young brought Stephenson various Canadian newspapers about every two weeks, and was introduced by Stephenson to his visitors such as Canadian politician Eric Nielsen, the journalists General Richard Rohmer, Bill Stevenson, Peter Worthington, and Dr Rodney Hunter from Winnipeg. Nielsen, the brother of actor Leslie Nielsen, was married in Stephenson's house.

Pauline McGibbon met Stephenson in the mid-seventies, while she was the Lieutenant-Governor of Ontario. When she visited Bermuda, she heard that Stephenson would like to see her. "I would never have called on him myself, but I heard that he wanted to see me," McGibbon recalled, "It was one of those magic things when two people meet and they click." She returned to Bermuda every year.

By this time, Mary was terminally ill with cancer. She was at their Paget, Bermuda home but confined to her bedroom and attended to by a full-time nurse, Elizabeth Baptiste. Mary Stephenson died in 1977 and was buried in a private ceremony. Baptiste and her son Rhys remained in Bermuda and looked after Stephenson. In 1983, he adopted her as his daughter.

Stephenson long had a reputation for preparing hearty dry martinis. Some people believe he developed a drinking problem after the war (David Ogilvy, Tom Hill) while others believe this wasn't the case. Excerpts of Coward's diary indicate the actor-playwright imbibed while with Stephenson. "Lunched with Bill Stephenson," Coward wrote March 21, 1949, "Too many martinis. Slept in the afternoon. More martinis."[18] After the Stephensons moved from Jamaica, Coward saw them less often, and it appears Stephenson became disappointed with the postwar decade and world events of the time. "I lunched at long last with Bill Stephenson on Thursday," Coward wrote in 1956. "We reminisced about the war years and discoursed gloomily on the present crisis in the Middle East and Hungary. The world is so idiotic," Coward continued, "There is so much superstition, graft, greed and general stupidity that I cannot feel any impulses to do anything about it whatever, even if I could."[19]

Similar postwar sentiments are echoed by Stephenson in *A Man Called Intrepid*, in which he says, "'The springtime of our hope was 1945. If the world had fully grasped the essence of the devastating experience we'd survived, we might by now have dispensed with secret intelligence and stopped the creation of terrifying weapons.' He paused again, lost in thought..."[20]

But Stephenson remained concerned with the future and seemed to keep in touch with modern developments "The farseeing James Schlesinger utters a word of warning with reference to danger of US entering an era of neoisolationism," he cabled to William Stevenson. "It's dangerous bringing up to today the fear that Winston expressed in his book *Triumph and Tragedy*. 'And as the great democracies triumphed and so were able to resume the follies that so nearly cost them their life.'"[21]

Until the end of his life Stephenson had sources which could give him quick results to such things as political conventions before they were available through regular channels.[22] He frequently sent messages using his telex all over the world to people such as Louis Mountbatten, who apparently visited him in Bermuda in March 1975.[23] In the late sixties Stephenson seems to have still been involved in some type of intelligence activities. Thomas Troy, with the CIA at the time, says Stephenson wanted him to join 'Olds', a line of communication which was monitoring activists.[24]

Apparently Stephenson's opinion was sought on Western intelligence and defence matters, and he received official visitors from Canada and the United States until his death. Reportedly he cabled the Israeli Prime Minister following the rescue of hostages from Entebbe, and he knew of the operation beforehand.[25]

Stephenson became disappointed at the turn of events in Washington during the early seventies and thought Canada had the potential to fill the moral vacuum that paralysed the American leadership. Cables of questions and answers dealing with preliminary work on *A Man Called Intrepid* with the author were interrupted by what Stephenson referred to as, "tears over Washington telephones." At about the time of the resignation of Richard Nixon as a result of the Watergate scandal Stephenson cabled to say:

WHAT A SAD DAY ATOP THE WORLDWIDE ANSWER NOW LIES SQUARELY UPON THE STRONG SHOULDERS OF CANADA STOP THIS IS NOT THE SUGGESTION TO GRASP LEADERSHIP STOP IT IS THE MOMENT OF DECISION THAT ONLY A NATION WITH A REAL SOUL AND COMPLETE FLUORESCENCE OF PER ARDUA AD ASTRA COULD ABSORB OPEN ITS MIND WIDELY TO ENCOURAGE ENCOMPASS AND ACHIEVE ITS GREAT DESTINY STOP WELCOME YOUR VIEWS STOP.[26]

Stephenson's antifascist stance, his lobbying and brokering on behalf of both Britain and the US, his attempts at postwar reconstruction, and assisting the developing world, could only be described as internationalist in nature. Yet he remained patriotic towards Canada. Robert Sherwood in *Roosevelt and Hopkins* wrote, "There was established by Roosevelt's order and despite State Department qualms, effectively close co-operation between J Edgar Hoover and British Security Services under the direction of 'a quiet Canadian,' William Stephenson." Stephenson later said he considered the simple designation in that book of being, "a quiet Canadian," a higher accolade than the British and

American honours he won for his war work.[27] It became the title of the first book about his espionage career.

A *Toronto Star* 1979 interview asked Stephenson if he felt "like the prophet who is without honour in his own land," as Britain, the US, France, and Belgium had honoured him, but Canada had never recognized him with the Order of Canada or any other major honour. "My personal balance sheet with Canada is much in Canada's favour," Stephenson replied. "It does not bother me. I am too preoccupied with the fate of the whole Western World."

Instead Stephenson used the occasion to warn of the Soviet threat. The 'cold warrior' told the reporter he thought Washington should be vigilant in the armaments race, and he quoted one military analyst who said, "There are tanks ready for action as far as the eye can see and what do we have? Without the neutron, they will plough through us as knife through butter."[28] He also advocated a close-knit coordinated intelligence service that was continually on the alert in every part of the world and could report accurately and quickly, as the best insurance against surprise.

According to many of his contemporaries, the lack of recognition from his home country did bother Stephenson. Although he was awarded decorations and honours for his role in two world wars, by European countries and the US, decades later he had still received no recognition at all from his own country, Canada. In Canada's centennial year 1967, the government created the Order of Canada in recognition of exceptional achievement in any field, and a quarter century after the conclusion of the war, an informal campaign began to see that it was bestowed on Stephenson. Some of Stephenson's friends helped lobby politicians in Ottawa for the country's highest civilian honour, the Companion of the Order of Canada (CC).

In October 1972, the journalist and writer William Stevenson drafted a letter to former Canadian Prime Minister Lester Pearson outlining Stephenson's career.[29] Pearson died later that year so was in no position to lobby. (Pearson should have been well aware of Stephenson's career, as he acted as a BSC contact person in a number of spheres, and he became Canada's Ambassador to the United States during the war.)

Over a year later, in December of 1973, Derek Bedson presented the case for Stephenson in Ottawa. The same month Peter Worthington wrote two columns in the Toronto *Sun* citing Stephenson's credentials for the award, and writing in his second column Stephenson should be honoured "not for Sir William's sake, but for Canada's."[30] Stephenson commented on the editorial afterward in a cable to William Stevenson, "Perhaps some indication at long last CC may be forthcoming."[31]

Six months later Worthington wrote about "The Forgotten Canadian," and said Stephenson was "isolated, forgotten, ignored." He said the former intelligence head, although he resided in Bermuda, was still a Canadian citizen and "is proud of his nationality and goes about his business expressing neither dismay nor rancour at being unrecognized in his own country."[32] A year later the *Sun* ran an editorial which said Stephenson's intelligence feats won the battle of the Atlantic, and in September of 1975, Worthington wrote a column which stressed, "our survival today hinged on Stephenson's activities then."[33] No award for Stephenson from the government of Pierre Trudeau was forthcoming.

The short-lived Conservative government of Joe Clark finally presented Stephenson with the Order of Canada in 1980. Due to Stephenson's failing health, it was bestowed away from Canada for the first time. Governor-General Edward Schreyer travelled to Bermuda, and Stephenson was named a Companion of the Order of Canada. Stephenson appears to have borne no grudges for the long delay. The cover of *A Man Called Intrepid* features a photograph of the numerous medals Stephenson was awarded from various countries. The front cover of *Intrepid's Last Case* depicts only one, his Order of Canada.

In September of 1983, Stephenson was awarded the William J. Donovan medal. It is bestowed to an individual who has rendered distinguished service in the interests of the democratic process and the cause of freedom, by the veterans of the OSS. The presentation took place on the aircraft carrier USS Intrepid which is permanently moored in New York. Stephenson appeared and spoke at the dinner, although at the time he was barely able to walk. US President Ronald Reagan sent a letter for the occasion.

The White House
Washington
September 12, 1983
Dear Sir William:

I was delighted to hear through Bill Casey that you would be the recipient of the William J. Donovan Award. I can think of no person more deserving. What an extraordinary life you have led in the service of freedom. Your career through World War I, World War II, and the postwar years adds up to one of the great legends, one of the great stories of personal valour and sacrifice for the sake of country and fellow men.

All those who love freedom owe you a debt of gratitude; but we, as Americans, are particularly grateful to you for all the warmth and friendship you have always shown to our nation. We want you to know that the friendship is reciprocated tenfold; and I want to assure you that as long as Americans value courage and freedom there will always be a special place in our hearts, our minds, and our history books for the 'Man Called Intrepid.'

Your accomplishments need little embellishment from me: they are your monument; they remain our inspiration. On behalf of the American people, I send you our warmest congratulations, our deepest gratitude, and our sincere wishes for many years of friendship and service together.

Sincerely, Ronald Reagan

Despite his strong feeling for Canada, throughout his later years Stephenson remained completely separate from his relatives in Winnipeg. For the most part, they heard nothing from him since about 1935. Stephenson returned to Winnipeg for a final time privately in 1980 and stayed at the Fort Garry Hotel.[34] Derek Bedson drove him around his old Point Douglas neighbourhood, but news of his trip home came out only after he departed, and while in the city he looked up none of his relatives. A radio interviewer, years later, remarked to family members, "this is almost as mysterious as his life was. Why did he come to see his birthplace and not contact you people that he grew up with?"

That question is difficult to answer. "They'd be talking and he didn't want too many people knowing about it," Reg Rimmer replied. Rimmer, the husband of Stephenson's niece, believed there was no chance of seeing Stephenson in Bermuda, and Stephenson's relatives had false assumptions about his security on the island. According to Rimmer, "You'd have to get through the mounted police ring to get to him."[35] Bina Ingimundson, Stephenson's cousin, had similar opinions. She was under the impression Stephenson lived on a separate island, away from the main island of Bermuda, which "was guarded very closely. Nobody went to that island except by invitation. What he was afraid of, or whether he was afraid of something. I don't know. But there was guards there all the time. There was no way anyone would go to the island without being invited."[36] Other relatives believe Stephenson moved to Bermuda for security reasons, although none of the family are sure where the information came from. "He was afraid of things that might happen to him, because of what he has done, you know, during the war. Being in the espionage and everything," Irv Stefansson said. "This is what is making us think that he's erased all of his past that he possibly could. That's what made us think that he didn't want anything to happen to anybody here because of his doing things ... I don't know. It's just a supposition."[37]

According to people who knew him after the war, the ex-spychief was concerned about his safety.

McKenzie Porter, the first journalist to interview Stephenson, thought the former espionage head was exceedingly excessive in his anxiety about security. "I thought, oh he's retired, he's out of it, he's finished. He's drinking heavily, this is some mistake. Some mistaken idea he's got. Some bug he's got in his mind. That's what I thought."[38]

Tom Hill, who worked with Stephenson during and after the war said, "I always thought the stuff about his paranoia for security after the war was a bit phony myself. It's one way of showing how important you are to people. At one point he went down to Jamaica and got the Managing Director to meet him at the airport with a gun, and so on. I don't think there was any threat to him at that point in history. I think he was merely trying to impress the MD who would then pass it on to the other directors how important he was."

David Young, Stephenson's friend in later life, says he was very concerned about being assassinated. He often mentioned to Young how easy it could be, pointing out the case of the Bulgarian who was killed in London by poison injected from an umbrella tip.[39] Stephenson covertly visited a Toronto hospital in the 1970's for his wife Mary's cancer treatment. According to Dr Phillip Hall, who was working at the Toronto hospital at the time, there was security for the ex-spychief—"a big burly fellow."[40]

Any information of Stephenson's security concerns that filtered back to Winnipeg possibly came through Lillian Stephenson, his step-brother Mindy's widow. Stephenson's sister-in-law was able to contact him. According to Lillian's son Gerald, Stephenson secretly visited Winnipeg in 1944 en route to elsewhere. Lillian Stephenson died in 1989, soon after Stephenson, and her son doesn't recall her opinion of Stephenson's low profile and the phony backgrounds in his biographies. Ironically, the only record the family has expresses concern about the publicity Stephenson had received.

608 Fifth Avenue
Suite 607 New York
January 14 1955
Dear Lillian,
We have just returned here from Washington. This is a brief note to acknowledge your nice card and to reciprocate your good wishes. I agree with you that there has been a lot of publicity and as much as I dislike publicity, I am afraid it is an inevitable consequence of agreeing to assist the province in development.

There was only one article that was irritating and inaccurate in the FP (Winnipeg Free Press). You will know the one to which I refer. I hope to get settled long enough in one spot in order to catch up on personal correspondence more fully. I will write to you at greater length. Love and best wishes to you both.
Yours, Bill

Derek Bedson said Lillian once got in touch with him before he was travelling to Bermuda to visit Stephenson. "I was going down there. I don't know how she knew."[41]

If Lillian had a way to contact Stephenson, she didn't share it with her relatives. A cousin, Margaret Mack (nee Breckman) visited Bermuda and tried to see him, but was unsuccessful. Irv Stefansson, the son of Stephenson's cousin was surprised that media people, such as Winnipeg radio talk show host Peter Warren, could contact Stephenson, "And we could never seem to get through. My mom sent a birthday card because she knew when his birthday was, and it was returned."[42]

Following the publication of *A Man Called Intrepid*, the author William Stevenson was in Winnipeg and appeared as a guest on a radio talk show in the spring of 1977. Stephenson knew of the broadcast, and requested a transcript of the Eric St. John show be sent to him in Bermuda. He was perhaps seeing what the reaction was in his hometown, to the phony Winnipeg background depicted in the book. There was little other publicity of the author's trip to Stephenson's old stomping grounds. "I did not see an article about him in the paper though, as was expected," wrote the show's producer Carolyn Rickey.[43]

It is difficult to deduce the raison d'etre of such a private person. Two biographers of the man didn't even find out his parent's names. Bedson, a friend for over thirty years, knew nothing of Stephenson's Winnipeg background, and had little idea about the espionage work that made his friend so famous.

The public account of Stephenson's life records only one major speech. It was organized by a press friend Charles Vining, for a May 31, 1954 presentation to the Periodical Press Association in Toronto.

Stephenson's address was entitled *The First Line of Defence*. In it he says the first true line of defence is information. He talks about the importance of intelligence services and gives examples. Napoleon, he said, was long regarded as a military genius and as having mysterious foresight. But historical research debunked the intuition idea and revealed he had good political intelligence and even had agents on the enemy staff. "You will recall that Hitler was supposed to have miraculous intuition," Stephenson's speech continued. He also talked of the value of code breaking during the war and of the fear of the unknown. Fear of the unknown or the incomprehensible doesn't always produce a sense of panic in an individual, Stephenson said. Quite often it produces the opposite: apathy.

Not all of the speech to the Periodical Association was published in the media, but in the files of William Stevenson is a draft of the conclusion of his speech. In it, Stephenson talks of his love of his home country, and in a way, he echoes the thoughts of two of his pre-war contemporaries, HG Wells and George Bernard Shaw.[44] Stephenson wrote:

> To my regret circumstances have kept me in other lands for more years of my life than I have spent in Canada but it may be this condition of exile has given me a sharpened appreciation of the good fortune one has in being Canadian and of what our country can mean to all mankind. In her institutions of law and order with freedom, in the character of her people, in the great endowment with which providence has blessed her.
>
> In a troubled world, Canadians have increasing reason to be proud and thankful. We also have increasing reason to recognize the obligations and responsibilities which are meant to accompany good fortune, whether of men, or nations. Of these things I have become more and more aware with the passage of time.
>
> I have no patience with those who seem to look upon the scientific age of our 20th century as a kind of Greek tragedy, catching all mankind in an inexorable finale of doom and destruction.

[He concluded his speech by talking about his convictions.]

> We Canadians have not the habit of speaking easily with each other about divine providence and the human soul, although I have heard in this respect one does not need to feel quite as diffident in the city of Toronto as in certain other communities. At any rate, putting diffidence aside, I beg to give you my belief that the most powerful force in the world remains what it has always been: the human soul attached by faith to its creator.
>
> I have faith in providence. I believe with Churchill that, "the destiny of mankind is not settled by material computation." I also believe that faith must be practical. That to receive the help of providence man must so conduct and exert himself as to deserve and earn that help.

Stephenson died January 31, 1989. He was buried in Bermuda in a secret ceremony at St. John's Church. According to his wishes, his funeral took place before his death was made public. He told his adopted daughter Elizabeth, "I don't want people to know that I am dead until I am buried."[45] Some local police acted as pallbearers. There were only a handful of people, five in all, at his funeral. Elizabeth and her son Rhys, Stephenson's doctor, his physiotherapist and Manitoba-born undertaker Brian Graham. The media reported he had no family in Winnipeg.[46]

10 Out of the Shadows

Although Stephenson's achievements during the war appear considerable, decades later his accomplishments were ridiculed in some media articles. Following his death he was tagged, "the Spymaster who wasn't," "an Intrepid Fraud," and "from start to finish a liar." However the criticisms are not based on research or interviews, but on the books that were written about Stephenson, especially *A Man Called Intrepid*. Stephenson's public persona became defined by a few articles, books, and reviews which warrant closer examination.

The first details of Bill Stephenson's espionage career became public in a 1952 feature story in the Canadian magazine *Maclean's*. It was written by British-born writer McKenzie Porter, who learned of Stephenson during the war and initiated the story. "I found out where he lived and got at him," the retired writer, now living in Toronto, remembered.[1]

Stephenson was wary of reporters and publicity in general, Porter says. Before the interview was arranged, Stephenson contacted the journalist a number of times for personal information and references. Porter said to him, "Well one guy I know that you know is Ian Fleming." Prior to the war, Porter worked for the British paper *The Daily Sketch,* and during the last two years of the conflict he was with the Political Warfare Executive (PWE) in Rome, Athens, and Vienna. After completing his PWE work, Fleming was one of Porter's editors, and eventually the writer moved to Canada and started working for *Maclean's* magazine.

Stephenson contacted Fleming about Porter and received a long telegram in response. Later he showed Porter the biographical information on him. Fleming's report concluded, "McKenzie Porter is a good second-class journalist." Porter retorted, "I never quite forgave Fleming for that."

The *Maclean's* interview took place at Stephenson's New York apartment on East 52nd Street and pictures were taken by *Maclean's* photographer Ronnie Jacques. The accompanying photograph of Stephenson on his balcony, with the United Nations in the background, is one of the few pictures of Stephenson publicly released. Porter also talked to some of BSC's former secretarial staff in Toronto and New York, and to Ernest Cuneo and Tommy Drew-Brook. Cuneo is quoted in the story as saying "Stephenson was the only man who had the unqualified support of both Franklin Roosevelt and Winston Churchill," which later became a point of contention for some historians. "If I said Cuneo said that, Cuneo said it," Porter emphasized.

The Biggest Private Eye of All appeared in the December 1, 1952 edition of *Maclean's* and revealed for the first time some of the exploits of "a mysterious millionaire from Winnipeg." The article opened:

"This is about a mysterious middle-aged Canadian millionaire who during the second world war became the mastermind of British intelligence throughout the Americas. His New York staff of more than a thousand hand-picked Canadian men and women spoke of his doorkeeper as 'Peter,' of his secretary as 'Gabrielle' and of him as 'God.' Only a handful of them knew him by sight."[2]

So began the public story of William Stephenson and British Security Coordination. The article credited BSC with training hundreds of Canadian and American parachutists for jumps into occupied Europe, helping to detect enemy submarines by pinpointing their radio signals, delaying Hitler's attack on Russia by six weeks with a few calculated indiscretions, neutralizing a vast Nazi sabotage ring in Central America, contributing to the smashing of dummy corporations and helping to sustain the American faith in British victory after Dunkirk. The article also marvelled at Stephenson's observation skills and his speed-reading ability.

The narrative concluded by mentioning that although Stephenson received a knighthood for his war service, he was more proud of the fact that it was conveyed by Churchill himself, with a written comment beside his name. The note was, "in green Churchillian ink on a list of candidates of honours that was submitted to George the Sixth. It read, 'this one is dear to my heart.'" Porter remembers seeing the document. "I saw that, yes," he said "I'm sure he showed it to me—that note from Churchill."

In Manitoba, people who befriended Stephenson in his childhood, and Stephenson's relatives, read the story of long-lost Bill with great interest. At least one contacted *Maclean's* to obtain his address, but early the next year he was told it could not be given out for security reasons. "It is probably a safe assumption to conclude that even eight years after the war it was discreet for Sir William to be cautious. Even in times of peace, life can be endangered through the actions of revengeful self-appointed assassins," WJ Lindal later wrote.[3]

No letters from Manitoba relatives were published by the magazine, in fact no letters to the editor at all were published about the Stephenson revelations. It later was written that this was an indication that there was little interest in the piece, as most long articles for the magazine received a few letters. However Porter says he received good response from the story and wished to pursue it further. It is possible Stephenson had some influence internally at the magazine, and public discussion was suppressed. Napier Moore, the managing editor of *Maclean's* for nearly twenty years, often commented on intelligence affairs in the fifties.[4] His wife, Marjorie Noble, worked for Stephenson during the war.[5]

Following the publication of the *Maclean's* story, Porter wanted to write a book about the spychief and BSC, and Stephenson indicated a book might be possible, but later he refused to give the go-ahead. Porter called New York twice about a future publication but Stephenson said, "I'm afraid something has happened and we can't go into the book at this time."[6]

The Quiet Canadian

By the end of the decade Stephenson was interested in having a history of BSC written, but he chose a professional intelligence officer and colleague to write it. The actual motives behind the publication of *The Quiet Canadian* (1962) are difficult to establish. Preliminary work on the book was done by Charles Howard (Dick) Ellis, an Australian and an employee of the British service, who worked for Stephenson during the war. Ellis, one of the founding members of British Security Coordination, was awarded the US Medal of Merit for his valuable help in the establishment of the OSS. Following his death, Ellis was publicly accused of being a German spy, and possibly a Soviet spy as well, by the British journalist Chapman Pincher and others.[7]

The start of *The Quiet Canadian* project can be traced to an August 24, 1959 letter from Stephenson to Ellis.[8] In it Stephenson thanked the Australian for a previous letter, and a copy of *Soviet Affairs*, and wrote that he was impressed with the amount of research the various articles entailed. "If you (Ellis) spent this kind of effort on doing a sort of 'journalist' history of 'our' war you would be adding constructively to historical records," Stephenson wrote. He proposed to pay Ellis for his expenses and then be reimbursed from the profits of the book. In the same letter, Stephenson said that *Time-Life* chief Henry Luce at one time offered him a $100,000 plus advance to tell his story, and that McKenzie Porter offered him the first $30,000 of royalties of his book. (Porter doesn't remember discussing the figure of $30,000. "I just said I think I could make some money if you'd let me write the book," Porter said. "And I was ahead of anybody else on the research."[9]) Stephenson added at the conclusion of his letter to Ellis, "Bob Sherwood said once: When the story of BSC and related activities comes to be written it should be titled *The Quiet Canadian* as I was described in his book *Roosevelt and Hopkins*."

Stephenson gave Ellis access to his records and helped with the draft, but he apparently was unhappy with Ellis's literary effort. According to Ellis's letters in the files of Montgomery Hyde, Stephenson was "for an all-out attack on various people and a *success de scandale*," and he criticized Ellis's draft because it lacked "ginger."[10] "Dick Ellis was not the sort of a chap to write a red-blooded book at all," according to his colleague and former BSC member, Bill Ross Smith. Ellis wrote in a dull 'governmentalese,' Ross Smith recalled.[11] (Ellis's working book title appears to have been: *Anglo-American Collaboration in Intelligence and Security: Notes for Documentation.*[12]) Eventually work on the book was passed to Harford Montgomery Hyde, who was teaching in Asia at the time.

Hyde was a politician, lawyer, former intelligence officer, and historian who also previously worked for BSC. He was the son of a Belfast magistrate and was called to the bar himself in 1934. Later he lectured in history at Oxford, and he became a private secretary to Lord Londonderry.[13] When the war started in 1939, Hyde was commissioned in the signal core and was an assistant censor at Gibraltar. He became a military liaison and censorship security officer in Bermuda and then worked for Stephenson's British Security Coordination as 'Assistant Passport Control Officer.' In 1944 he was transferred to the Supreme Headquarters with the Allied Expeditionary Force. Following the war he did legal work for the Alexander Korda group of film companies, wrote, and became an Ulster Unionist member of parliament. When Stephenson contacted him about a possible book, Hyde was a history professor at Punjab University in Lahore, Pakistan.[14]

The Quiet Canadian was released with much fanfare and syndicated in numerous newspapers around the world, including the *Sunday Times* in Britain, and *Weekend* magazine in Canada. Revelations in the book became news carried by the major news wires. Ian Fleming wrote a long preface to accompany the syndicated *Times* stories, and a rendition of it was printed in the American version of *The Quiet Canadian*, which was called *Room 3603*.[15] Publicity for the book in the United States drew comparisons between Stephenson and Fleming's famous creation. Newspaper advertisements read: "Ian Fleming says: James Bond is a highly romanticized version of a true spy. The real thing, the man who became one of the great agents of the last war is William Stephenson."[16]

After the release of *The Quiet Canadian*, there was a desire to publicize the BSC story further in film or television, but all attempts were quashed by Stephenson and his wife. Following the publication of the book, Ellis wrote to Hyde that Stephenson reportedly was alarmed at having entered the public domain as a result of the book, "and seems to want to hide himself."[17] A May 1963 letter from Hyde's agent, International Literary Management, to Hyde conveyed the sentiments of a Claire Degener in the United States. "I certainly think Cary Grant is a good idea to play Stevenson (sic) but it is insane to go to any major star until we have a much clearer picture of specifically what would induce Stevenson to a release. Frankly I could have sold the book thirty times in the last two weeks and my heart is broken for Hyde." Degener wanted to approach Alfred Hitchcock as producer.[18] Later Mary Stephenson cabled Hyde to urge a television program about Stephenson not to be done and Stephenson refused to have the book reprinted after the first edition was sold.[19]

Hyde did not become wealthy as a result of the book. He was paid a £600 advance for expense money to write it, but the professorship he left in Lahore paid him £3,000 annually and it cost him £800 to move from there. To complicate his finances, he was supporting his mother who was bed-ridden in Ireland. In July of 1963, after the release of the book, Hyde wrote to Stephenson and asked if he could repay the advance money gradually.[20]

Later Ellis approached Hyde for a portion of *The Quiet Canadian* royalties, but Hyde felt no obligation to pay him, as he didn't use the Ellis draft. From letters in Hyde's file, it appears Ellis did offer some advice. In one letter, Ellis urged Hyde to stress that "Anglo-American cooperation was a wartime development." He said to emphasize in the book that "not everything was started by Stephenson," and the US was bound by the Neutrality Act. To write otherwise, "... simply plays into the hands of those elements who consider that the US was seduced and led astray by FDR and the Limies in 1940."[21]

Ellis's financial difficulties were possibly compounded as a result of the publication of *The Quiet Canadian* and its revelations. Ian Fleming wrote in the *Sunday Times*, and in the introduction to *Room 3603*, that it was "the first book, so far as I know, about the British secret agent whose publication has received official blessing."[22] However this does not seem to be the case. There are clear indications that British intelligence circles were upset over the publication of the book, and Ellis was removed from his intelligence work because he was connected to it. In January of 1963, Ellis wrote to Hyde that, "The flap has died down here but I gather 'C' (chief of intelligence) is still sore, and the FO (Foreign Office) show no signs of reinstating me in the IRD (Intelligence Research Department) job."[23] Hyde, in a letter to Stephenson, reiterates that Ellis's trouble was a result of the book project. He says it was because he listed Ellis's help in the acknowledgments of *The Quiet Canadian*, which was "a normal courtesy, (which) got him into hot water at Broadway, not to mention the FO, and he lost one of the jobs he was doing for them."[24] Other letters in Hyde's files at Cambridge indicate the confusion was because MI6 vetted Ellis's version of BSC's activities, but not Hyde's more detailed account.[25]

Although Hyde is said to have had access to Stephenson's files, the ex-spychief didn't help fill in details of his personal life. Hyde corresponded with Stephenson's friend Tommy Drew-Brook to receive more information. Drew-Brook wrote back that "He tells me that in his opinion, McKenzie Porter's summary of his business career is quite sufficient."[26] Hyde's papers at Churchill College, Cambridge have little information on Stephenson's early life and, according to Montgomery Hyde's widow Rosalind, the biographer was unaware that Stephenson's Canadian background was fictitious.[27]

For some reason, perhaps related to concealing his Icelandic Canadian roots, in March of 1963, Stephenson cabled Hyde to try and halt the publication of *The Quiet Canadian* in Iceland.[28] Hyde cabled back to say the rights were a normal course of events handled by his British publisher and he could be sued for breach of contract if he didn't follow through. Hyde wondered why Stephenson objected to an English edition released in Iceland, and he replied, "there is a comie (sic) plot to handle publication and use that hotbed Reykjavik as a base to discredit us and create unfriendly relations Sweden and the whole of Scandinavia through Olason ... I am beginning to regret the whole thing."[29] Some of Stephenson's critics have used this cable as evidence that Stephenson was fantasizing and had impaired judgment.[30]

Why did Stephenson decide a book was possible in the late fifties, and not earlier? In a 1959 letter to Ellis Stephenson says, "the whole story is far enough behind us to be told fairly completely," but they would "have to talk about the OSA (Official Secrets Act) aspect."[31] Stephenson was also quoted as saying he was reticent because of the possibility, "the last war may not be the final one."[32] It has also been suggested that the publication of *The Quiet Canadian* was part of a Cold War propaganda campaign. In the introduction to *A Man Called Intrepid*, Dick Ellis indicates that the release of *The Quiet Canadian* was related to the defection of Soviet double agent Kim Philby. Philby knew of BSC's existence, but "was not aware of the full and far reaching purpose of Intrepid's organization. Thus just enough of the truth was revealed for publication to blunt the effect of any disclosures that Philby or his supporters might reveal."[33] Before that book was released in 1976, Stephenson, in a telegram (October 20, 1975) to the author William Stevenson, commented on the Ellis passage and said the release of

The Quiet Canadian "had nothing to do with Philby or general vetting."[34] Hyde, later quoted by the writer John Le Carré in February, 1976, said if *The Quiet Canadian* was simply "sand in the Russian eyes," it was without his knowledge, and the biography had started with Stephenson.[35] Following Hyde's comments, printed in the *New York Times,* Stephenson cabled Hyde and told him to "not allow himself to be quoted stupidly by scribblers," and express "derogatory views on subjects far removed from the serious work they know nothing about."[36]

Indirectly it is possible the release of *The Quiet Canadian* might have had something to do with the defection of Kim Philby and boosting morale of Western security services. According to some reports, "the entire community of BSC operatives were amazed Hyde had been able to write this book ... given the security that then existed and still exists now."[37] The full extent of the damage Philby caused to Western intelligence operations will probably never be known. He nearly rose to be the head of MI6 in Britain, and also spent a great deal of his career in the United States, liaising with the FBI and CIA. Philby first came under suspicion following the 1951 defection of Anthony Burgess and Donald Maclean, and pressure on MI6 from the Americans led to his recall from his Washington posting. In the 1950's Philby was asked to resign from the Foreign Office, and he was sent to Beirut to work as a journalist for the *Observer* and the *Economist*. He disappeared in January 1963, apparently after he received news from Moscow there was a CIA hit man on his trail.[38] According to Robert Ducas, who was with the *London Times* when investigative work on the Philby case was done in the late sixties, Philby knew the identity of every CIA operative in Europe. This provided the agency with the ultimate conundrum for their European operations. "They had to decide whether to forget the whole thing, or start again," says Ducas.[39]

When viewed in the time perspective of Philby, the shooting down of U-2 pilot Francis Gary Powers, and the Profumo Affair, it is plausible that a positive story about Western intelligence services would not be regarded as a negative. Whether or not *The Quiet Canadian* was related to that realm is a point of conjecture. Recently, it has been revealed the publishing of *The Quiet Canadian* caused "a tumultuous uproar" behind the scenes in various intelligence communities as it was much too candid.[40] A classified CIA review concluded, "the publication of this study is shocking."[41]

Stephenson's career was again in the public eye in the late 1960's when Shaun Herron, an Irish journalist and novelist who worked for Stephenson during the war, put together a radio series for the Canadian Broadcasting Corporation, *The Great Canadian Spy*. According to Herron, upon hearing Stephenson was about to retire from espionage, Churchill remarked, "the eagles have flown. Now the vultures will take over."

11 *A Man Called Intrepid*

I hope this book will be published as soon as practicable. I say this particularly in view of the long investigations that have been in process and promise to last indefinitely, of the operations of the CIA. The truth is that only a small fraction of the public or indeed of those who are vocal on this subject have any idea of the importance of clandestine operations.
—David Bruce (former OSS London) to Julian Muller (AMCI editor)[1]

If there was the possibility of cold war intrigue or espionage public relations involved with *The Quiet Canadian*, that likelihood was magnified with the release in 1976 of *A Man Called Intrepid*. It too began as a project of Dick Ellis, but the task was passed to British-born journalist William Stevenson.

Ellis, obviously using some of his previous material, began a new undertaking in the late sixties, and added to his draft. He contacted Colin Gubbins, the former head of SOE, in August of 1972, about assistance with a foreword for his book about the Stephenson organization. Gubbins replied:

"I am glad to hear you have written a book on the Stephenson-Donovan collaboration—on the vital role that Bill Stephenson played in the very highest quarters—at the top level in fact in the Downing Street / White House 'affaire' which led to such splendid results ... I moved only rarely in the rarefied atmosphere of the top circles where the two Bill's had their common stomping ground but Bill Stephenson's slightest wish to me is more than a command."[2]

Gubbins concluded his letter, "I remember well your own very distinguished record in the Service.[3]

Soon afterward it seems the Ellis book project was curtailed, but this time it wasn't because of the Australian's lack of literary flair. On September 11, 1972, Stephenson cabled Stevenson about Dick. "His electrical potential has turned from positive to negative like an overdrawn battery by reason of the unconcerned Dracula."[4]

At about the same time British intelligence writer Chapman Pincher reports, "an international authority on intelligence and defence affairs" heard negative reports about Ellis. The individual, who wished to remain anonymous, was involved in the setting up of Interdoc, the International Documentary Center, an organization involving intelligence affairs. Interdoc wanted a London representative and Ellis had taken on the job, but the appointment quickly came under fire from British intelligence. "In the early 1970's," wrote Pincher, "a representative of the Secret Service called on my informant (the anonymous expert) to ask if he had been responsible for recommending Ellis, because he was known to have been a spy for Germany and was suspected of being a Soviet agent too."[5]

Although obviously it is difficult to ascertain the validity of the accusations against Ellis, it does appear that each time he attempted to publicize the war work of William Stephenson, it didn't add to his job security. Ironically if Ellis's imposed unemployment was meant as a punishment for selling out to the enemy, it seemed to make him more vulnerable to foreign overtures. Ellis's trouble with his British employers—perhaps even losing his pension—made him more dependent monetarily on others. Ellis went to Stephenson for financial assistance, and Stephenson's former associate died owing him a large amount of money.[6]

At approximately the same time, William Stevenson was conducting a number of television interviews relating to British Security Coordination. The work on the new BSC volume was eventually turned over to Stevenson. Born in London in 1925, Stevenson apparently served in the RAF during the war and later became a journalist.

One book review says the author was Stephenson's assistant director of operations during the war, but this is not the case.[7] (As the writer was 15 when Stephenson received his New York appointment, his lofty stature in the organization is somewhat surprising—even apparently to Stephenson.[8]) His early journalistic background was similar to McKenzie Porter's, as Stevenson "first received a taste for international intrigue while working for the Kemsley newspapers of London, under Ian

Fleming," and he worked as a journalist in China, Africa, Canada, and Bermuda.[9] At some point Stevenson became a naturalized Canadian, although this is not always indicated in his books. The jacket of his 1986 novel *Eclipse* says he "was born and bred in England and lives in Washington."

Prior to *A Man Called Intrepid* (*AMCI*) Stevenson did two books about the Israeli military. He apparently knew fighting would start before the Six Day War took place in 1967, and he wrote *Strike Zion* soon afterward.[10] In 1970, he wrote *Zanek!: A Chronicle of the Israeli Air Force*, with the assistance of the IAF. At the time of the *Intrepid* research Stevenson had recently finished a book on the mysterious Nazi, Martin Bormann. Stevenson's *The Bormann Brotherhood* (May 1973) is dedicated, "For INTREPID." In the early seventies, he worked on a television documentary, *A Man Called Intrepid*, about Stephenson and BSC for the Canadian Broadcasting Corporation. The author-journalist refers to the *Sunday Best* documentary's interviews as the genesis of his book research. However, although the author's voice can be heard on the tape asking questions, and he can be seen in some of the interviews, nowhere in the documentary or the credits does his name appear.

From a perusal of Stevenson's papers at the University of Regina, one could draw many curious conclusions about a symbiotic relationship between certain journalists and intelligence work. Amongst Stevenson's files are newspaper clippings he collected from the *New York Times* (February 18, 1976 and others) concerning revelations that newsmen were used as stringers for the CIA.[11] In 1975, he wrote to Stephenson in Bermuda explaining what he thought the *Observer's* merits were to Britain's Foreign Office. The newspaper's value "has been that it could air some of the more trendy liberal notions and win over a few influential friends in the Third World, while extracting information not for publication. But the awful fiasco with Kim Philby has made this an even more delicate operation than ever."[12] Philby was working for the *Observer* in the Middle East. From reading his letters, there are a few indications that Stevenson may have been more than a casual chronicler of the cloak and dagger business. He said in a letter to Stephenson, that while he was working in Zanzibar, Tanzania, he was, "watching Kao Liang, the chief of Chinese intelligence in Africa and a guy I got the Indian government to expel three years earlier."[13] The Soviet defector Igor Gouzenko was an acquaintance of Stevenson's, and he kept Stephenson informed on his well-being. Gouzenko, in one Toronto meeting with the writer, complained about his treatment in the West. This reminded Stevenson of similar treatment accorded a Chinese defector who was convinced to come to Britain. "His (Gouzenko's) chief argument is that if the West treats people like himself in the way it does, few will ever come over from the Soviet side. I know that to be true too, because we coaxed a chap out of China and having emptied out on the floor, shaken all the value out of his skull, we let him fend for himself in England on the basis that letting him live there was largesse enough. The poor fellow ... ekes out a beggarly existence without help."[14]

In the summer of 1975, Stevenson wrote to Stephenson that the Intrepid book could act as a springboard for his career, from journalist to writer, but he didn't seem to have Hemingway's literary aspirations. "I want to make it absolutely clear that I do not depend on *AMCI* for financial survival, but that I do feel it opens the way to full-time writing, which I've not been able to do hitherto, and gives the opportunity to launch a counter-attack against communist and other subversive elements in the best way I know." In Stevenson's correspondence he frequently brought up a perceived Soviet threat, and it is clear William Stevenson was no fan of Soviet socialism. He frequently transposes historical references in the progressing *Intrepid* book, somewhat incongruously, into views on the Soviet Union.[15] The Chinese were also discussed in Stevenson's consultations with the Second World War espionage head. In a letter in the summer of 1975, the journalist thanks Stephenson for his support with his writing project. He continues, "When we lived in Asia, the Chinese Communists mounted a campaign through dupes to discredit me, and succeeded in getting me transferred to India. It's a long story, but I mention these examples to reassure you about my very keen awareness of how these bastards work. I told you a long time ago that I had a tough fight on my hands and needed your support and you have responded magnificently."[16]

When asked if William Stevenson, journalist, had any background in intelligence work, one of his friends laughed, and replied, "That's for you to dig into." He then added, "but I'll be surprised if you get that out of him."[17] As this tome is not a biography of William Stevenson, I am content to leave it at that.

Much of *A Man Called Intrepid* appears to have been written with the author in Toronto and the subject in Bermuda. There were numerous cables and letters between the two, which seem to show Stephenson did not know much of what was being written about him. He disagreed with some passages he was shown.

Before the book was published, the writer consulted a number of people about it's progress. By June of 1974, an early draft of *AMCI* was complete and Stevenson wrote to the then-publisher and Editor-in-chief of *The Globe and Mail,* RS Malone, and informed him about the book. Stevenson told him he was discussing the draft with the people "directly concerned—Julian Muller who runs the trade department, and Oscar Dystel who is the President of Bantam Books. Both are former intelligence officers. The publisher in London is Robin Denniston of Weidenfeld and Nicolson whose father was Alistair Denniston the chief of Bletchley Park wartime coding etc. ... Much of the basic material has come from Washington and London (the CIA historian and War Cabinet diaries, for instance)." Later in the letter he says, "I may continue on from New York next week with a copy of the MSS for Sir William, depending on publishing schedules."[18]

Stevenson also contacted David Ogilvy, a former BSC employee, and later an advertising mogul. Ogilvy seemed less than gung ho about Stevenson's book project. Replying to Ogilvy's concerns with the book, Stevenson wrote that he had "no wish to embarrass anyone (in the book) and do not think this is possible." Stevenson said he would use restraint in *AMCI*, and could "see no way to overstate Bill's achievements. I agree Bill needs no overstated tributes." Stevenson emphasized he was receiving guidance from a number of people who had an understanding of the situation. "My publisher was with me all day yesterday discussing the first draft," he wrote to Ogilvy. "He is a former US Navy intelligence officer with a tremendous admiration for everything British, and I have to restrain him ... Let me repeat that nobody named in the current book who as a result would suffer embarrassment. The last difficult task of this nature was a book about the Israeli Air Force which placed me under the most stifling security wraps—I survived ... I don't see how the OSA (Official Secrets Act) limits me, since my sources are documents in the public domain and men and women who have been told what can or cannot be said."[19]

A Man Called Intrepid apparently cleared more editorial hurdles than most biographies. On October 9, 1975, Stevenson wrote that, "All the security people who've read this are pleased by the spiking of Kim Philby's guns ... It should be emphasized that *AMCI* has been so thoroughly vetted now that it's clean as a whistle—including the formidable lawyers on both sides of the Atlantic and sundry gentlemen of the famous bureaucracies."[20] It seems somewhat peculiar, if the book was thoroughly vetted, that the Dick Ellis foreword was printed. Ellis was, according to unsubstantiated reports, a known, treacherous, double agent by this time. It seems Stephenson did not want the Ellis passage used and he requested that a passage from Colin Gubbins, or Ernie Cuneo be in the book. The writer responded by saying the two Stephenson contemporaries' comments were based on earlier information on *AMCI* and "had not been approved in connection to the final version of *AMCI*. The situation a year ago was we had a book more limited in scope." One might have assumed the book dealt with the war career of William Stephenson so his associates' comments wouldn't become obsolete or irrelevant because of turns in the book.

Later Stephenson sent the author a telegram to say, "Dick Margarine (Butterfield, a friend and business associate) begged me to pass to you in all seriousness his suggestion that you insert the (David) Bruce letter in place of Ellis in the same part of the book stop. I agreed ..."[21] Yet it is the Ellis passage that appears in the book.

The book is not footnoted and it contains a number of reconstructed conversations. Following its publication, there was a great deal of controversy in some quarters, due in part perhaps, to the style and depiction of events in *AMCI*. Stevenson's book *Zanek!* contains narration from a stranger called 'S' who could be in several places at once watching and listening and who could bring together several incidents that occurred on one day. "'S' could create one character out of several men whose identities had to be protected for security reasons."[22]

Stevenson's approach to *AMCI* seems similar, as the spychief seems to turn up almost everywhere. Surprisingly, he was even waiting in a desolate Scottish field one night to greet the Danish atom scientist, Niels Bohr, after he was smuggled there in a bomb bay of a plane on a secret flight from Sweden.[23] As the chief of a huge organization based in North America, one wonders how Stephenson found the time to loiter in Scottish fields waiting for secret night flights. Did he have nothing better to do? Many point to such instances to ridicule Stephenson, and to question his honesty, or mental stability.

However, there are Stephenson references to the Bohr incident in Stevenson's files at the University of Regina and nowhere does he say he waited for him in a field.[24]

At some point the Bohr story was changed. Why and by whom?

In a June 4, 1973, letter to Stephenson, the writer tells him, "You have a natural role at the heart of the story and it should be told through your eyes. *This does not mean of course quoting you* (italics mine). It means simply the main events between Dunkirk and Pearl (the chronological length of the original book draft) are recounted in relation to your activities. This requires that I reconstruct these events in the well tried manner of other recorders of recent history... "And, I may have to bother you with some further questions."[25]

More than a year later, after a draft of the book was complete, and sent to his editor, Julian Muller, Stevenson wrote to Stephenson saying, "Julian is entirely in sympathy with the philosophical thrust of the book but wishes there were more anecdotes. He feels the density of the material demands lighter touches ... *The second look is my responsibility* ... It means scissors and paste, rejigging actions, writing tighter historical bits, *keeping you in the middle of events* ... Julian's original estimate of six weeks more work has been revised downward. He thinks two weeks more work *by myself* (working flat out that is)."[26]

Countless critics of *AMCI*, even former BSC employees, have surmised Stephenson was hallucinating about some of the escapades in Stevenson's tome. "...Stephenson is quoted verbatim as though an eyewitness. Sir John Martin, who accompanied Churchill on this unplanned visit has no recollection of his presence."[27] "It is a tragedy that so much of the stuff that was written about him (under his own inspiration) ... was such a gross exaggeration of his achievements," wrote David Ogilvy. "It was probably booze that addled his brain."[28] The second look, keeping Stephenson in "the middle of events," if composed by the writer himself, indicates such summations may not be accurate.

It appears the writer Stevenson did receive some false information about Stephenson's life in Canada. A cable from Stephenson to Herb Rowland was forwarded to the writer, and concocts a 'subject's' life with a Scottish-Canadian background, which appears in *AMCI* . The 'subject' learns of the death of his father in the Boer war in 1901, about the same time as the death of Queen Victoria. Winston Churchill was visiting Winnipeg at the time on a lecture tour, the Stephenson cable said.[29]

A few of Stephenson's relatives in Winnipeg who heard nothing from him for decades, wrote the publishers of *A Man Called Intrepid* in New York to report biographical errors in the book and sent the correct information. "My mother-in-law registered the letter, and heard nothing," says Mary Jane Stefansson, who also wrote Harcourt Brace and Jonovitch. "I heard nothing. No one ever responded to having received it." According to Reg Rimmer, when Stephenson died, a Winnipeg radio station talk show host reported Stephenson had no relatives in the city. Rimmer contacted the station to report that he was a relative, but the station didn't pursue the matter.

Following the publication of *AMCI*, Stevenson met with more than the typical book reviewers in Canada and the US.[30] In January of 1976, he wrote Stephenson saying, "The meeting with the chaps in Ottawa was to map out some way of using the publicity on *AMCI* to further drive home the argument that intelligence is a vital necessity etc."[31] A few months later he reported, "Ernie (Cuneo) has arranged for me to speak to the Dutch Treat Club in New York ... before 'key figures in the communications media.' They want me to use *AMCI* as a means to defend the CIA et al today, and this I shall do along the lines already discussed."[32] He continued, "*AMCI* makes it clear that Allied intelligence saved us once and can save us again."[33]

The book ran into some obstacles in Britain in the very early stages of publication, when there were problems with expected newspaper serialization. In mid-March of 1976, Stevenson reported to Stephenson that London's *Sunday Times* was dropping plans to publish book excerpts. "The *Sunday Times* in London is rent with strife," he wrote. "Macmillan (British publisher) is taking legal action because the *Times* dropped an excerpt on the basis of someone challenging the facts re your World War I record. 'This smells of conspiracy,' in Julian's words, and indeed I'm quite sure we shall be smoking out those who would dismantle all intelligence apparatus and therefore launch attacks on *AMCI*. I hope you don't get any flack. I'll do my best to attract it."[34]

Stephenson's response later the same day seemed to indicate he wasn't surprised at the British controversy, and he expected more. "The *Observer* probably have half a dozen people busily writing eroding letters to the *Sun Times*, let alone the avalanche which will descend from the read (sic) enemy heard (sic)."[35]

A few months later Stevenson wrote that he thought his British publisher was subjected to outside influences. He wrote Stephenson to say, "Macmillan for a time inhibited by the attacks from Marxists and professional American haters like AJP Taylor."[36]

In August of 1975 Stephenson read a draft of *AMCI* in Bermuda. He disliked the "Dickensian model," of himself as a "waifish Tiny Tim," and questioned whether his house in Bermuda was accurately described. "You live only in Royal places if you consider this thing austere." He continued, "Perhaps the title should have been *The Secret War*." He also distanced himself from the book. "I trust that your, repeat your project, will prove rewarding to you," he cabled the writer.[37]

Stephenson complained about the negative depiction of Sosthenes Behn, the founder of International Telephone Telegraph Corporation, in *AMCI*. The writer Stevenson's response was unrepentant, "The ITT story in *AMCI* makes it clear that if Sosthenes had not been active in Germany, we might not have got the early indications of the ENIGMA coding machine." The book also portrays Behn as a Nazi sympathizer, who was involved in producing arms for the Germans, and refers to him as the "notorious Sosthenes Behn."[38]

After publication, ITT was not pleased with the portrayal of their founder in *A Man Called Intrepid*. Edward Gerrity, a senior Vice President wrote to the author April 23, 1976. He complained about comments in the book, and he blamed Stephenson for the story. Gerrity set out the case for Behn "with all due respect to Stephenson..."[39]

Stevenson responded to Gerrity about a month later, and explained that his book "was intended to demonstrate that secret intelligence accomplishes great things in the name of democracy." He concluded his response by implying he would change the text. "I am looking for some way to strengthen the reference to ITT's part in ULTRA in subsequent editions."[40] (No changes occurred.)

In fact, ITT provided invaluable assistance to BSC's communication network, which is not mentioned in *The Quiet Canadian* or *A Man Called Intrepid*.

The Curious Case of Dusko Popov

There are other indications William Stephenson's opinions may, in many cases, have been different than as chronicled by the writer Stevenson. In fact the *Intrepid* author was later quoted saying the exact opposite of what his subject told him.

Dusko Popov (1912-1981), was a Yugoslav recruited into the Abwehr as a German agent in 1940, and was turned into a double agent by the British. Among the information passed on by Popov to the Allies was a copy of a Japanese questionnaire requesting information including quite specific details about the American base at Pearl Harbor. When Popov travelled to the Western Hemisphere he came into contact with BSC (Popov remembered being met in Bermuda by John Pepper) and later was funnelled to the FBI.

According to Popov's autobiography *Spy/Counterspy* (1974), and some British sources, when Popov travelled to Washington he "forced" a meeting with J Edgar Hoover, and showed the FBI chief the Japanese questionnaire. Hoover, according to the story, was abrupt with Popov and chose to ignore the Japanese information, which heightened the catastrophe of December 7, 1941. Hoover didn't like Popov's lifestyle. He believed Popov was a playboy, and the code name Tricycle was assigned to him because he liked to sleep with two women at once.[41]

The Popov story has been repeated in over 30 books, mostly written by British authors, since the death of Hoover in 1972, but it is not necessarily true. John Masterman, who helped control German agents during the war, started the tale with the publication of *The Double-Cross System* in 1972. Masterman concedes, somewhat condescendingly, "We should certainly have risked a snub and pointed out to our friends in the United States what the significance of the document might be"[42] The British author Nicolas J Cull goes as far as to blame Stephenson for the entire disaster. Hoover, according to Cull, regarded Popov's intelligence as suspect as a result of BSC's propaganda tactics. "Stephenson had cried wolf once too often. The US Pacific Fleet picked up the bill."[43]

The Popov story came somewhat to a head in 1989 when the CIA historian Thomas Troy published *The British Assault on J Edgar Hoover: The Tricycle Case* in an intelligence journal. Published accounts of the neglected questionnaire, and the Popov-Hoover encounter have, Troy says, been propagated as examples "of the cleverness of British intelligence sabotaged by American incompetence."[44] Troy lists the numerous English authors who have repeated the Popov story, and the slur against Hoover, and points out that at least three are former British intelligence officers. The Britons, Troy wrote, have been joined in the attack by two Canadians, both familiar with the career of William Stephenson; the British-born author-journalist William Stevenson, and former British Foreign Office employee, historian, and author David Stafford.

According to Troy and former FBI director Clarence Kelly, Popov never met Hoover. Kelly wrote to *True* magazine about an excerpt from Popov's book *Spy/Counterspy* that after a "very careful study of the entire matter," he concluded Hoover could not have warned anyone of the Pearl Harbor attack. The FBI later released over a thousand pages of documents related to Popov's visits. Troy's conclusions stemming from the papers were:

- The questionnaire had a number of other questions as well, and possibly was a case of the Germans simply updating their files.
- If the British had knowledge of the attack on Pearl Harbor, why did they not inform the Americans through other channels? Why would they rely on the persuasive abilities of a 29 year-old Yugoslav who arrived in the US with thousands of dollars in his pocket and a desire to party?
- The documents related to Popov indicated the FBI *did* pass on the questionnaire to G-2 and ONI.
- Hoover never did meet with Popov.

Judging from the correspondence between author Stevenson and Stephenson, it appears the ex-espionage chief wasn't impressed by

Popov's exploits, and in 1974 after he read Popov's book, Stephenson cabled the author to say the young Yugoslav didn't meet Hoover.

"Popov Tricycle appears to be getting away with his usual cunning and his references talks with JEH (Hoover) pure imagination STOP Had thought of taking Ewen Montagu to task for his agreeding (sic) express favourable foreword but the whole affair is of such minor consequence that myself relegate tale to W P B (likely War Propaganda Board) STOP."[45]

During the writing of *AMCI*, Stephenson requested changes in a section concerning the double agent Popov, but didn't see any in the draft sent to him. Stevenson replied the changes were sent to the printer, but not to Stephenson. "When you mentioned this (Popov) to me I made the necessary amendments. Of course the clean copy you have now got from Julian did not pass through my hands, and I guess that he did not transfer to that copy the changes I had written into the one that went to the printers. The printers have the changes." This seems to clearly indicate Stephenson didn't see the book's final draft before it went to print.[46] The former espionage head requested passages in the book reflect his impressions of Popov's character, but the writer's letter to Stephenson two days later seems to show he didn't make the amendments his subject requested. "I enclose a copy of the changes made in the Popov section. I can't very well call him a scoundrel without risking a libel action."[47]

Strangely, after Stephenson's death the author had a completely different recollection of Popov's exploits. "Our conversation was not for publication at the time," Stevenson told the author Anthony Summers. "But he (Stephenson) was very clear. He said Popov had indeed met Hoover—he knew all about it. He thought it was a terrible failing in Hoover who had this straightlaced attitude that shut him off completely from realities. Stephenson had no doubts about Popov's credibility, and he thought the FBI had totally failed to pick up on what Popov was trying to tell him about Pearl Harbor."[48]

It is somewhat peculiar if there were such discrepancies in the telling of his career, that Stephenson would allow the same author to write another book *Intrepid's Last Case,* with his blessing. In fact Stephenson asked Hyde, and possibly others, to produce a book entitled *Intrepid's Last Case.* Hyde's account evolved into the *Atom Bomb Spies.*[49] The second Stevenson book which deals loosely with the Gouzenko case did not make as big a splash as *A Man Called Intrepid*. Stephenson told Canadian journalist Robert Collins, who was working for *Reader's Digest* at the time, that he went ahead with the second book for two reasons. "That it would bring active Reds and pseudo-Reds from the woodwork to attack me in every possible way. And it would clear Ellis. He (Stevenson) failed in that completely."[50]

The Reviews

Despite some eroding reviews, *A Man Called Intrepid* became a bestseller, selling millions of copies. A number of Stephenson's contemporaries—people who were aware of what Stephenson actually did during the war—were less critical of some of the book's contents. On February 6, 1976, Colin Gubbins, a former head of Britain's Special Operation Executive, wrote to the author Stevenson and said, "What a tremendous job you have done in matching up to the occasion to what INTREPID achieved. And I am so glad too for Intrepid's sake that at last everything that really matters for him has been told and what I mean that the remarkable achievements of BSC have at last been revealed, 'honour where honour is done.'"[51]

The same month Lord Louis Mountbatten wrote to Stephenson to say, "I am so glad that at last the story of all you achieved is being told in spite of your continuous cloak of anonymity up to date. It was always a great thrill meeting you and working with you and high time the world knew all about what you did."[52]

The historian Gilbert Highet wrote to say, "It was grand to see something like justice done to your magnificent career—at long last—in Stevenson's very careful book. It confirms my pride in having been associated with you at a great time in history."[53]

David Bruce, of OSS London, who later became US Ambassador to Britain, and a NATO official, wrote to the editor Muller, "Had it not been for Sir William's achievements it seems to me highly possible that the Second World War would have followed a different and perhaps fatal course. This is an amazing account of the influence exercised by one man on one of the great crises of history. I am grateful to you for sending the manuscript to me."[54]

John Le Carré in the *New York Times* Book Review, wrote, "I even wonder whether in our unconscious spiritual selves we hope that our old heroes will rise again and save us now. Until the autumn of 1942, "in the secret war, the job of saving Britain was left to a Scottish Canadian and an Irish American," and he referred to Stephenson as the defacto general of Anglo-American clandestine warfare against Hitler.[55]

The Critics

A number of what have been described by the *London Times* as "distinguished figures," entered into the debate on Stephenson's career, seemingly not based on the historical record, personal knowledge, or interviews with people who worked with Stephenson, but by the exploits described in the book *A Man Called Intrepid* and it's sequel. Two reviewers were especially vitriolic in their analysis of Stephenson and his career.

Hugh Redwald Trevor-Roper

The most prominent and vocal of the critics of the *Intrepid* saga is England's Hugh Trevor-Roper (b. 1914), historian, author, university professor and life peer. (He was introduced to the House of Lords as Lord Dacre of Glanton in November, 1979.)

Trevor-Roper obtained his BA at Oxford in 1936, and was appointed Regius Professor of Modern History there in 1957. He became Master of Peterhouse College at Cambridge University in 1980. Trevor-Roper is also a former intelligence officer who worked in Signals intelligence during the war. In 1945 he was sent to Germany to investigate the mystery surrounding the death of Adolf Hitler. His book *The Last Days of Hitler* (Macmillan 1947), was based on secret documents and interviews, and it won Trevor-Roper international acclaim. His academic career has been somewhat controversial.[56]

Trevor-Roper is often asked by the media to comment on espionage affairs. Explaining his background in intelligence, Trevor-Roper told the *New York Times* (April 24, 1977), "I was recruited as part of a package. A small body of which I was a member made some discoveries which were rightly regarded as of great importance; and to have them the Secret Service had to have me." He was an associate of double agent Kim Philby, and after Philby's defection wrote a book, T*he Philby Affair:*

Espionage Treason and Secret Service (Kimber 1968).[57] He was also an associate of Anthony Blunt, and in the words of Canadian journalist Peter Worthington, was "discredited" when it was revealed he may have accompanied the known Soviet agent to Europe following the war to recover letters (see Appendix A) from the Duke of Windsor to Nazi leaders.[58]

Trevor-Roper wrote in the *New York Review* that *A Man Called Intrepid* was "start to finish utterly worthless." To write such a book the author would have to understand British Intelligence, but the writer Stevenson was exempt from this precondition as, "It would be like urging a jellyfish to grit its teeth and dig in its heels."

He did say in the review that Stephenson was a friend and ally of Winston Churchill. He said he was the confidential liaison officer for ULTRA material sent to Roosevelt before the Americans were in the war. He also makes factual errors in his review.[59]

Following Stephenson's death, the *Sunday Telegraph* in England ran a Trevor-Roper story titled *The Faking of Intrepid*. The story's subheadline said Stephenson "was a fraud who fooled the world into believing he was a master spy."[60] In it Trevor-Roper, who is described by the Folio Society as "Britain's greatest living historian," wrote Stephenson was undoubtedly the source of all the anticdotes in *A Man Called Intrepid*.

"The author could be left to mug up the story of these operations elsewhere, but it can only be Sir William who put himself into them: for he had not been there before." He says a note described in the book from Churchill inviting Stephenson to his house must have been a forgery. "Such a document can only be provided by Sir William ... the implications of this forgery, which Sir William has chosen to ignore, are disquieting, even sinister," Trevor-Roper reports. (In fact, Stephenson said years earlier Churchill phoned and didn't send him a letter.)[61] The success of the Stephenson book in the United States was because the CIA needed a figurehead, Trevor-Roper wrote. "To the old OSS hands and their CIA successors, Stephenson was the mythical figure who in the heroic past had stood behind their semi-mythical founder Donovan." To rob people of heroes was a cruel act, Lord Dacre continued, "like robbing children of their cosy woolly bears."

Stephenson was not the only western espionage head who did not pass Trevor-Roper's scrutiny. Stewart Menzics, the head of Britain's SIS during the war was, at the end of his life, "suffering from delusions of grandeur," Trevor-Roper says. The historian attributes this problem to, "secret service insulation from real life, which can lead, in old age, to dangerous hallucinations," and, "publishers should flee from their approaches and friends should prevail upon them to be silent."[62]

He also wrote a laudatory introduction to a book critical of former West German intelligence head Reinhard Gehlen (see Appendix B), who released his memoirs in 1971. In *The General was a Spy* Trevor-Roper says Gehlen's organization after 1958 declined into a series of "small failures," followed by "great failures." One of the book's major summations is that Gehlen's chronicle "reveals himself as a victim of an outsize (sic) ego," and "The greatest service Gehlen could have done himself would have been to preserve his silence."[63]

In the sixties, Trevor-Roper appeared on a CBC radio documentary entitled *The Great Canadian Spy*. The historian had nothing negative to say about Stephenson. Surrounded by Stephenson's contemporaries (Lord Louis Montbatten, Montgomery Hyde, Malcom Muggerage, and Eric Maschwitz), in a documentary that heralded Stephenson's accomplishments, Trevor-Roper didn't mention that he thought Stephenson "was a fraud who fooled the world into believing he was a master spy," as his later literary efforts stressed.

David Stafford

British-born historian David Stafford (b. 1942) is a former employee of Her Majesty's Diplomatic Service in London. He served as a Third and Second Secretary with Britain's Foreign Office in 1967 and 1968, and shortly afterward, he moved to an academic career at the University of London and became a researcher and part-time lecturer. About 1970, he came to Canada and worked as an assistant professor at the University of Victoria. Stafford has also been linked with the University of Western Ontario, Concordia University in Montreal, Cambridge, and the University of Toronto as a "research associate," "visiting associate," or as a "visiting associate professor."

Stafford's specialization is World War II and espionage. He lectured at Canadian and American universities on Second World War events, and spy literature, providing commentary for a variety of media. The

British Foreign Office vet was the director of the Canadian Committee for the History of the Second World War from 1981 till 1984, and a member of the American committee. He has also acted as a referee for Canada Council research grant applications.[64]

Stafford researched the career of William Stephenson and British Security Coordination, publishing a book on Camp X in 1986. Stafford stresses career achievements of Bill Stephenson have been exaggerated by books and films. At the end of *Camp X* in a chapter titled *Myth and Reality*, Stafford concludes, "It is now difficult for the serious historian to give him (Stephenson) credit for anything."[65] Stafford says the Camp X 'myth' had been embellished by Canada, "in the service of nation building." Canadians, according to Stafford, "anxious to decolonize their past, have thus rewritten their history since the war to cleanse it of imperial heritage." He doesn't mention any Canadian writers doing this purging, other than English-born, RAF vet William Stevenson.

Following Stephenson's death, Stafford wrote *A Myth Called Intrepid*, for *Saturday Night* magazine. The cover read, "*Intrepid: the Spymaster who Wasn't*," and the story asserted "the amazing exploits of our favourite spymaster turned out to contain large doses of fiction concocted in the forgetful mind of an old man." Throughout the October 1989 piece Stafford refers to Stephenson as "the old man." He also wrote that the publishers of *A Man Called Intrepid* had "finally relented," and the book had been officially classified as a novel. (Subsequently the magazine wrote a correction that the British paperback publisher *Sphere* books had made an error on one edition in the early eighties, and that error had not been repeated. The book was not a novel).

The Stafford story on Stephenson led to the threat of legal action against the Canadian magazine. This appears to have been initiated not by Stevenson, but by the wife of the author, Monica Jensen-Stevenson, as Stevenson was away in Asia.[66]

The matter was settled out of court. A year after the story was published a handful of letters were printed by the magazine, most of which took Stafford's revisionism to task. The author Stevenson responded to the article in a letter and wrote mostly about himself. He flew planes in World War II, he said in rebuttal to the story that diminished Stephenson's career. (He flew Hellcats, "modified for 'lone ranger operations' behind Japanese lines at extremely high altitude." Stevenson got around—another report puts him in the Atlantic at the end of the war, "searching for a U-boat suspected of transporting (Martin) Bormann and his Nazi treasures to Argentina.")[67] His research was extensive, he wrote in *Saturday Night,* and he was not a tabloid journalist.

Oddly enough, Stevenson doesn't mention Stafford's connection to Britain's Foreign Office, or the 'red menace,' which is so prevalent in his correspondence with Stephenson. He too seems to conclude that controversy over Stephenson's career was Canadian-based. Stephenson "made enemies because he cut through bureaucratic red tape and offended the Liberal government of William Lyon Mackenzie King. It is shameful that these old enmities should be served up at the earliest opportunity following his death." This is a rather confusing connection. Stafford was eight years old, and living in England when former Canadian Prime Minister King died in 1950. No Canadian residents are quoted in Stafford's *Saturday Night* story criticizing Stephenson. When Stafford's article appeared, Canada's Liberal party had been out of power for five years. In all the research and interviews with former BSC people I have conducted, there is no record of problems with the King government. (In earlier articles RAF vet and author Stevenson has been rather nonanalytical of the critics of the *Intrepid* sagas labelling others, "miserable cockroaches," "anti-Semitic," and, "Canadians of convenience."[68])

Earlier in the decade Stafford was unimpressed by another espionage celebrity with a Canadian connection, Igor Gouzenko. "Gouzenko was not a modest man and throughout his life he displayed a tragic combination of massive ego and minimal self-knowledge." Gouzenko was also made into a myth by malleable Canadians, Stafford asserts. "How has it happened that Gouzenko found in Canada an audience that was eager to transform him from a man to a myth? In part it was Canada's relative naïvété in world affairs, and Gouzenko provided a rather brutal rite of passage into that arena," Stafford wrote in *Saturday Night.*[69]

Other 'Intrepid' Reviews

A number of other reviews did not acclaim Stephenson's war achievements, but questioned the accuracy of parts of *A Man Called Intrepid*. The English historian AJP Taylor, in the *New Statesman*, continually refers to Stephenson as Sir William Stevenson in his review, and criticizes the book for its lack of accuracy. "Nearly everything else in the book is either exaggerated, distorted or already known," Taylor wrote. "Great play is made with the BSC papers. It is not explained what they were or where they are." He complained there were no precise references and, "the only book quoted by name was *Casino Royal* by Ian Fleming."[70]

Sir David Hunt provided another negative review. He disputes whether a picture portraying a shadowy figure and Churchill surveying the bombing damage of the House of Commons could be Stephenson. The unidentifiable shadow in the photo was not Stephenson, but Brendan Bracken, he said. "Stephenson is quoted verbatim, speaking as though an eyewitness. Sir John Martin has no recollection of his presence and from Montgomery Hyde's book it appears he was in New York at the time." He also doubts that Churchill knew about the bombing of Coventry beforehand, which is mentioned in the book, but he admits this has also been discussed in *The* ULTRA *Secret* and *Bodyguard of Lies*.[71] Following Stephenson's death, Hunt discounted any possibility Stephenson could have known Churchill as Sir John Colville, Churchill's secretary for a short time, didn't remember meeting him. He continued, "I've also spoken to Alan Taylor (AJP Taylor, Beaverbrook biographer), and there is no evidence Stephenson even knew Beaverbrook, let alone Churchill."[72]

For his part Colville, who also worked for Neville Chamberlain, and Buckingham Palace (1947-49), doesn't explain why he would have known everyone Churchill knew, simply because he worked for him for a while.[73] If Churchill didn't know his own Intelligence Chief in North America during a World War, when his great desire was to have the Americans as an ally, his competency would have to be called into question. Colville doesn't explore this catastrophic breakdown of communication during England's greatest crisis.

On June 28, 1940, Churchill wrote to his American Ambassador Lord

Lothian in Washington, complaining, "We have really not had any help worth speaking of from the United States so far." In his postwar account Churchill wrote, "The rifles and field guns did not arrive until the end of July. The destroyers had been refused."[74] Bill Stephenson arrived in the United States June 21, 1940.

Weeks after Stephenson's death the *London Times* attempted to explain the 'Intrepid' controversy. The conclusion ascertained from the British scholars and "distinguished figures" interviewed, seemed to be that the former espionage head inflated his importance, and implied Stephenson was egotistical and loved drawing attention to himself. "The source of the information turns out to be only Stephenson himself— amplified by biographies whose authors he knew and whose writing he vetted."[75] Ironically, the picture depicting Stephenson accompanying the article was of someone else. The *Times* photo editors and, or, the defence correspondent who wrote the story, didn't know what this long-time publicity seeker looked like. (They were not alone. The Toronto paper *The Globe and Mail* in their year-end-review of prominent Canadians who died in 1989 printed a picture of William Stevenson the author, instead of the 'publicity loving' Stephenson.) The *Times* article also doesn't speculate why Stephenson, on his personal instructions, was buried before his death was publicly announced. As a result, six people attended the 'megalomaniac's' funeral, and local policemen acted as pall bearers.

Other British writers such as Nigel West and Chapman Pincher have commented about questionable historical references triggered by the book *A Man Called Intrepid*. West, the pseudonym for ex-British parliamentarian Rupert Allason, has pointed out that some photographs purporting to be from BSC's Station M archive are actually still pictures from a movie. He doesn't report that Station M was the BSC division in charge of false documents. The photographs from *A Man Called Intrepid* at the University of Regina have been classified 'restricted' by Stevenson, and can't be viewed by researchers.

Controversial incidents described in *A Man Called Intrepid* along with Trevor-Roper's, and Stafford's subsequent analyses, have influenced Canadian authors as well. The writer Richard Cleroux in his book *Official Secrets*, hypothesizes Stephenson became forgetful as he became older.

"By this stage in his illness, he (Stephenson) could no longer distinguish between fact and fiction and he misled a number of people."[76] The writer John Bryden in *Best Kept Secret* says, "Stephenson's warped version of events has directly or indirectly influenced dozens of histories, many of them by very competent writers. From first to last however, Stephenson was a liar."[77] *Spy Wars*, which J L Granastein co-authored with David Stafford, reduces Stephenson's wartime role to that of charlatan. Timothy Naftalli seemed to echo the opinions of Stafford and Trevor-Roper in *"Intrepid's last Deception"* for the publication *Intelligence and National Security*.[78]

Years after his death, this is essentially the public record of William Stephenson. A career misted in controversy, and a character so tight-lipped that two biographers could not even determine the names of his parents or date of birth. After working tirelessly to help save democracy in Europe, his career has been reduced in some quarters to questioning the dates he met people for dinner fifty years earlier, whether he knew his friends, or if he was an unidentifiable shadow in a photograph. Partially as a result, it was difficult to obtain a relevant grasp on the man and his accomplishments, even for those who were close to him. "What I'd like to know is what was true. And what wasn't true?" said his friend of nearly forty years, Derek Bedson, "I mean what *was* he appointed to? Exactly. In New York."

Most intelligence files related to Stephenson's British Security Coordination were destroyed and many other intelligence records remain closed. However during the war Stephenson surrounded himself with numerous people. Many of them had similar questions as Stephenson's friends and relatives, and subsequently they also provided some answers.

A Conversation

Pauline McGibbon, former Lieutenant-Governor of Ontario, Stephenson friend on the subject of *AMCI*.

The former governor of Bermuda Edwin Leathers is quoted as saying, "Sir William once told me we would have to wait a long time for the official history of his wartime activities to be written. In the meantime we will have to be content with the fictional one."[79] McGibbon said

Stephenson expressed similar sentiments to her.

"Let's say this, Bill (Stephenson) said the same thing. That (*A Man Called Intrepid*) was a fictionalized version and I really feel very strongly that the other Bill Stevenson did Sir William a great injustice doing that book."

"But why would he get involved with him again on the second book?"

"That I don't know. That I don't know. I also know that he turned over all his records to him. I think he was so damn mad at the things that were being said that were not true, that he wanted to make sure that somebody was going to write a true history."

Former Stephenson employees in Toronto said McGibbon once asked Stephenson why he didn't answer back against his critics. Stephenson replied, "One day the truth will come out."

"Yes," McGibbon said. "That's right. Oh yes. Bill was very, very, very closed mouthed and I know one time I asked him something and he just looked at me with a grin, and he said, 'I don't know, and if I did I wouldn't tell you,'" she laughed. "Oh, no. Right to his death he was a secret service person. He was very, very ... he would just never say anything."

SECTION II

The Unknown Agents

"But the leaders of the new order did not reckon with the indomitable courage of the individual. The urge towards freedom is irrepressible. Multiplied many times, it generates a force which cannot be measured in terms of tanks or machine guns firing hundreds of rounds a minute. Many times in the past it has slowed the onslaught of a tyrant and helped bring about his downfall. Tolstoy in War and Peace referred to it as the mysterious force of X"
—Sir William Stephenson

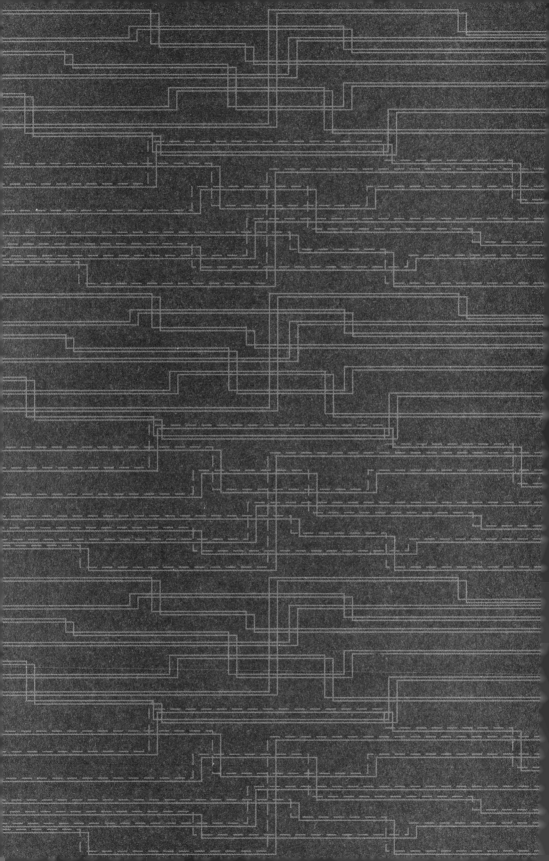

12 BSC Recruits

Winnipeg

Molly Phair

Marjorie Ferguson first saw the small newspaper ad. She trundled down to Winnipeg's Fort Garry Hotel for a job interview, and when it finished, recruiter Herb Rowland was impressed. He wondered if she knew of anyone else who would move to New York, "for British government war work." Marjorie told her younger sister Ruth, and she called her friend, Molly Phair. Ruth would go to the hotel to apply for employment, only if Phair went as well. "We were pretty young at that time," Phair remembered. Although they weren't keen on leaving Winnipeg, the duo went to the hotel for the interview. As time passed, they nearly forgot about the application completely. Then one day, a friend of Phair's in the Royal Canadian Mounted Police turned up at her door and said, 'Oh, so you're on your way to New York. I know more about you, than you know about yourself.' "The RCMP investigated us," Phair remembered. The trio passed their police check, and in June of 1943, a half-dozen Winnipeggers left for New York City to join the Stephenson organization.

On arrival in New York, BSC provided temporary accommodation at a women's hotel, but "the bedrooms were the size of broom closets." Eventually they looked for apartments, but there were restrictions on their movement and conduct. When they found a new place, the address had to be screened by the organization before they could move in. They were not allowed to go to Harlem. If the new employees needed medical attention, they were only allowed to visit doctors that had been pre-approved by Security Coordination. If they wanted an appointment with another doctor, they could only go after he was investigated and checked out by security people. "Other than that, we were quite free agents to do what we wanted to do."

But they were to keep their activities surreptitious. "I think the British security were pretty smart people," Phair says. "Three of us were living together, and none of us knew what the others were doing. They impressed us very much, but we did not talk about it."

Phair worked in BSC's communications department on the second floor of Rockefeller Center's International Building, near the statue of Atlas, and across the street from St. Patrick's Cathedral. "It couldn't be in a more public location." There was no uniformed security around the office and employees entered through an unmarked door.

The division dealt with the collation and dispersal of intercepted coded messages. Phair was in the Japanese section. Fourteen women were in her group, which contained a room full of 'TK' (telekrypton) machines. They received long sheets of teletype-like messages from an adjoining room and processed them. Phair's section counted portions of the tapes, cut them with a paper cutter, and sent them off by safe hand. Phair doesn't know where the messages originated, only that they were Japanese. "I was not involved with the de-coding, just the transfers of the messages." Herb Rowland, who hired her in Winnipeg, became her boss.

Marjorie Ferguson worked on the second floor as well. Her sister Ruth worked on the 36th floor for Wing Commander Richard (Dickey) Byrd, and later she came downstairs as the secretary of Benjamin de Forest (Pat) Bayly. Much of the younger Ferguson's activities involved basic secretarial work and accounting. Many of the messages that came across her desk were in code or ciphered. She remembers there was one telex-type machine in the office for important messages, that only two people were to touch, herself and Bayly. But almost all basic daily procedures were on a 'need-to-know' basis, and it was difficult to obtain any type of overview of the operation. Names such as Bill Ross Smith, Dickey Coit, and Cedrick Belfridge were not familiar to Ferguson, although they also worked on the upper floors with Stephenson. "People ask me what I did during the war," Ferguson says. "I can honestly say, I don't know. People think I'm teasing!"

Nearly all the people working with BSC were Canadians, Phair said, although there were a few English women, and British military men around. Many of the Canadians knew each other, because they were from the same cities.

The organization was known at first as the British Passport Office, but later changed to British Security Coordination. No employees revealed to anyone specifics about the organization or job descriptions. "If people wanted to believe that it was dealing in securities, or stocks and bonds, that was fine, let them think that," Phair said. "Because we didn't say what we were doing to people that we met."

When she was back in Winnipeg on holidays, a year after starting at BSC, Phair discovered people were interested in what she was doing. While at the race track, she met a friend with someone she didn't know. The stranger seemed quite aggressive, asked persistent questions, and asked her out. He came to a gathering she had the next day, as did Phair's friend in the RCMP, who knew she was working for BSC. When the Mountie arrived, he looked around the room, took Phair aside, and said, "What is that man doing at this house? Get him out!" The stranger left, and she never found out more about what had occurred. "That was sort of strange."

Contrary to some reports, Phair believes most employees were aware of who Stephenson was. "We knew he was the head, we knew what he looked like, if we saw him." Her section would see Stephenson occasionally when he would quietly slip in and out, but he kept a low profile. Every now and then a small delegation would tour the area. Noel Coward and Lord Mountbatten came through the office with Stephenson, Phair says. Bill Donovan was around, and his association with Stephenson was an important aspect of the entire operation. "I know during the war, while we were there, there was a very close relationship between him and Bill Donovan, who was the head of Strategic Services," Phair said. "Because of that relationship, the Americans worked so closely with the British."

Bill Stephenson, to the average BSC employee such as Phair, was a quiet individual who everyone held in high esteem. "He had the respect of everybody. A great deal. Certainly. Nobody would have criticized him. He was not the type who blew his own horn. He was the kind of person who would never talk to anybody about some of the things he had been doing." Although he didn't mingle with the personnel, Stephenson's covert manner was sensed by his staff. "I can never imagine him ever blabbing. He was a very, very quiet person." She thought some people made a cottage industry out of his career. "I am sure this has been done by people who are taking advantage of him."

Phair was surprised any information at all came out about BSC, let alone the saga of the international swashbuckler portrayed in *A Man Called Intrepid*. She believes the book's revelations had something to do with the defection of Kim Philby. She also thought Stephenson may have lost the ability to intellectualize and reason in his later life. Errors about Stephenson's career tarnished his reputation, which he didn't deserve, she says. "I think people are taking him at face value and that's not fair." Phair thought William Stevenson must have written *A Man Called Intrepid* in a great hurry. "He had a lot of inaccuracies in it," she said. "When he described Sir William had come from Manitoba, he said he came from Point Douglas, near Winnipeg—Nothing could be more Winnipeg!"

Phair remains somewhat reluctant to discuss her war work nearly fifty years later. She remembers a day in June of 1943, when she started to work for Stephenson's secret organization, and the preliminary instructions that were given. "The day we arrived, we were given a talk to the effect that, other countries, when a war was over, may reveal what they did. And he said you are never, ever, to reveal anything you did. And I don't think anybody that worked there ever said a word."

Some of Phair's former BSC colleagues gathered in Toronto in 1986. "We jokingly called it the 'Spy Reunion.' There were no records kept of staff or anything—afterward everything was destroyed, so the only way the people could go to the reunion was by word of mouth." Former BSC people in Toronto sent out notices to the former employees they knew, and those people sent back names of any BSC alumni they were in touch with. Stephenson was told about the reunion and he sent his daughter Elizabeth from Bermuda to attend on his behalf, and she brought a video message from him.

Phair left BSC in October of 1945. She was asked to stay on in the accounts department but as math wasn't her forte, she decided to return to Winnipeg. The Ferguson sisters eventually moved to the United

States. Molly Phair is the only former Stephenson employee who still lives in his old home town. She said she enjoyed her time with the organization and "would just like to reiterate the respect that everybody had for the man."

Toronto

Station M closed down and Camp X was phased out in May 1945. BSC's eight hundred Canadian women went home, forever sworn to secrecy about the details of their wartime work. But they would always remember with pride what they helped to accomplish—and, with amazement perhaps, the secrets they shared.—Canadians At War

Charmaine Manchee worked in BSC's inner office as one of Bill Stephenson's personal coding clerks. "It was called SIS," she remembered, "and you went through the passport control to get up to the office. There were two secretaries, and two coders, and all of Stephenson's correspondence had to come through us." They were in a central area and Montgomery Hyde, a Mr Baxter, John Pepper, and another had outside offices. She translated outgoing and incoming messages by hand from code books. "We weren't as proficient as Dorothy (Evenson). We did it all by hand in those days." The messages, once decoded, went straight to Stephenson. Most of the missives were sent via Bermuda, which was an intercept point, Manchee said.

A majority of the outgoing dispatches went to Britain she remembered. "They went direct to England, to Churchill, and 'C', and they came from all over." There was an outer area where the messages were evaluated. If they were designated as confidential, they came into the inner office where Kathleen Taylor (Kay) and Manchee decoded them. If the message was less urgent, it went to the outer office where it was transposed and sent to various other members such as Pepper, Hyde, Baxter, etc. "But his own personal messages were sent to us."

The coding and decoding went on around the clock, and the women worked in three eight-hour shifts. Messages had to be decoded and waiting for Stephenson each morning. She was paid $35 a week every Friday (A good bookkeeper earned about $20 a week at the time.).

There was no official record of the payment transactions, and no deductions. "It was all cash payment in an envelope. No payroll." Manchee eventually moved out of a women's hotel where she first stayed and into an apartment. The women employees paid their own rent and usually lived together.

Manchee was hired through family connections. She worked first of all in Washington for the British Purchasing Commission, or British Air Commission, and after about six weeks there she was moved up to New York. "When I arrived in New York I was told that I was on a very confidential job, and I was not to socialize with anybody." As a result she lived at the women's hotel and did little else, "simply walking to and from work each day," until others were sent down from Toronto and she made a few friends. For about the first two months she lived with Kay Taylor, the daughter of AJ Taylor, the close friend of Stephenson and one of the financiers of Vancouver's Lion's Gate Bridge and British Properties.

The BSC offices expanded after the American entry into the war, and on a lower floor in Rockefeller Center a separate office opened for Stephenson. "There was a set of offices with a door that was not used very much, and he would come in that door to meet various people such as Donovan and other dignitaries, or people that he was sending on missions hither and yon."

If someone asked her what she did for a living she said she worked for Passport Control. "That was the cover." But after a period of time the name changed 'publicly' to British Security. They were known by the staff security and most of the employees punched a clock.

Taylor and Manchee did the filing, coding, deciphering and distribution. Miss (Elizabeth) Richardson was in charge of receiving the messages and if they were marked 'Secret and Confidential' they were sent to the inner office for decoding, and to Stephenson.

"Could you read them?"

"Well, we'd have to decode them first."

"But then you would be able to read the decoded message?"

"Oh yes."

"Well you would know his contacts with Churchill or whatever?"

"Oh yes."

Stephenson "certainly did" know Churchill, she emphasized. He met with the British Prime Minister throughout the war. She and a friend in purchasing could tell when Stephenson was about to go to Europe because he ordered certain things. "And we knew just from common knowledge that he must be going over, and he certainly did go over to meet Churchill."

Another point Manchee could substantiate was that BSC planted propaganda in New York papers. The department was called Office of War Information (OWI). "We did that in our office, I'll remember the name of it eventually, but they did certainly curry favour, is that the right word, with the publishers of the papers and plant pro-British propaganda in the papers. You read that in all the books and it is very true...

"That's the one I'm trying to think of, Ralph Ingersoll and *PM Magazine*, they really worked on him."

∎

Helen Woolley worked primarily for Special Operation Executive's Richard (Dickie) Coit although the acting Western head of SOE changed from time to time. She did secretarial work and filing for four years. The files were about individuals and businesses, and agents who were sent abroad. Her immediate superior was Alexander Halpern, a Russian. She heard about the New York job through a friend, Marg Mowat.

"She was working at the National Trust, and I heard about this marvellous opening in New York, so I applied in early June of '41 I guess. What I remember most is being interviewed for the job, and they wanted Canadians obviously, and you had to have a reasonably good background, and we had to be investigated by the Mounties." She was interviewed by Tommy Drew-Brook, the Bay Street stockbroker who was a long-time friend of Stephenson. She met Drew-Brook again at Stephenson's office parties in New York, and asked him about her interview. "Apparently the only blot on my application was that my family was Oxford group (an anti-war peace movement), and it was supposedly a subversive organization. So I nearly didn't get the job. So I had to convince them that I wasn't a member of the Oxford group. My mother and my brother were. So when I got to New York, there was a file 'Oxford Group' and my brother's file was in it."

There was only a small organization in New York when she started, and she worked in an outer office and remembers Stephenson vividly. She was told the cover of the operation was British Passport Control, but was well aware few travellers visited Britain in the early forties during the war. "No one thought to ask me, 'who was getting a British passport in 1941? In the middle of the war?' and I always wondered about that."

They were told to live at the women's hotel and Beacmon Tower and they were given strict instructions not to speak to anyone about what they were doing.

Janet FitzGerald was in a records department primarily doing filing. At the time BSC was concerned with German shipping and sailors leaving ships who could possibly become spies and terrorists, she said. The organization had long lists of incoming Nazi ships and sailors to check, but she doesn't know how the information was obtained. In 1942, after the United States was in the war, FitzGerald moved to a new BSC office in Guatemala and did similar work. A major concern in Central America was keeping tabs on Nazi U-boats which were possibly operating in the Gulf of Mexico and near the Panama Canal.

A friend of hers, Betty Cook, went down near the beginning of the war and she wrote FitzGerald and told her it was great working in New York. Later she answered an ad in a Toronto newspaper.

The women were instructed to use specific doctors and dentists, FitzGerald says, and BSC would pay their bills. One of the doctors was William Rowland, the brother of Herb, who was an office manager, recruiter, and a friend of Stephenson's. "One woman had all her fillings taken out and replaced with gold ones," FitzGerald said with a smile.

Gwen Rollaston heard about the New York employment through her friend Margaret Mowat who was working for the Stephenson organization and enjoying it very much. Rollaston told her she would like to work in New York so when Mowat heard BSC was doing more recruiting she gave Herb Rowland her name, and an appointment was arranged.

In December 1941, she arrived in New York and worked in the Registry doing filing and clerical work, similar to the work done by FitzGerald. She remembered particularly large files on the German multinationals IG Farben and General Analine, and also on suspected Nazi sympathizers. In 1943 she also moved to a Guatemala office and did secretarial work. The BSC representatives in Guatemala worked with the British Embassy. "We were with the British Legation down there, working for the so-called Civil Attaché, who was actually SIS from New York, a Mr Neal." They made reports on all the Germans in the area that were 'suspect' and sent them back to New York.

The BSC subagents sent coded messages utilizing pages of books. *The Key To Rebecca*, a novel by Ken Fowlett, was remembered by Rollaston. "Now, it explains our coding system perfectly. We used novels."

The agent in the field was given a novel and the office used the same one. To convey the message, references were made to words in the novel using numbers, such as the third word on the fourth line of a page fifteen would be '3415.' The patterns could be reversed, and certain numbers could be transposed to represent other numerals. The women received all their code training in New York.

Rollaston remembers there was a high degree of anti-British sentiment when she arrived in the US. "I remember going out socially and being terribly insulted. An American was terribly rude to me. He hated anything to do with Britain and these destroyers. The lend lease that they were getting. It was terrible. I was shattered."

Nancy Thompson didn't go to New York until 1943. She had been working for the Royal Bank at that time and a woman she worked with knew Herb Rowland, and found out about a recruiting drive. Her interview was in a hotel room at the Royal York in Toronto, but she doesn't recall a tough interrogation. "I think all you really had to do was identify a typewriter, and you were in," she said. "Then they put the Mounties on you." She lived with three other girls in an apartment and they split the $125 a month rent. Thompson was a statistician. She did surveys on the time it took between when a message was intercepted, when it was relayed, when it was received in New York, and finally when it was received in England.

The clocks at BSC were on Greenwich Mean Time, and when Thompson first started she had a few problems. "I'm not very good about the International Date Line, you know, whether you go ahead, or behind, or whatever," she said smiling. "And there was no set rule whether you put the intercept station first, and then the date, and then the time. There was just this series of numbers across the top of the messages. So I would have messages received in Greenwich, before they had ever been intercepted."

Thompson was nearly fired a few days after she started working for British Security Coordination, as one thing the women could not do was reveal the office phone number. "My brother was in the Navy and happened to be in New York and he knew that I was working for British Security Coordination." When he was at Admiralty House in lower New York, he mentioned that he wanted to get in touch with her, and Admiralty House gave him BSC's number, and he called Thompson. "Well, we had the office manager. We had the personnel manager—everybody in there—wondering how this person had got hold of our telephone number," she remembered. "It was a very serious offense."

Thompson says the American Navy was using BSC facilities. "The US Navy right through the war used the British Intercept Services because they were apparently much more effective." The code room she worked in used three separate codes: Dumpy, Fido and Fog. She totalled numbers on an intercept page which indicated length and duration of the message, and charged the Americans at a set rate. "And every time Britain lost a capital ship, I would add another $5,000 to the US Navy bill," she smiled. ("I was just kidding," she said later.)

She worked on the second floor of Rockefeller Center. There was security to go through, and the department punched time clocks when they started work. She worked with a group of four and she was the only one of her group who didn't have to work in shifts. The women were to tell people they were nurses, which would explain why they came in and out of their apartment at strange hours. "We were really kept in great ignorance of what we were doing. They were very careful not to let us know."

Although the women worked, socialized, and lived together, they didn't talk about their work to each other. Most have stayed completely quiet. "I've learned more tonight than I have in the years since." They signed Britain's Secrets Act and were cautioned not to talk about what they were doing. On one occasion a woman mentioned what she was doing in a social setting, and was sent home.

◼

Dorothy Evenson saw an advertisement in a Winnipeg newspaper about employment interviews at the Fort Garry Hotel. She remembers the ad said the applicants had to be a British Subjects and one of her friends suggested they go for an interview. Evenson didn't tell her parents however, as she thought they would follow her to the hotel. She was interviewed at the famous Winnipeg hotel by Herb Rowland. "He basically just talked to us, and I think we were asked if we could type. But he just asked us our background, and what we did." Later in New York, Evenson asked Rowland how he screened people he interviewed, and decided who to hire. He told her he sought people who could get along with other people. "I thought that was interesting."

A week later she received a phone call saying she was to start work in New York on April 16, 1943. About a dozen people left Winnipeg in the spring of 1943 to join Stephenson's British Security Coordination.

Soon after her arrival Evenson was given an aptitude test and was asked to speak to Major Ken Maidment. He told her she was to learn a new machine because she was mechanically inclined. "I told him that I wasn't really at all," she remembered. "And he said 'yes, you are.'"

Evenson was sent to a small office and brought a machine and box. "This was the Type X machine." She was given a manual to read, and then instructed to take the machine apart, and put it together. Evenson studied the rotating drums inside, and turned them to change the coding of the machine. "So I struggled through that, and finally got it down. They gradually brought down more girls from Toronto, and I taught them the machine, and then they set up a section."

The section was at the back of the large telex room on the mezzanine floor of Rockefeller Center. The messages came in via long tapes, which were sent to another section and different staff. About two dozen people worked on the machines in her department, and the machines ran 24 hours a day. They used pasting machines, similar to those of telegrams which were separated with a preamble, time and date, and ended with a signature where they would start a new page. "And these then went into Miss Richardson. She was a lady, a titled lady. And she was very mannish in the British sense, and no nonsense. I was scared stiff of her, and she was very kind." After Richardson sorted the pasted messages, they were sent upstairs to Stephenson.

As the messages were coded, the women didn't know their contents. But they could see where the messages were coming from. They came "from all around the world." One woman recalled seeing some from Madagascar. "Station Two was Colombo."

On some occasions, the upstairs brass knew when important correspondence was going to arrive. They would get a phone call from the 35th floor and people would come down to wait for it. Periodically the communications department would get a call from Stephenson saying that he was bringing a visitor. He showed up with, among others, Louis Mountbatten, Noel Coward, and Lord Beaverbrook. "All these people would come down to look at the messages. And he would walk behind, with his hands behind his back. A little wee man, in a gray suit."

"And Lord Louis was up here," said Evenson, measuring his height.

"And gorgeous," said another.

"Oh yes."

"In navy uniform."

Evenson was asked if she worked on the microdot by Manchee, and it was obvious there was a great ignorance of what each person had done. "This was the secret of the whole organization," Manchee repeated. "Nobody knew what anybody else did."

"I think the whole thing about our organization was don't tell anybody, not even your roommate what you were doing. All we knew was what we were doing. So we couldn't tell anybody anything, because all we knew was this narrow little box that we were in every day."

However the Stephenson organization was very discerning and did know what the employees were doing, even after work. Evenson said BSC was aware of who she was seeing socially. "They watched who you dated. Because I was going with a 'Bill' somebody or other, and he had a car. And I was called in and asked who is he, because he was of an age to be in the forces. He was an American and he wasn't in the forces, so 'what did we talk about?', and they asked what he did. He told me, and as far as I know it was true, that he was the head of this Junior Achievement, which is still in existence in New York. And when you think about it, it is rather a funny thing for a young man to be involved in, so they told me to keep dating him. Ask him questions, and if he asks you questions—you know what to do." Evenson later discovered she was being followed. She was questioned after seeing 'Bill', and BSC agents knew where she and 'Bill' went for dinner the night before.

"I asked him questions. He never asked me a thing. He was just a nice young man. And then they told me to drop him."

"What did you do?"

"I dropped him."

■

Jean Peacock was a civil servant working for the Air Force in Toronto. She heard through a friend returning from New York about a variety of people with interesting jobs there. Peacock found out about a recruitment drive in November of 1943, and was interviewed at the Royal York Hotel by Herb Rowland and a 'Mrs. Shakespeare.' "If you sort of looked respectable you were in." She knew of two other women who were going to work for BSC at about the same time, and the trio lived together in the Bateman Tower which was recommended to them by the organization. Later they were free to look for their own apartments, but the new buildings had to be checked by BSC security before they could move in. "We knew that we had to be careful about what we said, and who we saw. And that was OK because it was sort of exciting to be a part of it, and also it was during the war, and we were all very patriotic and we wanted to make sure that we were doing the right thing."

She did shift work (9-5, 5-1 and 1-9) the entire time she was employed at BSC, and first worked in Dumpy section. The Dumpy messages had to be grouped in multiples of fifteen before they were decoded. The grouped strips of paper passed through a test tube-like mechanism with liquid in it, which made perforations in it, and then the tape was pasted on another paper similar to telegrams. Peacock doesn't know where the messages were coming from, but she was told once that they were shipping messages. "I never knew a thing, it was no problem not to talk about what you were doing, because we didn't know."

The communications department usually socialized together. They went for lunch on Seventh Avenue, or Broadway, or to Hamburg Heaven which was very popular at the time and full of the rich and famous. "We used to go Child's which was up Fifth Avenue, and we used to run into Walter Winchell up there. And he was a great fan, and I'm sure he knew what we were doing, because he used to write quite good columns concerning these Canadians who were in New York."

After a period of time the Dumpy code became obsolete and Peacock was transferred to a small Type X section, which was off the main room. The main Type X department was an absolute din of noise all the time, she said, and very hot in the summer, with salt tablet dispensers on the walls.

"So I was in this other section for a while and then after the atomic bomb fell, and all of a sudden everything was over and people were being fired left, right and centre."

"Fired, or laid off?"

"Same thing. Everybody was sort of anxious to get back to living again."

"Sent home."

Jean Peacock was with the last group to leave BSC's New York offices in December, 1945. She worked for British Information Services, which was a follow-up to British Security Coordination. At that time the Soviet Union was spreading black propaganda about British officials in New York, and that "came through our offices.

"I worked with British Information Services, which was a follow-up on this. There were things going through, to do with BSC through British Information Services. Because at that time the Russians were sort of blackmailing the high British people in New York, and that came through our offices. That's how I got the job. Then they asked me if I would work for British Information Services."

"What do you mean blackmailing?"

"Well, they were telling stories, which they always do, about high people. They would try and paint a black picture of them. At the time even the man I worked for. Cuneo. But it tied in with BSC."

In the late summer, Peacock's communications expertise was called on again. The top coding machine was needed to relay information about Igor Gouzenko. "I guess Dorothy had gone because she had moved over to that other section, but I was the only one left that knew how to run this machine and they apparently got worried that there was a message coming through, and it was about Gouzenko. So I had to stay around. They told me to go to the Beacman where I was living at that time, and to just stay there until they called me. So I stayed there and I went back to the office two or three times and then I decoded the messages about Gouzenko and I could read those messages. And that was in August or September, I guess it was in September '45."

"We didn't hear anything about that here until about January or February of 1946." (Gouzenko's defection was not made public until months after the fact.)

"So who were these messages going to then?"

"I don't know. Upstairs, but I don't know ... (they) probably had to report to Canada, due to the powers that be that were holding Gouzenko."

Peacock and Thompson visited New York in August of 1989, and were surprised a section of Rockefeller Center was still called the Passport Office.

Isolationism

There were large BSC files on the America First Movement, the large isolationist organization that tried to keep the United States out of the war.

"Because that was part of the problem—to get rid of that sentiment."

"That's right."

"That's part of the reason we were there."

"So they gave stuff to the newspapers. I think that's in the BSC history."

"And Mr Stephenson was influential in promoting that Lend Lease, the fifty ships, the tankers, British bases."

Canadians in New York.

"Did you let on that you were Canadian when you were out socially?"

"Some people thought we were from Boston."

"But you weren't told to cover up that you were Canadians?"

"Oh no."

"I didn't socialize much with Americans at all."

"We had so many of us down there, that we had a good time just with us ourselves."

Communications

"And another company that was very closely involved was Commercial Cables."

"Communications?"

"I dare say. I remember they used to have a marvellous Christmas Party. When you think about it, it was sort of questionable."

Colonel Bayly was in charge of communications, they said.

"He was a famous person."

"He was the one at Camp X too. He did something at Camp X."

"So he was the head of communications that figured out how to run this stuff?"

"Yes, he was the head ..."

"He was an agent that disappeared periodically and then came back."

Office Departments

"On the 2nd floor, it was a great big huge room with a row of desks."

"And there was a section where they parcelled things, mailing room, and another section was kind of glassed-in where (Ken) Maidment was; I've no idea what he did."

"My part was the Registry, everything out of Sir William's office, and then it went to Betty Cook's desk. She sorted it under headings and then she passed it on to the correct person who handled that particular area, such as you mentioned, the IG Farben or the Electrolux man from Sweden. (Axel Wenner Gren, see Appendix A) And also the isolationist groups in the States."

Maclean's Magazine Article

The *Maclean's* story talks about Stephenson being a speed reader who woke up at 5 am in the morning to start work.

"That would be true, I'm sure."

"And that he was particularly observant of things?"

"Very much so."

"In fact, the dictum was, we weren't supposed to go out with anyone in the office. We had an assistant called Walter Gallagher who asked me out to lunch. So we had to meet outside the office, and he took me to a French restaurant. We went back separately to the office and apparently Sir William was so smart, he caught on to the fact that we had been out to lunch together. He just smelt the garlic wafting through the office."

"How about his love for martinis?"

"Yes. I think that is true. I could be wrong. I have only one occasion that I remember a party and William was there and there were martinis."

"I think that was the drink of the time."

"Some places served only martinis."

Bill Stephenson

"Did you know he was a Canadian?"

"Oh yes."

"Because one of the things said, no one knew who he was."

"We knew who he was."

"That just a few people could identify him."

"He was a very inconspicuous man. He kind of melded into the background."

"I guess we were just told who he was."

"*Women spoke of his doorman as Peter, of his secretary as Gabrielle and of him as God. Only a handful of them knew him by sight.*"

"Oh that's garbage."

"Oh, well maybe later on. But in the early days we all knew who he was."

"Noel Coward. He was a good friend of Sir William's, and I remember going to a party that Sir William and his wife gave for the opening of his play."

Stephenson's code number was 48000, Manchee said, with 48 indicating the United States.

"The Mayan restaurant was one restaurant that we weren't allowed to go into."

"That was instant dismissal."

"At 63 5th Avenue."

"And we were never to take a course at Berlitz (language school). That was another thing that we weren't supposed to do." No one knew exactly why.

A handful of Toronto ex-BSC people continued to get together after the war. That nucleus organized a BSC reunion in 1986. The guest speaker, before the publication of his book, *Camp X*, was David Stafford.

Reflections on being in wartime New York with BSC
by Jean Peacock, 1986

We were an unusual group within an unusual organization— we weren't the Cynthia's etc. Canadians, because employees had to be British and we were the closest market.

We were a bit of history of WW II—a lot has been written about Intrepid's organization but not from our perspective.

The thrill for Canucks working in NY during that special period. People working shifts—unusual then except for nurses and production line women, which we were, seeing another side of NY life. The café society (movie stars at Hamburg Heaven, Sinatra from the Capital to the Waldorf, etc.) to Child's and Walter Winchell; and the low—all night cafeterias like Bicks and Walgreens. Out for graveyard shift lunches at 4 am.

Radio City Music Hall; the Rockettes; the old Roxy. Radio shows for free, if you got your tickets ahead, Fred Waring and the show he used to put on after the broadcast. Seeing the Rockettes in the AP drugstore, when a toasted English muffin order was "burn the British."

The glamour nightspots which we might see if someone turned up from out of town to take us—the Stork Club, El Morocco, the St. Regis Iridium Room with an Ice show, the Rainbow Roof, then there were the Zanzibar, the Copacabana, the Latin Quarter. The #5 Fifth Avenue bus all the way up to the Cloister. Movie classics at the Museum of Modern Art; pictures at the Museum of Modern Art. The Frick Collection.

The beautiful stores and store windows—Saks, Lord and

Taylor, Altman's Bergdorf; the gorgeous jewels in the window of Van Cleef & Arpels and Cartier.

The battle of the baritones on the radio. Second-hand clothes from the Dressing Room Shop. Lunches at the Stockholm. The Mayan in our building a No No. St. Patrick's Cathedral; 5th Avenue parades. Shopping at Klein's and Orbachs. Showing visitors the town. Shoes at Becks's and Kitty Kelly. 35¢ martinis. Broadway shows from the cheap seats (or even standing) The Blue Angel; Upstairs at the Downstairs. All those jazz spots on 52nd Street.

The Village; the East River; the Staten Island ferry to see the Statue of Liberty; the Automat; Jack Dempsey's. War bond drives on street corners with good entertainment. Uniforms. Central Park on Sunday afternoons; concerts at Carnegie Hall on Sunday afternoons. The itch to get home again and get on with our lives.

N.Y.—it was wonderful.

Elizabeth Wood

One of British Security Coordination's head secretaries, Patsy Sullivan, relayed a passage describing Stephenson by the late Elizabeth Wood, another New York Inner Office BSC secretary, who also worked in Washington. Wood wrote about her old boss:

"To those who didn't know him, no words are adequate; to those who knew him no words are necessary. 'Intrepid' is still the greatest mystery of all; no release from the Official Secrets Act 'thirty years after' will solve that one. Mercurial ... magic ... masterly ... magnificent ... these were the epithets used to describe him. Yet no one has ever properly defined him, and we cannot do so now.

"His most conspicuous quality was an inherent capacity to disappear, swift as summer lightning; or if he were confined to, say, an elevator to make himself invisible. We knew he had escaped from a German prisoner-of-war camp in World War I, but we didn't know it had been so easy for him! Like the magician's rabbit, he could melt into the mists of the night, or into the madding crowd of Fifth Avenue with the speed of a jet, without a sound, without a breath. No; he wasn't the magician's rabbit; he was the magic. Everyone felt it; no one could explain it."

Wood later wrote to Sullivan January 6, 1987 about the BSC Reunion in Toronto. "And *Stafford*! WSS is *furious*, but that is *Top Secret*." [1]

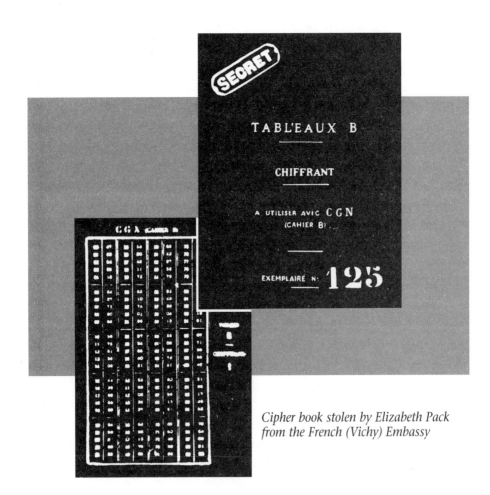

Cipher book stolen by Elizabeth Pack from the French (Vichy) Embassy

13 'Cynthia' and Marion

Elizabeth Pack, 'Cynthia'

During the war many agents worked for Stephenson, but the one with the highest profile was an American woman code named 'Cynthia'. Her exploits first appeared in Hyde's *The Quiet Canadian*, and a few years later he featured her in an extended non-footnoted book entitled, *Cynthia*.

'Cynthia' was born Amy Elizabeth Thorpe in Minneapolis, November 22, 1910, the daughter of a US Marine major, George Cyrus Thorpe and Coras Wells Thorpe. At the age of twenty, she married Arthur Pack, a secretary at the British Embassy in Washington who was nearly twice her age. She was in Spain during the Civil War and helped a number of Franco supporters to escape.

Pack began her espionage career in Poland, where she had a relationship with an aide to the Polish Foreign Secretary, Colonel Beck. Some of the information she obtained may have related to secrets of the German cipher machine ENIGMA, which the Poles were working on, and a prototype was eventually smuggled to Britain.

She and her husband later moved to South America where Elizabeth Pack, writing under a pseudonym, published propaganda sympathetic to the British cause. "It was at this time she was summoned to New York and given her code-name by the highly skilled spymaster William Stephenson, head of the British Secret Service in America."[1]

According to Hyde's account, the first major assignment for Betty Pack from BSC was to renew an acquaintance with Italian naval attaché Alberto Lais, who was stationed at the Italian Embassy in Washington. Her goal was to pilfer information from Lais. She is said to have discovered the Italians planned to scuttle their ships harboured in the United States in March of 1941, and warned the Americans. Her work may have led to the obtaining of the Italian naval cipher.[2]

In May 1941, 'Cynthia' was asked to concentrate on the Vichy French Embassy. Posing as a journalist, she arranged for a meeting with the Ambassador Henry-Haye. Before the interview, she met with the Embassy's Press Attaché Charles Brousse and he told her of the situation in Europe. "France's future requires cooperation with Germany," he reportedly told her. "If your car is in the ditch, you turn to the person who can put it on the road again. That is why we work with Germany." The two began a relationship, and after time, Brousse expressed a dislike of Laval which 'Cynthia' cultivated with guidance from BSC, and he talked more and more about Vichy affairs. In July of 1941, she told him she was an agent of the American government and he could receive money for information. She stressed this could help defeat Laval and the Nazis and he'd be a patriotic Frenchman. Eventually she obtained copies of nearly all the telegrams to and from the French Embassy, and 'Cynthia' was instrumental in securing the French Naval ciphers.

Published reports say one night the couple heard a guard at the embassy approaching and 'Cynthia' quickly removed all her clothes. When the guard saw her, he decided he should leave the two alone. On at least one occasion, BSC is said to have used the services of a criminal, 'The Georgia Cracker,' a Canadian safe expert who helped the couple procure information. By November 1942, Vichy Embassy officials in the US were detained in a hotel in Hershey, Pennsylvania. 'Cynthia' tried to join the personnel by posing as Brousse's daughter. However Brousse's wife began to put 'une and une' together and 'Cynthia's' tryst with the Vichy French came to an end. Elizabeth Pack eventually married Charles Brousse and they retired to France.

'Cynthia's' exploits for Stephenson's organization are said to have greatly assisted Allied European and African operations. The Italian ciphers may have contributed to the one-sided defeat of the Italian Navy by the British in the battle of Matapan. Ellery Huntington, who headed OSS special operations for TORCH, the invasion of Africa, was quoted as saying 'Cynthia's' work "had changed the course of the war."

Hyde wrote he first met 'Cynthia' in 1941.

"I had heard (only half believing I must confess) of some of her more astonishing exploits in Europe, and I was aware too that she recently engaged in some unusually strong and subtle anti-Nazi propaganda work in South America."

Hyde wasn't the only Briton 'half-believing' escapades of Bill Stephenson's most famous undercover agent. The English historian Hugh Trevor-Roper (Lord Dacre) wrote, following Stephenson's death, that the story of 'Cynthia' had "been proved fictitious." Noted British World War Two authority, Sir David Hunt, not only doubted 'Cynthia's' reported accomplishments—he questioned whether such a person ever existed.

It is difficult to obtain first-hand personal accounts to confirm the exploits of 'Cynthia'. Obviously BSC operated on a need-to-know basis, and according to Hyde's books, 'Cynthia' and her husband Brousse died in the 1960's. Hyde died in 1990. There is in Hyde's book, *Cynthia*, however, a nebulous reference to a BSC liaison person, who introduced 'Cynthia' to him during the war.

"She sounded so improbably romantic and fictional that I told her New York contact, whom I knew as 'Marion', I was eager to meet her. She would arrange it and so it came about."

Marion de Chastelain

The 'Marion' Hyde knew was Marion de Chastelain, mother of Canada's Armed Forces recent head, General John de Chastelain.

Born Marion Walsh, she grew up in Europe where her father worked for Standard Oil of New Jersey in Bucharest. Her husband-to-be, Alfred Gardyne de Chastelain, was a petroleum engineer and sales manager with Unirea de Petrol Company in Romania, a company controlled by Phoenix Oil and Transport of London.

...OUR MAN INVOLVED (in Romania) WAS READY COMPLETE OPERATION WAS PETROLEUM GEOLOGIST GARDYNE DE CHASTE-LAIN WHO MARRIED ONE OF MY NY SECRETARIES AMERICAN GIRL WHO HANDLED AND TRANSLATED ALL CYNTHIA'S VICHY PRODUCT STOP THE DE CHASTELAINS NOW LIVE CALGARY AFTER UNSATISFACTORY SOJOURN AUSTRALIA—William Stephenson to author Stevenson (undated, University of Regina)

Alfred de Chastelain was also involved in espionage. Early in the war he worked for British Intelligence in Istanbul, and he was in touch with various factions in Romania.

Marion and their children visited her parents in New York in

November 1940, intending to stay only a short time, but her mother became ill, and she received a job offer at BSC. "I got a phone call one day asking me in these words, would I care to do something 'for King and Country'? And I said why not? So I went down to Rockefeller Center."

She was interviewed by Alexander Halpern who was in SOE. He was a Russian-born naturalized Briton who previously worked for the Kerensky government in Petrograd. The interview was simple and over quickly as they knew of her through her husband. During the war British Intelligence had a tendency to employ relatives of people in the business, because they were familiar with their backgrounds.

"So I was with SOE for all of maybe two weeks, when Sir William whisked me upstairs to SIS and that was that. They were on a floor below us, SOE had a separate office from us, and SIS was upstairs."

De Chastelain, fluent in French, soon started working with 'Cynthia', who was then working on the Vichy Embassy. Unlike Hyde, she had never heard of her before. She was shown her picture and sent to meet 'Cynthia' in a Washington hotel. At the time Elizabeth Pack was separating from Arthur, her British diplomat husband.

"She was the type who revelled in espionage. She really loved it. And she came from a good Washington family so she had entree to all the embassies and places. So she circulated."

Although 'Cynthia' was an attractive woman, her allure was something deeper, de Chastelain says. "She was tall, I would say a dark blond. She wasn't a light blond. Beautiful figure. Not terribly good looking, but she had what I suppose Elinor Glyn wrote about years ago, and that was 'it'. Which certainly appealed to the males. She did very well for us."

"Is it true about the ciphers being smuggled out?"

"Oh yes. It's absolutely true."

'Cynthias' contact with the Vichy French, Charles Brousse, raided the Embassy safe regularly and handed over the contents. Later he supplied more and more material. He memorized conversations, took notes at briefings, and pilfered telegrams that were going to and from the Embassy. He forwarded the material to 'Cynthia', who gave it to Marion. "That was why I would have to go and collect them, and go back to New York, and translate them, and go back to Washington and give them back to her. I spent a lot of time on airways." De Chastelain usually collected the information in the morning, took the next plane back to New York, translated the papers and took them back the same day so Brousse could return them to the safe. He hauled out a variety of information, but BSC was interested mainly in the diplomatic cipher and the naval cipher. They used the naval cipher to help translate radio traffic to and from Martinique where there were a number of French warships. "The admiral that was there absolutely refused to have anything to do with the United States or Britain or the Allies. So we were monitoring his traffic constantly. From Vichy to Martinique."

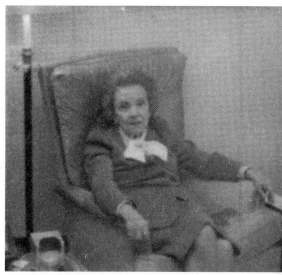

Marion de Chastelain interviewed in Calgary, 1989

De Chastelain usually met 'Cynthia' at the Wardman Park Hotel in Washington, which sat amidst several acres of park and had numerous entrances. She left a cab several blocks away, walked to the hotel, and would never enter or exit the same way. If the two women didn't meet at the hotel, they would arrange meetings at "strange places." BSC's Washington office was central, although it was small and located in a private house, but de Chastelain was not allowed to go there, in case she was followed. The two women met at regular intervals—at least once a week, sometimes more, depending on what she was getting from the embassy. 'Cynthia' was finished her work with the Italians when de Chastelain started working with her.

Stephenson didn't want 'Cynthia' in New York meeting with people in the organization, and that was one of the reasons de Chastelain travelled to Washington, she said. Although Hyde refers to trips 'Cynthia' made to New York on 'shopping' excursions, de Chastelain doesn't remember them. "I never saw her in New York. Never. I always saw her in Washington."[3] At nearly every meeting, sometimes numerous times in a week, 'Cynthia' asked de Chastelain if she could see Bill Stephenson. He always said no. "I think he saw her once, probably when she was recruited, but he would never see her again."

It seems Elizabeth Pack had strong feelings for Bill Stephenson. "I am already filled with nostalgia for the happiest days of my life," she wrote to Hyde in 1962. "They were packed with all sorts of emotions: the supreme desire to help the Allied war effort; anxiety lest I fail in the responsibilities entrusted to me; lonely despair when my moves went wrong; satisfaction when things took a constructive form. And in the end (it is with me still) the real anguish of wondering if, with more experience and better judgment, I could not have worked faster and done more." Hyde belonged "to that happy period that even in wartime exists for those who have a common cause and are especially united where there is a 'Quiet Canadian.' Long life to him, and to you!"[4] She later commended Hyde on his efforts, "My heart sings because at last someone has written about this remarkable man."[5]

'Cynthia' told de Chastelain about taking off her clothes to convince the guard she and Brousse were engaged in other undercover activity. "Of course she told me. Didn't surprise me in the slightest," she laughed.

"I got that the next day. She looked absolutely beat. She said, 'I've had quite a night,'" de Chastelain chuckled. "She told me the whole story. She was either top of the hill, or deep down in the valley. She'd look simply dreadful when I got there and she'd be so depressed. And I'd try to cheer her up." Part of the problem was Pack became very fond of Brousse, and he was living in the same hotel as she was, with his wife and children. Brousse and 'Cynthia' eventually married.

The safecracker used to open the embassy safe was handled in Washington, and de Chastelain didn't meet him. "That was a real James Bond sort of thing. I don't know why they had to break in. Unless, probably what happened was they changed the lock on the safe which would be normal practice in an embassy every once in a while, no matter how much confidence you had in your personnel."

When the Vichy Embassy staff was interned in Pennsylvania, 'Cynthia' attempted to stay at the compound in Hershey, "She was acting as Brousse's daughter, from another marriage or something," de Chastelain remembered, "to see if she could find out anything there."

There were also plans for her to go to France with the embassy staff.

De Chastelain left New York for England in November, 1943. Although 'Cynthia' also travelled to Britain, de Chastelain never saw her again. "By that time the thing was over." 'Cynthia's' espionage career was finished. Some accounts say she later tried to work in Europe, but was not allowed to.

"Her cover was pretty well blown by that time I would think," de Chastelain said. "In any event she wanted to drop into France. But with what she knew they wouldn't let her drop."

She does not know if 'Cynthia' was involved in obtaining ENIGMA secrets in Poland. "How true that is, I don't know. She certainly worked in one of the offices there in the intelligence department. And she may well have done. Then, there was another thing. Anybody who knew about ULTRA was not allowed to drop behind enemy lines."

Elizabeth Pack and de Chastelain got along well together, and she remembers her positively. "Well, she tried hard. And she was a very charming person. There's no question about it."

When she wasn't involved with 'Cynthia', de Chastelain worked in BSC's inner office and was a cipher clerk for Stephenson. She met with John Pepper, who was running the French section and the Spanish section. "And I had to do with him, simply because I took care of the French side of it." Grace Garner and de Chastelain had access to a safe containing one-time pads used in decoding messages from Britain and other places. "And apart from Bill himself, we were the only ones to have it."

The messages coming into the office were "Most Secret, Top-Secret, Destroy-before-reading type of thing," she laughed. Once the messages were decoded they went straight to Stephenson. Grace Garner, Stephenson's chief secretary for most of the war would be able to read what he read. Garner was usually the final link. "She would know what was transpiring from England back and forth. From any of our far-flung people in South America who were communicating directly with us."

According to *The Quiet Canadian*, BSC produced and distributed in the US an anonymous booklet titled *Sequel to the Apocalypse*, which told of "how your dimes and quarters help to pay for Hitler's war." It linked North American companies to trading partners, various subsidiaries, and parent companies operating in Nazi occupied Europe. Hyde's book says the managing director of Standard Oil offered $50,000 to find out who was behind the publication. Ironically de Chastelain worked in the inner office of BSC, and her father worked for Standard Oil. She was aware BSC spread black propaganda about them.

"Of course they did. Most of the big oil companies. They all had subsidiaries abroad. You take any of the major oil companies. Same as Ford apparently, and Baer and IG Farben."

Visitors

Stephenson received a plethora of visitors when de Chastelain worked there. The secretaries fielded all the guests and decided who advanced further. Charles Farquhar, Stephenson's old Winnipeg friend, discovered he was in New York's Rockefeller Center and decided to look Stephenson up when he was there. But he couldn't get past the first secretaries. "No one could," de Chastelain said.

Mountbatten was a visitor while she was at BSC. "He was only there once while I was there. Whether he came later, I don't think so, because after '43 he was pretty well taken up with other things. I don't think he came back." Bill Donovan was a frequent visitor. Once when she was there he was nearly hit by a message projectile flung from a vacuum tube. "As Bill Donovan walked in the door with his aide, one of these things came down and shot right over my head and just missed him. He said, 'I didn't think I was too popular, but I didn't think anybody wanted to kill me.'"

Pat Bayly came by and chatted to her, and tried to show her how a few of the communication machines worked. "He was in the office for some time in New York. He was definitely fussing around with the telecommunications ... And an awfully nice man too. And last I heard of him, I gather he was sent over to England to work on some of their towers or whatever they were putting up. He was an extremely bright man and a nice man."

Bayly had a reputation for not discussing his war activities. "I can't imagine him ever saying anything to anybody about anything. He was a very quiet man, but we got along very well ... He certainly worked at Bletchley."

Tommy Drew-Brook, the Toronto stockbroker and Stephenson's friend, was frequently in the office.

"And Beaverbrook was in and out like a yo-yo. I always knew, if I happened to be out of the office for a few minutes, and came back in. We had a sort of a reception room off of our office and when I saw that coat with the great big fur collar and the funny hat—I knew Beaverbrook was in there. They were interesting times."

December 7, 1941

The Quiet Canadian says Stephenson had success in penetrating the mission of Japanese Special Envoy Suburu Kurusu, who came to the United States to negotiate in November of 1941. One of Stephenson's men contacted a secretary of the Japanese envoy, and Stephenson sent translated transcriptions of the recordings of the conversations to the White House daily. Hyde's book also says James Roosevelt was sent to Stephenson with a message from the President which told him of the lack of progress in talks with the Japanese Special Envoy Kurusu, and Ambassador Nomura. The same day, November 27, 1941, Stephenson supposedly sent a telegram to Britain saying prophetically, "Japanese negotiations off. Expect action within two weeks."

Although she remembered meeting him, de Chastelain didn't recall James Roosevelt in the office. She was aware of many books and documentaries that conclude there was some prior knowledge of the attack.

"If they were monitoring a lot, it is hard to see how they missed it," de Chastelain said. "My opinion is that they did know, and unfortunately the poor Admiral and General in Pearl Harbor took the blame. I mean such foul-ups sending such vital news by cable. Instead of picking up the phone if necessary."

De Chastelain obviously was in a unique position, as she was working in the inner office of BSC at the time. "Now mind you Churchill was probably just as anxious, because I remember the day it happened, Sunday the 7th and I hadn't had a day off for about a month, and I said to my father, no matter what happens, I am not going into the office on Sunday. So I was sound asleep and he banged on the door and said 'you are wanted on the phone' and I said, 'tell them I am dead!' He said, 'their last word was turn on the radio'. So I turned on the radio and of course they were blasting this thing on and on. So I got dressed and beetled into the office just as the Japanese were being removed, because they had their offices in the same building we were in, a few floors down (the Japanese consulate). And then finally I got upstairs, and we had champagne and we sat on our desks and chatted."

The inner office staff and Bill Stephenson were all at work that Sunday. "He had probably been there for hours. I didn't get there till about 2:30 in the afternoon. Anyway it was quite a day. And then of course Bill Donovan was back and forth because he was setting up OSS."

"Would Donovan have known, too?"

"Bill, if he hadn't known, may have guessed. Bill Stephenson. And obviously Bill Donovan too. And Bill Donovan being in Washington was very close to Roosevelt."

It was a pivotal time for British Security Coordination as the Americans were then onside. "And that of course was Bill's first big job, trying to combat the isolationists."

Europe

De Chastelain's husband visited North America in July, 1943 to recruit Canadians with European ancestry for drops into the occupied continent. The scheme only met with limited success, and he himself parachuted into Romania, December 22, 1943 to help oust the pro-Nazi government. "What he wanted to do was to get the head of the peasant party to come out, but he wouldn't come." When her husband was in North America she realized she wanted to return to Europe. "I told him that I was going back, with the children being spoiled rotten by my parents and at this time, a little war would do them good. Besides I was bored." She returned to Britain in November 1943, and reported to her new espionage assignment just before Christmas. Her husband was taken prisoner on the continent and she didn't see him until after his release in 1944.

In England she worked for British intelligence in London. "I was Section 5 of MI6. That's counter-intelligence, and we were in the Charity

Commissioner's office building which dated from mid-Victorian I guess, on Ryder Street, just off St. James Street."

At that office she dealt with numerous intercepted and decoded messages. De Chastelain was surprised news of Britain's code-breakers success, the ULTRA Secret, was released in the 1970's. "I didn't see the necessity of publishing it anyway. What was the point? That's why Churchill's books are so peculiar. Now we knew that this was happening. How did you know that this was happening? I used to get piles of intercepts on my desk every morning from London to go through...

"From ULTRA. The German Army, the German Foreign Office. Of course you could tell from troop movements. And even orders for food that were put through. I mean a lot of it was awfully dull. A hundred tons of something or other. But then I passed them on to people who dealt with this sort of thing, and from that they could figure out troop movements in Europe. Right across Europe. So that's where it was so relevant."

The de Chastelain family moved to London in the late forties, as they couldn't go back to Romania. Following the war, "the Russians simply didn't want my husband back in, because he knew too many people, and they thought he'd be a problem ... so they ended up sending an Englishman in there. I think he was an Air Vice-Marshal, who didn't have a clue. So as far as the Russians were concerned, that was just fine."

Following the war, the oil business eventually brought the family to Canada. John de Chastelain, Marion's Romanian-born son joined the Canadian military and by the 1990's he became Canada's highest-ranked military officer, the Chief of Defence Staff.

Bill Stephenson

During the war Stephenson often bore the brunt of the costs of running the organization, de Chastelain says. "His years with BSC cost him in the region of $3 million of his own money. I'm sure he paid our salaries many times because it is very difficult to get money out of SIS. Or SOE for that matter.

"And of course we were paid in US dollars and they were very loath to let go of US dollars because they didn't have all that many of them.

And they were earmarked for other things. So I'm sure that he certainly spent I would say in the region of about $3 million, which he never regretted I'm sure."

De Chastelain remained close friends with Stephenson and his wife and visited them in New York and Bermuda on many occasions. The couple's apartment in New York was the whole floor of the building on East 52nd St. near the water. "He had one wall of the bedroom knocked out, it was all glass, so they could look at the United Nations."

De Chastelain knew nothing of Stephenson's background or work before the war. She thought his espionage career began when he reported on the Nazi build-up from Europe during the thirties. "He never talked about that sort of thing. He never talked about himself in any way. Sometimes it used to come up in conversation, something he had done in India or Germany or wherever. But never concluded, just passing remarks of that nature." She thought Stephenson may have attended university in Cambridge for a time immediately following WWI, but she knew few details. "And Lord knows I spent enough time with him. But we mainly discussed present situations or things that had happened when I was there. But he never discussed anything personal. His wife probably knew the whole story, I don't know."

Stephenson's fortune evolved from the can opener and the radio business, de Chastelain said. "But he had mining interests in Yugoslavia. He was heavily involved in the movie business with the Kordas—Alexander and his brother, and knew Merle Oberon extremely well and Greta Garbo."

She was surprised to learn most biographical information about Stephenson was incorrect. "I knew nothing about his early life. To me, he was just somebody I met in 1941. Out of the blue." Once Stephenson created his phony background, he must have made a decision to keep it. "By that time he'd certainly lived the life for so many years. It was probably second nature to him. I mean why go back and ... it was no point to it. I mean if he wanted to."

She thought it was "marvellous" that Stephenson was a difficult person to trace, and the spy hubris was maintained.

"Absolutely. No, he was absolutely made for it. And a lot of these stories that he's told people, if they knew him well they'd know that he was just ... pulling their leg," she laughed. "To see how much they believed."

Elizabeth, Stephenson's adopted daughter, was upset with press people descending on her after Stephenson's death. She went to England for three months and changed her unlisted phone number. "I don't think she'd see any journalists ever."

Some reports say his house was gone over by security people searching for papers. "She didn't mention it. She was so disgusted with the whole thing anyway, that all she wanted to do was get out. And I guess she had a pretty bad time there for awhile. Until she did the right thing, and just went to England." She planned on staying in Bermuda, and at the time her son Rhys attended school there.

People visiting Stephenson at the office during the war were frightened. "He had a cold steely eye. People were petrified, actually when they went in to see him, if they were called in. He intimidated."

Stephenson knew Churchill. "Of course he knew him. And the (North American assignment) meeting, I've gathered, took place at Beaverbrook's house. And why Colville should know about it.[6] Well there's no reason in the world he should know," she laughed. "He's another one of these with great egos who had to know everything ... I mean the whole thing is so stupid."

De Chastelain had little time for some authors of books and articles chronicling Stephenson's war career, and avoided reading much of it. She was surprised to receive a note from British Foreign Office vet David Stafford following the publication of his book *Camp X* which questioned aspects of Stephenson's career. "He had the gall to send me a thank you letter for all I did for him. I didn't do a damn thing for him, I wouldn't have given him the time of day."

She refused to read *Camp X*, and was "infuriated" at Stafford's 'A Myth Called Intrepid' story in *Saturday Night* magazine. "I can't stand him, and anything he writes. I could wring his neck.

"Bill made a lot of enemies during his time and a lot of people would want to smear his name," she said. She also knew the historian Hugh Trevor-Roper when he was doing British government work. "He worked right above my head in London in SIS. He and ... the spy who ended up in Russia, Philby. He and Philby were up in the attic above my head."

According to Philby, Trevor-Roper was threatened with court martial during the war by the head of Section V, Felix Cowgill. Trevor-Roper was one of the "formidable Oxonian" men who "outclassed Cowgill in brain power," he wrote in *My Silent War*. Like the former British intelligence department head, de Chastelain wasn't a great fan of Hugh Trevor-Roper's either, "Hugh Trevor-Roper is a little bit of a man with a big ego." She was quite pleased when his historical expertise was called into question and the supposed diaries of Adolf Hitler he said were genuine, proved to be forgeries. "That was one of the great days of my life when they found they weren't (authentic). And he had spent what? $400,000 of the *Times* money?"

De Chastelain says the Stephensons' move to Bermuda had nothing to do with security, or his previous activities. He moved to the island because he liked it there. "He loved Bermuda from way back, and when he had his stroke that is where he wanted to be." The couple lived in the Princess Hotel in Hamilton for two years while their house was built. He may have bought his property during the war, as he stopped off there on a number of occasions. "Lady Stephenson didn't particularly care for Bermuda, but anything that he wanted. She was a big-city girl ... Mary was just the right size for him because Bill was quite short and she was even shorter. I felt tall when I was next to her. She loved New York and she had lots of friends. And I imagine she found Bermuda fairly boring. And she had lots of society friends. Personal friends. And of course it must have been rather difficult for her, because Bill was not a man to socialize. You know, go to big parties. That wasn't his..."

Although Stephenson wasn't a party person, stories about his affection for generous martinis were true. "He made the wickedest martini that was ever made." But he didn't always drink them. She recalled in June of 1944 Stephenson had invited over former BSC New York people who were in London to his suite at Claridges for drinks. De Chastelain watched Stephenson all evening carry around an untouched martini. "He never drank it. He just carried it around, and then watched the results. He had the same one when we left as when we arrived."

The 1989 *Myth Called Intrepid* narrative in *Saturday Night* by David Stafford describes a doddering, seemingly senile, man living in Bermuda. "He wasn't out of it at all. I don't know what he's talking about. The impression of course could be due to this speech problem. Sometimes it was extremely good. And other times it wasn't ... that would give the impression that he wasn't quite with it. But if they had listened to what he said, not the way he said it."

One of Stephenson's great interests in later life was the potential harnessing of the Bay of Fundy tides. "That was very dear to his heart from when I saw him after the war until he died. He still thought that would be one of the greatest, cheapest forms of electricity that anyone could have. It would be very expensive to harness but when it's done, it would produce a fantastic amount of cheap power."

Stephenson longed for some recognition from his own country, and hoped he would someday be awarded the Order of Canada, de Chastelain said. But various nomination appeals from different sources during the seventies were ignored. She thought perhaps there may have been objections to the award from the Prime Minister during that time, Pierre Trudeau. "He would never have had it from Trudeau, I'm sure. I think Bill obviously knew a lot about Trudeau, and the fact that he didn't fight the war, and all those good things." When Stephenson was awarded the Order of Canada, it was during the short-lived Conservative regime of Prime Minister Joe Clark.

De Chastelain attended the BSC reunion in Toronto in 1986 and spoke on Stephenson's behalf. "David Stafford gave a long speech, and Grace Garner spoke on behalf of the women in communications. And she was in tears. So when it finally finished I said about ten words. That is it. 'Sir William thanks you. He loves you. He wishes you well.' And that was it. And I think everybody was relieved."

She knew few of the BSC employees who attended. "They were all in communications. Except me. And Grace. And a woman, I think her name was Butler. She was a Canadian girl ... I mean communications ... We went up the stairs and that was it. I don't even know where they were located. We never saw them."

The person most knowledgeable about Bill Stephenson's war career was his former head secretary Grace Garner, she said. "She probably knows more about it than anyone else. Because she was his secretary for the whole time. And a very good one. Although her heart was always in fashion magazines!

"Bill Stephenson was the only man who could have done the job at the time," de Chastelain concluded. "As efficiently as he did it. And keep his people reasonably in control. Because that's difficult. Especially when you have them all over the place ... South America ... He did an excellent job."

She thought Stephenson hadn't received appropriate credit. "But then there's something about Canada that doesn't like heroes. I don't know why. Can you imagine if he had been an American citizen? He would have been full of glory, and so on and so forth. And when they gave him that decoration (Donovan award), he did come to New York. And they had it on the USS INTREPID, anchored in New York Harbor. And gave him the decoration. And he was constantly having visitors from Washington. They were always coming down to see him. Right up to the end. When it probably wasn't very good for him. It was probably very tiring."

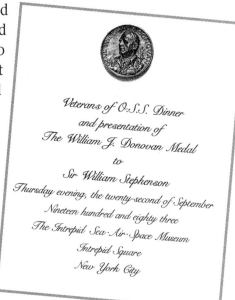

Veterans of O.S.S. Dinner
and presentation of
The William J. Donovan Medal
to
Sir William Stephenson
Thursday evening, the twenty-second of September
Nineteen hundred and eighty three
The Intrepid Sea·Air·Space Museum
Intrepid Square
New York City

Dolores Hogg

Former BSC employee Dolores (Griffiths) Hogg also lives in Calgary. She was recruited by Bill Stephenson's friend Tommy Drew-Brook in 1940, and did similar office work in New York as the BSC employees from Toronto. When she was working there she was unaware of which organization actually employed her. "I didn't know who I was working for," she said. In August of 1942, Hogg was moved to a division in Mexico City and she eventually married a man who was attached to the British legation there.

She said her husband's group discovered if an Axis attack was to occur on the United States, it would not be simply an attempt to storm the coasts. The attack was to come overland through Mexico. On one of her husband's covert raids, Hogg says, an actual map was discovered of a Japanese invasion plan for the west coast of Mexico.

14 Bill Ross Smith

Britain

AM Bill Ross Smith's career in espionage began through his friendship with Dick Ellis. He knew Ellis for a long time in Australia, and in England, and about a year before the war started, Ross Smith was invited over to Ellis's place in London for a number of stag dinners. "I didn't realize it then, but what he was doing, what the Service was doing, was recruiting." People attending the parties decided which men would be suitable for British Intelligence, and in which area. When the war began Ross Smith was anxious to contribute, but as a 32 year-old Australian in Britain, he found it difficult. In June of 1940, Ellis invited Ross Smith for lunch. Ellis told him he was going to America that week, and he wondered if Ross Smith and his wife would like to go along. "That was my invitation to join SIS."

Four days later Ross Smith and his wife sailed to Canada, and then travelled to New York. They met Ellis there and moved into a Madison Avenue apartment. Later Ellis introduced Ross Smith to his new boss, Bill Stephenson. "I had become one of the first four or five men, and three women to start British Security Coordination."

His first assignment for BSC was to deliver a thousand dollars to a French woman in New York, and tell her that her husband was okay. He had no idea who the woman was, as he had no reason to know. This was a basic security measure in the service. Ross Smith assumed the woman's husband was an agent in occupied France and she was being paid his sustenance. But no one told him. "Nobody said this is for that purpose, because it wasn't my business to know," he remembered. "Everything was safer that way."

Ross Smith is still unaware of the any essential priorities for BSC in the early stages. There were no office meetings to plot a basic strategy for covert operations in the US. In fact, he was unsure what he should be doing each day. "Stephenson gave me absolutely no guidance—didn't say here is a job, get on with it—precisely nothing." Eventually,

Stephenson told him they were interested in the penetration of foreign missions and whatever the Germans were doing generally. Stephenson was too busy to orchestrate Ross Smith's daily routines, and John Pepper was immersed in economic matters. One day Ross Smith asked Dick Ellis which organization he was actually working for, and Ellis told him, "It is an offshoot of SIS London. Don't leave too many trails to the door here." He could tell his wife everything or nothing, Ellis told him, but preferably nothing. The SIS veteran said there was a lot of interesting information in newspapers, so Ross Smith bought all the New York papers each day, and went through them.

The seemingly elementary reading of newspapers proved fruitful and BSC obtained numerous leads and intelligence from them. "That was a basic thing, because there were literally thousands of eyes and ears gathering news and unusual events," he remembered. The Australian chronicled many types of information such as arrival of ships, passengers, robberies, news of strategic elements, such as platinum, and he decided whether they were worth following up. The flow of certain elements was important because of their value to the Nazi armament industry. Platinum for example, was needed for magnetos in aeroplane engines. Two primary sources of platinum at the time were Columbia and the Soviet Union. Before Germany attacked the Soviet Union, they relied on Russian supplies, but afterward they were forced to buy it in small pieces wherever it could be found. As a result, the price rose astronomically and illegal trade began. "There were seamen and travellers, apart from the Germans themselves, organizing means of smuggling this out of the Americas into Portugal and Spain," Ross Smith said. BSC tried to stem the flow piece by piece. Ross Smith's first major assignment related to smuggling was to contact a subagent named 'Gray' and from there his activities developed mainly in shipping, and Iberian liaison.

His naval contributions to the Stephenson organization began when a prominent Portuguese shipping operator, Jose Bensaude, unexpectedly approached the British Consul in New York and asked to get in touch with British intelligence authorities. A great percentage of civilian trade between Europe and the United States came on Portuguese and Spanish ships, and Bensaude said there were many suspicious travellers on board. BSC decided to keep an eye on them. "This was the actual start of what became a large organization known as the Ship's Observer Scheme," Ross Smith said. With Bensaude's assistance at least one secret agent, and sometimes many, were put on each of his ships. Then Ross Smith began conscripting observers for other ships. The McCormick shipping line was approached through the British Consul and were told about German intelligence people in North and South America, and the possible threat to American ships and interests. Ross Smith then recruited most of the captains, some of the chief stewards, and others on the McCormick ships. "The bar man, if he was suitable, was a useful contact," said the Australian, with a slight grin. The recruits were told to keep watch on possible German couriers and suspicious travellers. Many supplies from South America were cut off by the British naval blockade, so smugglers were active in transporting a variety of small items that were vital to the Nazi war effort. The observers also watched for the movement of enemy ships on the high seas and in various foreign ports around the world. It developed into a worldwide reporting network of over four hundred. All of the observers were volunteers.

Information was procured in many ways. On one trans-Atlantic crossing from Lisbon to New York, a Portuguese captain announced to his passengers that there was a strong possibility the ship would be intercepted by British destroyers, so anyone with important papers or letters could deposit them in the captain's safe for posting in New York. The contents of the safe were handed over to Ross Smith, and BSC's censorship section looked at it all before it was dispersed. Another use of the observers was to spread rumours. Rumours were manufactured, usually in England, and spread throughout the world. Using ship's observers the same rumour could get back to Germany from Calcutta, Bombay, or Montevideo. "It was a way of spreading rumour or black propaganda. You tell something in 'strictest confidence', that's the best way to start a rumour."

BSC was located in an unobtrusive office called Passport Control in Rockefeller Center, and the growth of the New York intelligence net required an increase in physical space. The Passport Office consisted of an entrance lobby, where the general public could obtain visas and other travel information, and a regular passport section and staff. The annex of that eventually became a huge office area controlled by the

Stephenson organization, but in 1940, BSC was a small office on one floor. Ross Smith was unaware of a special rental agreement with the Rockefellers. Early BSC expansion depended on the benevolence of the office neighbours. One day Stephenson said the organization needed more space, and he told Ross Smith to persuade the people in the office next door to move out. "I went to them and said we needed it for the war effort and would they be very nice and find somewhere else. And they bloody well did !" Eventually that section of the secret office took up two upper floors of Rockefeller Center, with half of one floor occupied by OSS.

With the expansion, organizing and cataloguing the immense flow of information into BSC offices became a Herculean task. Super-intendent Edward Bavin of the Royal Canadian Mounted Police was a contact of Stephenson's, and as result, he borrowed a filing expert from the Mounties and had him seconded to BSC offices. "He set up the filing system which was superb, and one should be very grateful to the Royal Canadian Police for producing that man and the system they put in," said Ross Smith. "Because the filing system—this was before comput-ers—is the basis of every bloody thing. You put things together—suddenly a picture emerges. If the filing system is faulty, well you just can't do that."

The information-gathering network extended even to talk on the streets. Ross Smith found a good source of political intelligence was taxi drivers, especially in Washington. "People will chat simply because there's a taxi driver there who's got to listen." He says he learned a lot from Washington cab drivers, especially when Congress was debating the Lend-Lease bill.

One of the major problems BSC had to confront before Pearl Harbor was the massive isolationist feeling in the US. According to Ross Smith, one of the largest organized groups, the America First movement, had approximately 200 million dollars of German capital behind it. "It was a very, very clever thing, because what American could possibly argue with a thing called 'America First'—bloody wonderful." The group was used as a means of promoting Nazi slogans and propaganda such as, "England will fight to the last Frenchman," and lobbied against pro-British US decisions such as the Destroyers for Bases deal, and the Lend-Lease agreement. Isolationists were "egged on by the Germans, and the America Firsters, but they didn't realize they were being egged on."

BSC began to gauge reaction to the isolationists and American public opinion in general, through a number of channels. David Ogilvy, who later became renowned in commercial advertising, was with an opinion-research bureau in Princeton at the time and he indicated to Ross Smith that he wanted to become more active in the war, "even if it was shovelling coal into a battleship or something." He became a subagent of the organization, providing information on public intentions and public opinion. Later Ogilvy began working for BSC itself in the British Embassy working on financial affairs and economic warfare.

In early 1941, Germans and Italians began sabotaging their ships in American harbors and were banned from them. Thousands of German sailors and nationals, many of whom were skilled men, were marooned in North America. "The Germans wanted them back." Before the Soviet Union entered the war, they were returned on Japanese ships through Russia, across Asia, to Europe. One Saturday Ross Smith received a telephone call from an observer saying there were 700 German seamen on a Japanese ship sitting in port for half an hour before sailing. "These are the buggers who were just scuttling their own ships in American harbours," the observer told him.

Ross Smith went to Stephenson in the afternoon with a suggestion. "I said how about ringing (Frank) Knox, who was Secretary of the Navy and say to him, 'here are 700 men on a Japanese ship heading for the Panama Canal. They've just sabotaged their own ships in American harbours. Suppose they sabotage this one in the Gatton Lock? How would you like it?'"

Stephenson contacted Knox, and the Secretary of the Navy saw the danger in possible blockage of the Panama Canal. Stephenson suggested interning the 700 men in Kalong, and stopping any Japanese ships from going through the canal to prevent future sabotage. Knox did this and as a result Japanese shipping had to circle Cape Horn to reach the eastern US. "Knox was a hell of a good man," Ross Smith remembered.

Later the German sailors began to leave from San Francisco, instead of the east coast, for the return journey. There was an agreement with Japan by which the Japanese agreed that their ships would not carry Germans between 16 and 60 years of age of certain skilled categories, and the British would not molest the Japanese ships. This came about after the HMS Liverpool intercepted a ship in the Bay of Tokyo and found a number of German seamen aboard. Lieutenant (later Admiral) Madden of the British cruiser interned the men in Hong Kong, but the Japanese protested. The British Foreign Office arranged for the sailors to be released and agreed not to interfere with Japanese shipping, but negotiated the agreement that only certain people would be transported. "When these 20,000 men had to be transported, well they had different thoughts," said the Australian. Japanese captains were approached in San Francisco and, if skilled Germans were on board, they were told they would be intercepted by the Royal Navy in international waters and most of the passengers would be removed.

"Then the Japanese got a bit sly and they wouldn't give us a manifest to show who was on the boat at all. So we had to find ways to get that manifest, which we did on a regular basis every Thursday night." Later the Japanese complicated matters further. "They would have a manifest, but they would show 'Rudolf Hench:' painter, hairdresser, masseur or something like that.

"These bloody, big, beefy chaps were trying to ship home as hairdressers." The next step for BSC was to obtain the ship's manifest, and try to discover the true occupations of the German passengers to prevent their passage back to Europe. The actual occupations were obtained through "many surreptitious means," according to Ross Smith, and sent to San Francisco. "Then we could say to the captain, 'That fellow isn't a hairdresser, he's a tool maker working at Ford last week,'" Ross Smith smiled. "In the course of the war they got about 20,000 of those chaps off the boats and interned."

Kim Philby wrote in *My Silent War*, that British Security Coordination and FBI head J Edgar Hoover were sometimes at odds because of their unscrupulous activities in various harbours. "He (Hoover) was incensed when Stephenson's strong boys beat up or intoxicated the crews loading Axis supplies," Philby wrote.[1] Although he was aware of many covert shipping activities in New York at the time, Ross Smith denied any knowledge of rough stuff at the docks. "I should think that was absolute bloody nonsense," he said. "At least it certainly wouldn't be organized by us. Anybody might start a fight today, and blame you or me, but certainly we would never do anything stupid like that."

The activities of BSC's Dennis Paine were another point of contention with American officials. In early 1942, the FBI claimed to have definite evidence that Dennis Paine of British intelligence in New York was conducting a surveillance operation on assistant Secretary of State Adolf Berle for the purpose of getting 'dirt' on him, because he was thought the be anti-British. The FBI informed Berle that they had proof Paine had been conducting a campaign against him. The FBI wanted Paine out of the US immediately and if he wasn't out within 24 hours, they would arrest him. Berle called in Halifax and Stephenson to complain and Paine was sent out of the country. Halifax and Stephenson were reported to have thoroughly objected to the deportation and denied involvement, but Hoover was adamant.

Dennis Paine worked for Ross Smith, who believes Paine was set up, perhaps by the FBI, to encourage more State Department control of BSC and OSS. Paine was known to the FBI through a German-speaking American FBI informer who patrolled the dock areas of New York, picking up information in bars. "Paine may have used him as an informer himself." Ross Smith says Paine was his immediate assistant on the ship's observer scheme, and was not involved in any type of surveillance. Following the war Paine denied vehemently he was involved. Ross Smith said, "The real outcome of this was that Berle was then able to put great pressure to bring all British intelligence activities to end, and to try and bring British things under greater control. This was averted however by the intervention of Donovan." It was apparent to Ross Smith that if the Paine affair was not an FBI plot, it was a contrived attempt to get Berle to take action to try and get BSC under the control of the FBI.

"You see Hoover was jealous of the contact of other services, particularly Donovan, with the British services and that's the fact on that." Ross Smith said he spoke to *Camp X* author David Stafford about where he received his information on the Paine incident. According to Ross Smith, Stafford said he got the information out of Montgomery Hyde's book *Secret Intelligence Agent*. Hyde told Ross Smith he learned of Paine through Berle's State Department papers. "By gad they do appear in Berle's papers, as a permanent myth."

Ross Smith later learned Stephenson detailed Walter 'Freckles' Wren to escort Paine out of the country. Wren called Paine and told him to pack a bag, bring his passport, and to meet him at Grand Central Station. The pair got on a train to Montreal and checked into a hotel, but Wren didn't stay there for long. "Freckles said, 'Give me your passport', and then buggered off to New York, leaving him there. No explanation. Absolutely nothing." Weeks went by, and Paine's bills were paid regularly, but he didn't know why he was left stranded in Montreal. Ross Smith was in South America at the time. When he returned he wondered what happened to Paine, who used to sit next to him in the office. "I went to Stephenson and said, 'Where's Paine?' And he said,'You'll never see him again.' No explanation. I didn't hear about this thing until after the war. Long after.

"But that was just Stephenson. I didn't need-to-know. 'Get yourself another assistant,'" laughed Ross Smith. "He just says, 'Oh, you'll never see him again.' No explanation, but that was him. A few words. That's all it needed."

South America

In the early months of the organization Stephenson approached Ross Smith and asked him how many languages he knew. "Pretty good Australian, some English, a little American," he answered. "Not good enough," Stephenson said. "How long will it take you to learn Spanish?"

Although BSC was dealing with Western Hemisphere security, they didn't have appropriate linguists, or agents suitable for work south of the equator. "London was sending us all sorts of chaps who spoke German, French, Dutch, but not a chap with Spanish or Portuguese," Ross Smith remembered, "And so I learned Spanish under great pressure." He attended the Berlitz language school in New York an hour every morning for nine months. His language training paid off, as during the course of the war he travelled throughout Central and South America and established a good working relationship with Basque and Portuguese representatives.

Ross Smith's affiliation with the Basques began with a cable forwarded to him from an Admiral Burrows in Britain, which said basically, "look up the Basques and say I said so." In the late 1930's Burrows was captain of a British destroyer that rescued the Spanish government out of Bilbao. The spiriting away of many Spaniards who were under physical threat from Franco's forces endeared Burrows to the Basques. Ross Smith met with the Basque government delegate in New York, Manu Delasoto, and discovered he was educated in Britain and he was very interested in helping the Allied cause. Basque influence, contacts in the field, and other assistance soon proved to be invaluable to BSC and the Allies and reached throughout South America and into mainland Europe. "They provided us with a marvellous network in Europe, guides across the Pyrenees; escape routes. They were very, very helpful." Many presidents of South American republics were of Basque descent, as were several South American bishops. Many agents in the ship's observer project were Basques.

In 1941 an observer on a Spanish ship reported that the captains of all Spanish ships were carrying wallets containing very heavily concealed documents which were of such importance, if they were lost or opened, the captain could be subject to the death penalty. The captains took the secured document to a Spanish Consulate whenever their ships were in a port to certify that the seals on the document envelope were intact. "Well naturally I wanted to have a look at these things," Ross Smith recalled.

He told the Basque delegate, Delasoto, of the problem and they planned a theft. "I arranged for him to take Spanish captains out to dinner, until he could eventually get one of them sufficiently 'tight', and then to telephone me." After a few weeks Delasoto telephoned Ross Smith about eleven o'clock at night and said, "I've got one." He was at an all-night restaurant on 58th Street and Madison Avenue. When Ross Smith arrived he found Delasoto with an appropriate Spanish captain. "It was obvious that he had a bit more wine than usual, so I was able to extract the document from his breast pocket without him being aware of it." The document pouch had to be opened, photographed, closed and returned, all in a way that the Spanish authorities would be unable to detect. The Spanish captain would be unaware of what had been done. He called Dorothy Hyde, Montgomery Hyde's wife, who worked in Room 99, which specialized in opening and closing envelopes without detection. Ross Smith also contacted a photographer named 'Hall' and the trio hastily assembled at BSC offices in Rockefeller Center at about 11:30. The document package wasn't a typical envelope. "Dorothy took one look at the documents and said, 'God, this is going to be a hard one,'" remembered Ross Smith. It took her an hour to open it, Hall photographed the contents, and Hyde closed it up again. Ross Smith rushed the document pouch back to the restaurant where Delasoto was still at table, plying the captain with a drink every time he woke up, and he carefully replaced the envelope pouch in the captain's pocket.

The document inside was to be opened when a radioed code word was received, and the code word was on the outside envelope. The memorandum inside from the Spanish maritime chief, instructed the captains of approximately 700 Spanish ships to immediately sail to the nearest Axis port, as opposed to neutral, Spanish, or Allied harbour. The pilfered message indicated which side the Spanish government was on. "So with this piece of information, it provided Churchill with definite knowledge of where Franco stood. It also provided our navy with the code word." If the code word on the document was radioed and intercepted, the Allies could react and take action. The ships were to sail to the closest Axis port, so the Allies knew which direction the Spanish ships were to proceed and where to find them.

Manu Delasoto's family owned many ships prior to Franco's reign and at least two of the captains were still loyal to the Delasoto family. It was decided Manu, his relative Ramon Delasoto, who was chief of the Delasoto clan, and Hosio Antonio Deaguirrie Quobre, the president of the Basques in exile, should record a message to broadcast to Spanish ship captains if the code word was picked up. The message, recalled Ross Smith, roughly translated, "'Look, you've just received the word so-and-so which told you to open the document. The document tells you to take your ship to an Axis port. But don't be a sucker, boys. Bring it into Plymouth!'"

In February of 1942, BSC discovered that the Spanish captain's documents had been changed. A wire was sent to Manu Delasoto saying, "happy birthday," in Spanish which was a prearranged code word that meant new documents had been distributed. Ross Smith was instructed by Stephenson to try and obtain the new documents. This time it was a much more difficult task, as Spanish ships were no longer going into New York, they were sailing into Buenos Aires. Ross Smith met with Delasoto and told him that he could use the assistance of good men and crew in the Argentine.

"He did a remarkable thing," Ross Smith remembered. "He said that the Basques are either like that (he extended his arm with the palm up), or like that," (he extended his arm with a clinched fist). Delasoto gave the Australian the name of a contact in Buenos Aires and told him to say to him, 'Manu says ... like that' (palm up)." Ross Smith and Betty Raymond, who also worked in Room 99, flew to BA with a replica of the old document pouch to try and retrieve the new one. He met Delasoto's contact, took him by the hand and said, "My name is 'Miller' (his pseudonym at the time), and I put my hand like that—open, Manu says like that." There was an immediate kinship and Delasoto's contact asked what he needed. Ross Smith told him his problem. He needed help finding out which Spanish ships were available where, and who some contacts were.

A Spanish ship was soon located that was in port for an extended period of time and Ross Smith began to follow the captain whenever he was on shore. He noticed he frequented a restaurant called the Odeon, and he was always accompanied by "two rather tough-looking henchmen." One day Ross Smith went to the Odeon wearing a military raincoat and fedora hat, and waited for the trio about a yard inside the doors of the restaurant. When the Spaniards arrived, Ross Smith walked straight into the captain and at the same time he put his hands on the captain's breast pocket and felt for a document pouch. "Sure enough there was the document wallet there, which felt exactly the same as mine. He didn't notice a damn thing—it was over in a second." A few minutes later Ross Smith returned to the restaurant, but without his raincoat and hat (acting as a different person), and sat at a table where he could keep an eye on the Spanish sailors. After the captain ordered his lunch, Ross Smith followed him to the men's room. He noticed he took off his coat and hung it up on a peg before he went about his business, washed up, and returned to his table. "So I prayed he would be doing the same thing the next day."

The following day Ross Smith waited in the washroom. When the captain came in and repeated his routine, he was able to exchange his phony document wallet for the real one while the coat was on the peg. He took the document wallet to Betty Raymond who had her special paraphernalia laid out in an office set up by Jim Henman, an SOE representative. Behind closed doors, away from the men, she worked on opening it. Eventually she emerged to say she didn't think it could be opened because part of the glue seal was white of egg. She left the package under treatment while they ate dinner. When they returned Raymond was able to get it open. The document was photographed by a Basque photographer, checked with the original and the differences were sent back to Stephenson by cipher machine. The package was then resealed and Ross Smith was able to exchange it with the replica at the restaurant the next day.

The new documents changed little from the old ones. "It confirmed they were still going to go the German way, not our way," Ross Smith recalled. "Spain didn't come into the war, so it was never done, but it was there ready to be done." He received a personal commendation from 'C' in London for his work in South America.

In early 1942, because of the Berle situation and the implications of the McKellar Bill, Stephenson ordered a temporary shutdown of BSC's political activities. Around this time BSC handed over much of the Ship's Observers program to American control. Secretary of the Navy Frank Knox was present at the meeting. He was quite surprised at the scope of the operation and the fact there were some Americans reporting from American ships. Knox wanted answers from those under him, Ross Smith remembered. "He looked at the Naval intelligence intercepts and said, 'How the hell have these Limies put all these men on your ships without you being aware of it?'"

Camp X

During the shutdown, Ross Smith asked Stephenson's permission to attend the SOE/OSS training Camp X near Oshawa. He was a student at Camp X for a month and afterward he instructed in most disciplines, with the exception of parachute jumping and demolitions. He was taught self-defence by the infamous Captain William Ewart Fairbairn, a co-inventor of the double edged commando knife, and founder of many close combat techniques.

Fairbairn taught his students how to board and leave a train travelling at high speed, how to break into a house, and 'abseilen' (rappelling), but his specialty was silent killing. He learned his fighting techniques in China where he worked for the Shanghai Police Force, after a stint in the Royal Marine Light Infantry guarding the British Legation in Korea. Fairbairn, sometimes referred to as 'Dangerous Dan' or the 'Shanghai Buster,' is said to be the first Westerner to earn a black belt in jiu-jitsu. He is often credited with bringing the martial arts to the West.

Richard Dunlop, formerly with the OSS and a biographer of William Donovan, wrote later that Fairbairn "had an honest dislike of anything that smacked of decency in fighting." Another former student of Fairbairn's was Richard Helms, one of five past directors of the CIA who were OSS recruits.[2]

Ross Smith learned at Camp X how Fairbairn became an instructor. At the beginning of the war he was a man of about sixty and had recently returned to England from the notorious Shanghai police force where there were many problems, a huge population and relatively few police. "One man had to be worth ten men (in Shanghai), and he had contrived a means of fighting both physically and with knives and guns, which indeed did make one man

THE FAIRBAIRN SYSTEM is the most widely known technique of knife fighting among American combatants today. It embodies various slashing operations, with aim directed at vulnerable arteries at side of neck, lower center of stomach, h e a r t, below shoulder blade, above wrist, or at armjoint.

RESTRICTED

worth ten." When Fairbairn went to the War Office in London to volunteer they told him war was not a game for ancient gentlemen and sent him on his way. After Dunkirk, Fairbairn contacted the military again and said, "Look, we've got nothing now, most of the arms have been lost, and we've only got a few thousand men. I'll show you how to make each man worth ten men." The military brass he visited wondered how. Fairbairn told them to bring in a couple of tough young men and he would deal with them, to show how things could be done. Two majors were brought in and told they would have to fight the old gentleman. When they protested, Fairbairn said in effect, "Don't have a worry about me. I have to convince these dunderhead generals, that I, a gentleman of 62 years of age, can deal with tough young men like yourselves. I'm sorry," he added, "but I'll have to put the both of you in hospital." "Which he bloody well did in a matter of minutes," Ross Smith said. The quick and violent display impressed the military and Fairbairn immediately began to instruct a hundred men. "That was the start of the commandos." Fairbairn taught at SOE schools, and eventually was taken over by the American OSS.

Ross Smith said techniques were taught that could kill a person in seconds. Fairbairn taught how to kill and how to inflict injury on various organs and limbs. "He also had this marvellous method of shooting with hand guns. He maintained that the old-fashioned method of taking aim and firing—you're dead by that time." Fairbairn said a person had to learn to aim and shoot immediately. The quickest way to do that was to use a gun as a pointer. "It's natural to point your finger," Fairbairn's former student remembered. "He said to point your gun as you point your finger, and fire twice. That will stop anything."

Other instruction at Camp X wasn't as deadly. Operation VIC was harassment and dirty tricks. "Just as sex was the most fun you could have without laughing, this was the greatest fun that the resistance boys could have with the Germans without being caught." Several games were invented. If a wife of a German officer was visiting him in Paris for instance, flowers addressed to another woman would be delivered to his room. Ross Smith says there were countless variations thought up to aggravate or stress.

The Camp attempted to develop recruits mentally as well as physically. "There are other senses," Ross Smith said. "And you can learn to control them." Fairbairn and others taught that a person's ability to observe their environment visually, aurally and through general sensitivity could be focussed and improved. Ross Smith eventually lectured in sensitivity to the original OSS, some of whom were FBI agents, some of whom were lawyers and engineers, and most of whom were what he calls 'trained brains.' The course started with simple recall and observation. Ross Smith gave the class of about a dozen a test where they were told to put their heads on their desks and not look up. The first question was, "How many windows are in this room?" Then he would move from the class room to places the recruits saw each day—"How many windows are there in the common room? How many in your bedroom?" Many of the highly intelligent people couldn't answer seemingly simple questions about their immediate environment. But the ability could be improved. General sensitivity and awareness was not only used to increase observation skills—it could be developed to the stage where some agents could function in the dark. "Not everybody, but at least seven men out of ten, could come into a jet black room, jet black, no light at all, and hit a moving target five times out of six."

The Australian also became involved in the training of 22 Yugoslav North Americans who were to be sent behind enemy lines. The Yugoslavs were men between the ages of 36 and 56. "The older men did better than the younger men in the actual services because of experience and judgment. That's a useful thing to have."

They were trained in the entire syllabus of how a man operates as an undercover agent; how to handle propaganda, how to obtain information, codes, demolitions, and unarmed combat. Following the six-week course the recruits sailed for Cairo where they were to receive final orders and instruction, but their ship was torpedoed not far from Canada and a surfaced U-boat machine gunned them. Most of the Yugoslavs survived and were able to get to Montreal. The survivors were given the option of returning home or continuing and they all chose to go on. Eventually the group made it to Yugoslavia.

Ross Smith was unaware of their final mission, but assumed it would be to operate various intelligence and sabotage cells under the General Tito umbrella. "We started under Mihailovic and switched over to Tito."

Donovan

At Camp X Ross Smith met OSS chief Bill Donovan for the first time. Donovan was at the camp on business and was unpretentious with a good sense of humour, Ross Smith remembered. He was given a complete tour of Camp X, including demonstrations of a plastic explosive that could take out a telegraph post or a rail line.

Later when Donovan became more active in the European theatre, Stephenson asked Ross Smith to introduce Jose Bensaude to him. The Bensaudes were a prominent Portuguese family involved in the transportation business for many years. Jose Bensaude was a gentleman of the old schools, spoke a number of different languages and was honoured to meet the great General Donovan. He deemed the meeting a formal occasion and before the rendezvous he put on a top hat and a cut away coat and cravat. They met Donovan in his suite at the St. Regis Hotel and found him without shoes and dressed very casually. Donovan told the surprised Bensaude, 'Take off your coat and tuck up your feet and let's get down to business.' "Whereupon Donovan got up on the sofa and literally tucked up his feet under his bottom, and that was that. That was the start of a long and happy association with Bensaude and the Donovan organization. Eventually they (the Americans) decorated him." Bensaude, among other things, helped transfer supplies to people in occupied territory, and paid a great deal of money to Allied agents working in occupied France though his Portuguese office.

New York

With a staff of hundreds and a payroll in cash, vast sums of money were handled around BSC, but unobtrusively. Ross Smith remembers on one occasion Beryl Phillips, who was handling the accounts section, told him to go the British consulate and pick up $12,000 in cash, a huge sum in 1940. He and Ted Scott, a New Zealander who was a former professional boxer, journalist, and BSC contact in Panama, went to pick up the money. The two simply stuffed the bills into their pockets. "We had to be generous. The consulate weren't a bit phased," Ross Smith smiled. "They said, 'of course you won't give us a receipt for this.' I said, 'Hell no.'"

Stephenson received numerous requests concerning minor day-today operations from the British bureaucracy during the course of the war. Occasionally Stephenson showed them to Ross Smith. "Stephenson would get such telegrams as: 'His Majesty's Third Secretary of the Treasury, has noted, with pain and regret, that certain of your officers are using taxis to go to the Consulate in 25 Broadway, New York City, when it is known that there are other, and cheaper, forms of transportation available. Pray explain.' I ask you," said Ross Smith shaking his head. "In the middle of a bloody war!" Stephenson collected a few of the missives, and returned them. "Bill would save up about four of these and then he'd wire back saying, 'There's a war on.' That was another instance of him saying everything in few words," he laughed.

"Another time he got one: 'His Majesty's Third Minister of something or other, or something or other, noted that certain of our officers are using His Majesty's diplomatic bag for purposes other the His Majesty's Mail, vis the sending of silk stockings. Pray explain.' Well, you know, Stephenson had other things to do. And he sent this marvellous cable back saying, 'Not us. We only send pink elephants.'"

Ross Smith didn't have a precise job title or description and he only reported to Stephenson. "There were no exact positions for anybody. Everybody just headed up to Stephenson who was the one boss," he said. "He never interfered with anybody. All he wanted to know was successes." He and a few assistants coordinated the approximately 400 ship's observers and the men who contacted them at various harbours. All of the observers were volunteers but the contacts in the different ports were usually paid employees.

All of Ross Smith's office staff were Canadians. He thought one secretary, Eleanor Fleming, was particularly good, but one day he made the mistake of telling his boss. "I had found this super, superb, magnificent secretary in the Security Office which was downtown. Stephenson said, 'You have?' I said. 'Yes Sir.' He said, 'Fine. She can come to me. You find somebody else,'" laughed Ross Smith. Eleanor Fleming moved from his office and became one of Stephenson's inner office secretaries.

Ross Smith's final task before leaving the organization was to write the achievements of his division, which was to be compiled into the BSC history. He never saw the finished work. "I'd personally like to see at least my own section, to see whether it was accurate or not." But he did not submit everything he did for publication. "No, by no means of course not. It's the bare bones."

Ross Smith did not see Stephenson after the war. They talked on the phone occasionally and they exchanged Christmas cards, but he never saw his former boss again. "I regret never seeing him." Montgomery Hyde and his wife saw Stephenson quite often in Bermuda and when they returned to Britain, "Hyde would then report to us how the great man was." Ross Smith had many cables from Stephenson, particularly on the Ellis affair. He sent him strongly worded cables saying that Ellis was not a mole, and at one time he offered to sue the journalist Chapman Pincher who made the first accusations after Ellis's death.

Following the Philby defection in the early sixties, Ross Smith was contacted by Ellis about communist activities during the war years. There were some concerns about Cedric Belfrage, who Ross Smith believes was involved with political warfare for BSC. "Cedric Belfrage was an Etonian, an elitist, very, very nice. A literary sort of chap. I never knew whether he had any Communism. It certainly was never apparent around the office. He went to Mexico. The middle sixties I suppose, when there was that witch hunt generally, Dick Ellis contacted me and asked whether I had any feelings about Belfrage working for the Russians during the war, and I said, 'Hell no!' As far as I was concerned he was simply normal, one of the old chaps. But other than that I don't know about that at all. Except the charge laid afterward against Ellis, which I was telling you earlier was quite ridiculous."[3]

Ross Smith was disappointed and annoyed at the bad press Stephenson received. He believes the author of *A Man Called Intrepid* set out to make a bestselling book and as a result fleshed out the bare bones of the story, and may have added things that he may, or may not have run by Stephenson. "I can't see him (Stephenson) saying certain things were true," he said. "I refer particularly to the assassination of (Reinhard) Heydrich, which I believe had nothing to do with British Security Coordination."

But other instances could be factual. It was possible, for example, Stephenson assisted getting Danish atomic scientist Neils Bohr over to North America.

"Anything at all was possible with Stephenson. Frankly, one never knew what he was doing, except if it happened to concern me or my own particular organization. Then I can speak with my own authority of knowledge. But what Stephenson was doing in other directions ... like anybody else in the organization, everybody was individual. One had a 'need-to-know' law. Unless you happened to be cooperating with somebody else in the next office, you didn't know what in the hell he was up to. Whether Stephenson had anything to do with getting Neils Bohr out, he may well have done so, he may not."

"How about his relationship with Churchill?"

"Again, that's very high level stuff. I feel that it would be true."

As an example, Ross Smith remembered the Italian Naval Attaché Admiral Alberto Lais. In the spring of 1941 Admiral Lais was ordered out of the United States because Italian ships were being sabotaged and scuttled in American ports. Lais was granted safe passage out of the United States back to Europe by the Americans, who were still neutral, and they received assurances from the British that Lais would be allowed to return to Europe unimpeded. The British Embassy in Washington sent the following letter to the US Secretary of State Cordell Hull.

April 22, 1941

His Majesty's Ambassador presents his compliments to the Secretary of State and has the honour to acknowledge the receipt of Mr Hull's note of April 10th regarding the return to Europe of Admiral Alberto Lais, former Naval Attaché at the Italian Embassy in Washington, and his two Italian naval orderlies, Gaetano Canepa and Giovanni Burlo.

This matter has been referred to His Majesty's Government who have authorized Lord Halifax to give the assurance that the British authorities will not attempt to prevent the return of Admiral Lais or his orderlies to Europe.

British Embassy
Washington DC
April 17, 1941[4]

However according to the book *Cynthia*, BSC agent Elizabeth Pack met Lais in New York before he departed and wrote down the colour and dimensions of all his luggage. She knew the Admiral was going to be detained in Bermuda.[5] Shortly after Lais' ship departed, contrary to

British assurances, it was intercepted en route, and Lais was detained in Bermuda. American agent 'Beck' discovered the detention and wired the mainland:

May 1, 1941
STRICTLY CONFIDENTIAL
Understand Admiral Lais removed from Spanish steamship MARQUES DEL COMILLAS on the high seas now under detention here. In addition two women, one alleged to be a Nazi agent have been removed. Will report further if necessary. BECK.[6]

Ross Smith says Lais was detained because of Stephenson's intervention and an idea he had. The Italian Admiral was returning to Europe with a small staff and all his codes, records, and files. "Naturally we wanted to have a damned good look at them." But the Marques Del Camillas, a neutral vessel didn't go into the control of Bermuda. It was covered Ross Smith said, by a 'Naval serve.' The ship's captain was given his own specific route to cross the Atlantic and if he detoured off the route, he was subject to arrest at sea. Ross Smith went to Stephenson before the ship sailed and said, "Let's get the Navy to pick him up because he's bound to stray off, by a few yards at least, off his Navy serve route." Stephenson agreed, and he contacted the naval chief in Bermuda and told him to intercept the Marques Del Comillas. The Bermuda official said no. "The Admiral refused," Ross Smith remembered. "'Absolutely outrageous, arresting a fellow Admiral.' So that's when Stephenson phoned (contacted) London direct. And the order came to the Admiral, 'Do what you're asked.'" The ship was intercepted on the high seas.

"He was reputed to have a four-lane highway to Churchill and I'm absolutely certain in my bones, that it's true. Because, by God, he had influence everywhere. He was a very, very, very great man."

Publicly there seems to have been confusion as to why the Italian official was incarcerated, especially since he was granted safe passage home. The Associated Press reported from Rome that the British had detained the Admiral: "under the apparent impression that British diplomats were being held by the Italians in Albania."[7]

"Well what happened was very amusing, because in due course the

British destroyer discovered, 'Well, absolutely outrageous, the chap had strayed off his Navy Serve line,'" smiled Ross Smith. The destroyer put a party on board the crossing ship and then signalled to Bermuda. When the ships passed closer to the island, the English Admiral there sent a cable for Admiral Lais aboard the Marques de Comillas that said he had no part in this outrageous performance and that when the ship arrived in Bermuda, he would like the Admiral to be his personal guest, Ross Smith recalled. "Well this of course alerted the Admiral and the staff that they were being taken into Bermuda. So as they came up to Bermuda, five or six code books started coming out the portholes." Fortunately for the interceptors, this was anticipated. The Marques de Comillas was being followed by two small boats, ready to scoop anything up from the water. "He got two Naval pursers, armed with great bloody nets on each side—hand nets. They were on each side of the ship and sure enough as soon as things were thrown out of the port hole they went 'whoop,'" Ross Smith said, as he shovelled at the floor with his hands and laughed. "So we got the entire bunch of files. Codes. Every bloody thing."

On May 8, 1941 the *New York Times* reported that Lais was to be liberated because of American requests. "The State department made prompt representations to the British authorities for his release."[8] Five days later, American agent 'Beck' cabled the end of the affair. "Admiral sailed early this morning."[9]

A Man Called Intrepid

Ross Smith is unsure about some of the claims in *A Man Called Intrepid*. He believes Stephenson may not have been mentally alert at the time. He was surprised that some of the pictures in *A Man Called Intrepid* were from a training film, and an SOE map seemed copied from a book released in the 1960's. The Australian noted the source of the pictures in the book, 'BSC Station M archive.' "Do you know what Station M was?" he asked... (It was run by Eric Maschwitz, and it was the manufacture of fake documents.)

The critics of the book should be blaming the author and not Stephenson, Ross Smith said. He would have responded loudly to the critics of his former boss and the controversy when Stephenson died, but he was in Australia at the time. "You see all these chaps have the wrong end of the stick. Stephenson didn't say these things. Stevenson the author said all these things."

The simple truth, said Ross Smith, was that the real judges of BSC were the British government, the FBI, the American government, the Canadian government and Donovan. All of those groups honoured Stephenson. "Well. All these people recognized him! Well who the hell ...? These denigrators!"

A Man Called Intrepid begins with forewords said to be written by Bill Stephenson and Dick Ellis, but Ross Smith had doubts to their authenticity. He doesn't believe they were written by either man. "If you look at the so-called forewords in that book, they are so obviously not written by either Stephenson or Ellis. It is not their literary style at all. Stephenson had the ability, and invariably used it, of saying in one phrase what takes the average person three pages to do. Now I'll give you an illustration of this. On Pearl Harbor day plus five—that was a Saturday night (sic). He called me at about two in the morning, and said he wanted a 'Deal for a party at the Fat Boy's place.' It needed to be one page and on his desk by 12 tomorrow. Now that meant to me that he wanted a plan for basing an undercover organization in the Azores—the 'Fat Boy's' place. The 'Fat Boy' being Jose Bensaude, who came from the Azores. On 'one page' meant it would be going to either Roosevelt or Churchill."

(In what may be a coincidence, in December of 1941, after the Pearl Harbor attack, secret plans for Churchill's trip to the United States began. According to Churchill's *Grand Alliance,* escort ships sailed from the Azores and intercepted Churchill's crossing vessel. Ciphered communications were then transferred to the Azores ships for transmission, so the exact location of the crossing vessel remained secret.)

Ross Smith went immediately to work on the Azores assignment and he completed a report shortly before noon the next day, and delivered it to Stephenson. "I said, 'Look, the plan's perfect. It was originally forty pages. It's now down to eight.'" Stephenson took the pages and read them. "He picked up a pencil and wrote maybe three quarters of a page. One page. He read it to me, and said, 'Do you want to add anything?' He said it all 'like that,' in what I originally took forty pages. He said it all! Now that was his nature. Not stilted, but he just said the absolute essentials. Well if you read the thing there ... (the Foreword)."

"It's very long winded."

"That's right ... The author got him to sign that thing to substantiate, saying every word in this is true. It was never in his nature to say such a thing."

"Half of spying is lying, isn't it?"

"Well. Yes," he said.

Bill Stephenson

"He was undoubtedly a genius. And he had the tremendous ability that anybody would be anything for him. For instance I was going to South America on another occasion. No, I think it was Turkey, to get those things, I said to Bill, 'I really think this one is an impossibility,' and he said to me, 'If it can be done, you can do it.'" Ross Smith paused. "'If it can be done, you can do it,' he said with complete confidence. So you couldn't fail after that. He had this amazing ability. No pyrotechnics. There was no such thing as a staff meeting, anything like that ever. There was no organization, no orders. Everybody there had to be a self-starter. Had to be a self-starter."

"But he knew what was going on?"

"Oh, by God, did he know what was going on. Did he know what was going on! For instance, I was astounded by what I just told you, 'at our Fat friend's place.' I don't know if I ever told him he (Bensaude) came from the Azores, but he bloody well knew. Also one morning I said that I'd been in Harlem the previous night, and he said something which indicated that he knew exactly. We all thought that he must have a parallel organization, keeping eyes on each one of us. It seemed that way. I don't think it was so. But it seemed that way."

No one in British government commented on the controversy after Stephenson's death because, Ross Smith said,"the Service itself, and the government, never affirms or denies anything."

"Why?"

"Just tradition. You see, I took it up on Ellis's part, and had many letters published in papers, to putting the facts right in this thing. It didn't do any good. But never the less, it was in."

At the time of the interview the Russians had recently announced there was a 'fifth man' in the Philby, Maclean, Burgess, and Blunt chain of English traitors, and he had recently retired.

"There may be a fifth man," Ross Smith said. "There may be a fifty-fifth man. But one thing that's sure, is that it's Russian policy to always stir up trouble, and if you can get the intelligence services diligently putting their efforts into hunting for a fifth or fifty-fifth man, it's better that than looking into what the Russians were up to."

The Australian thought the Stephenson plan to assassinate Hitler in 1938 with sporting rifles mentioned in Anthony Cave Brown's book 'C' sounded far-fetched. "Consummate balls," he said. After he was shown the book, and he read the passage, he hesitated in passing a definite opinion. "Sporting rifles. It must have been in the open air, at some gathering. The choice of weapon. So much depends on whether the deed is going to be done. For instance, you wouldn't want to use a sporting rifle inside a house," he said. He looked at the book again. "It says they had a plan to assassinate Hitler—I find the thing a bit more acceptable, by putting that thing in there (the proposed weapon). But I have a feeling that Bill would have told me about that."

After the war Ross Smith worked for the German company IG Farben in the United States. "Which was very useful because I had a little part to do in taking them apart," he smiled. "So I went to work for them which was very good." The Australian maintained a residence in the US until 1960, but he spent a great deal of time in Britain. He wasn't involved in World Commerce Corporation, as many ex-BSC people were. He formed the Ross Smith Corporation on the New York Stock Exchange, which dealt with photographic printing on textiles, and the company did well for a period of time, and was written up in *Time* and *Life* magazine. Shares in the business rose from five cents to over five dollars. However the process remained in the preliminary stage, and Ross Smith eventually sold for long-term development.

Ross Smith knew little about Bill Stephenson and his Canadian life, and he went through clippings, photos, cards and obituaries with great interest. He often wondered about the circumstances concerning Stephenson adopting his nurse as his daughter and he believed his ex-boss's background contained an answer. "Extraordinary. What was done to him originally, he was repeating. He adopted this daughter and her son, as his godson. That's really repaying the kindness of the original Stephensons."

The Australian was surprised his former boss broke contact with the Stephenson family in Canada in the 1930's. "I wonder why he did that? Well, it's actually unimportant. It's the man himself," Ross Smith said. "You see, he was so remarkable that no matter whom he met, without making the faintest endeavour at all—he was the superior being—without making any significant move everyone who met him immediately liked him. Immediate respect. But at the same time he maintained a coolness. He was really a man apart. Completely a man apart."

It didn't appear Stephenson worked his way up an MI6 ladder. "Oh no. He was undoubtedly appointed by Churchill. Well, you see, Churchill wanted a man over there. That paper's (*Washington Post*, 1989 story on BSC) quite right. He wanted a man who could really get together with the top rungs, and top social lines, and American thinking. There's no doubt about it. Stephenson was exactly the right man, because he had all these terrific contacts and had this tremendous flare of influencing people, in an incredibly quiet way. An incredibly quiet way. If he could walk into this room now, he could sit down in that chair and, without saying a word, dominate this room. I tell you he was absolutely, bloody well, a genius. Inevitably he was phenomenal fund of knowledge.

"I bumped into him about 9 o'clock one night, on Fifth Avenue. He was with Mary. He was having a dinner at the Plaza, and I said, 'The Basques had just told me the German troops were mounting at St. Jean De Luz (in southern France). They think this might be a prelude to an invasion of Spain.' And he said, 'No they haven't got nearly enough people there to do that. But discuss it with me tomorrow morning.' He knew! It was absolutely incredible."

"So he was a real 'James Bond-type' character?"

"Well, James Bond never existed, he was a combination of one hell of a lot of people, but in reality he was no James Bond because he didn't go around killing people with his bare hands, or even with a gun. He dealt strictly with his brain and his personality. He used to start the day with 100 skips. A hundred skips in the morning. And lots of cold coffee for breakfast."

Betty Raymond (photo 1990)

15 Betty Raymond

In the 1930's Betty Raymond worked in a rural English hotel doing secretarial work, when she was approached by her brother-in-law Frances Ogilvy about joining British Intelligence. Ogilvy, formerly with the Air Force, worked at Whitehall. He and Walter (Freckles) Wren were approached by their superiors in the intelligence community who said they needed "two or three women of education, who they could trust," Raymond recalled. "Who would be good with their hands." She was interviewed by Frances Ogilvy and signed the Secret Service Act. "I said yes blindly and signed the lot." One of her friends, Dorothy Hyde, joined about the same time. "That's how they got Harford Hyde into it. Harford only came in because Dorothy was in it. But that's how he came into it."

Raymond began training soon afterward and her manual dexterity was funnelled into intercepting mail and forgery.

She learned the unique craft from an elderly man named 'Webb,' who began the art during the First World War. William 'Steam Kettle Bill' Webb devised a method of opening and then resealing envelopes without detection and controlled a large department in London. "He was absolutely wonderful and he taught us. But it was really one of the things you had to learn after that from experience." Years later when she returned to London, Raymond realized she was one of the few who could do all the various skills. Mail tampering had become compartmentalized. "Nobody was allowed to do them all. Typical. It was a rather civil servanty thing, you see. One could open some thing, and one could do another, and one could do another."

Tampering with mail that couldn't be detected was an acquired skill, rather than a formula. Some people were better at it than others, and improvisations could better the end product. Raymond says she and Hyde improved some aspects of what they were taught but "dear old Mr Webb," the teacher, remained proficient. "All his work was very good. Chamfering for instance. If you opened a letter that you shouldn't have opened. If you cut it open, then you had to put it back together again, as if nobody had opened it. This is a very difficult procedure which he originated. Called chamfering. It was not easy, but you could do it."

After a relatively quick training period in Britain, Raymond and Dorothy Hyde were sent to a major mail intercept station located in Bermuda. Working behind locked doors, six to eight women toiled in the Hamilton section covertly going through mail and packages sent to and from Europe and the Americas. With practice both of the women became experts in opening and sealing mail without detection. "Harford always said that I was Dorothy's assistant, but he didn't know very much. We were totally different, but we were a very good team. Both Dorothy and I moved up to New York, you see."

The process could be tedious, but occasionally their diligence was rewarded. In one instance an examiner had a hunch about a letter. "She didn't know to this day why she had a hunch. I can't remember her name. I wish I could. And she used to get these letters and send them off to be examined for secreting." (It was likely Nadya Gardner. According to Hyde's *The Quiet Canadian*, the letters were addressed to a cover address of the Gestapo).[1] In secreting the letters could be checked for invisible ink, but nothing was found. "She was absolutely determined there was something wrong with these letters, determined. So she went up to them one day and she said, 'Have you tried the Rd in the Indian?' 'Oh no, we haven't tried that.'" Secret writing appeared on the letter. "Later on we had an enormous job," Raymond remembered. "We had to open up all the envelopes with gloves. We tried to get fingerprints from them and everything, and it built up, and built up. When we were in New York they pounced on this ring." Gardner was singled out afterward. "They honoured her with a lunch because of the work she'd done. But she just hit it. It was a hunch, that was all. They rounded up a lot of agents. That was one thing that was worth doing."

There were regular scheduled ships and flying boats stopping in Bermuda carrying mail, and on occasions messages were purloined from couriers. "You'd have to get a sack open, and read it before the ship sailed the next day, and we'd do it all." Pictures were taken of contents of the mail considered relevant and sometimes, if there were suspicious couriers, of the mail bag itself. A 'Miss Birling' would often speak to couriers, Raymond remembered, and say, 'Oh you've got about four hours on shore. Now I will lock it up in my safe. It'll be perfectly safe.' "And off they'd go, and the moment their back was turned, it was out of the safe, over to us, with it." Soon the mail intercept people opened it, went through the contents, put it back together and it was ready for return. "Nine times out of ten the courier would take it, and they'd look at it with a spy glass to see if it was the exact way it was originally. They didn't trust us."

Envelopes were a complex process that involved "opening it all up and then cutting a bit away, and then chamfering it away fine, so you could join them up together so you couldn't see," Raymond said. "And the postmark would have to match. It was terribly complicated. It was terribly clever of him. (Webb). He originated that. It was very good, because there were some letters that were opened by mistake. I know there was one letter opened to a member of the Royal Family. Opened by mistake. There were panic stations. So it had to be chamfered and put back. And there were other things that were opened, and possibly had to go on. Shouldn't have been opened by censorship and rather that they thought it hadn't been looked at. All that sort of thing. We had all that coming through."

Hyde and Raymond started in Bermuda and eventually went to New York. Raymond travelled to Jamaica and helped start an office there, and spent about three months in Kingston where she continued to examine mail of random people and companies, and specific individuals. "There was a man there—I knew all about him! He didn't know I knew all about him, and we intercepted all his mail and everything. We were trying to check up on people."

At the end of the summer of 1941, Raymond left Jamaica for New York, where Dorothy Hyde and her husband were already working for Bill Stephenson.

New York

When Raymond arrived she stayed with the Hydes, and then moved to an unfurnished apartment on East 43rd Street, about 4 blocks from BSC. Raymond earned $40 a week in cash, from the espionage business.

"It was all very lax and very happy, until a very nice man, Brooks

Banks came and he was a civil servant, and he absolutely ruined it. We all had to sign on then and checking out, which ruined it. Because I don't think anybody worked as hard. We were clocked in and out."

Unlike some of the women working for BSC, Raymond's movements in the city weren't restricted by the organization, she said. But her fraternizing was. BSC employees and other people were not to be combined. "I would either go with the people who had nothing to do with it, or from the Office. But not mixed. Supposing the Hydes had some people over who had nothing to do with BSC—I couldn't be invited, you see. Only if they were office people, or people that weren't office people—we never mixed. For instance, if you got into an elevator at lunchtime, you got in—one day Bill was there. He'd got in at the same time from the floor above, or whatever it was. You didn't recognize each other. It would be very funny. You'd be chatting away outside on the landing, but as soon as you got on the lift, you didn't know anybody. It was a very funny little trick. It was very funny, I thought. But that was it. Mind you, I was with Dorothy, so we talked together. But you didn't acknowledge anybody else to your right or left, although you worked with them. That was the sort of security they had."

She later discovered she was followed in New York. "I still don't know who by until this day." Raymond went to a dentist near Central Park, and afterward someone made inquiries to the dentist about who she was, and what she did. Her dentist later told her about it, and she reported it directly to Bill Stephenson. He didn't seem to react at all. "He didn't appear to be the least bit interested about it—so tuned out. But he then put a man on, to follow the man who was following me. For three weeks, I didn't know. I had two men following me for three weeks! It was wonderful," she remembered. "I didn't know. I didn't know! That was the art of following."

On another occasion Raymond was assigned by Stephenson to follow her friend Marjorie Wren, as it was feared one of her friends was a German agent. She and a New York photographer she knew as 'Tiny,' followed Wren to try and catch them together. Tiny, who was enormous, was given a miniature camera for the task. Raymond soon found it was not an easy assignment, and the tailing was made more difficult as Wren knew who she was. "There's a great art to following people, and I never knew. It took weeks to catch the two together and take the required photographs. Then they discovered Tiny had put his thumb over every one. So you couldn't see a thing!" she laughed. The Marjorie vigil was quickly terminated when the German agent left New York, and the escapade wasn't revealed to the principals.

Raymond occasionally saw Bill Donovan, although he saw more of the Hydes. "He was really quite interested in what we were doing, because we were helping the FBI. Because they didn't know anything in those days, when we were over there. They were very new. They were very anxious to be spies. All of them very anxious, these Americans. They loved the idea of being a spy." In a Lima bar, returning from Argentina, she ran into an American agent. He said, "Here comes the opposition," when she appeared. "In a loud voice you see, so everybody there thought, 'here comes a spy.'" Raymond said. "They had no idea! No idea at all. They learned though."

Partially because of BSC's social restrictions, Raymond didn't meet anyone but BSC people in New York. "Because you didn't. So it was really a rather lonely life, but they were all there. It was an absolute hive of industry during the week. There was Ivor Bryce, Tommy Fairly, Ingraham Fraser, John Pepper, Cedric Belfrage. So many of them. Christopher Wren, Bill Gooch, Sir Alfred Ayres who recently died. Freddie Ayres. He was the philosopher, a brilliant man. He was there. There were two Wrens. 'Freckles' Wren, whose wife was Marjorie who I told you about. The other one was Christopher Wren. Last I heard Christopher Wren was in the Algarve. I didn't have anything to do with him. I must admit he was there, and we said hello, and we met occasionally. But he was on the other floors 35 and 36. We were really, really separate.

"We didn't know what anybody was doing. It was all so secret. It was very funny. I didn't know how important one was, or if one wasn't. Some of things we did were important and some of them were just routine. I think there was an awful lot of paper work. There was a whole lot of wasted paper. There always is."

Raymond and Hyde worked behind locked doors in a small office designated Room 99. No one was allowed into the office to see what they were doing except Bill Stephenson. "Nobody else was allowed in at all. Maybe Harford, but he never bothered. Dorothy and I sat behind our locked door."

Bolivia—Forgery

In May of 1941, BSC was worried some military figures in Bolivia may attempt a coup backed by the Nazis. BSC did not have enough concrete proof to link right-wing South American elements with Berlin, so a letter was concocted from Major Elias Belmonte of the Bolivian Legation in Germany to Ernst Wendler, the German Minister to Bolivia. Belmonte was, according to Hyde, a fervent pro-Nazi.[2] Montgomery Hyde travelled on Stephenson's instructions to Bolivia to glean the needed details. Paper and ink usually used by the Bolivian Mission in Berlin, and a suitable text was obtained through Hyde's South American contacts. A letter dated June 9, 1941, from Berlin written in Spanish, was put together in Canada with a typewriter that duplicated the print of one usually used by Belmonte. His signature had to be forged by Raymond and Dorothy Hyde. "A sample of it was given to Dorothy and myself and we practised it, because you must practice, and it was a desperately difficult signature to do." After much repetition, neither of the women could match the signature accurately. "We practised for weeks and neither of us were able to do it. Until one day we found to our amazement, she could do one half, and I could do the other. Now you don't break a signature in half normally, but there does come a break in the signature, if it so happens, and we found that this was how it was. This is the absolute truth. She signed one bit and I signed the other." After the forged text of the Belmonte letter was created, there was only one copy for the women to sign. "You couldn't make a mistake. There was only one."

Hyde says he took the women's handiwork to Ottawa and it was shown to RCMP experts. The Mounties were told, "We think this is a forgery," and it was compared to an original Belmonte signature. The RCMP studied it and concluded the signature was genuine.[3] BSC then decided it would go ahead with the ruse.

The letter from Belmonte talked about the moment approaching to liberate "my poor country from a weak government." It spoke of focal points of the proposed uprising, and said wolfram contracts with the

United States must be rescinded. He hoped to "save Bolivia and later the rest of South America from North American influence." The concocted letter said eventually a single supreme leader for all of South America would be required.[4] Stephenson devised a scheme, using false rumours and fibs, to authenticate the letter. He sent notice to Brazil and London that a German courier was expected with incriminating documents. Later the courier's secretary was bribed, and some details of his mission were released. The Belmonte letter was subsequently stolen from the courier in Buenos Aires, where a FBI agent reported the theft to Washington. Stephenson soon afterward handed the letter over to J Edgar Hoover. Both the British and American governments pressed for its release to the Bolivians. It was widely distributed in South America, and the letter's authenticity did not come into question—its contents appeared genuine.

"Photostat copies of the letter, whose signature was authenticated by the chief of the Bolivian general staff, were published in all morning papers (in La Paz)," the *New York Times* reported in 1941.[5]

"And that was done by two different hands—one signature," Raymond remembered. "That is unbelievable, but it is perfectly true. Harford didn't bother to ask me, and said that Dorothy had done it. It doesn't matter now. It's water under the bridge. But it was a much better story, because it happened to be true... Doing signatures is not an easy business.

"You have to learn how to do it, and you have to practice it like mad. Because you cannot pause. You cannot hesitate on a signature. Otherwise you are undone. Because nobody pauses on their signature. You just do it. And if there's the slightly hesitation, but the slightest—it is a forgery."

She would usually practice two or three hundred times. "But there were some easy ones, and they don't take any time at all."

The Bolivian letter led to the expulsion of the German minister, the closing of the German mission in Bolivia, the arrest of Nazi sympathizers, and the harassment of German officials in other South American countries. Wolfram continued to be exported to the Allies, and was denied to the Nazis. The German Foreign Office called the letter, "falsification in the crudest manner possible," and the Reich's government wrote all Latin American countries to complain about the forgery. The forged letter helped poison the climate towards the Axis in the Western Hemisphere. On July 29, 1941, Texas congressman Martin Dies warned that the Nazis had about a million soldiers in South America poised, "to produce a diversion to prevent our aiding Great Britain."[6] German diplomatic pouches started being stolen in Argentina, "with a typical show of Wild West bad manners," a Nazi spokesman complained.

Six months later, most Central and South American countries broke with the Axis powers at a Pan-American conference in Rio, and set up a common scheme for defence. That move was described by US Under Secretary of State Sumner Welles as "the decision that saved New World unity."[7]

Years after the war some people suspected the Belmonte letter could have been a forgery. Montgomery Hyde admitted the document was phony to American television (CBS, Mike Wallace) in August 1979, and later in the *London Telegraph* August 22, 1979.

Raymond says she didn't help on the letter which was purported to help put Italy's LATI airlines out of Brazil.

On one occasion, she was asked to forge Britain's US Ambassador's signature. "They came along and said Lord Halifax has to sign something, and I signed it on his behalf. I don't know what it was," she laughed. The top part of the document was covered so she didn't see what she was signing. "I just busily signed it. Had a little practice and signed. You know it's awful to laugh about these things. It was probably terribly important."

Room 99 only had signatures to deal with and never tried to forge handwritten notes. "We couldn't write letters, or anything. We could never get around to doing that."

Raymond taught the tricks of the trade to four Canadians in New York, and they were sent to various places in South America.

Argentina

Raymond's major expedition during the war was to Argentina with Bill Ross Smith. The two flew south to Buenos Aires to find a Spanish ship's captain with a document package. Spanish ships no longer visited New York, so Raymond and Ross Smith flew down together to South

America to try and pilfer another message packet. It was a five-day flight as aircraft were not allowed to fly at night in South America, Raymond says. During the journey she became ill with trench mouth, so she left the plane in Peru and was nursed back to health in Lima by the British Consul and a dentist, while Bill Ross Smith continued down to Argentina to find a Spanish captain.

When she arrived one of BSC's Argentine agents, who had been to New York, saw Raymond there. "Suddenly ... cables were flashed back and forth to New York Office, `I've seen Betty Raymond here. What is she doing?' And all this. It was terribly secret. And we were followed everywhere. It was horrid. Very unpleasant."

After a number of days Ross Smith obtained a document package and hurried to Raymond to open it. They set up shop at a British estate agent's place and Raymond discovered there was no envelope to open. The package consisted of one large piece of paper that had been folded and sewn up. "It was the most difficult thing I had to do in my life, because it was all closed up. All porous paper, very soft, which they sealed with dark brown glue and egg white. And they'd sewed a thin string right through it into a cross and right around and put a seal onto it." She got the package in the afternoon and worked on it until midnight she said, as they only had it for 24 hours. "We promised this man we would get it back to him ... ha.

"Bill got the captain at long last. It was the third one they tried. He got the captain to pass it over. He said somebody had a third eye, not to worry, it was quite safe. It wouldn't be touched. He would hand it back."

(This conflicted with Bill Ross Smith's sequence of events. He said he stole the package when a captain was in a washroom. Why were their stories not the same? Later Ross Smith said he didn't tell Raymond how he actually got the package. He lied to her. It was 'the need-to-know.' She didn't need-to-know where the package came from. If Raymond was captured, threatened or tortured, and eventually revealed where the package came from—it would be the wrong information. Her interrogators would know no more about the actual source, and if they pursued the matter they would be aimed in the wrong direction.)

When she finally got the package open the contents were in poor shape. "Absolute shreds," Raymond remembered. "And I handed Bill this paper. They had a camera waiting. And I handed it to him, and Bill went green in the face," she laughed. "He went green ... he thought this is the end, you see." Raymond slept for a few hours while the material was photographed. When the contents were returned to be put back together again, she told everyone, "All I ask is leave me alone. Nobody come near me, whatever you do." Raymond was able to repair the package and it was returned by noon the next day.

"Spain didn't come in, but the Argentine was very pro-German. We were trailed everywhere. It was most uncomfortable. Our rooms were searched every day. It was horrible. I was very glad to get out of there." Raymond thought they were not in actual danger, but people wanted to know what they were doing there.

There was nothing suspicious to find in the hotel room. She had only a few tiny tools to take through customs. She then bought a rubber ball at a toy store and cut it in half to get a rubber bowl. Her only other equipment was plaster of Paris and some oil. The camera work was done by others. There were at least three BSC people in Buenos Aires.

When the two were departing for New York the Basques in Argentina held a dinner in their honour. "They thought we were all so splendid and they looked at us in awe," she remembered. But she was not taken with the cuisine. "A very, very, funny dinner. It was, ah, octopus and deer's genitals, I think," Raymond chuckled. "It was absolutely ghastly! Bill fed me (later), but he was very noble. He ate it. I couldn't. But, it was a great honour. Very sweet."

Raymond made another trip for BSC to Trinidad. A ship was expected in Port of Spain that was laden with sacks of mail they wanted to go through. Trinidad had an intercept office, but they didn't have anyone experienced enough to do it all. "We had these ruddy sacks," Raymond remembered. "I didn't want to go." She spent about three weeks in Trinidad dealing with the mail, and nothing was in them. She returned to New York. "Some weeks later we had a most excited call from the FBI. A ship was in—'could we possibly deal with something on it?' It was the same ruddy ship, and the same ruddy bags that I'd already done, and I couldn't tell them!" The FBI contacts didn't need-to-know about BSC's activities elsewhere. Raymond redid the bags under the watchful eye of the Americans. "The utter frustration. It was that sort of thing you see. No. It was an interesting life."

Travelling from the Caribbean, through Spanish Honduras, to New York on a banana boat, Raymond thought she was drugged aboard ship. "I nearly got bumped off. One was very unimportant. But they knew who you were."

Before Raymond departed on one of her next assignments for BSC, Stephenson gave her a 'gas gun' for protection. She still has it.

"Well I'll show you," she said. "I'm not supposed to have it, of course, because it is a weapon, but Bill had one, and when I was going off on my trip—I forget which one I was going on, it was given to me and the thing is ... because Bill (Stephenson) had used it once himself ... If you get into a corner and you get trapped, as he was once. He told me he was trapped in a corner. You take out this little gas gun and as long as you are near the door..."

She disappeared into her bedroom and returned with a antique looking fountain pen and a small white box. She held the pen with two hands and feigned pulling on the clasp.

"If I shot the gun out to you, very close like this to your eyes—it would blind you. It would ruin your eyes. But the thing is, if you're over by the door and you're getting away. You just shoot it—the place is full of gas and you're just crying, you can't see, of course, because of the gas, and the person who shoots it goes away."

A gas spraying 'pen' weapon used by field agents as a means of escape from tight situations, given to Betty Raymond by WSS

(The pen seemed similar to John Krafchenko's pen. "News of the pen had caused every man in the audience to sit bolt upright with ears strained forward to catch this latest and remarkable phase of Krafchenko's craftiness." It seems Stephenson may have carried with him a reminder of the spirit of the Wild West.)

The pen saved Stephenson's life, Raymond said. "Bill used it. Bill used it. He used it either in Spain, or in Portugal. I'm sorry I can't remember, it is many years ago, and he said he got cornered. But he said, 'It was perfectly all right. I got to the door, shot my gun, and I got away. I walked away.' Because you can walk away like that, because they can't see for some time. Absolutely paralysed with this gas. And he said, 'I walked away, and I walked out of the hotel, perfectly safe.'"

Raymond said the pen made her feel quite safe but, she says, at BSC headquarters there was no security. You just walked in.

"Well I don't know what they would do to us all. We were just office people. There was nothing very much. We weren't any great problem."

She was not sure if Stephenson had extra protection. "Maybe he had a bit of security. I wasn't conscious of it. He was on the other side of the office, away from me. He was away from all of us. It was a separate bit he had so maybe he was very safe. I don't think anybody could come in from the outside or anything like that."

Eventually Raymond felt there was no longer enough work for Dorothy Hyde and herself in New York, and she wanted to go home. She returned to England before Christmas 1942. When she arrived back in London to continue her profession, she was tested and retested by MI5. She believes it was because of her connection to the Stephenson organization. "I went to the London office, and they were going to send me out to Turkey. You see, London Office was very, very, jealous of Bill Stephenson. Terribly jealous of Bill Stephenson," she said. "They hated him. So they put me through every hoop, to prove I couldn't do anything." She could do everything they asked of her. "Well, I was the best that they had. So that was very silly of them."

In the end Raymond wasn't allowed to go to Turkey for health reasons. She resigned from MI5, and Stephenson found her a job with the American OSS.

Raymond was employed by OSS in London for eighteen months, given a furnished flat on North Orderly Street, and was on call. But her workload was undemanding. "I never did a day's work for them. I never did a thing. But they thought it was very nice to have me, in case they needed some secret operation that I could do." She was given false American identification and once a month went to Grosvenor Street to pick up her salary in cash of 80 pounds, "which in those days was an enormous amount of money. I was on call, which was very nice, but I couldn't go away. They never called me," she laughed.

One of the few times her OSS contact, a Mr Murphy, sought her out, Raymond was in hospital having an operation. "I got a letter from them saying, 'we don't feel very nice, but I don't think we can use you after all.' That was the end of OSS. So I never had anything to do with them."

Stephenson

Raymond was a good friend of Stephenson during the war, especially when she was in London. "That's very funny, I say I didn't know him after 1944-'45. I never saw him again after then. Because I knew him all over here, when I came back to England, rather than New York. In the New York office everyone was terrified of him.

"In New York, you had this long, big office, with a desk at the far end and there was Grace guarding him," she said with a laugh. If someone wanted to see Stephenson, they had to go through Grace Garner. "One spoke to Grace and said, 'Can we see Mr Stephenson?' It was in those days, and Grace used to consult and see if we'd be allowed to see him."

People allowed to see the spymaster then waited outside the office. Most were intensely nervous while they were waiting. When they were called and got up to see Stephenson, they were actually physically shaking.

"So people would go along shaking. I never shook, because it was just one of those things. He used to beam at me, when I came in. But I was a girl, you see. It was one of those things that was a different matter," she laughed. "I was never frightened of him...

"They (visitors) were terrified. You see he never spoke. He sat there, and he waited for you to speak. It was a very great trick he had. He sat there just looking at you, with these hooded eyes. As I said, I thought he had a lot of 'Indian' in him. I suppose it was because he was Icelandic. He had these hooded eyes, and he just looked at you. And didn't utter. And you were pulp, you see. It was a very great trick he had."

When Stephenson did talk, he didn't say much. "He only said—," she paused, "He was very, very lean with his words. One word. Not necessarily two. If one did, he said one."

She doesn't think her former boss wrote the foreword to *A Man Called Intrepid*. "That's not Bill Stephenson," she said. "No. No it isn't.

He couldn't have done it, I don't think. No, socially he was much more talkative in Claridges (where he stayed in London).

"He did know the War Lords. I'm absolutely convinced he knew them over here. Because I remember one evening I was having dinner with him at Claridges. We'd been away for the weekend and we came back and he said, 'I've got the War Lords coming tonight. They're going to be down here to 'sweep' later on.' And I said, 'I'll go back down', and he said, 'Don't hurry, don't hurry.' He was in one of those chatty moods. Not about himself, but he was in a chatty mood and I kept on saying I must go, and he said, 'They can wait.' And he made them wait. He said Louis Mountbatten was with them. I don't think he'd have lied to me, I don't think there'd be much point. And he made them wait until two or three in the morning before he went down and saw them. He was a law unto himself, you see."

She also thought Stephenson met often with Churchill in London. "I'm absolutely convinced he did. I'm absolutely convinced he did. He knew them all. I'm sure he did.

"He had a really great friend called Alexander Korda. He was a very famous film producer, and Korda used to come down. Korda lived there in Claridges. Korda used to come down after dinner. And very happy evenings. He was very happy and relaxed and chatty but then it was very different, you see."

"What was his relation with Korda?"

"Just a friend, just a very good friend." Stephenson took Raymond to see Shepparton Studios during the war, but she was unaware he owned it. "One weekend we went out to the studios. He had friends, obviously. He had friends there, and they used to come and see him. As I say Korda liked him very much. I don't think he had any financial connections. He might have had. I don't think so. He was just friendly."

(According to information supplied by the studio, Stephenson likely owned it at the time. Alexander Korda purchased it from him in 1947. During the war much of an imitation invasion force was constructed there which was used to confuse the Nazis before D-Day.)

Stephenson came over to England every few months, Raymond said. When he was there, Miss AM Green, a secretary who looked after Stephenson's business concerns in Britain, came to Claridge's daily. She

didn't know Mary Stephenson. "But he adored her (Mary), I do assure you, absolutely adored her. He used to call her his 'Old Dutch'. His 'Old Dutch', yes, and he was absolutely devoted to her.

"He had an iron constitution. He drank Gin and French. And you wouldn't have known he had had a drink, until one day I gather, all of a sudden, it caught up to him and he couldn't drink another drink for the rest of his days.

"But he was a very good companion. He was a lovely person to be with. He never talked about his past, but as I say, he had a lot of important meetings at Claridges, a lot of important people. I know he did.

"Very important people as I say. He went off on D-Day, and viewed D-Day from somewhere. He did. I remember that. I don't think he knew any fear at all. I think he was fearless."

Stephenson was in London when the V-1 rockets started to attack England. "Yes. The one thing I remember about that ... V-1's. A V-1 came over, I can't remember the year. A V-1 came over and I was alone in my flat over there. And it terrified me. I saw this thing with a red flame, and Bill was over here. He was at Claridges, and the only time I ever rung him. I rang him up, and it was late at night. I said, 'Bill. I'm very frightened, what is this?' He said, 'Put your head under a pillow and put the phone down,'" she laughed. "Which was typical you see.

"It was going so slow," Raymond said. "There was a terrifying black object with flames coming out. It was the first ones. I'd never seen anything like it. At night. And they were very frightening in the daytime. I'd never seen one before."

"So he had some idea what it was?"

"Oh, he knew perfectly what it was. He was in at a meeting. I had disturbed him. He wasn't going to sympathize with me. 'Put your head under a pillow.'"

This was typical of Stephenson, Raymond thought. "This is how he got on so well. That was his attitude. He just put people off. He wouldn't mind. One evening we were having quite a big party in his suite at Claridges. He always had a suite at Claridges. And he was giving quite a good party, and he got a bit bored with it and he said, 'Now, young lady, I think you must go home.' I said, 'Yes indeed, yes.' I was thinking I'd overstayed my welcome, how embarrassing. And he saw me out to the lift, and saw me down, and saw me to the taxi, and he never went back to his party ever. He was like that you see. He was an extraordinary man, just left everybody there," she continued. "Everybody there, he didn't care. Yes, he never went back. He had the OSS people there and all sorts of things."

She thought Stephenson's major contribution to the war was alerting the Americans of the horrors of the Nazis. "Absolutely rightly. Roosevelt, as we knew, was very anxious to get into the war. He had to get in. We knew that, and Bill was very instrumental, I'm sure, in doing that. I think, in all, that he was marvellous.

"In those days you see he was only in his forties, and he was very active and very clear, as clear as a bell obviously and a very active, intelligent man. He was at the height of his powers then." Raymond said she thought Stephenson remembered everything she ever told him. "Every word.

"But about Bill Stephenson, there's very little I could tell you because, as you say, he never told anybody about himself. Never. I was devoted to him. I knew him very well. He used to ring me whenever he came over and I used to go over to Claridges and we had happy times together. We were in the services of friends of his a weekend or two and it was lovely. But he still never talked about himself. He was a very pleasant companion. He was absolutely charming."

"When did you see him last?"

"Well, I saw him when the war was coming to an end, and then the war came to an end. You see he kept on flying over in bombers. He used to fly over here very regularly. He came over a great deal and saw all these people. That's why I'm certain he saw Churchill. He always came to Claridges. He always had a suite."

CO-ORDINATION

Plate 1: Winnipegger William Stephenson, dispatched by Churchill, heads up the British Security Coordination headquartered in the International Bldg of New York's Rockefeller Center

Plate 2: William Stephenson (passport photo, 1942)

Photo: Courtesy Thomas Troy

Plate 3: 'Wild' Bill Donovan, head of the Office of Strategic Services, later to evolve into the Central Intelligence Agency

Inscription: To Bill Stephenson whose friendship, knowledge and continuing assistance contributed so richly to the establishment and maintenance of our American intelligence service in World War II — Bill Donovan

Photo: Courtesy Thomas Troy. (The above inscription had faded badly over time; Troy sent it to the CIA labs for restoration.)

Plate 4: Edward Travis, head of the Bletchley Park division of the Government Code and Cipher School

Berkeley Street   Entrance

Plate 5: The Government Code and Cipher School division in Berkeley Street, London. The arrow (drawn by William Friedman) points to the entrance beside Peggy Carter's hat shop

Plate 6: Toronto stockbroker Tommy Drew-Brook (William Stephenson's best friend) recruited Canadians for wartime work with BSC

Plate 7: Colonel CH 'Dick' Ellis, an Australian, was a member of MI6. He was William Stephenson's principal SIS assistant in the US

Some of Stephenson's 'Unknown Agents' and Friends

Plate 8: Robert Sherwood

Plate 9: 'Cynthia' (Elizabeth Pack)

Plate 10: Bill Ross Smith

Plate 11: Roald Dahl (photo, 1990)

*Plate 12: Below: Molly Phair on the roof of
The Manor in Tudor City, 333 E 43rd Street,
where she lived (December 1943)*

*Plate 13: Back row, left to right: Doris Ell,
Georgie Davey, Molly Phair
Front row: Mary McNeil, Mary Grant
(Pat Bayly's sister-in-law)*

*Plate 14: Left to right: Molly Phair and Ruth Ferguson with unidentified Canadian
servicemen at Billy Rose's Diamond Horseshoe, Paramount Hotel, NYC*

Plate 15: Benjamin de Forest Bayly (photo 1959)

Plate 16: Leaders of various Allied code and cipher departments
(March 13, 1944)
First row, second from left: Commander Edward Travis
First row, far right: Carter Clarke
Second row, third from left: Benjamin de Forest Bayly

Plate 17: HYDRA: Top-secret telecommunications centre at Camp X

Clockwise, from top: Alastair Denniston, Bayly being honoured by the Institute of Electrical Engineers, Gordon Welchman (with pipe) and Edward Travis

Plate 19: Allan Turing, eminent mathematician cited as, "the intellectual father of the modern computer"

Plate 18: Pat Bayly at home near San Diego, California (photo 1991)

19 June 1944

MEMORANDUM FOR THE PRESIDENT

Attached is a proposed recommendation for award of the Distinguished Service Medal to Mr. William S. Stephenson, chief representative of the British Secret Intelligence Service and the Special Operation Service in the Western Hemisphere.

All that is said in the proposed citation is absolutely true. Just as we have been insistent on the right of our country to have an independent secret intelligence service, so I would like our British colleagues to see that we recognize and appreciate the help they gave us.

For that reason I hope that you approve such a citation.

William J. Donovan
Director

Plate 20: Bill Donovan presenting Sir William Stephenson with the US Medal for Merit, 1946. Lady Mary Stephenson is standing next to her husband; Col G Edward Buxton, Assistant Director of the OSS looking on

Plate 21: Col. Tom Lawson and his wife Miggsie presenting Sir William Stephenson with the Order of the Buffalo Hunt, September 21, 1985

Plates 22, 23: The St. John's Parish Church cemetery in Bermuda where Sir William Stephenson and Mary, Lady Stephenson are laid to rest

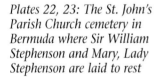

16 Astley and the Service

IF BORMANN NOT YET SENT ASTLEY PLEASE ADDRESS TO
MRS. J ASTLEY ON XX XXXX STREET LONDON SW 3 AND NOT REPT
NOT TO FOREIGN OFFICE AS PREVIOUSLY INDICATED STOP SHE
WAS PRINCIPAL WARTIME ASSISTANT TO GENERAL LORD ISMAY
AND SUPERVISED PREPARATORY ARRANGEMENTS ALL HIGH LEVEL
CONFERENCES ALLIES WINSTON ATTENDED
GREETINGS INTREPID[1]
Stephenson to Stevenson (following the publication of William
Stevenson's book *The Bormann Brotherhood*)

Joan Bright Astley

Stephenson's activities in Europe during the war will probably always
remain a mystery. In London, Stephenson, a conduit of secret information was in contact with Joan Bright Astley.

Born in Argentina, Joan Bright lived in South America until the age
of three, when her family returned to England. She began her British
government career when, following in her sister's footsteps, she started
working for the Foreign Office in Mexico. She left in July 1936, and
returned to London to look for a job. For a short time she worked for
Alfred Duff Cooper, helped with his book *Tallerand*, and had opportunities to work for British Embassies in Rome, Vienna, and Paris. Instead
Astley moved from one temporary post to another. During the Munich
crisis of 1938, she worked in the headquarters of the anti-aircraft unit of
the territorial army.

She also had an offer from the British Consul-General in Munich to
live at the home of the enigmatic Nazi leader Rudolf Hess, and teach
English to his family. (See appendix A) She later regretted not taking the
post. In her book, *The Inner Circle, A View of War at the Top*, Astley
remembered the Nazi leader's arrival with a certain regret. "Rudolf Hess
arrived in May, his parachute swinging him down mad and alone on his
private peace mission. I imagined myself sent for by the Foreign

Secretary. 'Miss Bright, you alone in England know this man. Go and see him. Here is your ticket for Scotland.' Yes, certainly I should have accepted to go to the Hess family in Munich in 1938."[2]

Astley found more permanent government employment when a childhood friend told her to go to St. James Park underground station at a specific time wearing a pink carnation. From there, in a roundabout way she was led to an office and interviewed by the military. She was informed of the methods of torture of the Nazis and signed the Official Secrets Act. After the interview she was led to a window and a lone figure on a street corner was pointed out. She was told he had been watching all morning and not to let him see her. "It all seemed like good clean fun and I was pleased to be joining an organization in which fact and fiction played so smoothly together."[3]

Bright began working for the most secret departments of Britain's war effort with: Colonel JCF Holland, Colonel Colin McVeagh Gubbins, Major Millis Jefferies, and Commander Dymock Watson in the Military Intelligence Directorate of the War Office. She then worked in Section D under Colonel Lawrence Grand. "Grand's section D deeds would be done by undercover men spies and saboteurs who, if caught, would be neither acknowledged nor defended by their government," she remembered in her book.

Her responsibilities grew during the war. When Winston Churchill decided his generals needed easier access to covert information, he instructed Pug Ismay to establish, "a special secret information centre in the Office of the Minister of Defence which Commanders-in Chief could visit whenever they came to London." Ismay got Joan Bright to run it. She became the director of the information centre that collated and distributed confidential material to British war commanders. Before and during the June 1944 D-Day landings in Normandy, the Allies feigned an invasion at Pas de Calais so Nazi strength would concentrate there. In Anthony Cave Brown's *Bodyguard of Lies* Sir Ronald Wingate, the deputy chief of the main deception bureau of the invasion, remembers Joan Bright informing them of the ULTRA intercept that indicated Hitler still believed the deception. The Nazi leader was stopping the flow of Panzer and infantry divisions to Normandy, and sending reinforcements to Calais. As a result D–Day would be successful.

"We looked at the ULTRA—and there it was! Hitler had cancelled Case Three. We'd won, and what an astonishing moment that was! We knew then that we'd won—there might be very heavy battles but we'd won. The PM came in with Stewart Menzies and the PM said this was the crowning achievement of the long and glorious history of the British Secret Service—or something like that."[4]

Astley attended all the major Big Three conferences, and eventually she was appointed the Manager of the British Delegation at the Allied Conferences. The cover of the American version of her book is a circular picture, as if viewed through a spy glass, of Winston Churchill in Tehran in 1943, celebrating his birthday with Joseph Stalin.

Many prominent people corresponded with Bright during the time, including General Archibald Wavell and Admiral James Somerville, and she socialized with both Peter and Ian Fleming. According to Peter Fleming's biographer, he planned to use forged correspondence between Wavell and Bright in a planned deception during the Allied retreat from Burma.[5] She introduced Winston Churchill to Ian Fleming following his famous 'Iron Curtain' speech, and had entertained some thoughts of marrying the future spy writer. She married Philip Astley in July, 1949.

Joan Bright was a friend of William Stephenson. She refers to Stephenson in her book and implies he was instrumental in convincing Bill Donovan in 1940 that the United States needed a centralized intelligence organization.

> "The contact with Mr Stephenson and this visit convinced him (Donovan) that when the United States entered the war it would be profitable to draw into one body the many intelligence agencies which worked independently of each other in the department of War, Navy, and State and to include in the body the study and implementation of unorthodox methods of war such as were now being pursued in England."[6]

Astley and two of her friends, Walter and Katie Bell, together discussed Bill Stephenson.

Bell worked in passport control when Stephenson arrived in the United States in 1940 and became one of the first members of what became British Security Coordination. He was with Foreign Office for most of his career, stationed in New York during World War II and then transferred to Mexico. He was also on embassy staffs in Washington and various British missions in Africa. According to one report, Bell relayed information from the chief of British Security about the 1944 assassination attempt on Adolf Hitler to OSS representative David Bruce, because he "had important contacts with the conspirators."[7] Bell and his wife were also associates of Donald Maclean, the Soviet double agent.[8]

Walter's wife, Katie, was the daughter of American General Carl Spaatz.[9] (Spaatz was a prominent figure during the war. Among his assignments was Berlin in May, 1945. He signed the surrender documents on behalf of the United States ending the military war against Nazi Germany.)

After the trio learned of Stephenson's Canadian life, they offered some of their observations.

"Well, he was just someone I met during the war," Walter Bell said. "I was just in the passport office in New York working with passports." He made a stamping motion with his hands. "This little Canadian fellow arrived, and no one knew who he was.

"David Bruce had a tremendous regard for Bill Stephenson," Bell said. "He told us how Bill took him to Cheatley (Beaverbrook's house) for tea. Bevin was there and Dalton, and Bill brought Bruce. Well, Beaverbrook stood up and started making all these anti-American comments. Repeatedly. Eventually Bill Stephenson just got up and said, 'Look, our guest is a distinguished American. He's a guest from a remarkable country, and I didn't bring him here to be insulted. We're leaving.' And they began to walk out. Well Beaverbrook got up, ran after them to the door, apologized, and pleaded and pleaded with Bill. He begged them to stay. You don't do that in Beaverbrook's house without knowing him very well."

"I don't know how well he knew Churchill, but I do know this," said Astley. "If 'Little Bill' rang up General Ismay, Ismay would clear his desk. Immediately. I think that's important. Very few people could even get in to see Ismay.[10]

"He may have seen Churchill a few times. I don't know. I don't think it matters," she added.

The consensus of the trio seemed to be it was easy to read too much into the espionage business and Stephenson's career. "We're so close to it, we know what hockum a lot of it is," Astley said.

But were there not certain security precautions and guidelines within the 'hockum' such as 'need-to-know'? For example, Canadian BSC women in New York couldn't attend Berlitz language schools during the war. Bill Ross Smith, when he was dealing with South American assignments, learned Spanish at Berlitz in New York. Everything was on a need-to-know basis. No one else at BSC needed to know Ross Smith was taking Spanish for South American contacts. "So no one can go to Berlitz?"

"Oh, I think that's ridiculous," Katie Bell said. "They couldn't go to Berlitz, because they might see Bill Ross Smith there. Come on."

To BSC people certain restaurants were out-of-bounds as well. "That's just so they don't see their bosses drunk there," Astley said. "Oh, don't get caught up in that nonsense! The war was won by the people on the front lines."

Astley said the secrecy seemed a bit much at times. Employees were to walk into her office with their heads down in a certain way, she said, and once in a while she would look up at someone she knew and shout 'Boo' at them. "People read too much into this spying business, don't they Walter?"

"Well, yes," Bell said. "But don't call it spying. It's the Service."

"What about ULTRA?"

"Oh, that wasn't espionage really," Astley said. "You know Winston felt a little guilty about ULTRA. He was very much a man of fairness. ULTRA was a bit like cheating."

Later Walter Bell spoke about Bill Stephenson. "We had no idea how to approach the Americans," he said. "The most valuable thing he did was talk sense about the Americans. The British feeling was the Americans were just a bunch of salesmen. The disquieting thing was that they were all rich," he laughed. "Stephenson cut all that out. He said that's all bullshit. They're our friends. They'll help us. And we need them if we're going to win. Which is what Churchill thought. Of course, he was right. Absolutely … he was an invaluable person."

Following Stephenson's death no one from British officialdom spoke up for him amid negative press reports.

"Well, British Intelligence never acknowledge anything, one way or the other," Bell said. "Never. And the government? Well it happened so long ago who would really know, without a lot of researching.

"I submitted something for (HH) Hinsley's book, *British Intelligence in the Second World War*, that would have refuted one of (Hugh) Trevor-Roper's criticisms. But they wouldn't put it in," Bell said. "National security, they said. National security. Nonsense.

"In many ways Stephenson was very uncouth," Bell continued. "He knocked the establishment and the rules and pretty much did what he wanted. He wasn't being paid or anything. So if he didn't like what you were doing, he'd tell you to bugger right off. I can't say I was a fan of his. I wasn't a fan of Fleming's either. All this 'James Bond.' He shook his head.

"But on the other hand, I do know this. He did an incredible job."

A biography of Jim Thompson, a British silk merchant from Thailand, stood out from Astley's bookcase. According to *Donovan,* by Anthony Cave Brown, Thompson was a secret OSS agent, and following the war he became the Thai contact of World Commerce Corporation which Stephenson headed. By the end of the evening, Astley said she was *sure* Thompson worked for Stephenson. "Everyone did! Don't you see?" she said, raising her voice. "And even people who didn't, said that they did. I'm certain that one day, an aboriginal will walk out from the far reaches of the outback, and he'll say, 'Oh yes … I was working for Sir William,'" she said in a low raspy voice. And she laughed.

A day later, a message was relayed from Katie Bell to this author by Grace Garner, Stephenson's wartime secretary. "They couldn't go to Berlitz because that was where people were trained for drops into Europe."

■

Astley thought any new Bill Stephenson publication should deal with his early years, and not the war. "Bill covered up his childhood. I find that so sad," she said, "and to me that's far more interesting than anything you do about the war. If you could do any kind of character sketch as to what made this man tick over. What made him into the character and the personality he became, because he did—why are we talking about him now?—I think if you could go through such research, such as parish registers and that sort of thing and find out what sort of man. Why? What it was in him. As a serious study of a personality. I think it would be absolutely fascinating.

"I figure about these silly old people who wonder if Dick Ellis was a spy or wasn't a spy, or whether Bill was liked by Churchill or not. I think all of that is so unimportant. But what made Bill tick? Why this lonely little fellow as a small boy—." She wondered about his mother, and other family. "He's got no brothers and sisters alive?"

Behind her computer desk, she started sifting through her files. The keeper of many of the war's top-secrets retained many personal papers. "I think it would really be something to put an end to this. 'Little Bill.' Here's a file now." She pulled up copies of letters from Montgomery Hyde and from Edwin Leathers,[11] "who's very concerned." Astley questioned if certain instances in *A Man Called Intrepid* were true, such as Stephenson being an unidentifiable silhouette in a photograph with Churchill at the bombed out Houses of Parliament.[12]

"This is William Stevenson (the author, making the claims). I've heard from friends and I think this is true, that Mary Stephenson was frightfully against *A Man Called Intrepid*. She didn't want it, and if she'd been alive I don't think that book would have been published."

Astley knew the ex-wife of the author Stevenson, and saw her in Bermuda. She read *A Man Called Intrepid* while she was there as a favour. "I said, 'I promise you,' I said, 'I'm devoted to you Glynnis, and I don't want to be mean about your ex-husband, but I'm going to settle down and very quietly read it.'"

She walked to the bookcase and retrieved a copy of *A Man Called Intrepid*. "Oh really, on the first two pages. Let's just pick any page." She started thumbing through it. "'*Area of disaster ... Coventry ... Roosevelt discussed with Stephenson the dangers of knowing too much*'. I don't believe that for a minute. '*War is forcing us more and more to play God ... I don't know what I should have done.*' *Churchill chose one.* etc. *Bletchley obtained the German order to destroy Coventry.*' I don't believe it. And then these are the main street maps of Europe. Here you see. SOE wasn't even formed when observer units went undercover to defend England in case of invasion."

After stressing her concerns about Stephenson publications, Astley talked about her career during the war. The surreptitious work of her office at the beginning of the conflict was brought on by Britain's crippled circumstances at the time.

"I was in the Office before it had become SOE, a branch. It was very straightforward. The war had to be fought that way. We didn't have an army. And the decision was, there were only three ways to wage the war in the beginning. By economic warfare, you know, by interception of ships, etc., and bombing. And by subversive operations, and commando raids, and that sort of thing—while the army was being built up."[13]

Astley at the time was working on a book about former British SOE chief Colin Gubbins, but didn't see Stephenson about him. "No, I had no business arrangements with Bill at all. We were friends. I knew him in the war and then I married, and we lost touch and that type of thing and then when I published my book (1971) somebody must have sent him a copy, because he sent me a telegram. He was absolutely thrilled with it. And then he kept in touch every Christmas, and then after my husband died, I think I went altogether three times. He put me up at the Princess Hotel about ten days. It was always very measured. You didn't see him every day, but you would get Elizabeth or someone to ring up and could you come at 11 and that sort of thing." She met some of Stephenson's friends in Bermuda who were not involved in espionage, such as Derek Bedson. "He was very sensible ... You saw Walter Bell the other night. Once you've been involved with intelligence, you become very cagey." She didn't think Bell's name should be mentioned in any publication. "He's retired. Put John Brown."

Bell emphasized Stephenson was a very good liaison with the Americans.

"That you could say without quoting him," she said. "That you could quote anyone saying, about that. I think that is absolutely true. Anyone who signs the Official Secrets Act. They get very angry, you know."

Astley said she was careful not to put certain things into print. There was a huge signals organization for example and she got wrapped up in coding of all kinds. "I am very careful in my book not to reveal the actual system. Coding can go on forever. If the key can be found. Even a hundred years after, it would be interesting."

Stephenson attended the Quebec Conferences, Astley said. "Well sure he was there. Very likely. It would have been very odd if he wasn't. When you say 'at.' There's a great deal of difference from being 'at,' a member of the delegation, which he wasn't, and being called and coming up, or being important enough to say, I'd like to see you, while in Canada."

There would be no need for Stephenson to attend the other conferences. "He was in charge of the Western Hemisphere. He wasn't a spy. He wasn't spying, really. He wasn't a spy. He ran a large organization covering from the Argentine up to Alaska. You Canadians, as well, you know."

But Stephenson was made aware of the major decisions.

"Well of course. Naturally. I don't see how possibly you could run anything, unless you had a certain number of people who have to know. You can't, of course. I mean ULTRA, very few people knew. Bill Stephenson knew. He would have had to know." Although Astley dealt with ULTRA messages, stored and distributed them, she says she was unaware of their source. "I didn't know about ULTRA. Ian Jacob, my boss, one of my bosses, swears he didn't know. Because there was no need for him to know. He didn't need-to-know. Only the people who needed to know knew. So this is sensible. A lot of us juniors, we all knew the date of D-Day long before. I mean, you'd certainly find out if you did give it away. You're relying on people's honesty, confidentiality."

"You said that Ismay would make room for him?"

"Oh, always. Bill was a senior operator. If you wanted to give ranks, he would have been a Major General or an Air Marshal or Air Vice Marshal. That would be his rank, and as such result he would have entré. And Churchill he might have rung. I wouldn't know. There would be no need for him to see Churchill. He had nothing to do with intelligence matters. I mean he was Prime Minister.

"People get extraordinary ideas about things. Intelligence is not as exciting, or secret as it appears to be. Intelligence is what you glean in order to mount an operation. You can't mount an operation without first finding one what type of guns the enemy have on the other side, or what the people are thinking. Therefore Bill would be gleaning the intelligence. He would be passing on what he thought was important. The same as the Directors of Intelligence in Washington and in Canada, and Australia, and the headquarters in India. You wouldn't tell India about the intelligence in France."

Grace Garner thought that Bill Stephenson knew Bill Donovan before the war, and meeting him in North America wasn't set up in London. Astley's book suggests otherwise.

"I may have been wrong on that one," Astley said. "Well, maybe I'm wrong there. Perhaps he did know him before. I'm trying to think who I talked to." She went to her files and bookcase and started to go through a few things.

"I used to lunch with him and Mary after the war," she said. "Mary didn't come over during the war. Travel was very restricted, I suppose. 'Dined with Bill and Mary. Claridges.' I often look back. I suppose he used to come into the Office. I suppose he did. I had my one operations room, and wasn't privy to everything coming in. I was running my own show. How awful if I'm wrong here. I loathe being wrong." She started to read from her book to confirm her Donovan story. "It's not very polite of me to say at a much lower level. *At a much lower level—at what even may be called a personal 'subversive' level—collaboration had begun between the two countries earlier in the year.* I don't know who I got this from. I never met Donovan.[14]

"As Walter Bell was saying so rightly. For example, Desmond Morton. Industrial Intelligence. Bill would have been used. He was a high-up man then, and people would have said get a hold of Bill Stephenson. You see in the years between 1930 and 1938, he was a hired man in that business."

Astley went through notes she made while in Bermuda visiting Stephenson and watching the *A Man Called Intrepid* telefilm which featured David Niven as Stephenson, which was loosely based on William Stevenson's book. She didn't believe it was accurate. "Talks about Gubbins and ENIGMA. Poppycock.

"Gubbins shows Bill Stephenson the pill that kills. Stephenson and Gubbins who were as busy as bees in New York. The film was awful. It was all made up, wasn't it? I don't know who made it (Lorimer)."

She looked at further notes she had made previously about the 1979 made-for-TV film, and recalled a telephone call she received to try and halt its broadcast in England.

"Nigel West a 27 year-old BBC producer, called as a result of Intrepid giving him my name, you see, to discuss a crime being committed by ITV. A reporter writes about a Canadian film *A Man Called Intrepid* in which David Niven plays Stephenson. I can't remember who plays Colin Gubbins. He wonders if it could be stopped. I don't understand this. He, West, is working on a 20-minute obituary film on Stephenson." Then she added, "Stephenson hadn't died yet. 'I would like to see the film. I must make inquiries about doing so. I cannot see what could be done. If Colin is portrayed inaccurately. What can one do, unless it reduces him?' This is all to do with what Nigel West said."[15]

Astley was Stephenson's guest in Bermuda in 1979 and 1981. She continued to scan her files of those visits. "Camden House, a presentation by me. Poor old Bill, it was part of his hubris at the time. Nothing there. I'm not trying to hide anything! Let me be quick to say. Nothing about Bill there! We had to listen to some of his fantasies such as him and Colin Gubbins blowing up the heavy water ferries. In other ways his memory is perfectly okay. Chapman Pincher. He goes on and on about these old chestnuts. Pincher was very much a journalist. It's all there. Very boring."

Although some aspects of Stephenson's career may have been "very boring," years after the war Astley was still concerned about the ex-spymaster's welfare. In the April 1973 Astley wrote Bill Stephenson a letter thanking "dear Intrepid" for his telegram at New Year's and for not forgetting his old friends. In the letter at the University of Regina, she talks about what she and her family have been up to.

But the end of the letter has a completely different tone.

"I should love to see you again. I am sure you are wise enough never to come to England. But I hope, if you did, you would tell me." The last paragraph is hand-written, "And so with my love and thanks—and keep away from random and purposeful bullets. Joan."

17 Roald Dahl

A Question of Honour

People from a variety of backgrounds and occupations worked for Stephenson's BSC. There were professional intelligence officers, secretaries, businessmen, military, police and professors. There were also writers.

Roald Dahl was born in Wales the son of Norwegian parents, and was educated at a British private school in Derbyshire. He started working for Shell Oil in England and in 1937 he was transferred to Tanzania. When the war broke out Dahl joined the Royal Air Force in Kenya. He was shot down in Libya, and suffered a skull fracture, spinal injuries and a smashed hip. Eventually he moved to Washington, as an Assistant Air Attaché at the British Embassy.

The novelist Cecil Scot Forester asked Dahl to jot down a few thoughts about being a combat pilot for a story he was doing. Forester, who created Captain Horatio Hornblower, was impressed with Dahl's writing and decided to submit the young Briton's notes as a story. Dahl says the *Saturday Evening Post* paid him $1,000 for his article, which he later lost playing poker with Senator Harry Truman at Washington's University Club. Dahl became a writer, and he produced an eclectic body of work. One of his short stories, 1943's *The Gremlins*, was made into a movie by Walt Disney. Eleanor Roosevelt took a liking to Dahl's work and soon he was a regular guest at the White House and Hyde Park.

CS Forester was doing a number of things during the war. He covered the Nazi occupation of Czechoslovakia in Prague and was a member of British Information Service. "During World War II, Forester devoted himself to writing propaganda for the Allied cause, much of it for American consumption," the Cambridge Guide to literature reports.[1] During the war Dahl was an agent working for Bill Stephenson.

When Dahl was contacted about contributing to research into the life of William Stephenson, he wrote he was willing to talk about Bill Stephenson's work, "while in the saddle," and he thought Stephenson's work with British Security Coordination was "outstanding." But he had some reservations. He later said he was unsure of some of the claims in the books about Stephenson, and Dahl believed in his later life, the ex-spychief was trying to get attention. But he was interested in his old boss's background, and he was surprised people from BSC were talking.

"Aren't they worried about the Official Secrets Act?" he asked over the phone.

It was pointed out many of the people were Canadians.

"Well. *We* do," Dahl said.

He extended an invitation to discuss the life of William Stephenson at his house, but he made a point of saying he would reveal no secrets. "You won't get any from me!", the renowned children's author said emphatically, and then he paused, and sounded more subdued, "It's a question of honour really."

Lunch at Dahl's

Dahl sat down and immediately started talking. Before any questions could be asked, he remembered 1941.

"Bill always affirmed that he had chaps in the next hotel room to the—I don't know what he was, the Japanese Foreign Minister, who came over just before Pearl Harbor to Washington. Do you know who it was? (Special Envoy Saburu Kurusu.) He was a very big shot. And they were talking in this room and they had tapes of them discussing the actual date of Pearl Harbor. And he swears, he did to me anyway, that he gave that transcription to FDR. He swears that they knew therefore of the oncoming attack on Pearl Harbor and hadn't done anything about it."

"Do you think that's right?"

"I don't know," Dahl said. "I have no way to judge, except Bill didn't usually tell stories like that. That's the end of that little story. That's all I know and heard about."

"What date would that have been?"

"Whenever that chap was visiting. I don't know, shortly before Pearl Harbor."

A number of sources imply certain officials possibly knew about the oncoming attack, but Dahl was still a bit incredulous. He wondered how the base could have been left so unprepared if they knew the situation. "FDR was a very sensible man, and I knew him well. I mean there was no way he'd let the Pacific Fleet be destroyed if he could avoid it. The whole thing doesn't make sense.

"Not with the destruction of the Fleet," said Dahl. "If you'd have been FDR or I'd have been FDR and we got hold of Nimitz and we'd said, 'move most of the battleships away for Christ's sake, the day before. And just leave one or two if you want. You don't want the whole bloody lot destroyed.' There's many many ways to do it."[2]

Dahl then didn't want to talk about Pearl Harbor, he wanted to talk about Bill Stephenson.

"Much more interesting to me is this very secret man, all through the war, and he was very, very secret," said the writer. "Very private was the main thing. An extremely private man."

He remembered the wartime BSC offices, and Stephenson's relationship to staff. He didn't deal with subordinates in his office, he only talked to very few designated people and they were seldom called into see him, "unless a big thing came up and he wanted to hear your version specifically." Some people who worked at BSC never saw Stephenson, because he didn't go through the large cluttered area in front of his office. "He was a very, very private man," Dahl repeated.

Dahl thought that following the focused frenzy of the war, there was a let-down and a somewhat troubling void for Stephenson. Over five years he had built up a huge organization and used all of his connections. "Then the war finished, and then although he got a knighthood, he got no publicity whatsoever. But then people in the Secret Service, the SIS, don't expect to get publicity.

"I think he felt he did expect to get it, myself," continued Dahl. "Even before his first stroke. And was a bit nulled by it all. And my own opinion is that he set the machinery rolling. And he did hire people to write books about him."[3]

Dahl thought Stephenson was interested in promoting himself, and said if Stephenson made a speech after the war he sent copies of the text to "anybody he could think of. I got the bloody things. Everyone got them. He circulated them. You know of a lot of people like that, but we don't have a very high opinion of them."[4]

Dahl thought the books were full of mistakes, "Because Bill didn't bother to check them. Or he gave false information. Or his memory was at fault. Well, the question is whether he made the mistake in telling us about the Pearl Harbor thing too. You know, there's other things there."

"What did you do exactly? Or are you going to say?"

"I'm not telling you. No."

"Honour?"

"No, of course I'm not," he said smiling. "I'm not a Mr (Peter) Wright (*Spycatcher* author). All I'm here for is to give you my own opinions of Bill Stephenson. No. No, you won't get anything out of me on that sort of thing."

From interviews he did decades earlier, one can piece together some of Dahl's work for the Stephenson organization. When he first arrived in Washington, the young RAF pilot had no idea who Stephenson was, but he soon realized that everyone in any position of power from the British Ambassador down or on the American side knew about "this extraordinary fellow up there." During the war Stephenson was a silent secret, "a kind of unknown small creature, hiding in a dark room somewhere up in New York," Dahl said. Stephenson didn't outline a job description for the former pilot. "When he hired you he expected you to know what your role would be." Dahl worked for Stephenson for over a year before he met him.[5]

One of Dahl's contributions was purloining information from prominent people. The socially active British Air Attaché became friendly with a number of Washington politicians including then-Vice President Henry Wallace. Once while visiting his friend Charles Marsh's house, Wallace left a position paper for postwar Asia, and Marsh showed it to Dahl and asked for his opinion. Dahl quickly phoned a friend he knew was a BSC contact in Washington, and told him to meet him outside Marsh's. The BSC contact arrived within minutes and the position paper was photographed and returned as quickly as possible. While he waited for its return, Dahl hid in the basement bathroom.

The paper *Our Job in the Pacific*, called for "the emancipation of colonial subjects in the British Empire countries of India, Burma, and Malaya, and the French Empire of Indo-China, and the Dutch Empire in the East Indies." The paper also outlined plans for creating an American monopoly of postwar commercial aviation. The Wallace draft is said to have incensed Winston Churchill. For the 1944 election Wallace was replaced on the Roosevelt ticket by Senator Harry Truman. It is not known exactly the extent to which BSC played a role in Wallace's downfall, but "Stephenson could be very devious."

Dahl later confirmed in writing that the 'Wallace Affair' incident was accurate.

Wallace knew Dahl worked for British Security. After the war, Wallace wrote in his diary Wing Commander Dahl told him of the very close friendship between Bill Stephenson, his chief, and Bill Donovan. "He spent most of his time trying to convince me that the United States should continue the Donovan Secret Service setup. He thinks a combined American-English Secret Service is necessary to prevent destructive possibilities of the atomic bomb." (Wallace was unconvinced and thought the agency would be under the thumb of the English.)[6]

In 1943 Dahl started working for British Security Coordination full-time and described his job as, "to try and oil the wheels between the British and the American war effort." He was a frequent guest of the Roosevelts and would ask informally what FDR or cabinet members thought about a variety of subjects and relay their off-the-record comments to Stephenson.

He also shared information with the prominent columnist Drew Pearson. On one occasion, details of Britain's Ambassador Lord Halifax's telegrams to London about the situation in India appeared in Pearson's *Washington Post* column. The Embassy didn't know the source of the leak and eventually London sent word to Stephenson to locate it. Stephenson designated Dahl to find it. Since Pearson was a friend, Dahl soon discovered the columnist's source was a person in the India High Commission. This served as an indication that future telegrams sent from Britain's Washington Embassy may not be safe and could also be compromised.

It appears Dahl may have previously discussed what he could say about the war with British Intelligence, before he was quoted in the past. A letter from the author William Stevenson to David Ogilvy says Dahl "checked with what he regarded as the proper authorities before talking on film. I know this, not from Dahl, but from the consulted."[7]

Dahl thought Stephenson had a brilliant mind. "There's no question about that," he said. "I mean the fact he became a millionaire about the same time as Beaverbrook and at about the same age, 27 or 28. Came over here and took over Pressed Steel for Christ's sake, at that age. Which is the Morris Works in Oxford. And it was not so easy to become a millionaire as it is today. He became rich as soon as he wanted to, more or less," he concluded. "And that was it."

Stephenson was always drawn to intelligence and intrigue. It was through his company connections he saw Hitler building up militarily, and he started informing Churchill who, Dahl thought, Stephenson didn't know at the time. "But he would have had a connection through Beaverbrook."

The connection could also have been through Desmond Morton.

"It could have been too, through there. But he didn't know Churchill personally then, I don't think. But he got the notes through. He got them through for patriotic reasons, number one, and secondly, with his absolute cleverness, he spotted Churchill as a future leader. Christ, he could have sent them to Chamberlain, but he didn't. Yes, he could have sent them to Halifax or Chamberlain. But they were both idiots, and he wouldn't have got anywhere," he said. "And he picked the right man to send them to, and Churchill, when he came to getting a chap for America said, 'This is the chap for me.' It was on that I'm sure. And I think Max Beaverbrook advised him to do it too, because they were both Canadians. He was a close friend, a really genuinely close friend of Beaverbrook. No question about that. I've been in Beaverbrook's house in Jamaica with him and they were absolutely like that," he said crossing his fingers. "A couple of Canadians, a couple of old Canadian millionaires, who were both pretty ruthless."

Toward the end of the war Stephenson wondered about Dahl's financial situation, and he gave him some investment advice the writer remembered. One day they were chatting in his office.

"Do you want to make some money?" Stephenson asked.

"Well, everyone does," replied Dahl.

"Do you have any?"

"Not much, I've got about £3,000 saved in England."

"Well, I'll tell you what to put it in," said Stephenson.

The spychief then told Dahl about an entirely new type of pen his agents in Argentina had found out about. "It's called the ball point," Stephenson said. "This is going to sweep the world."

The rights to the ball point pen were owned at the time by a small British aviation company and he advised Dahl to buy their stock. At the time the shares were worth about three shillings, and he put all of his money into the company.

"He was absolutely right about the ball point pen. He couldn't have been righter," Dahl recalled. "But the trouble was this little fucking company that had the patents sold out to another company, and the whole thing was fiddled and my company disappeared," he laughed. "So I lost all my money!" He keeled back on his chair. "The interesting thing was his intelligence was good. It must have been—it swept the world."

At the conclusion of the war Dahl was a fairly successful magazine and story writer. Stephenson wanted him to help write a history of British Security Coordination. Tom Hill was in charge of the operation and Grace Garner, Eleanor Fleming, Harry Smith and a few others packed up the files from the New York office and transported them in a convoy of vans to Camp X near Oshawa. "We don't dare to do it in the United States, we have to do it on British territory," Stephenson told Dahl. The reason being security. "You're going to open these things all over the bloody place. Room after room of God knows what. And you know he pulled a lot over Hoover particularly. He didn't pull anything over Bill Donovan. And he didn't want any of that seen. He pulled a few things over the White House too, now and again. It was secure, and he was protecting SIS anyway." Dahl didn't know if Stephenson pulled anything on Stewart Menzies, the head of Britain's SIS. "I wouldn't be surprised, but I wouldn't collaborate that at all," he said. "He was a schemer."

In Ontario, Dahl found the sorting and summarizing difficult. He was a fiction writer and didn't want to organize the files into a readable history. "I wrote a little bit of crap, and I said, 'Christ, I'm not going to do this, it's an historian's job,'" he recalled. "And I called Bill and I said, 'I'm packing this in, I can't write.' And he said, 'Okay, come on back'. And that was it. And this famous history of BSC through the war in New York was written by Tom Hill and a few other knocks."

Dahl thought the finished product was circulated to Members of Parliament and others. He had a copy for a period of time, but wasn't sure where he'd put it. He was surprised it had been leaked in the fall of 1989 to the *Washington Post* by the author William Stevenson.

Dahl was primarily in Washington during the war following his accident and knew the Roosevelts. He went to dinners at the White House and for weekends at Roosevelt's retreat at Hyde Park, New York. Mingling at the various gatherings, he met Cabinet Members such as Secretary of the Treasury Henry Morgenthau and Secretary of Commerce Will Clayton and others. The President took a liking to the young British Embassy attaché and Dahl drove around with the President alone in his specially designed car. Security men would carry Roosevelt to the driver's seat where the President operated the gas pedal and brakes from controls on the steering wheel.

"I was just a sort of clown for him in his relaxing time. I was just a young man, 26 or 27, who he found fun to talk to, when he wasn't doing business. That's all. Exciting for me, but not for him particularly."

"And he'd tell you what to tell Bill?"

"No! Never. Never," Dahl said. "I never got anything out of FDR. Nothing at all. I don't think he even knew I worked for Bill. I was sort of an attaché at the British Embassy. That's all he knew. He didn't care, I wasn't that important."

It's possible Dahl's value was not only liaison with the US official-dom, but general liaison—public relations. At the beginning of 1942, Anglo-American relations were at a low ebb and certain members of the US government thought foreign espionage services should not be allowed to operate on American soil. There was also a rising feeling in the US that Britain was 'sitting on her rifles' in the war; and the value of British lectures on 'London Can Take It,' and the exploits of the RAF in Europe were wearing thin in a country greatly concerned with the Pacific conflict. Stephenson sought opinion from a variety of sources on how to improve relations with the Americans. A February 10, 1942 paper from 'VW' in BSC's Washington Office to WSS had a number of ideas. The final suggestion:

"The appointment to Washington of a tough and invigorating personality, who would make an end of the present almost hermit-like seclusion in Washington, would be a step in the right direction, especially if he were not one of the official governing class, but more or less a man of the people, as there is reason to believe the President would desire. But the present decline in Anglo-American good understanding would not be checked if such a change were seen to be merely a political reshuffle or if the new appointment were not supported by a drastic reorganization of Cabinet Offices at home with a thorough burning-out of all dead wood."[8]

Not being of 'the official governing class,' it's possible one of Dahl's Washington assignments from Stephenson was to be an 'invigorating personality.'

The writer felt Stephenson kept everyone at arm's length in BSC, except John Pepper, and Pepper was the only person in on all of Stephenson's plans. (Pepper later denied this, but offered no elaboration.) The BSC chief often ask Dahl's opinion on things? "He used to confide in me a lot. And sit and chat. 'What will we do about this?' But I was very young."

The English writer knew nothing of Stephenson's background or that he had very little formal education. "You mean he was lowly educated? Well the old mind worked all right, I'll tell you that." But he questioned many of his ex-boss's reported achievements. He doubted if Stephenson was actually involved in scientific developments in the 1920's or whether he actually won medals during the First World War.

Newspaper clippings from a 1921 *London Daily Mail* which described Stephenson as a brilliant scientist, and a WW I Winnipeg newspaper clipping headlined: "Wins Military Cross," were available and shown to the writer. "No! I'm an old man. I don't want to see that crap." He then said Stephenson had likely planted the telegraphy information.

"I believe it. But I'm sure he disseminated that information. I'm sure he did. Yeah, I'm sure he did."

"He'd just got off the boat from Canada."

"Yes, but you misuse the words 'brilliant scientist' because he was never a scientist…

"No, he wasn't any brilliant scientist," he repeated. "You're getting yourself into —," he paused. "I'll tell you what's interesting, about what you're doing, which you should pin-point. You'll find contradictory statements everywhere you go about this man. Don't you? You do!" he said raising his voice. "And that's interesting, you see. And that's not to do with the fact he was in the Secret Service. It's to do with the man himself. I think."

Dahl was one of the few ex-employees who remained friends with Stephenson after the war, and he often received telegrams and telexes from him. "He never wrote letters." Dahl visited Stephenson in Bermuda and stayed with him there. But he hadn't seen the spychief since the early sixties following Stephenson's first stroke. He was shocked, as Stephenson's speech had been greatly effected. This was around the same time as Dahl's son Theo had a traffic accident. Dahl suggested Stephenson see his neurosurgeon, Sir Kenneth Till. The writer talked Till into going to Bermuda, all expenses paid, and treating his old boss.

Immediately following the stroke, Dahl was told Stephenson's survival was uncertain. Newspaper executive and former BSC liaison Ernest Cuneo said Stephenson appeared deathly ill after the stroke, and simply remained in bed most days, waiting to die. But one day Cuneo was at his bedside talking to him and all of a sudden, "just like that," Stephenson got up and went back to work. Cuneo told him, "We need you to fight the Reds, or something like that," Dahl remembered, and then Stephenson perked up.

Dahl said he learned nothing from Stephenson, "except what I disapprove of, the art of secrecy. He was a very secret man, like I've been saying. No, he was a totally uncultured man. Totally. His background would lead to that."

Music and the arts didn't seem to captivate Stephenson immeasurably. "He pointed at one painting he had in his New York flat, by well-known Canadian painter Cornelius Kreigoff, and said, 'Look at that. Look at that.' That's the only painter's name he'd ever heard of, I think. No, he was a totally uncultivated man. And, ah ... not a pleasure to talk to really. If you met him socially he never had any conversation at all, really. He talked to Max Beaverbrook about business. I think they probably had a ball talking about which companies they were going to take over, or bust or whatever. To ordinary people like us, he had no conversation at all. Absolutely none.

"He's an enigma all around. This man is an enigma. He was interested in business. And to him SIS was a business, but he was not interested in any of the arts at all. He was intrigued by writers, and he tended to hire writers to work for him. And you know perfectly well quite a few writers were working for him in New York."

Former members of BSC and the official history of the organization indicate the spy agency curried favour in the American media. Playwrights such as Eric Maschwitz, Benn Levy and historian Gilbert Hyatt worked for Stephenson. The playwright and author Robert Sherwood was present when Stephenson received his Medal of Merit from Bill Donovan. "Winchell?"

"Yeah, quite a few. Well. Winchell, he wasn't a writer, he was a fucking columnist… Winchell. Christ."

"Was Fleming writing then?"

"No, he wasn't."

"His brother was."

"Yes, Peter was writing then. Peter was writing. But he wasn't really working for him, Ian Fleming … I mean a whole bunch of people who said they worked for Bill weren't working for him. Noel Coward kept saying he worked for Bill, you know. Bill would ask him to do the tiny little things, because he passed through New York. And Noel Coward would go all over the place saying, 'I'm working for Bill Stephenson.' They all did that. I mean Coward made a huge thing of it." Dahl lowered his voice to a whisper, "And he'd turn up in the salons in London and say 'Now, shhh, You've heard of this chap Bill Stephenson.'

"You know it's true. Any celebrity that passed through, Bill would try to see. And he'd give them some piddly little thing. 'Where are you going?' Or, 'you're going to Africa for ENSA to act for the troops, why don't you find out what so and so is doing and give him something'. He got thrilled by it."

"How about Greta Garbo?"

"No, it's bullshit. The whole thing is bullshit. All those stories are bullshit. It's a very funny thing that a man with that kind of character is intrigued. It's a weakness. It's a weakness to be intrigued. Rich people are the most seductive of all. To most people. Most people are totally seduced by rich people. I mean look at Churchill and all those pricks.[9] Rich. Purely rich idiots."

Stephenson never flaunted his wealth the writer said, and he was one of the first people to spot the West Indies as a tourist resort. After the war he bought a house in Jamaica and told Beaverbrook about it, and eventually Noel Coward and Ian Fleming also bought there.

"How about his relationship with Fleming? Do you know anything about that?"[10]

"Yes, because I knew Fleming very well indeed. And there wasn't much. I'm quite sure."

"Fleming liked him though."

"Yes, of course, Fleming. Very well. Anything to do with secrets Fleming would like to use, himself.

"This man is a total enigma," Dahl continued. "And that's the interesting thing. He is an enigma. And how much wool did he pull over people's eyes, and how much truly good work did he do? But there's no question he did some truly good work."

Stephenson told Dahl during the war, that his greatest achievement was the destroyers for bases deal with Franklin Roosevelt. He recounted flying from New York to Washington to see FDR virtually every day and he negotiated the proceedings, 'on behalf of Winston.' "He said he did personally with FDR. Well, I always doubted, myself, if you want to know whether he had met FDR. I did."[11]

Stephenson had an extraordinary relationship with his wife, Dahl remembered. "He loved her and they had a very, very good marriage, I think. But, she was frightened of him." Stephenson and his wife, Mary, had a traditional relationship. She would fuss, and frequently bring her husband things, almost acting as a servant to him. "But they got on very well together."

Beaverbrook often talked about the women he'd slept with, but Stephenson never would. "He loved Mary." In fact Beaverbrook wouldn't talk about women the same way around Stephenson. "In a lot of ways Stephenson wasn't 'one of the boys' as they say," he said. "In a lot of ways he was a man apart."

Future advertising mogul David Ogilvy lived with Dahl for a time in

Washington and Dahl thought Ogilvy would have a lot to say about Stephenson. "You'll get every sort of theory under the sun from David. You would."

Stephenson is listed in one of Ogilvy's books *Blood, Brains, and Beer*, as one of his heroes, but he doesn't go into great detail about his assignments. "He was always going on about Gallup. He said Gallup's the answer to everything."[12]

It seemed apparent the organization employed numerous good people, and many had successful careers following their stint in British Security Coordination. "That wasn't Stephenson who lifted them up," Dahl said. "He didn't give them a hand.

"He used to pick people out and seduce them away from what they were doing, and into BSC. I mean he did that to me. I was just a simple air attaché in Washington, and I started playing the game he played with Winston, of sending him snippets of hot stuff. And when I got the sack from, ah—because I insulted a lot of Air Marshals and I sent word up to him, 'Look I'm getting going back home.' He said, 'Don't worry about it.' This did show power, I was impressed by the power he had then. Because I was a squadron leader and he said the moment you get home from seeing 'C,' or whatever it was, go and see so and so. I went and saw him and this chap said, 'You're going straight back to Washington as a Wing Commander, and you're going to work for Bill Stephenson.'

"I said, 'Well, all right. Thanks. That's nice.' And I did. The day I arrived back I was at a cocktail party in Washington with the Air Chief Marshall, who sent me packing because I insulted him. I'd actually revealed a crooked racket going on with Sir Richard Fairey, the aviation man, who was running a special airplane to take his friends across the Atlantic. So I got booted out by the big boys. I turn up at this party and this Air Chief Marshall strode up to me and said, 'Dahl, what the hell are you doing here? You're sent home!' I said to him, 'If you want to know what I'm doing here, you'll have to talk to Mr William Stephenson in New York.' He paused. And that was it."[13]

"He had a bit of power," Dahl continued. "I don't think he was ever in touch with Halifax. They were just two totally different people. In fact any Halifax stuff, I did it. He despised him. He was a different man,

Halifax was. A gentleman, a courtly English gentleman and Bill Stephenson..." he laughed. "And he moved very slowly indeed. And he engineered Munich and Christ knows what. And he had no time for Halifax at all."

On the Moon

Roald Dahl, the writer, served Intrepid after his Royal Air Force career was cut short in a Spitfire crash. Dahl reported from Washington in 1944: "You should know that the Americans are planning to land a man on the moon.

"Everyone thought that I was mad, but I never heard that Intrepid laughed."

About 25 years later, a telegram (from Stephenson) was delivered to Dahl's cottage in Buckinghamshire, England. It said: "Congratulations. You were right." It then quoted the serial number and date of Dahl's original memo."

—*Toronto Star*, May 27, 1979

When Dahl was questioned about the above he replied. "Your letter of July 25th. The story about me and Bill Stephenson and the men on the moon is totally true. That I can confirm."—Roald Dahl, letter to author, August 3, 1990.

■

John Pepper

Following the publication of *A Man Called Intrepid* John Pepper, who Dahl thought was in on Stephenson schemes, wrote to his ex-boss.

"INTREPID has become a household word in these Bahama Islands and I am basking in your well deserved and reflected glory. You're the most famous man I know, Bill. And I bet it's not doing your namesake any harm either. There must be a little in it for him. Will put him on the map as an author, too. He should be grateful for all you have done for him, but he can't be as grateful as I am for all you did for me. John AR Pepper."[14]

When this writer was able to locate John Pepper, he was living in the Bahamas and in Switzerland. He denied he was in on all of Stephenson's schemes. After the war he was one of the Vice Presidents of World Commerce, but says he was not involved in all the activities. He had seen the former spychief only a few times since the war. "I'll help you as long as it doesn't get involved with MI6," he said. A short time later he sent a one-sentence letter. "You know more about Sir William Stephenson then (sic) I do. Kindest regards, John Pepper."

Soon afterward he seemed to have moved from his Swiss home. Unfortunately, he didn't clarify why he was grateful to William Stephenson.

■

David Ogilvy

David Ogilvy was involved in economic warfare during the war, and although he often visited BSC New York, he was based in the British Embassy in Washington. One of his duties was to give the OSS reports from South America, as the United States had few resources in Latin America. His American contact was Francis Miller, who had been a friend of his aunt, Zoe Fairfield. He left Washington in 1945 and bought a farm in Pennsylvania. Toward the end of the war, he suggested former members of BSC get involved in a trading company. This eventually became British American Canadian Company and then World Commerce Corporation. Ogilvy thought the trading company would be a good idea, as "we all needed jobs in civilian life." Stephenson liked the idea and circulated copies of Ogilvy's paper to some of the wealthy people he worked with during the war, and some of them put up capital. "I am absolutely sure that nobody involved envisaged that the purpose of BAC was espionage," Ogilvy wrote. "I don't know who started this canard. Tripe." After a few months Ogilvy left the company as he became bored, and with some assistance from his brother Francis he got started in the advertising business.

Ogilvy thought Stephenson became an alcoholic after the war and as a result, some postwar publications were a "grotesque exaggeration of his achievements. It was probably booze that addled his brain.[15]

"I was devoted to WSS. A good leader. Laconic. Sense of humour. Ruthless. Loyal to his staff. Discreet in those days. More popular in Washington and Ottowa (sic) than in London.

His *worst* shortcoming was his inability to hire good people or see through bad ones."[16]

Ogilvy suggested reading Lord Dacre (Hugh Trevor-Roper) and Sir David Hunt to learn more about Stephenson's career.

18 Grace Garner

If anyone wanted to see Bill Stephenson in New York during the war, they had to go through his head secretary Grace Garner. She too, was from the Canadian prairies, born in Qu'Appelle, Saskatchewan and educated in Regina. Garner moved east, and for a time did some writing and editorial work for *Saturday Night* magazine in Toronto. In February 1941, after replying to a newspaper ad, she moved south and started working for the Allied war effort.

She first worked for the British Purchasing Commission at 25 Broadway in New York. The Commission was brought under the Stephenson umbrella, Garner says, and a small group of people evolved into British Security Coordination. The inner core of the organization at the time was Beryl Phillips, a cashier and principal secretary, a passport control officer, and a coding clerk. In the front office was a receptionist, Willie Wilson, and an assistant night guard. When Garner arrived, Stephenson's inner secretariat consisted of only three or four, and there were a handful of others. Then it began to grow. "Sir William had only come over in May 1940," she said. "He had the vision, and he saw, and probably a commission, as to what he was to build this organization up to." He soon moved the office to Rockefeller Center.

The purchasing commission had a nucleus of British people under contract to the Ministry of Economic Warfare and the Foreign Office, who were in charge of contracts and contacting suppliers. There were also Canadians working there. British Columbia businessman A J Taylor worked for the commission. Taylor, a business partner of Bill Stephenson, hired his daughter Kathleen to work as a secretary. Others followed from the west coast of Canada. Vivian Jones and Elizabeth Wood, who worked for Taylor's solicitor in British Columbia also joined the organization. "Those were the first three girls recruited. Then they began getting girls. Richard Coit's daughter who was in the coding department came in. Ellis's wife was also in the coding department.

Then they began bringing the girls down. Tommy Drew-Brook put an advertisement in, and word of mouth."

British Security Coordination emerged from the supply commission and a few other British Intelligence people. Bill Ross Smith was among the first in 1940, as was Dick Ellis, Richard Coit, and Walter Bell. "As far as Walter was concerned, our cover was British Passport Control," Garner said. "It was still on the front doors, British Passport Control."

Dick Ellis moved to Washington and became the senior man there. Barty Bouviere acted as the London and South American contact in the American capital. Peter Dwyer was the chief FBI liaison. Ivor Bryce was in Washington working with OSS people, but the DC group didn't get much bigger. "It was just a post office, really." The Americans were preoccupied by the Far East. "They were particularly concerned with China and Chiang Kai-Shek. That was one of their big concerns because the war in the Pacific was very big with the States. They were involved in that. It was their area of war, really, before they started the massing of troops for the onslaught of Europe."

Dolores Griffiths Hogg, a code officer, came down about the same time as Garner through Drew-Brook. Hogg, who was later transferred to Mexico, said her husband found a map while he was stationed there, about proposed Japanese plans to invade the United States through Mexico. "Yes, that was quite true, because you see they moved all the Japanese on the West Coast of the States and Canada. That was very possible," she said. Garner also knew Hogg's husband. "He was a second generation. His family had been in the consular service there before, and he was stationed down there in Mexico."

Although BSC's Washington office remained small, the New York organization began recruiting businessmen, police, journalists, lawyers, and hundreds of secretaries and coding people. BSC people worked with the similar sections of Britain's Foreign Office, Americans, Canadians and others. "The intelligence was gathered on all sorts of fronts," she said. "In formulating foreign policy you need to know about economics, as well as the effects on industry, and sources of supply, and so on and so forth. Well, that's mirrored in the organization." Nearly all BSC people were from Canada. "The easiest and quickest British subjects were from Canada. That's why we were brought in." Stephenson's friend

Tommy Drew-Brook did most of the recruiting, Garner says. He and his wife remained active in other areas. Often their house in Toronto was used as a stopping-off point for people going to the secret Camp X in Whitby or over to Europe. Much later Herb Rowland did some recruiting.

Most of the BSC employees were women, and when they first came to New York many would go to the Barbican, a women's residence. As the organization got bigger, Garner isn't sure how they were settled. "Probably Tommy Drew-Brook arranged for them—they shared flats." Recruits also came from the Canadian government. One report says Charles Vining, the president of the Newsprint Association of Canada, helped facilitate BSC connections to the Canadian government through his friendship with Defence Minister JL Ralston.[1] BSC also placed more advertisements in newspapers.

"They began to get girls recruited from the civil service in Ottawa, because you see, with one advertisement, I don't know how many people answered the ad. It was really through (Lester) Pearson and (Tommy) Stone and people in the civil service in Ottawa. He (Stephenson) wanted state secretaries and people who were skilled typists and office staff."

Stephenson also worked through External Affairs, as they were his closest Canadian contacts in the United States. Eventually all sorts of Canadians were united into the Stephenson organization. "They were bringing down Canadian girls of course. And not only that, the Canadian businessmen, all sorts. (Arthur) Purvis and (AJ) Taylor (in British Purchasing Commission). And then of course Tommy Stone used to go down to Washington and be Canadian Embassy liaison with the British Embassy. Later on, of course, there were the (military) service personnel, and Canadian Security, and the RCMP."

If someone asked Garner what she did, she told them she worked for the British Purchasing Commission. But she was seldom out to places where people could be inquisitive. "We didn't have much time for a social life. You didn't meet many people. People who came down from Canada to New York, and friends coming shopping or that sort of thing, they weren't very interested in what you did. They just said, 'oh, aren't you lucky you have a job in New York.'"

When Garner arrived in New York circumstances looked particularly grim for Britain. The United States was still not fully in the conflict and Nazi U-boats were cutting the supply line to Europe. "You see, they were used to bring over food, and there was a very severe crisis in the beginning. Late '41, '42 when we were losing so many ships it was dreadful. We had torpedoes right into the Bay of Tampa around by Florida, and the trade between New York and the South American ports, Rio and Montevideo.

"That's where Bill Ross Smith came in, because those crews, you see were South American Germans. There were an awful lot of Germans in South America, particularly in Rio and Argentina. Montevideo was quite British, but the others had a lot of Germans and German crews."

BSC faced an uphill battle in a pre-Pearl Harbor America. The United States had no corresponding intelligence network to deal with. Not only was the United States neutral, there were strong anti-British sentiments. With Stephenson's assistance, an American organization began to evolve.

"David Bruce was one of Donovan's first recruits," she remembered. "They were in the same law firm. One chose one's nearest, most trusted friends. Because at that time, you had to be very, very careful of the Americans, because there was so much anti-British feeling. The America First, and there was also the large Central European first generation immigrants there. Germans, Swedes, Yugoslavs, Poles, the lot. There was a terrible anti-British feeling, the Hearst newspapers, and so on. But the irony of it is, after he (Stephenson) moved out of the St. Regis, he moved into the penthouse that Hearst had for Marion Davies in West 53rd Street.

"William Randolf Hearst and the *San Francisco Examiner* and others were terribly anti-British. Lindbergh was very anti-British. He had hero status.

"(Adolf) Berle was one of those conviction politicians. But they were only some of the people. There were these bunds, the German bunds. Middle America was largely populated by the central Europeans who went into the coal mining, in central Pennsylvania and Ohio and places like the that.

"Spanish (immigrants) were in pockets of California and Texas and later when they came up from Cuba, but at that time they were not the significant racial strains that you think of in the American melting pot. So that was one of the things that you had to constantly defeat or try to alter. You couldn't bring the Americans into the war with the strength of the anti-British feeling."

Inside the Office

Garner didn't remember any precautions taken at the office for security reasons. "Well, I wasn't given a course, or anything like that. But you were pretty wary if you had any sense." One of the rules was not to have an American boyfriend. One woman married a US Marine and had to resign. In the office however, the security seemed relaxed. "They all came through a perfectly open security thing and we had an awful lot of people in the outside office.

"But to be quite honest, we didn't think about—it wasn't in the days of hijacking and gangsterism like now. One knew that you probably would be followed, if people knew. I dare say we were all marked people, because you went up and down. I remember the Bulova Watch Company had the floor above us, the 37th floor because we had 36 and 38 and it used to amuse us because these girls were always beautifully dressed, and looked like the girls behind perfume counters. They were all beautifully groomed and everything, had Bulova watches. To get on the elevators in the morning, they always won—shoved and pushed in and we would always be the last people and this would make us rather annoyed.

"As Ellis says in the foreword there, it's amazing the cover for British Security Coordination was maintained for so long. The Americans were naive too. I mean, they wouldn't know. They must have seen this organization growing, but they didn't know what we did. They were not particularly curious. I think they'd be much more curious in Europe than they would be in the States and Canada. As I told you we had the Bulova Watch Company above us and we had all these girls who all worked at Bulova and they all used to get into the elevators before we did. They were good tough Brooklyn cookies who could elbow their way in, you know. But I don't think it ever occurred to them that—why are all these ... (Canadians) ... what are they doing? You know, it wouldn't rouse so much suspicion. We were much the same."

Stephenson was very observant of the proceedings outside the building, and in the corridors. "Patek Phillipe, the famous Swiss watch people, had an office near us and I think Sir William knew something about them. I think he might have even recognized people he'd seen in Switzerland and so on." One morning Stephenson arrived at the office and told Garner, "Get Hall." He thought he recognized a Swedish agent lingering at the foot of the elevators. "Now Hall was a New York private eye," Garner said. "He was a real Dashiell Hammett character. He was a photographer and a personal investigator, and that. A big, burly chap ... He was a very nice man, and we used to get him to do, you know, sort of discreet jobs, and he knew a lot of characters." Garner couldn't reach Hall so she took the elevator down to check out the agent herself. She hung around the window of a lingerie shop downstairs and looked for suspicious people. "I saw this chap who had dark, rather darkish skin, swarthy and he had on a black and white tweed coat. A tall chap. He was hanging around for a while. Finally he went out on the doorway that led through to the Radio City Music Hall." She returned upstairs, told Stephenson she couldn't get Hall and described the possible agent to him. "He said, 'Yes that's him,' and sent a telegram right away. He had spotted him as an agent because he'd known him."

"Although Sweden was neutral, Swedish ball bearings and Swedish ore and Swedish things were very important in the war. I always understood Sweden was much more pro-German. They were pro-market wherever they could sell. Swedish steel is the finest. Surgical instruments are made with Swedish steel. Yes, a very high standard."

"What would he have been doing there?"

"I have no idea." The cable Stephenson sent simply reported the Swedish agent was in New York she recalled. Stephenson spent time in Sweden before the war. "There was an incident in Sweden I do believe is true. Ellis more or less confirmed that, when he and a man in Sweden escaped. It was some incident about ball bearings, some shipment of ball bearings that were very crucial that were lost. It's in the midst of my memory as something I had been told."

The nimble-fingered staff of the lingerie shop downstairs were put to work by at least one BSC employee. "We had a girl who rather took things easily, and she worked with another girl in Coit's office and her job was to wrap up the papers for the diplomatic bag, which you put in a pile in brown paper and they were wrapped up in string. They used to be sealed with sealing wax, and they had the official British Embassy seal. Dorothy Markus, that was her name. Dorothy was a girl who was mad keen on underwear and things like that. She used to spend her noon hour going down (stairs). She became very friendly with the girls in the (lingerie) shop down there, as she couldn't be bothered doing the parcel up. She used to take the contents of the diplomatic bag downstairs and they'd wrap it up for her and she'd bring it upstairs. I mean this innocent child. I mean the whole thing is a hoot. That's the kind of thing ... Now it's killingly funny, I think."

One of Garner's tasks was to line up Stephenson's appointments. Many prominent people came through, "From Mountbatten down or up. We had the famous meeting of Craig, Stratton and Moll. They were MI5 officers who came over to inspect the security of the United States. That was immediately after Pearl Harbor. We had very senior personnel. Bomber Harris came over. We had a lot of Air Force personnel, Chiefs of Staff. Senior people. On their way to Washington, they would come and talk to Sir William. They went to Washington to liaise with the military people and so on who were perfectly 'en clair.' Then we had all sorts of specialist people came over. Then they began to recruit. We also had SOE. When they began to get these people, which was before America entered the war, they were looking for UK nationals or European nationals to infiltrate into Europe and one of the heads of the department who did that was a man named Halpern, AJ Halpern. He was a Russian, an international lawyer. In those days people worked under alias. They had two names.

"We began to get people to staff that organization, at the same time we also had various Fleet Street journalists." Journalists Sydney Morrell and Doris Sheridan, who had been with the *Daily Express*, came over to work with British Information Services. "This was propaganda, or at least putting forth the British case. Sheridan liaised with the Arab sections in New York, keeping in touch with foreign nationals. The English playwright Eric Maschwitz was recruited to write propaganda and scripts. University professor Bill Deakin worked for the office, as well as the philosopher A J Ayer. There were also bankers—Berings of Berings Bank and Sir Charles Hambro." Stephenson also saw many people in Washington who didn't come to New York.

Garner remembered meeting Lord Beaverbrook at the Waldorf Astoria, "the end of 1943, and the beginning of the V-1's and V-2's. He was at the Waldorf Astoria with (AJ) Balfour and (Del) Maysfield, who later became head of British Airways. Sir William seconded me to go over to his suite in the Waldorf Astoria to do some secret—to do some typing and things for them." At the time flying bombs, the V-1's, were attacking southern England. "They used to have daily cables about how the bombs would come, and where they had landed. Beaverbrook used to be wandering in the corridors, and every time he saw me he said, 'Good evening.' No matter what time of the day it was."

One article in the *Times*, after Stephenson's death, said there is no proof Stephenson ever met Beaverbrook, "let alone Churchill."[2] Garner says this is ridiculous. "Don't forget that Beaverbrook was one of the many Canadians over here, who were all in it. Their various interests, the cement, Beaverbrook's cement is where he made his fortune in Prince Edward Island. Stephenson in cement and Pressed Steel. The Canadian Pacific Railways, the big banks, the stock exchange. It was a time when Canada mattered. There was a time, before the satellites and planes, and that sort of thing when the CPR, the CNR, the Canadian banks, particularly the Bank of Montreal, the stock exchange, the Winnipeg Grain Exchange was one of the great things of the world. You know those were times when Canadians had a significance. To say that he didn't know Beaverbrook, is like saying you don't know your own aunt or uncle. Yes, I have seen Lord Beaverbrook."

As the organization grew it handled not only the incoming of the press, the Ministry of Information, and government officials, but technical people as well. The atomic scientist JD Bernal, a professor at Cambridge, came through the office. According to Anthony Boyle's *Climate of Treason*, Bernal was a committed Marxist.

"He could have been a Marxist," Garner said. "There was a great deal of feeling among scientists that they should change these views before the war. That science is international. You know (Alan) Nunn May and those, always made their defence that until the hostilities broke out, what was found to be the truth was for the whole scientific world. I think most of them probably were (Marxists)." Bernal was a dead ringer for Harpo Marx. "You could have walked him straight onto the set. Wild. He had a funny hat on, and this saggy, greeny old coat on, bulging with documents." She gave him some American money as he had none, and he insisted on going to Washington as quickly as possible.

BSC kept files on individuals and a black list on people to watch. Harford Hyde's job was very important, she said. BSC had people in Bermuda, Trinidad and in South America linked to censorship. When people travelled or emigrated to the Western Hemisphere, by air from Europe, they flew from Lisbon and stopped over in Trinidad or Bermuda to refuel. When the planes landed, censorship offices in Trinidad and Bermuda went through the passenger lists, which were cabled before-hand from the offices in Lisbon or known departure points. This was cross-referenced with a watch list of suspect characters. For example, the fashion designer Elsa Schiaparelli was suspected of smuggling essential oil, Garner says. "They knew pretty well who to watch, and what they were doing. So they would be taken and interrogated ... And they would talk to prominent business people who were coming over and so on.

"Wren, Leonard Silverston, Mary Graham and Angela Drew were in Trinidad. Those people all worked with him, on assessing the sensitive cable intercepts and interrogation or route because Bermuda and Trinidad were the two transit stops for the planes."

The intelligence that was gleaned from the travellers was sent to the New York office, where it was checked with registry files. They would act on the ranks of names, update the files and possibly alert people, and follow up on the new information. A section of women oversaw the files. Dall Hunty, a Briton, was the first. She brought over the original system from the central registry in England. She was succeeded by the secretary of a high-ranking air force official, who was replaced by a Canadian woman, Meryl Cameron.

Stephenson was surrounded by a secretariat of Garner, Eleanor Fleming, and Eleanor Little. As well he had another group that handled much of his personal coding which included Charmaine Manchee, Marion de Chastelain, Elizabeth Hunter, Kathleen Taylor and Patsy Sullivan. Because of the difference in time zones, some worked shifts and there could be activity around the clock. Garner didn't work shifts, although usually she came in at 7 am and didn't leave till about eight in the evening. "We just worked until we more or less finished." There were also three very competent switchboard operators, Garner says, who always seemed able to make swift connections. BSC's phone numbers were unlisted, but British Passport Control was in the book.

Bill Donovan was in frequent contact with Stephenson. "The Americans were supplying Chiang Kai-Shek and they were taking it 'over the hump' into China. And who knows what happened in there. So it took a lot of people to keep in touch with the Far East and that's where a branch of Donovan's organization was very active because of the Americans' interest in the Pacific. Increasingly a number of SOE people came in and because they were connected with all sorts of people in the field."

Stephenson's connection with Donovan, like Hoover, was also through Gene Tunney, she believed. "Sir William had known him anyway, but Donovan was also well-known. I remember him coming, a very shy man, very nice, very modest man coming to see Sir William in those first early days." Tunney didn't come in but he did a lot of good work for BSC countering defeatism. "You see, after I first went there, we had the fall of Singapore and the sinking of the Prince of Wales. We had a series of the most terrible, terrible things. A series of disasters and people felt that Britain was going to lose. And you had to try and counter that, build up confidence and get the arms. You know, as Churchill says, 'Give us the tools and we'll finish the job,' and Roosevelt's famous fireside chats. And there were these articles that were put in the press."

Garner remembers the activities of the BSC agent 'Cynthia' soon after her arrival in New York. "Marion de Chastelain was brought in to be a liaison between John Pepper, masterminding under Sir William's direction, who was managing this 'Cynthia' operation. What they wanted to get was the Italian Airlines. They wanted to get them out of commission. And also we had the Free French. Don't forget we had that little problem. You see Hayes (French Ambassador) and those people were very anti-British. So Marion used to go down as a courier to Washington and deliver messages and instructions to 'Cynthia', and that's how she was very useful because she could be very discreet, a very sophisticated girl." Garner's friend Elizabeth Wood also met with 'Cynthia,' she said.

Roald Dahl came over in about 1943, after he was invalided in an air crash. For a short time he was Stephenson's personal assistant. "Then I think he got rather bored with that and moved back to Washington where he liaised in Washington for a short while. He wasn't in the New York office very much." Later he was in Oshawa to help write the history, but he didn't write much. "I think he was too much of a butterfly." David Ogilvy was in the Ministry of Economic Warfare attached to the embassy in Washington and he came to see Stephenson. "He used to swing his legs on the edge of my desk and talk to me. He was a chef on the Majestic, with his stories of Paris restaurants and that sort of thing. He was a fascinating man. A great deal of charm." Economic warfare dealt with the constriction of supplies and contraband. "Seeing that people were keeping to the rules."

Gilles Playfair did general propaganda and he also contributed to the BSC history after the war. "He rewrote … after Highet's draft was delivered to him. And Christopher (Wren) and a man called Friend were brought over during the war, because they were injured and out of the army. He first went to Trinidad as a Passport Control officer and censorship and he did what Hyde did in Bermuda and that was to interrogate these people as they crossed over. Then he came to New York and he was in charge of that and Gladys Silverstone and Mary Graham. They used to assess the reports and sift out the names that were on the wanted list or people who were interesting. These people came from all over Europe and they would tell how conditions were and that sort thing, but also searched for money and any contraband they were carrying. He returned to civilian life after.

"Peter (Dwyer) was with Friend and he was to liaise with the FBI. He would have been able to tell you, not only about Bill Stephenson. He would be able to tell you about the FBI. He worked very closely, particularly with the Washington FBI. He was in a bad train crash and very fussy, he always had to have a seat in the middle of the train."

Playwrights Ben Levy and Eric Maschwitz, and Bill Deakin all came at the same time. They were recruited through the Ministry of

Information and worked with public relations and newspaper people. "They knew people. That's the sort of thing. We had people who could help counter things."

"Walter Winchell?"

"Oh yes. Walter Winchell became very important. The contact for Winchell was an international lawyer (Ernest Cuneo) and "the mouthpiece for the CIO" (the labour organization). The lawyer was up on gossip and celebrity. "He knew everybody." Cuneo told her he once took a two-week holiday in 1935, and he missed a lot when he was away. "He could never catch up on the weeks he'd been away. He knew Walter Winchell and the rendezvous for them was the Stork Club, this famous night club. Every celebrity went there. Walter Winchell used to have a table every night and at lunchtime and he would see all the celebrities and get all the gossip. He would be given stories and inside information on what was happening in Britain and so on and so forth. Very influential and a good friend.

"Drew Pearson was not a good friend. Drew Pearson was anti-British and much more critical. And Berle was definitely anti."

Garner thought stories of BSC agent Dennis Paine trying to denigrate Berle were probably true. "All sorts of things could be done to embarrass an agent. Maschwitz was writing a paper on all the things you could do." It has been referred to as operation Vic. "There were all sorts of things you could do, telephoning people in the middle of the night, sending anonymous letters to their wife. They even had a colouring, giving people something to drink making them urinate blue. And they'd think something's terribly sick. Pranks! Yes they were up to that sort of thing. Yeah, it was very funny. You couldn't take that seriously. These were the sort of harassing things."

She remembers Paine thought he was doing a good turn by trying to get the dirt on Berle. This ended up being an embarrassment and he was whisked, within the hour, over to Canada, because the FBI would have been after him. "I only knew he'd overstepped the markers. I could only tell you what I heard at the time which was, as far as I knew, that was the case. It could have been an FBI plant. There were other things they got up to."

There was some tension between the FBI and BSC. "For no other reason than we were operating in another country, a foreign country. It was their province and the FBI was very proud. Hoover built up this huge organization. They were responsible for gangsters and security of every kind and he was a megalomaniac anyway. He was an empire builder."

Garner didn't meet Hoover, although he was in New York all the time, she says. Stephenson usually met with the FBI's New York man Percy (Sam) Foxworth and Garner often spoke to him on the phone. On one occasion Foxworth couldn't make a meeting with Stephenson at a hotel. The spychief couldn't be publicly paged and Stephenson waited about a half hour before returning to the office on the subway.

Foxworth died in a Caribbean plane crash early in 1943. Garner believes he was shuttling secret information to American general Mark Clark in North Africa. The plane crash was an accident, Garner says, "it had very far-reaching effects because it delayed the operation."

Stephenson was briefed on such overseas operations. "I think when he got that information, it didn't come through on a cable, it was when he was briefed in England, or maybe at the Embassy from the Joint Staffs. I don't know because he used to go down to these meetings. But that would not be for us to pass on."

Garner met Ian Fleming, who was with the director of Naval Intelligence (DNI) Admiral Godfrey. She also met Mountbatten a few times, who was with Robert Harling. (Harling later wrote a few books and became the editor of *House and Garden*). "Mountbatten would not come to the office frequently. Fleming came in from time to time, and of course they were both so good-looking that just like dominoes the girls would go down—whoosh, like that."

Mountbatten was organizing his post to South East Asia and India, she said. "They went out to Singapore and so on, after the fall of, after the Americans came into the war. That's when Fleming was there, but he certainly did come into the office and I remember seeing the Minox camera (miniature spy camera) and things like that. Very affable, very amiable."

Bill Ross Smith was very active with Ship's Observers—especially before Pearl Harbor—because of heavy ship traffic, the Grace Line, and fruit boats that plied the West Coast of the United States down to South

America. "They were manned by every nape—all sorts of characters, a lot of Germans, and they used to go into these German ports and so on." Garner remembers on one occasion Ross Smith attempted to get a sailor onto a ship and down the hall, Richard Coit was trying to get the same man off the same ship. "They were international characters." One strange thing they watched for was secret information being transmitted under butterfly wings. "They used to have magnificent brilliant blue butterflies, that were native to Brazil, I think. There was quite a trade in making paper weights or framed pictures out of these beautiful butterflies and then to put them in a gold frame. Well somebody had the idea that the German agents were putting messages under the butterfly wings of these pictures."

Colonel Louis Frank, a Belgian banker, was brought over. "Sir William said, 'Tell so-and-so he's the greatest arbitrage expert in the world. I never heard the word arbitrage, and I thought it was arbitration. So I told somebody, I think it was actually Foxworth, somebody high in the FBI, he was the greatest arbitration expert in the world. That was a boo-boo. But he was famous for that. He was a great banker. He came over. He headed the SOE operation in New York. He was in charge of international finance. They were the people who could block bank accounts, transfer funds and all that sort of thing."

The astrologer Louis de Wohl was brought over from Britain. He had a big following in the daily papers, and propaganda people thought they could bring him over to the United States as an authority and tell him what to predict. He didn't come to the office, but Garner was aware of his set-up in Washington. "He was very expensive. He demanded to have suites of rooms and so on. There was a very beautiful lady sent over to be his sort of hostess in front ... he didn't last very long. That was one of those Eton prankster 'think-ups.'

"Vincent Astor was attached with OSS, just as they had David Bruce, the Rockefellers, the wealthy people that they brought in. Because they knew them and they had contacts all over the world, and so on. He was not an anti-person, he was pro."

Lord Leathers was around. "He was one of Beaverbrook's people. He was in Ministry of Supply also. He was on the Embassy side."

James Roosevelt, the President's son, did a few things in the way of propaganda for Britain, and he appeared at meetings. "He was not anything sinister or secret jobs." He could have also acted as a courier, but she doesn't recall him in the office. "I know Sir William saw him. He was in the very early days."

Nelson Rockefeller may have given BSC a break on the rent at Rockefeller Center Garner said, but she was unaware of a formal agreement. "It could possibly be that was one of the things that was a concession to Britain. And Sir William might have very well negotiated that, because when they first came over, they were operating from this little office down on Wall street. The Passport Control used to be on Wall Street near the docks. It was there because of passports, near the Statue of Liberty, and the shipping offices. The British Purchasing Commission was down on Wall street and also Bill Ross Smith's Ship's Observers scheme—Sir Connop Guthrie used to head that. That was an MI5 proper thing, and Sir William knew that was perfectly inadequate for what he wanted, so he took this space in Rockefeller Center. The whole of the 36th floor. So it was very possible that Sir William, through his various contacts, decided this would be the move and approached them."

Herb Rowland came down from Canada as an administrator and personnel man. "He was not in any way a diplomat or engaged in agents or anything like that."

She remembered Zoltan Korda, a set designer who worked designing camouflage, but she was unaware of Stephenson's precise involvement with movie studios. "I only know that I got plane seats for (Alexander) Korda. He was in the office. I got a plane seat and cigars for Korda. I remember one day Sir William sent me over to Dunhill to get some cigars for him. A certain kind of cigars. I came back in a panic and said, 'Sir William, they're six dollars each!' He roared with laughter and he said, 'Oh yes.' So he got a case," she laughed.

Allen Dulles moved into Rockefeller Center after Pearl Harbor. "He was one of Donovan's first appointees. He was another lawyer. Later he was to head the postwar Central Intelligence." John Foster Dulles, his brother, was on Roosevelt's staff. "He was not a great friend of England."

Garner recalls Neils Bohr, the Danish atomic scientist who was spirited away from occupied Europe, but doesn't remember BSC's involvement. "I remember the name Bohr. I remember him being an atomic scientist in the early days. I remember there was something in the file. Vessel used to carry valuable materials and VIP's from Sweden. Yes, I remember about that. It was very early on."

Tom Hill came down about 1942. He was brought in when BSC needed a lot of desk people, but she doesn't remember the details. "They worked on various programs, either working on information with Middle East or whatever they were doing but he was brought in and worked with a man called Patterson." She didn't recall BSC's Western Hemisphere Weekly Intelligence Bulletin, which Hill edited. "It was probably one of the things they put out through the propaganda."

Cedric Belfrage was brought in as one of the propaganda people." He was a known communist." John Paul Evans was brought in and worked for Halpern's staff. "A very nice chap. There's a chap called Dan Hedical. I always think of the two together. The recruitment of aliens.

"Rex Benson was the attaché in Washington. He was very nice. He was the stockbroker over here. He was a very urbane man.

"H (Henry) A Benson was SOE's second-in-command in New York. He was a nasty piece of work. He was a nasty sort of a miserable little nit-picking man.

"Gilbert Highet was again in propaganda with Belfrage in the same offices, before Pearl Harbor. He was an historian at Columbia. A very nice man. And he wrote one of the first drafts of the history of British Security Coordination. Tom Hill compiled and administered the compilation of it. I don't think he wrote a lot of it."

When she started there were a few English secretaries at the office, and Garner didn't consider them workaholics. "I complained to Mr Taylor one day, Kathleen Taylor's father, about the money. We were paid quite generously, but the English girl my co-secretary and the other girl were getting quite a lot more. And I mean, they worked sort of on the Foreign Office system. You know what I mean. They had 'Pending Baskets.' I'd never heard of a 'Pending Basket' in my life, and they'd never answer the telephone. They'd let it ring two or three times and they'd hang it. Well anyway, so I said to Mr Taylor, 'Look, I know it's their war but...' Well he fell about, he ran into Sir William like a scalded cat and told him and the two of them were killing themselves laughing. But then, sobering down, Sir William I think he thought, well that's the attitude of these people, you see. They think, well ... it's ... they had the feeling that the British let it happen."

"How do you mean?"

"I mean I could never understand why the British seemed to be so unprepared. If you'd read anything, you knew from the build-up of Hitler and that sort of thing, that it was going to be inevitable and you see with the fall of Dunkirk and that sort of thing, it looked as though it were an accident waiting to happen." She was told there was British intelligence about the rise and military buildup of the Nazis, but it was either not believed, or vetoed by people such as Sir Neville Henderson, Britain's Ambassador to Berlin. "Ellis was over there, and I said to Ellis, why did they not know about Hitler. And he said, 'Oh, we sent them the reports.'

"And the other thing was the attitude of the British officers was very—I don't think they put their back into it."

"In North America? Or all over?"

"No, no, no. I'm only speaking of my own organization. Some of them worked hard but a lot of it was ... well, the English work in a different way. When I came over here, you could never go into an English office to interview somebody and start right in. You had to ask sort of how their family are, or some conversation and then you get down to it. And they would for instance, just a small thing, but on Sundays they would come in casual clothes. I felt some of the English secretaries didn't work the same, with the same sort of drive, should I say. They were very knowledgeable and carried the dignity of the English office and so on. They were ladies, and people and so on. And they weren't having any upstart girls who were whiz on the typewriter, but didn't know that Jack Barkley was the world's largest importer of Rolls Royce cars. You know. We didn't know that. But when we came, we didn't ask people where you could see the Indians. After all, people weren't so well-travelled.

"People only used to get two weeks holiday. How do you get over to Europe? People didn't have the money to travel. It wasn't within the means of people. It was a big thing. Students, Rhodes scholars, academics, business people, and so on. People didn't travel to that extent."

"So there was a real cultural shock, almost."

"Not so much shock, after all one was well-read. I remember being brought up on *Girl's Own Manual*, *Boy's Own Manual* and English novels and all that sort of thing, but it's not the ambience, people living in a very sophisticated, multi-cultural."

"So they viewed North Americans differently?"

"Yes. Because we had the North American work ethic. For instance they used to have afternoon tea in the office when Sir William first came there. There was a young office boy who was outside, a sort of 'dog's body.' That's an English expression. He was the dog's body for the Passport Control people and he used to bring around a tray of tea, and one day he dropped the tray outside Sir William's office. Crash, bang. Well that was the end of the tea. And there was no more tea. Nobody was going to have a cup of tea in the afternoon," she laughed.

Garner talked with Noel Coward on the phone a few times, when he stayed at the Waldorf Astoria. On one occasion she helped him get a visa for the United States. Coward had been in Cairo and visited American wounded at a hospital there, and officialdom were unsure of comments he was making—viewing them as possibly coded or defeatist. In Africa, Coward "talked about the American boys who were sick for home, amid the alien corn," she remembered. "The Americans didn't know the reference to that." When they received the telegram at BSC, Garner knew what Coward was talking about. "I said to Sir William, 'that's the *Ode to a Nightingale*'. She and Alex Halpern decided the poet. "I said of course, it was Keats, and they asked me to recite it… that's the wonderful thing, 'when the sad, sick for home, she stood in tears and stayed in the alien corn.'[3]

"You know the poem—its absolutely lovely, well anyway, they took it out of context." Eventually Coward was allowed to come to the United States, and he did a few things for Stephenson. "He was a propagandist and he was used, like a lot of people, just to go around to cocktail parties and go around and spread the word. That was all. He was a glamorous figure." At the parties Coward would build up the Allied cause and try to counter defeatism. "They just go on talking to people and say: 'The Germans win? Go on. Not bloody likely.' You know, that sort of thing."

Stephenson was continually seeing people. "He was a par excellent listener," she said. "You know the old saying, 'A wise little owl sat on an oak. The more he heard, the less he spoke, the less he spoke, the more he heard. Why can't we all be like that bird?' Well, that was Sir William."

External Planning

Stephenson made numerous trips across the Atlantic during the war. He was in Britain before the ill-fated landings at the Dieppe raid. One report of the Dieppe raid was that the Allies tried to capture Axis radar information. "It could have been," Garner said. "It could have been to test the radar, to test the German, how sensitive, how good they were. You see people forget things like Mulberry, the invention of the Mulberry docks, the invention of all that sort of thing."

Stephenson attended the Quebec conference. "I think he was at the Atlantic Conference, but I couldn't say whether he was at Yalta or Potsdam, because I can't be sure. But I do know that he went over at, or around, the time of the Conferences, to London." She knows he was in Quebec because she had to put together a number of files for shipment to Canada for it. "We took the documents to the Pennsylvania Station, which were left on the top of the filing cabinet. They were supposed to have gone with the others. We suddenly discovered them and tore down in a taxi, Sydney Morrell came to hold the gates and they held the train until we pushed them through." Garner didn't go to the conference herself, but she went to Quebec afterward.

Garner learned many code words during the war, but was unaware of the operations.

"You would hear the code word, but it didn't mean anything to you. I remember one was Cossack. I remember a telegram came through: 'Get in touch with Cossack Morgan.'" (In the middle of 1943 the Allies set up a headquarters for the planned invasion of Europe. Its head was General Frederick Morgan and he was known as COSSAC Morgan, from the initials Chief of Supreme Allied Command. The first operation of the group was to plan the feigning of an attack on the continent.)[4] "And I said to Sir William, 'That's a funny name, a funny pen name for Morgan.' I thought it would be a pirate, or a Dead-eye Dick sort of thing, because you think of Pirate Morgan. And there was deathly silence. I knew that I stepped on a mine. But that was the operation to deceive the Germans on the exact landing of the D-Day landing."

"From Calais?"

"Cossack was the name of the operation. And Torch (invasion of North Africa) was a very secret word."[5]

Stephenson travelled across the Atlantic at least twice a year. "Well I came in March '41. And he went over that November, or December. He went over in the winter time, I remember. And he went early in the Spring or beginning of '42. He went at least eight times when I was there, probably more. Not all that often."

Stephenson is quoted as saying he went to Europe over forty times during the war. "Well, I don't think he went that often. He came over in '40. He probably made three or four trips before I came along. He probably went over, to report back on the thing, and so forth. Travel to Europe was not easy. He had to go to Quebec and across by bomber." Stephenson didn't travel on regular flights, because of scheduling and security. She made some arrangements and recalled one he made with Desmond Morton and Alexander Cadogan. "They were not easy, comfortable flights. They had to have oxygen, and it was cold." Numerous couriers leaving BSC went on regular flights with diplomatic bags.

Stephenson was in New York when the bombing of Hiroshima and Nagasaki took place.

"Would he have known that those were coming?"

"I think probably he would. He would have known about the planning. Once the Germans had been defeated in Europe, they had to concentrate on the other. And there was the question of whether they slugged it out to the last man or ... I think the strategy, he would have been party to that."

"How about the destroyers for bases deal? Do you think Bill had much to do with that?"

"I think he had a role in that. He was in that, I think, through (AJ) Taylor and probably (Arthur) Purvis—through the Purchasing Commission. And the Foreign Office would be making deals, after trading the Atlantic bases, would be like the Falklands. You give away a base for ninety-six years. No, he certainly had an influence on what the needs were."

December 7, 1941

Stephenson's office moved twice. One move was into the Japanese Consulate after Pearl Harbor. "That was a fascinating story, the day that happened, Sunday. When we went home that night I was literally shin deep in flash bulbs from the photographers.

"They'd been standing outside and waiting for the Japanese Ambassador to come down. And we went down about 9 o'clock at night, because we were very busy. We had to wade through these broken flash bulbs. They got out in 24 hours, 48 hours at the most, and Sir William had arranged to have their offices, and they were on the 38th floor two floors up. In the meantime, this famous man Professor Bayly came over... he was to be in charge of our communications, the coding machine, and the transmission of the actual messages. Because at this time the traffic was very large. At first it was through Western Union, then it was still Western Union, but it had to be handled in a much bigger way than just writing telegrams and sending them. So Sir William had the vision to take offices on the 35th floor, with Bayly in charge. He had two or three people, a man called Maidment, a very, very nice Englishman, and there were people who actually vetted the things coming in and out.

"When we went up to the 38th floor, we still retained the 35th because there were huge installation of machines. When we went up, there were stamp marks for the Japanese passport on the wall, and they even had a temple in the corner of their office, which had become our office. They had a Shinto temple built in the corner.

"It was about 11 o'clock in the morning. I remember Sydney Morrell, the *Daily Express* newspaperman, to the last. He came in on a Sunday and I remember, I could see what he was wearing, and everything. He had a long strip of the telex machine and he came in to see Bill. Bill wasn't there, he was off seeing Kathleen Taylor's father, and he didn't come back until about 5 in the afternoon, because they were incommunicado. He came and we had to get the two Japanese experts. It was a weekend. I had to bring them in and then of course, that changed the whole thing. Then he was down in Washington, and of course once the Americans came into the war it was a different ball game, because then you had quite different priorities."

One of Churchill's and BSC's wishes was to get the Americans involved in the fight against fascism, but Garner says there was no outward elation at the office. "We were very sober. It was a day of sadness after all, it was a terrible disaster for the Americans, not only loss of life, but for their morale. And the fact they were caught napping and all this."

Certain documentaries and books imply more people knew an attack was going to take place than has been publicly acknowledged. "There are certainly things which one doesn't talk about, and there are actual recorded incidents of what happened."

"Roosevelt was pro-British."

"Yes. And Donovan was a good ally. Oh yes, without a doubt. Donovan recruited very top people, like David Bruce who later became ambassador. A very charming man. And the Americans became very much involved in the Far East. People in this part of the war (Britain) are blinkered. Unless people here had relations in the Far East or had fought in the Burma war over there, they didn't have much interest in the Pacific. It was the Americans' theatre of war. We used to read the *Herald Tribune* and the *Times* and hear about the suicide dive bombers, the sacrifice Japanese bombers, the Kamikazes. And you had all of those things. Guam and all the way down the Pacific. Those were terrifying stories. I don't think the British over here felt the Americans were participating in that. But was a terribly wasteful, dreadful war. Then Singapore fell, and we had MacArthur. I think MacArthur did come through (the BSC office). Wilkinson, Wilkinson was his liaison. He came through."

The Quiet Canadian and the BSC history both quote a telegram sent from BSC to England on November 27, 1941. The message read, "Japanese negotiations off. Services expect action with two weeks."

"We sent that telegram, yes," Garner said. "It was ahead of the Foreign Office intelligence.

"The significance I remember, about the information, related about the Japanese and the strength of their massing, their plans about a massive attack on Pearl Harbor was passed on to the Americans, and presumably passed on to their General Staff and they didn't pay any attention. This was the problem. This was the thing. And the Japanese attacked, as you know on a Saturday night, which was because they knew that was the most vulnerable time."

"Sunday morning."

"Well Saturday night, after they'd been having parties and so forth. Early Sunday morning. But the warning was passed on a good ten days before Pearl Harbor."

According to published accounts the Allies also received a survey regarding Pearl Harbor information from double agent Dusko Popov.[6] "It came from various sources and observations, and actually watching what was happening in the Japanese Embassy in Washington. To-ing and fro-ing, and what was going on. And the intercepts. The code intercepts, this was what was happening. They knew from the code intercepts what the instructions to the Japanese Fleet, what was happening. You see Japan and Germany were in the Axis and the fact was if you attack one, you attack all. I mean it was a progression. I wouldn't have thought anything was a cause for surprise there. They didn't have to declare war on the United States. The Germans were perfectly well aware that America was arming to join."

Although BSC's principal sphere was obviously North America, she said they were also aware about activities in the Pacific.

"They knew what was going on. Yes, in that you had your international feedback. When Mountbatten went to be South East Asian Command he took one of our principal girls."

Bill Stephenson

Garner said Stephenson moved silently and seldom moved his arms. "He had the very dark piercing eyes, and the uncanny stillness of the man. When he walked he was very quiet and still. The man who most looked like him, and was most like him in physique was Sir Michael Edwards, the man brought in from the motor industry. He was a very small in stature, neat man and very neatly put together, didn't move his hands or do anything like that. A very still person."

Stephenson went by "like a panther. A black panther." And sometimes he seemed to arrive in places very quickly. "Oh, yes. Incredible. You see he moved very fast. He really would be out of that office like a bullet. He moved fast, but it was silent and like—the only thing is like a panther. All of a sudden, he'd be in Washington. He'd get there. He used to catch planes. I don't know how he did it, but he managed. It was incredible how fast he moved. Elizabeth Wood was to go and meet him at the airport and give him a document, and she went out to meet the appointed plane and she came back to the office, and he was in the office, sitting there laughing at her. She said, 'You weren't on that plane.' He said, 'Oh, yes I was.' She said, 'Well, I looked, and I didn't see you.' He said, 'You saw that lady carrying a Berndorf Goodman bag,' or something. 'I was behind her.' He thought it was a great joke but ... he probably saw Elizabeth there perfectly well, but he thought, he'd not teach her a lesson, but just play a trick on her. He had that quality of blending into a crowd. You wouldn't see him. You wouldn't notice him. He was not of conspicuous height or build or have any distinguishing feature. No buck teeth or anything like that. He certainly had the most wonderful eyes. Interesting eyes.

"He was so swift and so silent. He was so quick, this was the thing. And he'd put down the telephone and while the receiver—you know, hit, he would be out of the office. And he'd be in Washington. I still don't know how he did it. He used to, as I say, he was like Batman.

"In the most incredible way, he would catch a plane. We used to have Eastern Airlines or American Airlines or we would have to go by Pennsylvania railway. He had to get from 36th, in traffic, down to Grand Central or Pennsylvania Station for that. And he'd be in Washington. They'd have a car to meet him probably, or he'd get a taxi. But he would be there in the most incredible speed ...

"He certainly took in things in an instant, and he got to the centre of a thing. But that's what makes executives what they are. They decide. They see enough of the crux of the thing. Like Churchill. He wouldn't put up with long documents. He was supposed to have a sheet of paper, 3 or 4 by 5, and he put all on it. He wouldn't stand for gobbledy gook. Sir William's style, his English was flawless, his style was terse, tense and to the point."

Garner was familiar with Stephenson's writing style, and as a result, she didn't think the foreword of *A Man Called Intrepid* was written by Stephenson. "He doesn't write like that. Incidentally he (Stevenson) mentions (in a book review) that he was with British Security

Coordination. That was not so. None of us ever heard of him. There was no connection."

Her former boss didn't dictate letters or cables. He would write things down to be either coded or typed. "Only later I wrote a few personal letters. People like Noel Coward, and Ted Leathers and people like that. But he did not dictate cables. He wrote them out by hand.

"But it was the stealth of the man," she repeated. "I mean, I'd be typing and the first thing you'd know he'd be at your side. And it was his peculiar stillness, as I said. He didn't flail his arms around or move.

"No one has ever brought up his background. I never questioned he had the DFC. He never wore his medals. He never wore a uniform. He was not a boastful man. And he was not a generous man. He might have been a millionaire, but he didn't throw it around. I remember one time he brought me a beautiful box of chocolates, and I shared it with the girls outside. And he was mad, because he had bought it for me," she laughed. "He had bought it for me, and he was a bit annoyed. I was glad to share them. But I thought that was strange. I've never had a penny from him, nothing. There was no present. (Richard) Gambier-Parry took me to lunch at the 21 Club and gave me a watch, a gold watch. And I was a bit embarrassed about it. It cost about $60 or so. But he was the one who said, come over (to England), you're worth your weight in gold, I'll have you at Bletchley. You know, that nonsense, you don't pay any attention. He was not a man who took us all out for lunch, or ever had a party for—he was not a social man at all—but he did have cocktail parties. After the war and when he was in New York he used to have people, when he saw people arriving on the ships. We used to get the ships' sailing lists cabled ahead of time and he would pick off people he wanted to have invitations sent to. And he used to have cocktail parties. But he never entertained us or had us out. At Christmas time we had presents. I remember Lady Stephenson gave a lovely dressing gown and slippers from Lord and Taylor, and a compact. And one time he said he was going to give us all hankies and we said, 'No, Sir William, we always use Kleenex. If you pay six dollars each for handkerchiefs we'll all have a fit.' You know, $75 blown on handkerchiefs. There was nothing at all."

Garner didn't feel any curiosity about Stephenson's background. "For one thing I was too busy. He had no family, no children—it was only his wife and she was very much a homebody. She didn't take part. I don't think she even did things like working with some of the women who worked for the English-speaking Union. I don't think Mary ever took part. Now it might have been security reasons, you know. People asking what her husband was doing, and so on and so forth. But she was a very quiet like, little mouse thing, like that.

"She was never at the office. I'd spoken to her on the telephone. He brought over his housekeeper Nancy and she was a character. An Irishwoman who was widowed. They were bombed during war and he wrangled getting Nancy over in about '42 to run his house. When he left the St. Regis, as the organization grew and was bigger he had to spend more time at the office, he took this apartment on 53rd street. It had been Hearst's. A love nest for Marion Davies. He brought Nancy over as his housekeeper and then he began to have people over for sandwich lunches and he used to give cocktail parties, that sort of thing. That's when the famous martinis came into it.

"I remember they used to have a little Scotch Terrier like Roosevelt's Fala, and I remember Nancy went for a weekend. I went over and fed the dog and that sort of thing. He once had me over for lunch and I couldn't swallow, because I just felt so ... Well. He just looked at you, and you thought he watched the piece of salmon sandwich going down," she laughed. "The only other time we met Mary was when we were working late, we went to the Three Crowns restaurant, which they liked.

"I don't think I've ever heard him speak of an art collection, or anything like that at all. He didn't take any interest in music or art. Never. I never heard of him going to a concert, a play. Where he got his electronic ability and that sort of thing, I don't know. I certainly know he had a very quick intelligence. He certainly saw through to the heart of a problem. I don't know if he was a very good judge of people. Not awfully good at it, I thought."

"No?"

"No."

"He got a lot out of them though."

"Oh yes. He could do that from people. He expected a lot. And he did get a lot from people. People certainly did work very hard for him.

"Funny enough, he didn't like tall people. He said their brains were too far from their feet, you know. He had a thing about tall people. That's funny, but you know many men, brilliant businessmen, Napoleon, are small men or short in stature. They're neat and well put together. Well, not always, I mean you take people like JK Galbraith, there's a man with a brain there, but you know what I mean.

"He went through things quickly. He read quickly. And you had to get through things, and put them together, with his language sectors. He had this English girl, but she was used to the basket, the Pending Basket, and he had to have people who worked quickly. And funny enough, the girls who gravitated to the top were Western Canadians. Isn't that extraordinary? Patsy Sullivan came from Medicine Hat originally. I was a Western girl."

People were frightened coming in to see Stephenson, Garner said.

"Yes, because he was a very … well he was the head of the organization and he was rather an intimidating man, in that he could present a very cool eye. He would obviously be a man who wouldn't stand for any waffle. You would have to give him the facts straight, and no messing. He would question people on their facts, and question them on their evidence, on why they thought a certain thing. He would want to know.

"You didn't know if you had done the wrong thing. If somebody just said, 'Come down to my office down on Broadway,' or somewhere … You'd be inquisitorial, should we say. It was subconscious, but there was a sort of reverence for a powerful organization. You felt you were caught up in something. You realized that it was a much bigger thing than you had … and you see, Canadians aren't used to that kind of thing. We're not used to codes. Nor did you have agents, nor did you have … a war was going on, and people dropped in and you heard terrible things happening. I remember a wonderful man, a terribly nice man. I actually saw him packing rifles in the office on a Sunday. He was dropped into Yugoslavia and was killed … I mean you knew the results. People disappeared."

Stephenson was knighted before the end of the war following the D-Day landings. But knighthoods come in various levels and he didn't receive the highest. "He didn't get any CMG. I think that hurt. But, as I say, he never boasted. He never used it. He never used DFC after his name. But I think that really hurt him, and I know that after the war he became an absolute recluse. He was the first person I know to have an answering machine, and that gave a great deal of offense to people.

"This was right in '45, because people weren't used to them. After he gave up the flat in the penthouse, he had a place on East 53rd Street and people used to ring up and get this answering machine. And it put them off. He didn't see anybody. Very quiet, and then he started this business association. But he started out with (Ian) Fleming, (Ernie) Cuneo, and I think (John) Pepper was in it too. It was International News Media.

"It didn't last long, but he did start something up, and then he picked up his business interests. So I don't know what to account for ... he was a man of very few personal friends. He knew who they were, and that sort of thing."

Although she was close to him for a number of years, Garner knew little of Stephenson's financial affairs. "I don't know how he financed himself in Bermuda. They did live at the St. Regis in New York. But he certainly didn't throw it around. Living at the St. Regis couldn't have been cheap. It was a very expensive hotel, as it goes, and he lived there. But he had very modest tastes. He didn't eat a lot. He was not a man who was a great gourmet, or wine man, or anything. Not at all. In fact he used to have wine from California, Napa Cabernet, before California wine became a thing. We used to get our wine from Chile or from California. He said the California wine, the burgundy particularly, was very good, and this was long before it was hyped-up.

"He had a wonderful sense of humour. He liked the wry side of life and I used to bring him things from the *Herald Tribune*. I remember there was a wonderful story one time about a man out in Brooklyn who phoned up police and said there was an elephant at the bottom of his driveway. And they said, 'Go back to bed buddy, and put some water in it.' And minutes later they got another chap, and after that about ten neighbours phoned—there *was* an elephant there. But the way it was written was a marvellous story. He loved something like that. He'd laugh at something like that or jokes, if you had a cute story. Some of the things were happy. Some of the things like the Marx Brothers in the Foreign Office, or the chap trying to get the chap on the boat and the other fellow trying to get him off. You know those things are good for a laugh."

Garner does not know if Stephenson financed some of BSC's operation. "Hyde says he did. I wouldn't know about that. Payroll was a woman named Beryl Phillips, and she managed the whole thing." Phillips was the secretary of the Passport Control Officer in New York, and the money, Garner believes, usually came by courier from Washington or from one of the New York banks. They were paid cash.

"I just know about these companies he was involved in—that sort of thing. And he never, never, never used government cables for his own business. That was never done."

"Did you see any cables from Churchill or 'C'?"

"Yes. But they're not sent like that. They're not signed, 'Yours, Churchill.'"

"How did you know where they were from then?"

"Well. I can't tell you. There were various ways in which a telegram is addressed in code."

Stephenson's number was 48000.

"Yes, it was. It's a rather stupid thing, I would have thought. Because there were 48 States, but there you are. That was his number, yes."

The zeroes designation were similar to those used in James Bond—a licence to kill.

"I think all of that ... Bond was the name of a famous ornithologist. That book was Fleming's reading matter."

The Public Account

Garner commented on a 1952 *Maclean's* article on Stephenson which was the first public notice of her former boss and the organization. "He was very observant?"

"Oh yes."

"*During the war a Canadian girl secretary who pricked her forefinger and covered it with a tiny square plaster came into the office and without looking up from his desk Stephenson said, 'What have you tried to do, kill yourself?'*"

"That wasn't you?"

"I remember a girl came down, a secretary. She was in the office one day and Sir William was walking home on Broadway, and he saw her in,

I think, Jack Dempsey's, which is on Broadway, and the next day he had her sent back. He was as observant as that."

"The pace at which he reads is also legendary. I've watched him reading a novel, says close friend Tommy Drew-Brook and it reminds you of a man rifling through an index for a reference." "He was a speed reader?"

"Well, he could read quite quickly, yes."

"One girl on his wartime staff handed him several sheets of closely typed manuscript, he flipped the pages, grunted and handed it back. 'Clearly,' she said,' you haven't read it properly?' He gave her a succinct resume of it's contents reciting several passages." "Does that sound like hokum? Do you remember stuff like that?"

"No. Eleanor Fleming might have done that."

"His New York headquarters (were) staffed with more than a thousand hand picked Canadians. Men and women spoke of his door keeper as Peter, of his secretary as Gabrielle, and of him as God. Only a handful of them knew him by sight."

"Well. I think he was known as God. They used to tease you and say 'Is God at home?'"

"Who would Gabrielle have been? You?"

"Probably. Eleanor and me." She laughed. "The man who was Peter might have been John Pepper. 'Peter picked a peck of pickled peppers.' Because he was always around. He could always get an enter and nobody else. He used to have lunch with him."

The article quotes Churchill's notation written beside Stephenson's name: "This one is dear to my heart."

"Yes. That was the story that was told by him, yes."

Garner didn't believe there were any significant errors in Hyde's book, *The Quiet Canadian.* "There are things in *Camp X* that I would quarrel with." She disliked the book *A Man Called Intrepid,* and thought it tarnished Stephenson's reputation. Stephenson's former secretary didn't even read it all. She commented on some details BSC may have initiated.

The magazine called *Sequel to the Apocalypse* was produced by BSC and profiled businesses in North America profiting from dealing with the Nazis. It was called the *"Uncensored story of how your dimes and quarters pay for Hitler's war."*

"Oh yes, that was a book that was brought out as a sort of pseudo-true thing, you know. It was just popular."

BSC came up with a bogus letter that helped get Italian airline LATI banned from Brazil.

"I remember it was going on. It was one of the things that Pepper was engaged in. That was an important thing, because it got the Italian airlines out of Brazil."

It also has been reported that BSC fabricated a map that graphically outlined the proposed Nazi occupation of South America. The map was even referred to in a speech to the nation by Franklin Roosevelt. "You thought Dorothy (Hyde) had done that?"

"Yes. That was a ruse. But that should not have been told. That was important in bringing to the United States, the threat. It was a very real threat of the Nazi plans for world domination. As I said, Latin America was stiff with Germans. There were a lot of them. Brazil particularly, and Argentina. They were not pro-British, despite the fact that in Argentina they'd been good friends. I think I told you that all the railways, beef interests, big companies were built with British money. They put a lot of money into Argentina. There were a great deal of pro-Anglo Argentine families—when Britain stripped its money. They never got that money back. All those foreign funds were confiscated and moved over to the British Treasury.

"The thing about the exposure of that map of South America and so on, shown to the President. That should never have been written in the book," Garner stressed. "Harford should never have done it, and this man Stevenson shouldn't have done it. It's not a need-to-know by people. You know people are going to read it fifty years later. How does it affect the thing? It doesn't."

"So before Pearl Harbor they tried to put by a few things?"

"Yes. To waken the Americans really, to the threat."

"Would Donovan be in on it?"

"Oh, I'm not sure if Donovan was in on that. I don't think anybody was in on that at all."

A Man Called Intrepid implies BSC had something to do with the assassination of Nazi henchman Reinhard Heydrich. This has been a point of contention with many critics of the book. Heydrich was ambushed in Czechoslovakia in March 1942, and died a few months later. It is generally accepted that this was a European operation.[7]

"That's one (inaccuracy in the book)," Garner said. "And also a lot of it was out of context. I have to reread it but there was a lot of hyperbole. We never claimed about Heydrich. I remember things like, 'could this man not be eliminated?' and things like that. We knew about the plot for Hitler, but so did the *New York Herald Tribune*. That came out. I don't think there was any prior knowledge of that. I don't think there was anything sinister."

Another point of contention in some criticisms of *A Man Called Intrepid* was Stephenson's reported relationship—or lack of—with the American President. Garner saw continual memoranda to and from Roosevelt regarding meetings. "Yes there were numerous things, where he'd come back and dictate (sic) cables, after he'd seen Roosevelt and so on. Gave a verbatim account of what he'd said. He talked with Sherwood and with Donovan, of course, and later on with Cuneo. So there were those sort of things. (If) you said, 'Did you ever see him (Roosevelt) with him?' No, I didn't. But I know he used to go down there. I don't know how much he saw him through Halifax, with Halifax, or what went there. But you talk about forty-four trips across the Atlantic—the number of times he went to Washington was countless."

After the war, in the late 1940's, Garner crossed the Atlantic to see the Britain she'd only read about. She found the residents still shell-shocked. "When I came over here, right after the war, people were ... they were numb. And they were sort of shocked to talk about it, it was very bad form. And you dare not say anything about the Prince of Wales. You could not talk about Edward the Eighth at all. Not the sort of people I knew. I mean, it was a terrible faux pas. They couldn't talk about it, and for a long time. I heard about people's personal stories about being covered with gas, awful stories. But a long time afterward. They wouldn't talk."

She thought subsequently the Edward VIII story had become twisted. "Yes, it's been turned around and around, and upside down." (See Appendix A)

No one in British government or establishment circles came to Stephenson's defence following a number of negative press reports at the time of his death. Trivial details, even Stephenson's code name 'Intrepid' has come into question. "I did remember the name 'Intrepid' during the war," Garner said. (see Appendix B) One of the reasons Stephenson received little recognition, and even abuse, in England was that he was an outsider.

"I can only say he was not 'one of us', as Mrs. Thatcher would say. He was one of a peripheral organization. He was not in the mainstream of the British Foreign Office. He was not a career man. Many, many people had a wonderful war. I think that's part of it. I think part of it is the natural ... well not an economy of the truth, but an economy of praise for anybody who wasn't British. Even Harford Hyde in his book does not give any praise to the Canadians. Does not single them out. He singles out all the people from Britain who were names. All the big merchant bankers and British who had names. Not the unknowns."

"So it's more a nationalism?"

"It's a nationalism, yes. It's pride. It's grudging. When I came over here I was incensed at the lack of appreciation at what the Americans had done in the war. There was no gratitude for the generosity, and the wealth that was spent on this country. The Bundles for Britain, the food, the things that were donated. Very little of that. There was a wave of anti-Americanism. There was a time when, 'Oh, everything from America was wonderful. The nylon stockings, and then there was a, 'Oh, it's American is it?' and you couldn't do this and couldn't do that. And I remember, they would say, 'Oh yes, the Canadians. Their boys were wonderful over here. They were wonderful. They used to give us this, and give us that.' But never the fact the Canadians held their border edge at Caen. Some of the hardest fighting was done by the Canadians. And they wouldn't want to be with the Americans, 'They're soft, they're overfed, they're oversexed, they're over here.' You know, that sort of attitude. And they resented the fact they were so well fed. They were reluctant to give America credit.

"When the Marshall Plan came, after the war, when aid was given to Europe, and the French got all the building up of the ruin. And the success of Germany. The Germans after all, to give them all credit, their country was in rubble and terrible. But they rebuilt with their own hands, and their energy, and their strength. They built it up. But they had American money to re-establish themselves."

Garner chose to remain in Britain after the war. She visited Canada on a number of occasions, and was astonished at the political conditions in her home country. She and a friend drove through Quebec after the province made it against the law to have an outdoor sign in English. "We couldn't stop laughing," she said. "We laughed about it. I despair for Canada. I really do.

"I feel strongly that Canada—Canadians would be interested because he was a Canadian, was born a Canadian, but how much ... so much damage has been done by that book *A Man Called Intrepid*. It's very difficult to rebut that. It only takes one big flaw like that to make the whole thing suspect.

"What I felt about *The Quiet Canadian* is it still does not give any adequate recognition to the Canadian contribution to British Security Coordination. I know it was given the title British Security Coordination, the funds were British, the expertise, and the system was British but it was staffed by over 400 Canadians and had contributions as I say from Lester Pearson, who was our Canadian High Commissioner, to eminent lawyers, to industrialists and so on. Because they aren't world figures. They aren't the big bankers and those sorts of people, there's very little credit given. And they worked terribly hard."

Garner remembered seeing documentaries in 1984, the Fortieth Anniversary of the D-Day landings and learning things about the war, "things they didn't tell us." Many men died right off the landing craft, weighed down in deep water, because they couldn't manoeuvre close enough to the shore." They show these pictures of the assault, on those landings. Well, it was absolutely devastating. I just couldn't watch it, it was so awful. We didn't know that was war ... they kept that away from us.

"The carnage," she said. "The terrible things, that when the Entity Bee, the motor boat landed, the men had this heavy weight—fully armed men went into the sea, if it didn't land in the right place. Hundreds were lost like that. Now that was probably censored out of the news."

After the war Garner worked for *Harper's Bazaar*, worked for Bill Ross Smith, and did public relations work in Britain. "I didn't stay with the

Foreign Office. I went away like puffed rice. I wanted to get out of that."

Garner has few momentos of the war. She still has her old typewriter with the BSC stamp on it and her security armband labelled 'CD.' The initials stood for Civil Defence—*American* Civil Defence. Even New York practised brown-outs during the war,

Grace Garner's wartime armband

she said, and in emergencies wearers of the armband would be allowed to pass through police lines. From its humble beginnings, BSC grew to be regarded as an essential component of the defence of the United States. Garner also has a certificate thanking her for her service from Bill Stephenson.

'Intrepid'
Igor Gouzenko lawyers

Gouzenko always had a theory that before the Russians would kill him they had to destroy his credibility, because they never kill anybody unless they destroyed their credibility first—any person in the public eye.—Nelles Starr, Gouzenko's lawyer, *Gouzenko: The Untold Story*

He (Gouzenko) was trying to protect his reputation … They have always felt the Russians had two tactics. One was to simply kill people they did not like. And the other was they would try to ruin them. Ruin their reputation … if you ruin someone from the point of view of their reputation to the point of ridicule and where everyone doesn't care about them, I suppose that's as good as killing them physically.

… and that's what they've always been conscious of, that they protect the reputation at all costs.—Alan Harris, Gouzenko lawyer, *Gouzenko: The Untold Story*

Following the Cuban revolution, the United States pondered what to do about their socialist neighbour. In the years following the revolution there were reports the CIA considered many ways to discredit Cuba leader Fidel Castro, including slipping him chemicals that made his beard fall out, and exploding cigars. According to some accounts, assassination was also considered.

In the early sixties US President John Kennedy played host to Ian Fleming, of whose writing he was a fan. He invited the English spy writer to the White House and during the course of the evening he asked the former naval intelligence officer what to do about Cuba and Castro. Fleming, according to his biographer, told Kennedy the US was making too much fuss about Castro, "inflating him instead of deflating him." Applying one or two ideas would "take the steam out of the Cuban," the author told him. Kennedy wondered how this could be accomplished.

"Ridicule chiefly," said Fleming."[8]

■

There has been much conjecture about some details of Stephenson's career, and the validity of what has been written about him. Even Stephenson's supposed code name 'Intrepid' has come into question. It was not Stephenson's official code name, the author Nigel West has written, but a name that referred to the entire organization.

The writer Mary S Lovell has pointed out it would be natural for a person sending a cable to BSC New York to say, "Send this to Intrepid," and the name would stick to the head of the organization. In the same manner, if a message to 'Intrepid' was intercepted, it is likely those who intercepted the message would not assume it referred to a huge espionage agency hidden in the heart of New York. They would assume it referred to simply one man. A man called Intrepid. It appears the name of the book was actually based on a message.

Report AS/783/25X to Red Army Intelligence HQ, Znamensky 19, Moscow, USSR, dated 23.1.1944, concerning Hermina Rabinovich and the assistant Soviet Military Attaché (cover name Lamont) in Ottawa: "Funds were delivered to William Helbein of the Helbein Watch Company of 6, West 48th Street, New York, NY, the firm known to 'Hermina' when she was stationed in Geneva. This completes SMERSH Plan Destruct..."

Report AB/3/97X to the Fuehrer of the Third Reich, Adolf Hitler, from SS-General Heinrich Mueller, otherwise known as "Gestapo" Mueller: "Liquidation of the man called INTREPID is now assured." The date on this file recovered from wartime German archives is exactly one month before the Soviet intelligence report quoted above.

The above reports are followed by a narrative that says orders for the destruction of the Intrepid "Anglo-American" secret operations were first issued by 'Gestapo Mueller' when Hitler and Stalin were still bound by their peace pact and Hilter was about to invade Britain. According to the narrative, Mueller—actually working for the Soviet Union—reported to Moscow on Hiltler's plan to combine the old British Empire with the new German Empire to dominate the world. The Fuehrer's future collaborators were named. "The laws of libel prevent their publication except in the case of the British Ambassador to Spain of that time, Sir Samuel Hoare, now dead."

"The biggest single obstacle to Anglo-German imperialism apart from the public hatred of Hitler in Britain was INTREPID. He was thus described in the Mueller dossier and this story is taken from the strangest manhunt in modern times."

Intrepid, the narrative continues, virtually unknown outside a small collection of people who ran the world's affairs in 1939, was sent to North America by Churchill, "to build up the largest secret operation in history" and organize America's first intelligence agency.

Intrepid was Bill Stephenson, who, for a time was the sole link between Churchill and President Roosevelt when the two leaders conspired to preserve freedom.[10]

What is this synopsis?

It is the original outline of *A Man Called Intrepid*, dated June 5, 1973, in the files of William Stevenson at the University of Regina.

When shown the pages, Grace Garner didn't question the contents.

It's a challenge to confirm whether or not aspects of this outline were in fact true. The first document quoted refers to the Canadian Royal Commission into the espionage activities of the Soviet Union following the defection of Igor Gouzenko. It was headed by Robert Taschereau and RL Kellock. In the formidable mound of transcripts of the 1946 inquiry, there is a reference to a cable dated January 23, 1944. There are also references to details such as 'Hermina,' Heilbein Watch

Company, Lamont and Znamensky 19. 'Hermina' was Hermina Rabinowitch, who for a time was stationed in Geneva with the International Labour Organization. The contents of that specific cable are not spelled out in the released papers, although any money being delivered seems to have been destined for Switzerland. The Gouzenko transcripts weren't widely released in any form until years after the publication of *A Man Called Intrepid*.[11] No reference could be found to the second report AB/3/97X, and an official at the Imperial War Museum in London could not place the quotation.

In *A Man Called Intrepid*, 'Gestapo' Mueller is not even mentioned. Soon after the first outline was composed, the author decides there is a "basic story which is filled with political intrigue in high places," and "It does not seem necessary to complicate matters with cutaways to what the Germans were doing to stop Intrepid." He says it has not been proved that Mueller was a Soviet agent, although Stephenson believed this on the basis on his own files, and it was best to leave Mueller out of the book.[12] (In later letters it seems Stevenson the writer is perhaps justifying a pro-British slant in the American-published book. In a July 24, 1974, letter to Stephenson he wrote, "It should be said that all Julian's (Muller) comments have been within the context of his own admiration for Britain and his anxiety that an American audience be captured by the fact an Anglo-American alliance saved the world from tyranny."[13])

Gestapo stands for Geheime Staats Polizei or State Secret Police. In Nazi Germany, the SS became almost a state within a state, duplicating almost every aspect of state administration. The Gestapo was its spearhead. Lt. General Heinrich Mueller reported directly to Reinhard Heydrich, and the organization dominated all of occupied Europe, and contained numerous sections and subsections over a wide range of areas.[14] There does appear to be Soviet influence, if not connections.[15]

Following Rudolf Hess's flight to England, Mueller carried out a purge of those around him. Even his chauffeur was arrested. Mueller disappeared at the conclusion of the war, much like Martin Bormann. He was possibly seen in Moscow and died there in 1948.[16]

Soviet military counter-intelligence during the Second World War consisted of two successive organizations, the Special Departments of the NKVD (OO/NKVD) until April 1943, and after that date the

Third Main Directorate for Counter-intelligence of the People's Commissariat of Defence (GUKR-NKO). The latter organization was given the nickname SMERSH, or Smiert Shpionam (Death to Spies) by Stalin himself (Soviet Military Encyclopedia). Stalin thought the organization should not deal only with German spies, but the intelligence services of other countries as well.[17]

The existence of SMERSH became wide-spread public knowledge in the 1950's, in a somewhat unique fashion. The possibility that elements of Soviet intelligence were in favour of attacks on Western intelligence figures following the war, was revealed in the same book. An author's note refers to names, numbers and places.

"Not that it matters, but a great deal of the background to this story is accurate.

SMERSH, a contraction of Smiert Shpionam—Death to Spies—exists and remains the most secret department of the Soviet government.

At the beginning of 1956, when this book was written, the strength of SMERSH at home and abroad was about 40,000 and General Grubozaboyschikov was its chief. My description of his appearance is correct.

Today the headquarters of SMERSH are where in chapter 4, I have placed them—at No. 13 Sretenka Ulitsa, Moscow. The Conference Room is faithfully described and the Intelligence chiefs who meet round the table are real officials who are frequently summoned to that room for purposes similar to those I have recounted."

A Soviet intelligence meeting is reconstructed in the fourth chapter. A selection of Soviet officials engage in a round table discussion about future plans, and how to possibly weaken foreign intelligence organizations.

"It is not just a question of blowing up a building or shooting a prime minister," one concludes. *"Our operation must be delicate, refined and aimed at the heart of the Intelligence apparatus—hidden damage which the public will perhaps hear nothing of, but which will be the secret talk of government circles..."*

The intelligence services of the Swedes, Italians, Spaniards, and French are rejected. The Americans are dismissed as well. Although they are often technically superior and have had successes, they have no understanding of the work, and do everything for money is the conclusion. "Good spies will not work for money alone, only bad ones, of which the Americans have several divisions," was the analysis.

The consensus concludes the English service would be the target of a terrorist action, not because of an overt superiority, but because of underlying factors. "Of course most of their strength lies in the myth—the myth of Scotland Yard, of Sherlock Holmes, of the Secret Service. We certainly have nothing to fear from these gentlemen. But the myth is a hindrance which it would be good to set aside.

"... And now for the target within that organization. I remember Comrade General Vozdvishensky saying something about a myth upon which much of the alleged strength of this Secret Service depends. How can we help destroy this myth and thus strike at the very motive force of this organization? Where does this myth reside? We cannot destroy all its personnel at one blow. Does it reside in the Head?"

"... He is an Admiral. He is known by the letter M. We have a zapiska on him, but it contains little...The public does not know of his existence. It would be difficult to create a scandal around his death. And he would not be easy to kill. He rarely goes abroad. To shoot him in a London street would not be very refined."

"... But we are here to find a target who will fulfill our requirements. Have they no one who is a hero to the organization? someone who is admired and whose ignominious destruction would cause dismay? Myths are built on heroic deeds and heroic people. Have they no such men?"

There was silence around the table while everyone searched his memory, "... It was Colonel Nikitikin of the MGB who broke the embarrassed silence. He said hesitantly, 'There is a man called Bond.'"

—Ian Fleming, From Russia With Love

19 Benjamin de Forest Bayly

Pat Bayly

Since 1941, the most secret member of Bill Stephenson's wartime staff was former University of Toronto Professor Benjamin de Forest (Pat) Bayly. He is not mentioned in either of the Stephenson biographies, yet it seemed obvious during the course of this research that he held a senior position in the organization. Former BSC employees refer to him as the "famous Professor Bayly." Yet for much of his life, even for years after the war was over, his position was such that he could not be identified by name. There are brief references to him in material related to Bill Stephenson, but not much. The first published glimpse is in McKenzie Porter's *Maclean's* article in 1952.

The spider's web extended from Stephenson's BSC headquarters in Rockefeller Center to a legion of undercover men had at it's core the most efficient communications system in the world. A Canadian electronics expert, whose name cannot be given, designed the equipment which coded and decoded messages in seconds, thereby saving hours of human effort. BSC business in code made up more that 50 percent of the traffic of the normal trans-Atlantic cables and kept a secret transmitter in Canada operating at full capacity day and night."—Maclean's, December 1, 1952.

The first few details of Bayly's career appeared in Gordon Welchman's 1982 book, *The Hut Six Story.* When Welchman, usually regarded as one of the two main conquerors of the Nazi's ENIGMA machine, started to work with Bayly, it was a promotion. A few other writers have paraphrased what Welchman said about him, but Bayly himself never spoke to anyone about what he did during the war.

No look at the extraordinary life of William Stephenson could be considered complete without reference to the mysterious communications centre that popped up, from nowhere, that was relied on by all Allied nations. It guarded the cryptographic secrets such as ULTRA, and helped to win the Battle of the Atlantic. Bill Stephenson is considered to be a father of the CIA. Pat Bayly laid the groundwork for international cooperation in communications intelligence and cryptography. From his war work evolved the murky spheres of North America's most covert organizations—Canada's Communications Security Establishment, and America's National Security Agency.[1]

The most direct route to finding Pat Bayly was through Harry Smith, Bayly's friend, former accountant, and a Camp X Alumni. But writers who have written on BSC or wartime communications, such as William Stevenson, David Stafford and Nigel West, got no further. "As far as people contacting Bayly, ever since the wartime, people who wanted to get a hold of Bayly, mostly have come through me," Smith said, "And I've pushed them off. I wouldn't give Stafford or Stevenson any clue as to how to get a hold of Bayly. I have always keep Bayly's name out of it. Nigel didn't get Bayly from me at all. It's one of the things Bayly asked when he left and moved to California."

Pat Bayly was the Deputy Director of Communications for British Security Coordination and the second in charge of the entire organization. Bayly was in charge of Camp X for the duration of the war and afterward. When Stephenson retired in 1945, Bayly became the BSC director.

David Stafford did an entire book on Camp X, and did not indicate Bayly was in charge of it. "Well, he didn't know," Smith said. "You're the first person I've ever talked to who seemed to know Bayly's connection at all. No one else has ever got that deep as far as I know, because if anyone was chasing it, and chasing it through me, they didn't get anywhere."

The First Mayor of Ajax

Benjamin de Forest (Pat) Bayly was born in London, Ontario, June 20, 1903, the son of Benjamin Moore and Alice de Forest (Seaborn) Bayly. He grew up in Moose Jaw, Saskatchewan, where his father was a medical officer and he always considered Moose Jaw home. For a time the young Bayly attended school in Shrewsbury, England, but he later returned to the prairies. There he helped start a Moose Jaw radio station called 10 AB. There was no commercial radio in Moose Jaw at the time, and he and a few people began the amateur station and broadcasted church services and other events. Eventually Bayly entered law school at the University of Saskatchewan in Saskatoon. He graduated at a young age in 1923, but after a period of articling, Bayly was unsure he wanted to pursue a legal career. With the encouragement and support of his Moose Jaw friend Margaret (Bun) Grant, he decided to leave the legal profession. Grant, originally from Hamiota, Manitoba, told him she didn't like a guy who didn't like what he was doing. "And I didn't like law, but I couldn't afford anything else, so she said, 'Why don't you put yourself through University and take engineering?' Bayly told her it would mean holding off their wedding for several years. "Better than wishing the rest of your life that you did," she told him. "So we did."

Bayly left the legal career alone, moved east, and entered the University of Toronto in electrical engineering. His proficiency in the field was noted by the university administration. When an electronics and communications professor left the university to work in the new talking motion pictures industry, the faculty didn't look far for a replacement. Bayly was asked to teach to the fourth year students, while he was still enrolled in third year. "I had been a lineman and I had my signals training in England." When it was time for him to graduate from the university, the brass had trouble deciding how he should complete his degree. The issue eventually had to filter through the full bureaucracy. "The board of Governors decided that I didn't have to write my (own) exam. I could give myself an 'A'," he said with a smile. "Some of the university people didn't always have a sense of humour."

He continued to teach at the university following his graduation in 1930. To earn money Bayly often played the piano, sometimes at theatres. During college, he had his own radio program on the commercial station CFCA in Toronto. However Bayly was compelled to drop the show by the head of the university, Cannon Cody. "When I became a professor, he said he hoped I would drop the program, 'Pat At the Mike.' He didn't think it was a university professor job," Bayly laughed. Bun, nicknamed because of the rabbit-like way she used to wrinkle her nose as a child, moved with Bayly to Toronto. After six years of informal engagement, the two married, May 19, 1932. They were happily married for fifty-four years until her death in 1986.

Bayly stayed at the university until the end of the decade. He also acted as a Consulting Engineer for the Tariff Board of Canada 1938-1940, and as a consultant to the National Electric Corporation. At the outbreak of war, he trained for a time in Winnipeg, and began working behind the scenes on Canada's war effort.

One of his jobs for NEC was to rig antennas onto small bombers ordered by the Free French, but France was occupied before the bombers were ready. The planes were eventually offered to the British through Lend Lease, but since all the controls were in metric, they were given to the Russians. During the antenna installations, Bayly was asked if he could hook up bomb racks for the planes as well. He contacted American officials and was able to obtain French blueprints for the racks through covert means with the assistance of the FBI.

In 1941, Bayly was approached by Toronto stockbroker Thomas Drew-Brook, and his career was diverted into the shadowy world of espionage. Drew-Brook didn't know Bayly, but he researched his qualifications, contacted him at the university, and met him downtown for an interview. "He explained what he was doing, and would I come along, and I said I would.

"Tommy was asked to find a man who understood something about commercial communications, and who would have enough security clearance to buy top-secret radio material. The point is that the English were, at the moment, developing all sorts of secret radios. They didn't want to divulge what they were buying through normal commercial channels. So I was asked to come down and do that." Later Bayly realized why the stockbroker received his unique recruiting position. "He was Bill Stephenson's best friend. They had served together in the Air Force."

Bayly travelled to England in November 1941, learned the British communications setup and about their progress in analysing Axis covert messages. He spent most of his time with Brigadier Richard Gambier-Parry, the SIS Communications Division Chief. He was introduced to Stewart Menzies, the head of Britain's Secret Service, and other top people in Britain's intelligence community. He visited the covert decryption centre, Bletchley Park, and Whaddon Hall. The professor from the harsh Canadian prairie "damned near froze to death in England" that November. Britain was a nation under siege, and he had to obtain a clothing ration card before he could buy warmer clothes. Eventually he managed to acquire a pair of unglamorous combination overalls to see himself through the British sojourn.

In England, progress was being made in the breaking of the Nazi cipher machine called ENIGMA. At Bletchley Park some of the best brains in Britain were at work trying to decipher the millions of variations possible from the portable coding machine. Two men in particular were responsible for the British success, following preliminary work done in Poland. Gordon Welchman is considered the man who perse-vered, believing the millions of statistical variations of the machine could be deter-mined, and figured out how to break the apparently unbreakable ENIGMA. Alan Turing invented the machines that helped with the solution, and in the process created the first computer.

ENIGMA: German cipher machine

During the war the Government Code and Cipher School, as the department was called, was headed by Alastair Denniston and later by Edward Travis. Winston Churchill knew the importance of the information produced by GC & CS, which was delivered to him regularly by Stewart Menzies. When some of the top staff at Bletchley needed more resources they wrote him personally, and quickly received the support they requested. "Action this day," the British Prime Minister demanded. Churchill referred to the scientific aspects of the conflict as the Wizard War. "This was a secret war, whose battles were lost or won unknown to the public, and only with difficulty comprehended, even now to those outside the small high scientific circles concerned. No such warfare had ever been waged by mortal men."[2]

The English quickly took to Bayly. Gambier-Parry wrote to New York to say that he was "more convinced than ever that Bayly was the right man for the job."[3] Later Bayly thought the British were impressed for wrong reasons. While waiting in Menzies's office, he came across his personnel file on the spychief's desk, thumbed through it, and was disappointed in its contents. They seemed overly impressed he had a portion of his education in England. "There was no mention about my present 'technical skills.' There was no mention of teletype, or things that were necessary in anything I did—most of it as a lineman—before I did signal corps training. There was no mention of that at all. I'd simply gone to the right schools."

Bayly signed Britain's Official Secrets Act, and the need for secrecy was stressed. He was told how intelligence could be passed on as a result of any type of disclosure. One example he was given was David and Goliath. "I said, 'That's six thousand years ago.' And they said, 'We're telling you that to show you that time doesn't necessarily influence security. Anybody who is fighting in Arab countries knows that if you go up against a sheep herder, he can use a slingshot, as accurately as a rifle, up to about a hundred yards. And the reason that everybody knows that, is because of the story about David and Goliath.' I was quite impressed because that was six thousand years ago."

The security of certain Allied ciphers was very poor at the time, Bayly discovered, and he was not impressed with Allied communications in general. When he started the job at least one ciphering system was pitifully obsolete. "The British were still using the Playfair cipher, which they had started in 1914, and which we then could break in two minutes," he laughed. He spelled out one of the consequences of poor communication—the hasty retreat of British troops from Europe at Dunkirk, France, in 1940.

"Dunkirk happened for one good reason. I had been a signal officer in the Canadian Army. Of all things, a cavalry signal officer. They only had one, and they gave it to me. I was trained in Winnipeg, and I had a WWI radio set. It had a distance ability of 15 miles. By 1940, the German tanks could go 15 miles in half an hour. The British were still using radio communication that had a range of only 15 miles." he laughed.

"The British were completely out of communication. Nobody knew where anybody else was. The tanks had come in so fast at Dunkirk, that nobody knew where anybody else was. So the British finally decided, let's get the hell out of here, and they landed at Dunkirk, and they couldn't get enough naval boats there. So everybody who had anything longer than 15 feet tore over to Dunkirk and brought as many people home as they could. But it was entirely a complete lack of communication, and even of a decent cipher. The communication of British Army was just a disgrace—having been a communications officer in the Canadian Army I knew exactly what it was, because we were taking our orders from the British."

Later in the war Bayly was given British identification. He spent a lot of time dealing with British Security, and this was partially to circumvent Canadian law. "The British decided if they wanted to shoot me, they didn't want to argue with Canada," he remembered. He was given the army rank of Lieutenant Colonel.

The new communications officer sailed back to North America where his real assignment began. There were no available flights, so he returned on a converted Norwegian banana boat. Although the ship, formerly used to transport fruit to Scandinavia before it ripened, was one of the fastest on the Atlantic, it was delayed by days of strong south-west gales and his return to North America took over two weeks.

Bayly arrived in New York City on a Sunday, and he hurried to the office of his new boss, Bill Stephenson. He was increasing his espionage network and Bayly was to help institute secure communications. The Moose Jaw native had his plans well-prepared, "I know exactly what I'm going to do," he told Stephenson at their first meeting. "The hell you do," Stephenson curtly replied and he handed Bayly a cable. It was from President Franklin Roosevelt and it detailed American damage in Hawaii. Bayly's first day at work was December 7, 1941. As the United States was no longer going to be neutral, his communications agenda was already changing.

But talking safely to Washington remained one of Stephenson's priorities, and Bayly made sure the spychief stopped using the telephone for any security matters. "He couldn't do it on the telephone, because he knew that everyone would be listening. Not only the FBI, every mayor of every town in between." Telephone communication in those days was not at all private, Bayly says, and the scramblers used to conceal speech "weren't worth a darn." He told Stephenson to use a teleprinter and one-time pads.

As Bayly was working in the United States, Stephenson arranged for him to meet with American government and military officials. But first he had him checked out by Hoover's FBI. The Bureau organized an interrogation of Bayly and invited Canada's Royal Canadian Mounted Police to participate as well. The meeting made Bayly's "hair stand on end." The RCMP sent down Inspector George McClellan, and during the questioning the Mountie frequently interrupted ominously, 'I know your face from somewhere.' "Every time he said this, the FBI would sort of scramble for notebooks," Bayly recalled. The interview continued for a half hour, with the new recruit getting more and more nervous, thinking the Mountie's recollection was regarding some sort of illicit activity. "I don't mind saying, I was perspiring freely." Finally McClellan said, 'Hell, my mother was your first music teacher.' "And she was. He'd come from Moose Jaw, and Mrs. McClellan was my music teacher. And after that we got on much better."

The FBI involvement in BSC's communication at the time was extensive and, in retrospect, very unusual. The American domestic police service was transmitting the Stephenson organization's secret messages to England on their channels. Not only was the foreign spy network allowed to exist in the US, the FBI was working for them. Bayly admits the FBI was "in a very funny position," and Stephenson had brokered the deal with J Edgar Hoover. "The communication with England, for security reasons, wasn't carried through normal channels. It was being handled by the FBI, handled personally by the bossman of the FBI, whom I ended up liking very much in spite of the fact that he had a reputation as being everything that was wrong in the world." J Edgar Hoover wanted out of the communications deal, as he was unsure what would happen if Congress or the press found out what he was doing. "He finally decided it was too dangerous, and it was going to get him in wrong if it was found out, because it was still a neutral country. And he was sort of exceeding his duties."

British Embassy channels were not used, but Bayly was somewhat vague as to why. "Lord Halifax was known as Lord Holy Fox, and he was not popular in intelligence circles. Most Ambassadors hate any intelligence going on in their embassy, because they are not allowed to know what is going on, and know that if it's dynamite, it could blow up in their face. So I was brought in really to handle the communications for BSC."

■

"Why didn't I want to talk about these things? Let me go into detail again for a minute. Let's put it this way—all liaison between countries is, first of all, subject to a treaty. And all the treaty says is that you may do 'this.' But from then on, the liaison is a very personal thing. If they like you, and believe you, then you have good liaison. It doesn't matter what the treaty is. If they don't like you, there's no liaison. I was very generously treated in Canada, the States, and England, and I would feel very badly if it sounds like, if in any way it appears, that I was starting to shout my mouth off.

"Because these things do hang on, and they do have political repercussions. For instance, you take Hoover, if he were still alive, and it was found out he was doing BSC's communication while it was still a neutral country, politically that would be dynamite. And there are many things like that which exist, so I decided that the best thing for me to do was shut up."

■

Well versed in Britain's covert communication methods and decryption successes, Bayly wanted to know what the Americans were up to. He had a book by Gilbert S Vernam, who had worked for Bell Labs, that described encipherment of characters using teleprinters. Bayly thought this would be a good system to work with. Then he contacted Barty Bouverie at BSC's Washington office. He told him to find William Friedman.

William F Friedman was possibly the greatest cryptographer of all time.[4] However, in the USA, the evolution of cryptography has been somewhat staggered. American code breaking went through periods of being shut down, or forced underground, as some politicians concluded 'gentlemen did not read other gentlemen's mail.' When Bayly tried to find Friedman he was given the run-around. "We got the story that Billy was now a librarian, and he was no longer head of the cryptographic division, because there wasn't one."

Eventually Bayly met with Friedman and explained his situation. Friedman told him to get in touch with Western Union, who had a machine called the telekrypton, which was the teleprint machine that Vernam had worked on. BSC bought two of the

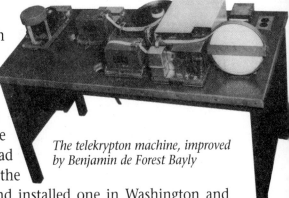

The telekrypton machine, improved by Benjamin de Forest Bayly

machines from Western Union and installed one in Washington and one in New York. But Bayly knew quickly they were insecure, as the units simply ran a short rotating code tape. "After ten minutes any cryptographer could open the machine." He had both ends use one-time pads, which contained coded sheets and tables that weren't used again. "You tear it off so that there is no way it repeats itself, and lends itself to statistical breaking." The pads combined with the machines made the system secure, but the process was time-consuming and involved a lot of coding and decoding. Bayly then set about constructing the fastest, most secure cipher machine ever devised.

Cryptography vs. Espionage

"Bear in mind that the way you get an understanding of other people, is to find out what they are saying—not to go and watch them and guess what they are saying. In other words, cryptography has taken the place of espionage." He remembered Edward Travis, the head of Bletchley Park, gave a demonstration of this when he was visiting New York. The two looked out the office window and took an interest in what was happening next door. Workers with a crane at the RCA building lifted an immensely heavy object. "It took them ages to lift it, and set it down inside the building, and Travis said, 'What do you think they are doing?' and I said, 'Well it looks as if it is heavy enough to be a vault door.'" Travis tried to find out what was happening next door and eventually, by phoning around, he found someone in an engineering office who could tell him. He was told the heavy object Bayly thought was a vault door, was a new air conditioning system they were installing. Travis said, "Now there is the difference from espionage. Here am I, as a perfect agent, and I've watched them putting a door on the vault, and it wasn't a vault at all. It was an air conditioning unit. And me, as a skilled watcher, watches this thing, and I don't tell them anything useful. But when you could find out what they actually were doing, by talking to the man in charge, you get so much more information. That is the difference between espionage and cryptographics, a factor of hundred to one or something. The same piece of information, it is so easy to—even if you see it—it is so easy to misjudge what it is. But I thought that was a wonderful example."

■

Although the purchased Western Union system was not secure, Bayly was convinced that utilizing punched tape and teletype was the best way to run all BSC's covert communication. It was secret, unlike telephone, and it was nearly as fast as telephone—about 68 words a minute. Bayly took off the tops of the Western Union machines and installed a long cipher tape that would run for two hours, and never be repeated. The receiving party was sent a duplicate tape to run simultaneously, and characters were added at one end of the tape, so they could be aligned with a new one. The cipher tapes were transported by courier between the two machines, often in diplomatic bags. "This was now secure because it was not using a repetitive tape." The new machine was the prototype for the machine later dubbed the Rockex. (The actual Rockex machine was different as it could be used on commercial lines.) "It was a fine machine to be used, say, in between New York and Washington but useless for running, using commercial facilities in between," Bayly explained.

The Bayly network started from the two converted telekrypton machines and grew from there. "We started using machines to Ottawa (likely the Examination Unit)[5] and then we used it on the cable to England." For the trans-Atlantic communication BSC had to have privately accessed cables as the system was dependent on having synchronized connection, and they couldn't rely on other operators in between. The coding tapes had to be aligned properly. If the circuit was broken, the tapes were not in synch and the messages had to be started over again. As a result BSC had to have control of the transmitting facilities. The organization leased cable and then approached the heads of ITT and had a terminal of the Transatlantic cable installed in their

Rockefeller Center office. "That way facilities were in our control—so there wasn't any option." With the hardware in place, the Allies began relying on BSC's resources.

"That's really what started the whole thing. This grew because we had very quick communication to England. We could send—if you went through the embassy, and have them encipher it, and the Foreign Office then decipher it—6 hours was a minimum one way. That meant that to get an answer back, it took at least 12 hours. Where, with our automatic encipherment, it took a minute. Bil! Stephenson and Churchill wouldn't stand for it, once they had discovered that they could talk instantly, in other words you could talk to someone, and have them answer back, because there was no delay—but you couldn't take 12 hours to get an answer. So that's what started the whole ball rolling. So my original job became a non-entity. What happened then is we had to have secure communication to every place that we needed to, for Bill Stephenson. That's where I had radio circuits, and cables, and everything else, talking to Canada, Washington, and London. Not only London but to Bletchley Park and all for Bill Stephenson's communication. When we had those facilities, we started doing other things with it."

When he arrived in New York BSC's communication was handled by two people. "It ended up with a thousand people on the mezzanine floor of the International building there. But this growth was just the necessities of getting on with intelligence."

The area he started in was small, on an upper floor of Rockefeller Center. He and a few other Stephenson officials had private offices there, but the rest worked in an open area. Bayly spent a lot of his time commuting between Ottawa, Camp X, London and Washington, so he approached Elizabeth Richardson, who was involved in decoding incoming messages and told her he would move out of his office, and she could have his space. "You go into the office. I don't mind moving out here," he told her. Afterward Richardson became his "devoted admirer," he says, and when he moved downstairs to the mezzanine floor, she moved with him, and became part of his department.

The British sent over a university professor, Ken Maidment, to assist him. Maidment had no electronics background but he understood what to look for in intercept messages. "He had a marvellous detailed knowledge about what was going on everywhere in the world, about spies, or anti-spies." Originally he came over to show Bayly what to look for in espionage communication networks. BSC was looking for Fifth Column activity in the US, and if there was any connection to people in Britain. "We were still trying to find out whether the Germans were using radio amateurs in the States to communicate with England. It turned out there weren't any to speak of." Bayly's assistant then changed his focus to interception of other signals such as army, navy and diplomatic. Maidment had a tremendous mind for detail, Bayly remembered. "He could tell you what frequency, what code name, what everyone was doing."

But Bayly suspects the British shipped the university professor to North America, simply because they wanted him moved. "Why he was sent over was to get rid of him, because he was a professor and people didn't trust professors, so they put him with me. Everybody in the office was from somewhere in Canada, except for Ken Maidment who was the only Englishman in the communications division, along with Miss Richardson."

Bayly remained convinced that utilizing punched tape and teletype was the best way to run all covert communication. It was secret and about as fast as normal speech. It was also simple to train competent personnel. In about half an hour a good stenographer could become a good teletype operator. Bayly approached the US government, the US war production board, and the Teletype Section of AT&T, persuading them to put in two production lines of teletype. Machines were converted and his network expanded quickly. His secret communications central, on the mezzanine floor at Rockefeller Center became a beehive of activity. "At one time I had 105 teleprinters." It took four people to run a teleprinter round the clock—three eight hour shifts, and one person off. The amount of heat that is given off by 105 teleprinters was extensive. "The operators were just about dying of the heat," he remembered. Bayly later worked out a deal to use some of the cooling system of the Radio City skating rink in the summertime to cool the area.

The top machines created by Bayly became known as the Rockex. He and Edward Travis named the devices after seeing the Radio City Rockettes out sunning one day.

The Rockex was unbreakable. At the height of the war, Bayly invented a machine that was a cryptographer's worst nightmare. Bayly's machine created no letter frequency peaks at all. "If you intercept this (enciphered message), it's completely random, in the sense that if you copied all the letters from A to Zee ... if you copied each of the letters, each of them would be there one twenty-sixth of the time. Which proves that it's completely random, and if it is, you could prove mathematically that this is unbreakable." If the Nazis had intercepted Rockex messages and plotted them, they would "know perfectly well it's a very high grade cipher indeed, that doesn't show peaks where letters occur."

As a result, eventually his network guarded many of the war's secrets, including ULTRA and MAGIC material. "There was no use giving the enemy back their own stuff," he said with a slight smile. "They'll spot the fact we're intercepting everything, and breaking it."

■

"The Rockex machine was produced quite early in the war and it's not actually much of an invention. It's just taking what other people had done. I quote for a minute the Massey Harris binder. I asked an expert on patents, one time, 'who had patented the Massey Harris binder?' And he said, 'You obviously don't know anything about developing a machine. That goes back for five hundred years with at least a hundred people doing it'. Well, it was the same as Rockex. I invented the last 'ten minutes' of years of development on machines that did similar things. And they couldn't handle teleprinter communication, just clear English, or they used the English alphabet. I invented a way of taking the 32 characters that you get in a teleprinter and only sending 26 characters. So we could use commercial cable companies to send them."

Roald Dahl
Radio Documentary, *Tuesday Night*
"The only telegrams that didn't leak were the ones that Bill sent from New York, because I'm sure you heard he had all these fantastic ... coding machines up there. Yeah. You had to have ... whole roll of lavatory paper at one end, and another the other, and with the same size and number of holes in them (laughing)."[5]

Harry Smith

"Rockex was really partly Pat's invention. There's no doubt about that. He worked on that code system, and Rockex I guess, is used today by, I would say, all the embassies in the world—even the Russians, you know."

■

For security reasons Bayly's secret machines, such as the Rockex, were not converted or manufactured by outside sources. "I set up a machine shop—right there in Rockefeller Center." Machinery was put on shock mounts to help curb suspicious noise. Bayly's BSC people doubled drive mechanisms on some teleprinters. "We made a whole lot of machines. You could take Morse tape (perforated tape) which came in off the radio, and you could put that onto teleprinter code automatically, so you didn't have to have an operator doing that. (Gordon Welchman wrote, 'Pat was in some way responsible for the operation of a high-speed Morse code radio link between Canada and England.')[6] We made machines like that, so that we were just cutting down necessary man power. We made all sorts of funny things."

Unknown even to some of the people who worked there, BSC offices were monitored and protected by plain-clothed policemen of Canada's Royal Canadian Mounted Police. "The guy sitting at the desk in my office—he looked like a hobo. He was never well dressed. He was a Mountie and he knew who came and went."

At Camp X, Bayly put together radio linkages. "We couldn't put radio stations in the States because the war wouldn't let us, but we could put radio stations in Canada because they were licensed to me."

For security reasons large commercial transmitters weren't purchased. Amateur radio operators were approached and asked to turn in their equipment. "We couldn't go out and secretly buy $1,000 in commercial transmitters, but we could seize radio amateurs' stations, and pay for them on our own and use them 'under the table,' so to speak."

Would not that equipment be useless on a trans-Atlantic scale?

"No, funnily enough, it isn't. If you take 24 hours a day, and you have a 100 watt transmitter, you could probably get through one hour of the 24. If you then went to a kilowatt then you could probably get another 3 hours out of the 24, and if you went to 71 kw, which is about what they use across the Atlantic, you could probably get 16 to 18 hours. You have to change frequencies, and this business of fading is quite a problem."

With the help of the RCMP and Canadian Government radio inspectors, a major Allied communications link was completed. "We could get the government inspector to say so and so has got a 500 w radio transmitter he would probably sell you, because he can't go on the air now during the war, etc. etc. So that is what we did. We bought amateurs' and gradually increased the power so that it was something useful."

The largest transmitter they found was in Philadelphia. A newspaper owner had a radio station connected with his newspaper, and the FCC cancelled his license. "We bought that, tore it down, and moved it up to Camp X. The whole trick of our operations was that it was a fast way there and fast way back, and that we could do with ease within this continent when we wanted. To do it for England, we couldn't do it as fast as we might have liked it, but at first we were able to do it for radio and get a lot of words for free. Or you rang them. Free means that it wasn't costing us 10¢ a word or something, and that is a normal commercial rate across the Atlantic. When you've got half a million words to send, and relatively quite important, depending on the business they were about, it could cost a lot of money. Not only that, you were giving away quite a lot of facilities that people knew about. We didn't want people to know we had a hundred thousand words to send a day. But really, at the heart of the whole thing was that we had a network of fast communications and that's what Stephenson needed, and it was completely unbreakable."

Two-hour tapes were distributed between Camp X, Ottawa, Washington, New York, and England by courier. The facilities at Camp X Bayly called HYDRA because with OSS and SOE training going on, and RCMP and Communications people around, the place seemed to have many heads. He also arranged that radio transmissions could be adjusted for atmospheric conditions. "We had quite an installation at HYDRA. We had three transmitters and they steadily did about ten hours a day. You couldn't work them at night—mostly by day and about ten hours a day. So that we had very good communications."

Remarkably, Bayly's communications links were set up and running within months of Pearl Harbor. "That was really all I did from the beginning."

BSC's communication system had the unbreakable Rockex. It had automatic encipherment, where a stenographer could type normally and the letters would be automatically coded, and later decoded just as quickly. The cable messages could be coded automatically to radio transmitters. There were cable links, radio links, and trained staff. They all combined not only to provide communications security, they provided speed.

Meanwhile, the American Army and Navy chose to focus on radio. They were impressed that radio could run at 300 words a minute, Bayly remembered, and felt teletype was too slow for their purposes. Staffing was more of a problem however, as it involved undulater tape and Morse Code. "It takes two years to teach a good undulater. I decided, as I had worked with both systems, that this was silly."

Soon after Pearl Harbor the American military "discovered that running along with high speed Morse didn't work worth a darn, and they began to work with teletype, and there was a shortage of teletype. They discovered that I set up the teletype production line, and got enough (US) government assistance to do it. The war production board allowed me to, because I'd done this—to have first go at the teleprinters, which we wanted. The Signal Officer in the Navy, who's name I can't think of now, discovered this. He discovered also, that I understood this business. He and I became quite good friends and he made it much easier for me to deal with the cryptographic people and this sort of thing. Navy communication." Shortly afterward the American military decided to use Bayly's communications network as well.

As the war progressed, with a few exceptions, the Allies had increased success breaking Axis codes, as the process and machinery gradually became more efficient. But in cryptography, there can be no mistakes in a 'raw' intercepted message. Often messages were recorded by hand, by relatively simple equipment, and errors were easily made. "We'd intercept in ten different places," Bayly said. "We'd intercept the German signal, and the people we had intercepting would give us ten different versions of the story. Because they were intercepting it by hand, and in small facilities, and mistakes would happen. And if you are trying to bust cryptograms, you must have no mistakes, because a mistake makes a cryptogram unreadable to everybody, including machines, and so we began to need better and better communication facilities."

It was decided to funnel the raw intercepts into BSC for distribution to various countries. Signals came in from all over the British Empire, from the South of Africa to the Falklands. "Anywhere the British Empire had listening posts." The signals usually went to Camp X and then onto New York. There they were sorted, and sent to the crypt bureau of the country that was working on that particular code. "The US had every bit as good interception as we had, only we had it in different places. If you happened to be at the right angle from where people were going, and with this fading business that goes on with telegraph radio, we happened to be in better position than they did and they had better places than we had. But not necessarily. So frequently we could trade parts of the Pacific with them, and they'd be only too glad to play ball with us, because we were adding to things that they didn't have. They would give us part of the communication which we could send to England to back up. In cryptography you're always trying to break fresh codes, as well as old ones, so interception, even if you're not breaking it, can be very important, so that you get accurate messages."

Many of the Axis messages picked up in North America were actually communication from Europe because of the strange bounce of short-wave skip signals off the ionosphere.

Some radio signals were picked up and analysed in the Western Hemisphere before the message was received by the intended recipient. After the US lost much of their Pacific Fleet at Pearl Harbor, the Japanese Navy sought to assert it's dominance. One of the first major objectives was the island of Midway. American cryptographers broke the instructions to the Fleet, figured out the proposed plan, and took countermeasures that sank the attacking force. "At Midway we knew the Japanese admiral's instructions before he knew them. He was still asking for repeats. And we knew them. And the difference was, we were able to put our aircraft right on the top of his battleships—Bang." The Allies were searching the Pacific skies for foreign transmissions, Bayly said. "And in this case, the Japanese captain was asking for repeats, because he was listening on a little antenna on a battleship. We were looking at it with mile wide (sic) directional antennas on shore and we had it broken out, and knew what was being said while he was still asking for repeats."

The Japanese lost four aircraft carriers, 2,500 men, and over two hundred aircraft at Midway, which turned the war in the Pacific around. "And that was the difference between winning the Pacific and losing the Pacific, and that was done by cryptography and nothing else."

Midway was the most remarkable success for codebreakers and the US Pacific Fleet. The most infamous debacle in the region was brought on by a lack of communication and ignorance, Bayly said.

"The whole history of cryptography and the US Senate is a disgrace," he said. "The US Senate decided that doing cryptographics was not a gentlemanly occupation and the United States was not going to do it. And they told the Army to quit it, and they told the Navy to quit it, and they told the Coast Guard to quit it and they told the FBI to quit it. The Navy said well to hell with that, and the Army said to hell with that, and the reason we didn't know about Pearl Harbor is the Army had half of it, and didn't dare admit they were doing cryptography, and therefore didn't tell the Navy, and the Navy got half of it and didn't dare admit that they were doing cryptographic work, in case the Senate found out, and didn't tell the Army. And the result is Pearl Harbor went on. We could have, if they were talking to each other, known exactly what Pearl Harbor was doing. Or was going to do."

Bayly said he often told the US Army what the US Navy was doing. Gordon Welchman says this occurred because of inter-service rivalry in Washington. (Welchman says that both he and Bayly were the go-betweens, but Welchman was only briefly in the US in 1944.)[7]

During the war the American Senate wanted to know from the American military exactly which foreign codes they had, and what they were breaking cryptographically. "And the generals said, 'I have taken an oath that I will not do this, whether you're Senators or you're not Senators, and I'm not doing it.' That would be about the year after Pearl Harbor. Right in the middle of the war.

"Just an absolute disgrace. Because of the Senate, Billy Friedman had to quit being a Colonel in the Army, resign from the Army and become the resident librarian. This was the sort of nonsense. In a time of war. This isn't just a couple of kids playing in the back street. This is a country at war, and the Senate was insisting that we shouldn't do cryptography and they would discuss what cryptography was being done. In spite of the fact we weren't doing any."

The Plumber

Bayly had no code name during the war, but he had a code occupation. He was the plumber. His task was not to know what a particular message was. His assignment was to see that the messages kept flowing. "My job was to see that there was running water, but what happened to the water was none of my business. And so I never at any time let any of my people see the breakouts of any secret documents. We just simply got coded documents and transmitted them.

"I was just myself, because I functioned almost publicly in the sense that being just a communications man, I didn't have to worry about identification, or who or why or what. Being a plumber, I didn't count in the organization for security. The joke about that was that the communications man knows who you are dealing with, how important the communication is, and what it is in the background, even if you don't know the wording, but I had no security clearance to speak of."

He had a code number, but doesn't recall exactly what it was. "It was 48 something, because Bill Stephenson was 48000 ... I wasn't allowed to kill anybody."

Few references to Bayly exist anywhere, but in the papers at the University of Regina, there is one cable from 1974 from William Stephenson to William Stevenson. It appears to refer to a book on ULTRA by Peter Calvocossi, or else comments he made on the CBS television program Sixty Minutes on the ULTRA Secret. It reads :

PETE (Calvocossi) SPARES NO CREDIT TO MAGIC REPT MAGIC THE AMERI-
CAN MACHINE ALSO TO THE FACT THAT OUR ARRANGEMENT TO SUPPLY
THEM FREE OF COST THROUGH CANADIAN WATSON OF IBM WITH
COMPUTER OF OUR DESIGN WHICH SAVED THEM MILLIONS OF MAN
HOURS NOR ANY REF OUR TRIANGULATION U-BOATS POSITIONS AND
OUR TELEKRYPTON IMMENSE TRAFFIC DIRECTED BY MY PROF. BAILEY

(sic) WHOM BISON (Herb Rowland) WORKED UNDER STOP BAILEY WAS MY RIGHTHAND ELECTRONICS MAN AN AUTOMATON WHO GAVE GREAT PRACTICAL HELP TO ALL HOME COMMUNICATIONS OPERATIONS INCLUDING ASPIDISTRA WHICH BUFFALO KNOWS ABOUT.[8]

The U-Boats

"Nor any reference of triangulation of U-boats positions ...?"

"That I was concerned with, because we had now got to the point where we could break the coding of the submarines, and Hitler had insisted the submarines give their position reports twice a day. So if you could break the code, you knew where the submarines were twice a day. Every Navy had to know where submarines were, so they could send ships or aircraft with depth charges. You could move a submarine completely if you could drop depth charges within so many hundred yards of the sub, the shock was too much for the submarine. The timing was essential, and it was handled through the US Army which had 30 million (letter) groups a day in their headquarters. It was decided that this was too slow. I was given the job of giving submarine position reports to whatever Navy could be anywhere near that particular place, to tackle these submarines. We were allowed a minute and a half, from the time we got the information from the station, to get it to the Crypt Bureau of the Army or the Navy or which country could then alert the Navy to where the submarine was.

"So that was one of our things. I had devised a method, because everything came in on punched tape. I devised a method by just punch-ing the right holes in the tape could give the code in English, so that any operator knowing it could see that this had 'sub' or something in front of it, and that meant a minute and a half—get rid of it. This method was so that inept people could code the stuff and hand it to the next person, whether they could read the tape or not. Most of the girls could read the perforated tape as well as they could English. You get pretty experienced in that ...

"But because of this, we were given the job. And that was kind of an important job, where all these subs were. We got rid of a lot of subs that way. Bill was very pleased with that. He thought it was proper use of our facilities. It was "an important job." Describing the importance of

ULTRA and the Atlantic, Peter Calvocossi said, "I would say it was the decisive element in the Battle of the Atlantic. This was extremely important because the Battle of the Atlantic was obviously decisive about the war as a whole. If we hadn't won the Battle of the Atlantic in the winter of 1942-43 we could have been knocked out. We, I mean England. If we had been knocked out, and France had already been knocked out, what happens to the Americans? What happens to you? You can't cross the Atlantic because the U-boats are still there. If you do cross it, where do you go?" (CBS Sixty Minutes interview, 'The Ultra Secret.')

When the Allies couldn't break the ENIGMA code, they used direction finding. Various listening stations could report the location of a U-boat as being at such and such direction, in relation to their location. The more signals that could be received, the more accurately they could zero in on a precise locale. "At first we didn't know that the subs had to report into Hitler twice a day," Bayly said. "We only learnt that three years on, by mistakes. Up till that time we just knew from the tones on the transmitters, and the noise that the German subs made. We could tell from the noise, the power noise, and by one thing and another, we could tell that was a German sub, even if we couldn't break out the communication."

From the report of only one ship or station, very little could be deduced. "We wouldn't know whether it was right or wrong, but if you have ten of those, from ten different places, you've then got what we would call a 'cocked hat' which means these are places … they all try to go through this point. Then you would say that the centre of these is the probable place."

When the codes were broken the process became easier, and if the subs were not destroyed at least convoys could be diverted. "You would then listen, and the subs would say, I'm at latitude and longitude so and so, and we didn't need the DF-ing. But this came much later. But in the times that I started this, we weren't breaking the code. We just knew that this was a sub, and we had to handle that as quickly as we could to give the approximate position.

"I didn't have charge of that. I was just one place where they could push the stuff in one place, and do something to it as it went by." BSC didn't plot the location of all the U-boats, they dealt with the distribution of their location messages. "We didn't organize it in any way, but we had to know what Navy could be in that area, or close to that area, to make sure that everybody knew that we had this submarine reported at such and such a latitude and longitude. It wasn't much good to be twenty minutes later, because by that time he might be ten miles further away. It had to be done as fast as possible."

The American Navy's top code machine was considered so secret, it was not to be even viewed by any foreigner. Bayly had one in his office. "This was just an exchange, and we did this completely unofficially in the sense that we would never admit that we could do it. I had the Navy code machine—the top code machine—in my New York office ... and if that had have been known, all hell would have broken loose. We had it sitting there so that they could send the stuff to us on that machine and we could break it out, and in turn they would have our code machine in their office. This was very practical—it worked, but it only worked because people trusted each other, and that's one of the reasons I've been quiet about writing books. When you've been dealt with that way, you feel that you would like to keep it that way. We had very good personal relationships with the people, which is the only way I've discovered anything works. It doesn't matter how many laws people pass enabling it—if you don't like each other, business just doesn't happen."

Aspidistra

"WLW radio station had obtained, through political pushing around, a license for a 500 kilowatt station, at a time when 50 kilowatts was the thing. By a little political manoeuvring had got the FCC to license it, and they had purchased it through RCA, and RCA had built the station. It had a front panel 200 feet long, I might add, and was quite a thing. The output tubes stood 11 feet high. They had enlarged the output from 500 kilowatts to 1000 kilowatts because they thought they were going to sell it to Mexico. The Americans decided they didn't want such a huge transmitter in Mexico.

"The FCC got cold feet and wouldn't license it, so RCA had this immense transmitter, the biggest transmitter that's ever been built, and nothing to do with it. And I happened to tell, of all people, the Queen's mother's brother David Bowes-Lyons that we had this station. He was in charge of propaganda and he said, 'That's exactly what I want. I want a station that is so powerful it can't be interrupted with.' He went back to England and he pulled some wires there, and they said yes, you could buy this station. RCA quoted us, I think it was a million, two hundred thousand. This is a story of Enid Bence that I had forgotten all about. But in any event, we had bought the station and it was known as 79 80. In those days we were using hand-communication on the radio and mistakes happened, and 79 80 would get abused and we wouldn't know what they were talking about. I said, 'Quit using a number and put a name on this thing.' And they said, 'Fine. You pick the name.'

"Bun and I had been to a play with Beatrice Lilly. Beatrice Lilly sang a song, 'the biggest aspidistra in the world.' The English boarding houses always had an aspidistra. It was a sign you were nice people, if you had a big aspidistra plant. We'd listened to this song the night before and I'm having lunch at home with Bun, saying, 'I've been asked to give a name to this thing. What'll we call it?" She said, 'Well, last night was the thing. Bea Lily called it the biggest aspidistra in the world. Let's call it that.' So we called it 'Aspidistra.' My wife named it.

"The first use it got was an interesting one, and very rarely known. Probably most people didn't talk about it. The Germans came over with bombing raids, and we had people who could speak German so fluently that they could imitate the voices of the normal people giving the bombing raids their orders. By using Aspidistra, we could completely overcome the German orders that they were giving to the bombers, and tell the bombers what to do next. A thousand kilowatts—you could smother the thing so it didn't matter what head office was telling them, we just wiped it out." On occasion, he said, the flights were so confused they went over Ireland.

Aspidistra was put underground in the south of England and when the invasion of Europe came, the Allies were able to issue orders to the invasion troops. "They didn't want another Dunkirk, and so they wanted a transmitter big enough so the troops could get their orders without any chance of being smothered, and I'll get to Enid Bence now," he said. He gave his secretary Enid Bence a cheque for a million dollars to pay RCA. "And I can still see Enid clutching her purse to her breast," he smiled. "She had a check for a million dollars in this thing! She came back, still breathless and horrified, and all the rest of it ... But that's how Aspidistra got it's name. You know, you remember the funny things."

ULTRA and Bletchley

"It was quite a thing when they released ULTRA to the general public, because it had been so secret. The reason it was so secret wasn't what was in it, but the method of production. Most of the ULTRA work was merely the results of cryptographic breaking-down of German communications, and Japanese. But it was secret. Very secret. Not as I say, because of the stuff itself, but if you used anything about ULTRA in Germany, or Japan, they would be certain as to where the information would come from. And we didn't want anybody to know where we were breaking their codes."

"So they said it was from a spy close to the scene?"

"Yeah, they always invented a way of defining ULTRA. But that was why ULTRA was so very secret, and I made sure that we handled it. The material was sent across in our communication, probably because of the speed of it—if you're giving something to the Americans, if it was two weeks old, the Americans would say, 'why the hell didn't we know this two weeks ago?' So they wanted to make it fast and that was why I handled it. But at no time were any of my people, except the girls running the terminals themselves, in on it. So we never saw ULTRA. We didn't even know it was ULTRA."

Canadians handled Bayly's machines, even at Bletchley. "They were almost always Canadians," he said. "All the girls in England, in Bletchley, were Canadian girls they had sent over there—Bobby Griffiths was one of them."

Bobby Griffiths was from his home province Saskatchewan. "Bobby Griffiths' father was a friend of one of the bank managers out in Moose Jaw that I knew very well. I used Bobby Griffiths as the first operator of it, because I trusted her. I had known her since she was a youngster." She later married Kevin O'Neal, who was with Canada's National Research Council, which also was involved in covert activities during the war. O'Neal subsequently became head of Canada's top-secret Communications Security Establishment. Griffiths was one of the proficient operators of Rockex at time, and Bayly sent her to Britain to handle the Bletchley connection.

Aside from trusting Canadians, Bletchley Park had trouble with the English Post Office, Bayly said. A branch of the Royal Mail handled telecommunications. This could present employee problems and working situations dictated by postal people, not by the existing emergency in England. "The result is that Travis and the Post Office would make arrangements, and those arrangements would become written in letters of fire. You couldn't change them," Bayly said, "it was most uncomfortable.

"It would be the Post Office which would tell us what to do, which was why I sent girls in England that would handle the ends of the cable, to keep them out of the Post Office. The Post Office was union, even through the war, and the union allowed them to do this. The Post Office was most indignant when I put in operators and teletypes that they weren't allowed to go near. The English were so ... I found England's planning very uncomfortable, because it had happened long before the war, and it was now established, and you couldn't move it. Even Travis would have a hard job trying to change what went on."

Bayly knew few of the successful decrypts at Bletchley. "I deliberately kept away from that, as far as I could." But one day in England, he was shown a notation from the Nazi Fuehrer to the Italian dictator Benito Mussolini. "This was a message from Hitler to Mussolini, bawling the daylights out of him, for having sent some very secret stuff by courier from Italy up to Germany, and saying, 'Do not take a chance. Your courier might be intercepted. Send this by radio.' We intercepted this. I thought this was amazing, because we were breaking radio. And we could not catch couriers."

Across the Atlantic

In England, even though he was often on secret flights, Bayly had to go through Customs as everybody else. However, he was what the British called 'minimum interrogation,' which meant the British authorities were to leave him alone, and not search baggage. He would contact London before going over and tell them of his expected arrival and they would communicate with Prestwick, Scotland, or his expected port of entry. "If two people telegraph them from London, or somewhere else and tell them, 'Bayly is coming in at such and such ... Minimum Interrogation is required', they give you pretty decent treatment. I would get Censorship, Cryptography and two other people to tell these people, 'Bayly. Minimum interrogation.' You got the royal treatment. You got red carpets and all the rest of it."

On one flight he was accompanied by the British Minister of Transport, Lord Leathers. The minister was unaware of how to coast through customs. England was under rationing, and Leathers brought back a ham from North America. He wasn't allowed to take it into the country, and had a kerfuffle with custom officials when it was confiscated. Exasperated, he finally asked if there was anything he could do with the ham. "Give it to him," the customs agent replied, motioning to Bayly. Stephenson's Communications head could bring anything he wanted into England, so he took the ham and gave it to the Minister of Transport later. Leathers was more surprised as they made their way back to London. Bayly had a car waiting to take him to the train station and a private carriage on the train. "He was quite impressed," Bayly remembered, and said, 'In the next war I am not going to be a Cabinet Minister. I'm going to be a damn security officer!' He was Mr Transportation. He could have anything that he wanted, but he hadn't raised an 'advance,'" Bayly chuckled.

Late in the war, Bayly found out the American OSS had a shuttle plane waiting for trans-Atlantic arrivals in Scotland. The Americans made him a member of OSS, so he tried to hitch a lift, but he was stopped entering the plane. Why did Bayly, OSS, have a British passport? He simply answered, "You know better than to ask questions like that," and the American apologized.

Washington

Bayly was in Washington about three days a week. He was in Ottawa once every two or three weeks, which would include the trip through Camp X. "This was just liaison work, getting on with people, seeing if they had problems and weren't writing them, and that sort of nonsense. If you have four hundred girls in one place, there are lots of problems that they wouldn't write ... but if you talk to them offhand, you can quickly grasp if there is trouble."

In Washington the American military took over a Lady's College and turned it into the US Army Crypt Bureau. "And the Officer commanding it had a button on his wall. It had been one of the bedrooms in the Lady's College, and the bell underneath it said, 'If You Urgently Need a Mistress Ring This Bell'," he laughed. "The Officer commanding had refused to let them take that down. He said, 'I want that in my office.'"

He attended numerous meetings in the American capital regularly, mostly to do with communications security. Other meetings he frequented were not to talk about communications security, and that was why he was there.

There were 57 joint committees, Bayly said, so they were known as 'the Heinz.' Some came and went quickly. One committee was to unify Allied phonetic names used for letters, such as 'Able' for 'A', 'B' for 'Bailey' and so on. However certain words were viewed as being rude in England, or in the United States, and the committee soon became bogged down as they moved through the alphabet. One night the British delegation got drunk in the Mayflower Hotel, Bayly remembered, and they invented a code. "It started 'A' was for 'Arses', 'B' for 'ham', 'C' for 'colanders', 'D' for 'dung', ... and 'L' for 'hell for leather,' and they presented this to the US committee. The committee never met again."

Bayly also sat on the top-secret radar counter-measures committee. The Allies discovered shredded aluminum strips dropped from aircraft could confuse radar and the code word for the project was 'windows.' But Bayly didn't know the details of the project. He was on the committee simply to terminate any talk about trans-Atlantic communication and telephone security. "I was in the position, if they got mixed up in telephone security, I was to say, 'Sorry boys. I've got orders for you to stop ... can't go on any further.'" Bayly didn't enjoy the discussion. "I remember sitting as a member of the committee, I'm bored to tears and darned if I'm going to ask them what 'windows' is. But they kept telling me about 'windows.'"

Later he received a cable from England wanting the committee report: "Please give us copies of the Radar counter-measures committee. We need them urgently." Bayly wasn't sure about that one. "So I phoned the head of G-2 (Military Intelligence) in the States and said, 'Can I get

on this radar counter committee? There's a guy in England who wants (the report),' and Carter Clarke said, 'I can get it for you. But it will take months. We just cut that to the minimum. But I'll phone you back.'"

Clarke returned the call soon afterward, laughing. "He said, 'Hell, you're one of the 13 people that gets that damned thing.'" Bayly regularly received all the information of the committee, but he hadn't read the reports, and simply stored them in a filing cabinet. He then walked across his office and retrieved them from his files. "Carter Clarke was one of the top men in G-2, with a rare sense of humour. I was glad it was him. He was a friend of mine, and not somebody else more official. Did I feel like a chump! This was the most secret 'holy of holies.'"

Gordon Welchman and British scientist Henry Tizard also sat in on some of the Allied committees, Bayly said. Not all the scientific ideas were used, or were as useful as radar or 'windows.' He also met Geoffrey Pike in Washington. The Allies were losing a lot of shipping in the Atlantic, so Pike's idea was to construct a frozen ship using water, wood chips, and a mould. The ice vessel would last long enough for a voyage across the Atlantic and then it would be unloaded. "Pike was a screwball if there were ever one," Bayly remembered. "You just froze the ship. You had a special dry dock which froze the ship and you loaded it up with what you wanted, and shipped it across. Then it would melt. That was Pike's idea."

Pike didn't make a full-sized model but he constructed something that was big enough to impress people. "But it came too late in the war to actually get used."

Bayly met a number of prominent people travelling between New York and Washington (See Appendix C). He worked with many more. "You find that people that are famous and important, treat you like a human being," he said. "But people who think they are important are regular SOB's."

People
Mountbatten

Several people Bayly worked with during the war impressed him. He considered Stephenson and Hoover as two of his heroes, and another stopped off in New York on his way to Asia. "This fellow had been a communications officer in the British Navy. He went from that to the Captain of a destroyer and then kept on moving up."

Lord Louis Mountbatten, assigned to Asia, wanted to use Rockex while he was there. He toured BSC's secret communications center to learn about it. He told Bayly, 'I want to know about Rockex. I'm going to use that, and I'm going to depend on it. I'm a communication man and I want to know about it.' "He wanted to find out, so ask the guy himself, 'so here I am.'"

Bayly showed Mountbatten a terminal for a teleprinter cable to London, and his guest sat down beside the operator and said, "Okay dear, move over, and show me how to run this one". Mountbatten spent the day there learning all about Rockex in one way or another, and made quite an impression on some of his employees. He was with an aide-de-camp, who was there to see that everything went well, and afterward Bayly asked some people on his floor about him and they said, 'What aide-de-camp?' "They just saw him," Bayly laughed. Mountbatten's assistant had been a captain in the British Navy, but didn't register at all with them.

Mountbatten was a man he took to immediately, he said. "He was a real guy. You couldn't meet him for two minutes, without being impressed that he was just a hell of a nice guy, who did his job to his best. He was one of my heroes of the war."

Stephenson arranged a lunch for Mountbatten, Noel Coward, Brooks Atkinson, of the *New York Times*, and Bayly, soon after Noel Coward's film *"In Which We Serve"* was released. It was the story of a virtuous British naval captain and loosely based on Mountbatten. During the lunch Atkinson commented on the film. "Brooks said to Noel Coward, 'I liked everything about your picture immensely, except the speech the skipper gave on the deck of that sub before going into action. That was so corny! I'm quite sure that no captain would have said that,' and Mountbatten says, 'Well! I'm sorry you feel that way, because that is the speech I made on that occasion verbatim.' There was dead silence around the lunch table." Bayly glanced over at Stephenson. He was keeled over laughing. "Bill Stephenson was just about busting a gut. He knew the whole circumstance.

"The English gentry were really something," Bayly said. "They really were. But there's nothing left. Two World Wars have killed them all off."

Colonel Barty Playdell-Bouverie

"Barty Bouverie was a fine English gentlemen, proper order, and one of the nicest men I knew. He'd been with the Cold Stream Guards and his hobby was needlepoint. And if you'd see him, with rolls of medals, going on the plane to England … American officers were sitting there staring, while Barty was doing needlepoint."

John Pepper

"Pepper did a good job of work, but his motto was kiss people on all four cheeks."

He was not in on all Stephenson's activities, as Roald Dahl thought, Bayly said. "His job was office manager. He might have handled some of the other, in preparing reports for Bill to submit. But his job really was office manager. There were two of them. He was one of the two. There was a lot of office managing to do. You had salaries, clearances.

"He was in on everything, in the sense he was sort of Stephenson's personal assistant. Garner knew more than he did, but Garner wouldn't go out and interview people, and that sort of thing. If there was anything like that, Stephenson would probably pick on Pepper.

"Bill Stephenson trusted him implicitly. He was never particularly observable."

Dick Ellis

"Dickey Ellis was MI6 and the only professional, the long-term professional in the business. He had been in MI6 for years and years. He's the one they thought must be a Russian or German agent, which I regard as entirely unproved, because I had known him quite well. He visited us in our apartment in New York quite often. He was a musician and he just didn't ever give an inclination that he was that way concerned.

"The only thing I knew about Ellis is that he was a very good musician. He used to come over to my apartment, and I played the piano, and he would talk about things and he had a marvellous knowledge of classical music. And I think he played the cello or the viola. He never played it in my presence but he knew the scores of the viola and the cello. And I liked him very much. I liked Dickey Ellis immensely. And if he could have been a spy, I wouldn't have known the difference.

"And as I say, we were very lucky we didn't have a breach of security, a bad breach of security. I'm quite sure if Ellis had been a spy (we would have known). I'm suspicious of the people who said he was."

Eddie Hastings

Eddie Hastings did liaison work for Government Code and Cipher in Britain and was an assistant of Edward Travis. He was frequently in North America. "I'll tell you about Eddie Hastings, Eddie was a gentlemanly confidence man. He had been to Eton, Oxford, he had come from a good Old English family and he was a captain of the British Navy. And I didn't trust him an inch. He made his living riding horses for his gentleman friends and he was a complete confidence man.

"Gouzenko always said that there was another man in the British (security organizations) who he called 'Elli,'[9] and I'm quite sure that what he was trying to say was 'Eddie,' and I'm sure this guy was it, and I've never had enough information that I dare say that, but I wouldn't trust Hastings as far as I could pitch him by the ears."

Part of the problem, Bayly said, was the English seemed to screen people using schooling and background as parameters. "Because they'd been at Cambridge, therefore they were safe, and they were almost known German agents at that time. I think Eddie Hastings was probably Russian. Bill didn't like him at all," Bayly continued. "Eddie did such things that Travis finally decided he didn't trust (him) and kicked him out."

When the war was over, Bayly gave Hastings a few accounting problems. "I had borrowed three transmitters, which I used in Camp X, because the original transmitters which we had bought from amateurs were sloppily put together. They were running 24 hours a day. They just didn't stand up too well. I got talking to one of the US Air Force communications officers at one stage in the war, and told him the problem, and he said, 'Hell we've got a lot of those 71½ kw transmitters that we aren't using. I'll sent three of them down.' So he sent me three of these and we set these up in Camp X." The transmitters were acquired through Lend Lease and under those terms, the British had to pay the American Treasury the dollar value specified for each item they had used, or given away. Following the war, Hastings was to help arrange the transfer of any English wares at Camp X to Canadian government control. Hastings simply gave away the transmitters. "Eddie discovered these transmitters, I think were $90,000 each, and he had to go to the British Treasury and say I've just given away $270,000 worth of US Lend Lease." Bayly believes afterward Hastings was not held in such high esteem. "That was what finished Eddie.

"I'm afraid I was a little bitchy about that," Bayly remembered. "Because I hadn't told him they had been on Lend Lease. You couldn't trust Eddie as far as you could pitch him. He would tell you one story and two seconds later he would tell somebody else a different story."

Grace Garner

"I was very fond of Grace, in the sense that I admired what she did. She was a good secretary. Stephenson didn't understand women much. Grace Garner was very fond of Stephenson.

"She asked him one day if he'd get her a job as an editor somewhere. He did, and she never forgave him for it, because that meant she wasn't working for him any longer.

"It always scuttled me as to why Grace would feel so badly about Bill Stephenson letting her go."

Halifax

The British Ambassador in Washington, Lord Halifax, was one of the few people with a private aircraft. Once he gave Bayly a lift to Washington and told him that upon arrival, he would have to review a guard of honour. "So I, as a half-Colonel, had to inspect the Major Generals, and their guard of honour," he laughed. "This was in the Mayflower Hotel lobby."

Stephenson and Halifax "were two men as different as day and night." On another occasion Bayly flew with Halifax across the Atlantic. "I came back on an aircraft, BOAC, with Halifax and we ran into a bunch of bad weather. Really, really bumpy. And Halifax got down on his knees on the floor and started praying. And the pilot came back and said 'You get the hell off that floor, or I'll break your damned head.' Because everyone else on the plane was wondering why Halifax had to pray. He was a funny guy. He was a very sincere man, but he was," Bayly hesitated, put his nose in the air and imitated a posh English accent, "very, very English."

Carter Clarke

"I'll give you an example of the kind of man he was. British Officers did not get Army Gold Badges and if you didn't have an Army Gold Badge, you didn't get into the Mall entrance of the Pentagon Building. You went in the back entrance, which is half a mile away walking from where you could get in. I'm late to a meeting, apologize, 'not having a gold badge.' Halfway through the meeting, his secretary gave me a Gold Badge and it had my picture on it. He asked me to turn it in, then he says, 'Hell, keep it, you'll be coming back.' He was quite a practical guy and if he believed in what you had to do, he would back things and keep you going."

(Later, while going through his possessions, Bayly pulled out his US Army Gold Badge. It seemed to be one of his most prized mementos of the war. "It's unheard-of for a foreigner to be given a US Army Gold Badge," he said.)

Ivor Bryce

"Ivor Bryce I liked. He was a nice guy. Bill Stephenson didn't trust him too much because he was English."

Montgomery Hyde

"He was a writer and he (Stephenson) wanted writers around because he'd get them to write. Propaganda and what have you. Bill wasn't too reticent about getting any publicity he could. He liked to get plenty. He was in a position at first, before Pearl Harbor, where he didn't dare get any because we were teaching OSS in a neutral country. And you couldn't very well get a lot of publicity about the fact they were breaking every law that you could think of."

J Edgar Hoover

"I am certain that he wanted one thing. He wanted the best federal police force that there was in the States. He would talk about this, if you were talking to him. He would explain the Secret Service, which now just looks after the President's safety, had once been a police force, until Congress had pulled it apart to nothing. Treasury then became one of the top-secret things, and Congress pulled that to nothing. Now they look just for counterfeit money. He went on pointing out all these things, and he said, 'I've decided that if they want to play dirty, I'll play dirtier than they do. But I am going to have the best police force in the United States, in spite of Congress. Congress don't want good police forces around.' So it ended up ... I kind of liked him.

"I liked this guy just as much as Sir William. He was very sincere, in spite of all the stories about him now. At the time I knew he was a sincere guy who was going to have the best federal police force in the United States. And it was going to be over the dead bodies of Congress. And he liked Sir William.

"Hoover, I'd discovered, had bought machines. We were then using a thing called the telekrypton which was a background of my later Rockex. But telekrypton was an automatic code machine that was pretty high grade, hard to use, but high grade, and we used that for all our communication, and we heard from Western Union that Hoover had ordered two of these machines." The machines would not have worked without the proper code tapes and synchronization, but Bayly viewed the situation with concern. "So I went into Bill Stephenson, and I said, 'Hoover's going to try to intercept our messages, but I'm sure he can't do it because he can't break our codes. He ordered two telekrypton machines and is going to intercept (our messages). What do you want me to do about that?' And Bill laughed and said, 'Well why don't you take two of our code tapes, the latest ones, and hand them to Hoover and say, 'Okay, you wanted these. Here they are.' I know perfectly well what Hoover will tell you, but try it and see.' So I went over to Hoover and I said the machines are no good without these tapes. Here are the code tapes we are currently using. He said, 'Well, thanks very much.' And I'm just halfway out of the office and he says, 'To hell with you. If I have those code tapes I am agreeing to everything you people say to each other. This is something I don't want any stake of. Good-bye!' And he sent the telekrypton machines back to Western Union. He wasn't going to be stuck with Congress knowing he knew exactly what we were saying.[10]

"He and Bill were very close but they were very discreet about it, because he didn't want to be mixed up with Donovan's outfit. Hoover was in a delicate position, from a US government—I mean from Congress. If Congress could have tied Hoover to any illegitimate or touchy thing like the educating of OSS, they would have hung him on it like a million dollars. They hated his insides for obvious reasons."

"Back then they hated him too?"

"Yeah. Well, he saw to it that they did. In my opinion, I went into a little hero worship in regards to Hoover. He sincerely wanted to have the best federal police force there was and he would let nothing get in his way and he used any means he liked to ensure that. And when you talked to him you realized he really meant it."

"Including blackmail?"

"Including blackmail and anything else. You just name it," he laughed."Well, there was no straightforward way of doing it. There isn't any now. He didn't like a lot of people around, because he didn't trust them. But he was to my knowledge, because I dealt quite a lot with him in the beginning, a very, very, sincere dedicated man, and that's rare in high policemen."

One reason BSC and the FBI got along well was Stephenson helped with US security, Bayly said. At one point Stephenson found out information about German spies landed in the United States. "He gave all the details to Hoover and then let the FBI take all the credit. The FBI thought that was very nice of him."

Menzies and Leadership

Bayly eventually got to know the head of British SIS, Stewart Menzies, quite well. Menzies once told him, "It's the most amazing thing. You speak like an American. But you think like an Englishman."

"My trouble was not 'getting on' with the English. I had no trouble with the Americans at all. They sort of felt the British Secret Service was something to be coddled, so I had no trouble with them. I had trouble with the English people who came over. I had to tell them how to get on with the Americans, which meant I was entertaining the English people lavishly in order to keep them quiet and happy. I had to entertain the Americans, but I didn't have to mother them."

Bayly spent uncounted hours commuting overseas and on one occasion he was stranded in Labrador waiting for a plane across the Atlantic with England's Minister of Transport Lord Leathers. They started discussing Stewart Menzies. The MI6 chief did not impress Bayly with his knowledge of the field, and he expressed some surprise that he was in charge during a World War. "I said, 'How in the name of fortune did Stewart Menzies,' who knew nothing about espionage, or counter-espionage, 'how did he get to be the head of SI?' Leathers replied, 'For one reason. He was a Scotch gentleman who everybody trusted.'"

That's how you pick a leader, Bayly said. The leader of anything. "Someone that everyone trusted. The head of a covert material thing is somebody you have to trust. The English would not put a man in charge who wasn't allowed to have his own way and not be backed by everyone. I thought that was an interesting thing. The Americans never found that out. They never found out that was the way to pick the head of something."

Igor Gouzenko

The Soviet defector Igor Gouzenko lived at Camp X for a few years in a farm house, but he was handled by the RCMP and Bayly kept out of it. "I had a deal that he didn't know who I was. He probably did, but I never addressed him in any way or gave him any orders. I just simply turned this place over to the RCMP and they ran it."

There was a lot of false information floating around that disguised Gouzenko's whereabouts. On one occasion Bayly and his wife heard on the radio, as they were driving from Oshawa to Camp X, reports that Gouzenko was likely staying somewhere in the Laurentians north of Montreal. "Everybody was heading there. And here's Gouzenko sitting on a deck chair outside the house, just as we drove up. I thought that was quite amusing. Poor old Gouzenko. He had no more brains than a peanut."

"How did he write that book then?" (Gouzenko's *Fall of a Titan* won the Governor-General's award.)

"I think his wife did it. She was quite a girl. It was his wife who advised him what to do. The Military Attaché at the Soviet Embassy got Gouzenko to decode one of his messages because he didn't feel like doing it himself. When Gouzenko decoded it, he saw it was instructions for him to be sent back to the Soviet Union, because he wasn't trusted. He'd be bumped off on landing," Bayly said, "the way the Russians were running things in those days." Bayly says Gouzenko then asked his wife for advice. "'What do I do now?' And so she told him, 'Go into the vault and steal every secret thing you can put your hands on, and change the combination on the vault and lock the door. It'll take six weeks for the Russians to send somebody over to chisel the door of the safe open to find out you've taken all these things. Turn yourself over to the Canadians.' So at the time the Prime Minister, King, said he wasn't going to be mixed up in that kind of Russian politics, and gave strict orders to the RCMP. Norman Robertson, who was the Secretary of External Affairs, told this story to Bill, and what King was doing. So Bill Stephenson headed up to Ottawa, borrowed my Buick from Camp X, drove it up to Ottawa, arrested Gouzenko (military arrest) and said, 'If you don't want to try him, we'll try him over in England. How would you like that?' King said 'No, I don't want that,' so they gave this guy protection. When he went back to his apartment the Russians were just breaking into his apartment. They'd had finally got somebody over.

"Norman Robertson was behind it all," he said. "Bill was protecting Norman Robertson." There was no easy way for Robertson to overrule his boss the Prime Minister, so he contacted the only person he thought could—Bill Stephenson. "King was his boss and Norman Robertson could hardly have turned Gouzenko in. So Bill Stephenson invented a story leaving Norman Robertson out of the thing.

"Bill was up because Norman Robertson tipped him off. He flew up and as I say, he wanted to get around and there wasn't a car available. So he took my Buick from Camp X and pinched Gouzenko. It was quite a thing."[11]

Although Gouzenko was at Camp X for an extended period and Bayly controlled the camp until 1948, he didn't want to have anything to do with him. "I got out of that as fast as I could, because the Russians were looking all over for Gouzenko, who spent the last two years at Camp X. I didn't want to get mixed up in that one. The Russians for years afterward would have gladly bumped him off."

Beaverbrook & US Security

A visit by Lord Beaverbrook to New York was particularly memorable to Bayly. The Canadian-born British minister knew that the Queen Mary's trans-Atlantic passage had been interrupted by a huge thump. Wanting to know what the ship had hit, Beaverbrook contacted his friend. Stephenson however, didn't want to deal with any more questions from Beaverbrook, so he sent Bayly over to the Waldorf with instructions not tell him. The Queen Mary had, in fact, hit a U-boat, Bayly was told, and the Americans were gleaning information from it.

"I almost perspire when you mention U-boat, and I think of myself spending the afternoon with Beaverbrook and not telling him what the Queen Mary had hit."

A lot of information was obtained from the Nazi submarine and it helped with ENIGMA deciphering. "They couldn't destroy their documents. It was all they could do to save their own lives, and get on deck because the battery acid had spilt and when battery acid and salt water reach together—bang! There was chlorine all over the place and they could just get topside. They just rose suddenly and everyone came above, and they didn't have anything. They couldn't destroy the documents, they couldn't get back down or anything. The US Navy took it to port, blew the chlorine out of it, and found all her papers intact, all the navy ciphers and everything else. That was why it was so secret, because if we had told the Germans that this had happened, they would have changed the ciphers before we could have worked some more stuff out."[12]

"Beaverbrook was just curious. He was a newspaper man and also had been very, very busy with the British Government. So he just wanted to know and Bill Stephenson didn't dare tell him. Sicced me on to it. Actually, Beaverbrook was quite nice about it. He was a little irritated for a minute, then he kind of grinned and said, 'How are you? I see I've run into something I should keep my mouth shut about.'"

"He was even in the war cabinet."

"Oh yes, he was a very important individual. He didn't suffer fools gladly, I can tell you."

"It's strange the way the security works."

"Well this wasn't our security," Bayly said. "If it had been British security, or any secret in the world, everybody could hand it to him and gold-plate it. But this was US security. We weren't even supposed to know this ourselves. Somebody had broken this to us. You didn't monkey with US security. I mean, if we had blown US security, we'd have been very wrong with everybody."

Bayly dealt with the security of three nations. He was a member of America's OSS, a director of British Security Coordination, SIS, and the head of Canada's Camp X. He even put his own people into Bletchley.

"I was as international as a person can get. I was a Canadian who had done business with FCC in the States, and in the English Government at the moment. Because of that I was very lucky, and could do the job because the Canadians didn't resent me, and the Americans—I talked with an American accent for all intents and purposes. The only person, as I say, was Stewart Menzies who said to me one time, he said, 'I just can't understand you, you talk like an American, but think like an Englishman.' But I was lucky in that way that I'd been to an English school, so they would accept me as an English person. We ran a very international (apartment) ... practically a bed and breakfast place."

Turing and Welchman

Two frequent guests at Bayly's were his friends Gordon Welchman and Alan Turing, the two men most responsible for solving the Nazi ENIGMA machine. When Welchman came over he familiarized him with the American organizations. "I introduced him to the Navy and the

Army Cryptographic bureaus. They were interested in knowing what he had done with the ENIGMA machine, and how he had done it and that sort of thing and the 'bombe,' which was their way of breaking ENIGMA and they had several bombes in the Army and the Navy, and Welchman wanted to see their design and compare it to his. The Americans had an entirely different mechanism but doing the same thing, and Welchman wanted to see whether their particular drives were better than his."

When the Churchill-Roosevelt link via telephone scrambler was compromised, Turing was sent to New York to devise a method to fix it. During that time, Stephenson's BSC was his home base and he lived with the Baylys for a number of weeks, while working out a solution at the Bell Labs.

"That was Turing's job. He came over and lived with us for a while and one of his jobs was to re-design that telephone link, so that it was secure. He was able to fix it. He spent six months in the Bell Labs, and they tightened up that line so that it was secure. Apparently they knew that the Germans were intercepting it. There was always a voice scrambler on the line, but telephone scramblers were never as secure as enciphered messages. The trouble with scrambling telephone conversations is that if you get it right on anything—it suddenly makes sense. You hear a man say 'Yes', and if he says 'yes,' that must be right, that part of it. But on a enciphered message when the man says '3-5-2', you don't know that is true encipherment, or actually '3-5-2.'

"Most scrambled calls are gibberish to the ear. The minute you break any part of that gibberish, even if it's just a guess, you can see immediately that you've done something useful. You may only see for a moment that you've done something, but you can recognize that as language. But with encipherment all you get is a bunch of figures, and you can't tell if those figures you get are true."

Turing, one of the great minds of the century, was at times a confusing house guest. He stuttered, but apart from that, Bayly thought there were also times when his brain seemed to be working so fast, he couldn't speak at all. Turing would try to talk but only strange clicking sounds came out. On other occasions Turing cranked himself up to talk and "he'd put his finger on his throat and say 'peep peep.' And then you could talk, and he'd wave his fingers and say 'peep peep.' This is the way he taught himself to talk, and we used to just scream with laughter when Turing would be at the dinner table and want to talk, he'd say, 'peep peep' and away he'd go. He was a complete madman. But he was very brave."

Gordon Welchman eventually moved to the United States after the war and remained involved somewhat in top-secret research and development. In 1982, he published *The Hut Six Story*, a book about some of the activities he initiated at Bletchley Park and the breaking of the ENIGMA machine. He thought he could publish the book, and checked with what he thought were the proper authorities, but as a result of the publishing of the book he lost his American security clearance and his consulting job with the Mitre Corporation.

"Welchman was a great friend of mine indeed. Welchman's book got him thrown out from Mitre Corporation because he hadn't cleared it. He'd cleared it with the English and hadn't realized he hadn't cleared it in the States. They just cancelled his security. So he couldn't work for the Mitre Corporation." Welchman was hurt financially as a result. "In fact, he died really hard-up."

Turing and Welchman, two eminent people—instrumental in winning the war—lived in anonymity with no financial or employment security. Churchill's wizards were not rewarded.

"I'll explain something else. Turing and Welchman were extremely important, because they had broken the German ENIGMA and most of our intelligence was coming from the German ENIGMA. It was really important. So he and Turing were highly regarded, and very important people. After the war the best thing that Turing could get was an assistant professorship at a third rate, Birmingham or something, Engineering school.[13] Everybody says he committed suicide because he was gay, which, as far as I'm concerned, is just so much nonsense. He committed suicide because you couldn't go from being one of the most important people in England, to just nothing at all. And Welchman felt the same way."

"Is that why he came to the States?"

"Yeah. And he had quarrelled with the people. They had moved from Bletchley to whatever city it was, and he was quarrelling with people, because he had been their senior and by this time the ENIGMA was past history, and he wasn't getting on very well. He came over to the States where he had a much more responsible position. And it's a funny thing. If you've been important, it doesn't do you any good psychologically to become unimportant."

Bayly thought Stephenson suffered a similar postwar void.

BSC Security and Planning

"There is one thing I'd like to say. The females of BSC kept their mouths shut better that any group I have known anywhere. They were first class. We never had a breach of security right through the whole blooming war. Men know better. They don't live up to the rules because they know this won't hurt, or that won't hurt. But the girls, if you told them not to talk about things, they just didn't. Which is surprising in the female. But I have the greatest regard for the personnel we had there in New York.

"Almost everybody else did (have a breach of security); the British Office in Ottawa, the British High Commissioners office had a bad one, and the Embassy in Washington had a bad one. I think the embassy, or whatever you called it in New York, had a bad one or at least thought they did. But I was very fortunate we didn't have anybody. The people who did the recruiting for us in Canada were pretty good.

"There was very little planning at any time. You planned by what happened, rather than deciding this would be the smart way to do it. Something worked easier done today, or something had to be done today, and that became part of the routine. It was the most unplanned thing you ever saw in your life.

"You didn't plan and go down and have elaborate meetings to decide this week we will do this, and do the other, it was just that some need would come up and somebody said, 'Could you do this for us?' and we'd say well, we'll think it over—lets try it out, and suddenly it became routine. This applied to both Canada and the States."

Bill Stephenson

"You've cleared up importantly, something that always puzzled me," Bayly said. "I was the only Canadian, really of position on his staff. Because of this he trusted me. Bill didn't trust the English. I don't know why. He would talk about things to me. He'd just be talking out loud for somebody to talk to, if he had something on his mind. If I got on the subject of his early upbringing in Winnipeg, he would close up like a clam. Just change the subject. Obviously didn't want to discuss it at all. I couldn't understand this, because he was so forthcoming in everything else. He would talk about anything, without hesitation. Not Winnipeg. So you've rather solved that one.

"I worked for him for two years before I realized he knew anything about radio at all. The first two years he thought he'd get on better with me if he pretended he didn't know anything about radio, because that was what I was doing for him. I mentioned it, and he just put it off. Laughed, and we never discussed it again. He was keeping it under his hat so that he could check up on me if I advanced funny things.

"I trusted Stephenson implicitly. I liked him as a person and as a boss. There's one thing about a boss. If he backs your play, gives you a say, and gives you a fair hearing, he's a good boss. If Bill told me something he didn't like he'd say no, don't do that, and that would be that. But if he liked it, he'd back you, and if you got in trouble he'd still be there. I liked him. He was good.

"He'd back you, even if you got in trouble. If you annoyed somebody and stepped on somebody's toes and annoyed people, you'd explain to Bill why, and if he liked it, he'd back you."

Bayly thought Stephenson's major contribution to the war effort was not a specific achievement, but the friendships he created and nurtured with many people across the international spectrum, "the fact that he got along (with people).

"Bill would always have me over for cocktails. At five o'clock he'd be entertaining these people. So I met everybody from soup to nuts, and you met so many of them.

"You'd meet almost anybody. Bill knew an awful lot of people, especially in the same line as Walter Winchell, because he was using them for propaganda stories and what have you. Bill entertained lavishly when he entertained those people. You met Admirals, Generals, heaven knows what. Not only American, but French, Canadian and British.

"He liked propaganda. And propaganda was really one of the important things he did. He saw to it, before even Pearl Harbor, that the anti-British feeling there was squelched by writers. He got all sorts of people to write things that helped that. And I know. Because I met them at cocktail parties."

Bayly met people like *Time* and *Life* head Henry Luce, Walter Winchell, and playwright and Roosevelt speech writer Robert Sherwood at Stephenson's place.

"Winchell was a man who actually got a reputation for being a very straightforward person, and he did a lot of propaganda work for Bill Stephenson. If Bill could sell him on why the US should do this, and if it did that, then Winchell would be your man. He thought very highly of Winchell."

"Robert Sherwood was about six-foot four and I once heard him say after a cocktail, 'If I have another cocktail, I'll just call timber and fall on my face.' Sherwood would be there all the time. Bill liked Sherwood.

"And as I say, it's amazing how many people, and good people, that he had working for him on that," Bayly said. "And he'd sell them on the idea that it was a good thing to do. He didn't pay them to do it. It was just a question of ... He was a good salesman."

One person who didn't come to Stephenson's gatherings was Bill Donovan, the head of the OSS. "Because he didn't want the public to know that Bill was educating OSS. It was touchy in those days because the US until Pearl Harbor was a neutral."

Stephenson worked without a salary Bayly believes, and contributed some of his personal fortune into the running of the organization. "I'm quite sure that he put some of his own money in here and there, because in those days he was extremely wealthy. And his wife too.

"On a couple of occasions I wanted to do something and he said, 'the Treasury will raise hell about that, but I'll fix it.' That didn't mean that he was actually going to pay for it. But I suspect that's what happened.

"I had for all practical purposes an unlimited expense account. Bill Stephenson fixed that for me, so I never gave detailed expense accounts. I just told them $900-$1,000 for a month or something like that and that was that. Bill Stephenson realized that I couldn't put down expenses for entertaining English people, but I obviously had to do the job. The easiest way was not to account for expenses but just to estimate them."

Stephenson's deputy was told his former boss made a lot of money through his Earls Court investment once the can opener stopped making money. He didn't think Stephenson was made rich through wireless photography, as Montgomery Hyde has written. "Hyde was very impressed with that, but I don't think it made that much. There wasn't much of a market for it really."

There were many squabbles at the multi-headed Camp X, and Stephenson's financial clout helped smooth out the supervision. When he got irritated at some of the bickering, Stephenson shut the training camp down. SOE were putting up some of the money for the operation of the Camp and thought they ran it, Bayly said. "Bill Stephenson just got mad one morning, and cancelled the whole thing, and said, 'Now you are in charge.' Cuthbert Skilbeck wasn't going to have that. He said, 'We put up some of the money for this place,' so he went down to New York, and burst into Stephenson's office and he said, 'This is quite a deal, and I've told Bayly he has to get out,' and Stephenson said, 'Oh, you did? Well. Just wait a minute.' He phoned me downstairs, and I came upstairs and he said 'Cuthbert Skilbeck, I'd like to introduce you to your Boss.'" Bayly smiled. "And this is me.

"Bill was putting up a lot of the money for these things. I never did find out how much. But he never had to worry about Treasury. He could tell them to go jump in the lake and they would jump. So I figured that Bill was financing a lot of that deal."

Following the war it was imperative the Communications Centre at Camp X Bayly created was kept in operation, but it was uncertain who would be paying for it. Bayly was actually in charge of the remains of BSC, but he had no money. "When I took over (because he had closed up the BSC) I had to go on running the radio station for a while, to live up to some of our obligations in Canada and the States. So Bill guaranteed the expenses. I found that I'd taken over a payroll of $5,000 and I had about $2 in the bank. I had to tell Bill, and he said, 'Well, that's okay', and he sent the money up."

Bayly felt nobody knew exactly what Stephenson's link was to espionage before his New York posting. "I don't think the British had any idea of what his connection had been with that in the past because ... MI6 was in a great deal of trouble with the British Government for many years before World War II. Just in the same way that the CIA is in trouble with the politicians who just don't like having it around. It embarrasses them to have it around and it embarrasses them to think that their country is doing things that are covert. Therefore they must be wrong, or they would tell parliament about it. I think the same thing existed to a certain extent in England."

Stephenson's relationship with SIS was 'perfect,' Bayly said. "Stewart Menzies and he got along very well. I think there was a little jealousy because I have a suspicion that somebody else, probably Churchill, saw to it that Bill Stephenson took the job. I have a feeling he was sort of wished on Stewart Menzies. But I never heard Stewart Menzies give him anything but praise, and on a couple of occasions, when I had a fight on my hands in England, I called up Bill Stephenson on the cable, and I'd tell him to put in a word, and it always worked. When he said something ought to happen, it happened. He really had a lot of power."

"Why, do you think?"

"He knew an awful lot of interesting people ... at his house, and you'd meet, you'd meet any number of people, you didn't expect to meet in such a place. He was liked by people and they had an immense regard for his influence. On top of that I expect he was very rich."

Bayly chose a quote from a John Pearson biography of Ian Fleming, and read it aloud. "'For Fleming, Stephenson was almost everything a hero should be. He was very tough. He was very rich. He was single-minded. Patriotic, and a man of few words.'[14] That, in spite of the fact I don't believe in Fleming one inch, is a very good description of Stephenson.

"Very tough. Very rich. Single-minded, patriotic, and a man of few words. That's what I think of him. Yeah. That's how I'd sum him up."

Toward the end of the war Stephenson wanted Bayly to document the evolution of BSC's Communications division. Bayly didn't think he should. "I got in very wrong with Bill Stephenson because he wanted me to write up my division (Communications Division), and I wasn't having any of that—because I had been treated extremely well by Canada, the States, and England, far beyond what was necessary. I was welcomed into places where it was absolutely necessary that I be, and everybody's been very kind. And doing so, we'd go out and have a couple of drinks and they'd tell me political things that really shouldn't be free, and they were really quite outspoken. I came to the conclusion at the end of the war that the best thing I could do was shut-up. Because if I did, I would unwittingly mention things that would have been political."

He gave an example of his preferential treatment. In BSC's office they had an American stamp from the US War Production Board which could print 'high priority' on BSC's orders. Bayly often met with the American head of the board, "I was asking for directives and 'high priority' for things, and he would give them to us. He said to me one day, 'Look. I ordered two of these darn stamps, that stamp priorities in coloured ink. Stamp it right over the document so you can't forge it.' He said, 'Here. You store this. If we want it back, if this one gets destroyed, bring it back. But you just store it, and stamp any damn priority you want on your stuff.' That's what we did."

BSC's purchasing department was covert and didn't go through the English. "We had a purchasing department there that bought everything we needed and was supposed to be secret, and we didn't go through the British Supply Commission. This was a harmless enough thing, because we were buying so little in comparison, that the War Production Board didn't give a hoot what priorities were put on the thing. But that sort of thing, if you told about it, might still cause a lot of political trouble. They'd say, 'That guy had no business giving out that.' Now that's just one example of the sort of silly thing that you can talk about. So I just decided that I wouldn't write a book. Most of the books that were written irritated me, because they were incorrect."

Subsequently Bayly was not involved in the compilation of the BSC history at Camp X at the end of the war. "Tom Hill I knew very slightly, because he was concerned with the 'Bible', as it was called and I wasn't. I didn't have any part of it, or want any part of it. I arranged it with the people in England that I not be cleared for publication in any of those. Nobody could write histories of my section officially without going to England and getting their permission specifically."

He said Gordon Welchman was not aware of this arrangement and that was why Bayly's name appeared in *The Hut Six Story*. There is a communications section in the BSC history but Bayly couldn't vouch for it's accuracy as he submitted nothing to it.

"No. No, I had nothing to do with it. I didn't approve of it, like it, and didn't want to be part of it. I didn't want to be mentioned in it. Bill Stephenson believed in propaganda. If you didn't talk about things, then nobody was going to, so it should be talked about. He used it with a fair amount of discretion. But I have a feeling that the powers that be must have screamed blue murder, knowing that volume exists."

Bayly thought Hyde's *The Quiet Canadian* was accurate. "There were some exaggerations in there ... but in the main not exaggerating seriously. Bill believed in propaganda. He wasn't one who wouldn't advertise, although he was very closed-mouthed. He saw that the right people knew the right things." Bayly thought Stevenson's books were inaccurate. The 'Intrepid' books left him "colder than learning to ride a horse in 40 below at Fort Osborne." He thought David Stafford's *Camp X* "made an attempt at accuracy, writing under difficult situations. He made several mistakes or omissions, but I think pardonable under the conditions." One major mistake in the book was the date the Camp opened, as "it was in full operation before Pearl Harbor."

Activity at Camp X continued long after BSC New York shut down. "What happened was, BSC quit. We closed up for all intents and purposes. And Camp X was still actively sending communications because we were still intercepting a lot of material that was going through there and rather than set up commercial channels I just kept on handling it."

"From who? From the Russians?"

"From all over. Just anything that we wanted to intercept."

"Just spying on everybody?"

"Well you had to, for a very good reason. The top people (in governments). In other words, if the Germans were talking to someone they liked, they used very high grade ciphers. In fact they used my encipherment, the Rockex."

"After the war?"

"Yes. Japan was still going, but the European thing had folded. Some of the original messages would be unbreakable, but if the original message was sent to other locations, it was usually sent in a less secure cipher. So the way you could break the original message was to wait until the people who received the high grade message passed it on to the next one, and then you knew from the serial number and the ratings and so on what the original message was. So we were intercepting stuff from all over the place, and my communication network had three radio channels at Camp X. We had two leased cables across the Atlantic and were running about a million and a half words a day."

"You sent it to SIS?"

"Yeah. Or the Cryptographic Bureau there, or whatever bureau we were running. Canada and the States had two big bureaus and a third, smaller one and our job was simply to distribute this material to whoever could use it. What they were currently interested in, and what they could break. So that was highly specialized."

"So they still do that, I wonder?"

"Yeah. Canada took over Camp X."

Following the war Bayly was asked by the British government to stay involved with covert communications on a development contract. He convinced a number of Canadian engineers to quit their jobs and work with him on the five-year deal. Bayly's task was to transform the success of the Rockex into a coding machine not just between two people, but for portable multiple use. However the whims of Britain's government changed and the agreement was terminated.

Although the contract was for five years the development agreement was abruptly cancelled at the end of one year. Bayly was dismissed with five days notice. "It ran for five more years, and the Labour party got in and said, 'Sue us if you like, but you're finished as of next week.' They got into some sort of a cook-up or other, and I found myself facing a government that hadn't hired me, and didn't want to hire me and weren't willing to. It was a very dirty deal. But I wasn't in a position to argue with them." The unbreakable machine for multiple use was never completed. "It still isn't done. Nobody else has (done one) either. It was going to be a horrible machine to use. It had 21 rotating cylinders."

Finding work wasn't a problem for Bayly after the cancellation—he was still a professor at the University of Toronto—but he was concerned about all the people he had hired. He convinced them to leave their jobs and work with him. "I had persuaded a whole lot of people to stay and work for me, who had finished their war leave of absence. They couldn't go back to their jobs and that's why I formed Bayly Engineering. Because I had to employ these guys."

Bayly Engineering worked on numerous electrical and mechanical devices, many of them top-secret. "Just anything we could get our hands on." The company started out in Oshawa, and then moved to Ajax.

One man Bayly eventually hired previously worked for Germany during the war. He hid nothing, and told Bayly what he had been doing. He said, "I've been doing counter-espionage work in Germany, and I've heard that you would know about this sort of thing," Bayly remembered. "And he said, 'I'd love a job. I'm a good maintenance man, and good with electrical equipment.'" Bayly hired him. Afterward the new employee started to tell Bayly about a few things he worked on during the war. He mentioned sonobuoys so Bayly said, "We get them in here for repair. You'd better do those."

The sonobuoys were microphones attached to a radio beacon that were dropped into the ocean and used to detect U-boats. The U-boats were rather noisy underwater. If a trio of sonobuoys were dropped in a triangle around a sub, the engine noise would be louder in one than the others. The buoys beamed the sounds up by radio to passing aircraft. "German subs were noisy, and we didn't want them to care whether they were noisy or not," Bayly said. "So the sonobuoys were still pretty top-secret, even after the war was over." But his new employee knew all about them. The Germans had recovered them early on and took them apart. "He got the first one the Germans had and recovered the circuit, and had redrawn it and all the rest of it." Canadian security officials arrived at Bayly Engineering one day and said the German couldn't work on the top-secret buoys. However the new employee stressed, "I knew about these things before you people did," Bayly remembered. "And he was quite right." The security officials eventually backed off.

Bayly left the University of Toronto in 1951, as Bayly Engineering was doing well and was taking more and more of his time. It expanded in an abandoned Shell plant in Ajax, near Toronto. He lived in Montreal for a time doing contract work but made the Ajax area his home base.

Bayly Engineering was the largest business enterprise in the district and he began to get involved in municipal affairs. Eventually the locals decided to incorporate into a new town. Pat Bayly was elected the first mayor of Ajax, Ontario. Later he sold the company and retired to southern California.

Bayly felt some of his contemporaries were not nearly as fortunate as he was following the war, and he frequently referred back to them.

"Poor old Turing had been one of the most important people during the war. This is a tough thing. Psychologically. He and Welchman had been extremely important people during the war. They had broken the ENIGMA machine and everybody thought highly of them, and they were working their fool heads off. When the war was over, Turing could only get an assistant prof's job at a second rate university. And it really hurt."

"Why was that?"

"His mathematical genius applied to one job that they weren't interested in. The same thing happened to one of the top men in the US bureau."

"Not Friedman?"

"No. Billy Friedman was a good friend of mine. But he ended up all right. This guy was in the Navy and he had been the Dean of Mathematics in a very good university and when the war was over he just couldn't find a job that pleased him at all. He just went downhill right and centre.

"It's tension (war work). A flap occurred every ten minutes. I can't think of anything more nerve-racking than that sort of job. When you work at that for years, and then you go back to a faculty meeting where somebody spends an hour deciding whether you put in a 'semi-colon' or a 'comma' there. It gets you down."

From the government of Britain Bayly received five days' notice before being fired, and at approximately the same time, the Order of the British Empire. He received the OBE in 1946. Press reports said he was "of an organization working with the Foreign Office," who was awarded the OBE "for reasons unspecified." He didn't think much of the honour, and never used the designation.

The American government wanted to award Bayly with a medal but were told by British officialdom that they couldn't. 'Colonial officers' could not receive foreign decorations, the Americans were told. When US officials wondered what else they could do for him, Bayly said he would like to become a fellow in the Institute of Electrical Engineers. He received a fellowship shortly after the war. It was presented by Herbert W Armstrong, often considered the inventor of radio.

From Canada, his own country, Bayly received no recognition or form of thanks whatsoever. In 1989 the University of Toronto contacted him about appearing at an alumni function, but he couldn't attend for health reasons and heard nothing more about it. But in the spring of 1991, Bayly received a plaque in the mail, completely out of the blue, from his alma mater. It reads:

Membership in the Hall of Distinction is accorded to Benjamin de Forest Bayly Class of 1930—Electrical Engineering
His useful radio hobby helped co-found a Moose Jaw station, and led to phenomenal communications feats during World War II. From Law, University of Saskatchewan, 1923, he came to the University of Toronto and such was his expertise that in his third year he lectured to the fourth year. He was on the staff until 1951 with war leave. In 1941 under the close association of the British Director Of Security Coordination, Sir William Stephenson, he became Assistant Director with the British Army rank of Lieutenant Colonel. He set up communications center Hydra at Camp X near Oshawa and designed special equipment to link New York, Washington, Ottawa, and Britain. To handle confidential traffic he invented the cipher machine Rockex now used worldwide for diplomatic communication and his activity influenced Canada's radar development. Acknowledgment came through the award of OBE '46 and fellowship in the Institute of Radio Engineers '47. Bayly Engineering Limited established '46 Oshawa moved to Ajax in '48 where his municipal leadership led to incorporation, with him as first mayor, 1955.

It was dated 1989 and signed by the President of the University, the Dean of the Faculty and the President of the Alumni Association.

"They'd done a lot of research," Bayly said about the award. But there was not even a cover letter with it, and he received it in the mail two years after it was dated. He had no idea who was behind the plaque or why it was sent. Bayly wrote to the university, thanking whoever was responsible, but he received no response, acknowledgment, or further details. He concluded someone may have found it in a closet somewhere and decided to send it down.

Bayly Engineering, now Bayly Communications Incorporated (BCI) is still in Ajax, Ontario, designing and manufacturing, according to a company release, "state-of-the-art digital multiplex equipment for access to voice and data transmission services." One of the main thoroughfares passing through Ajax and adjoining Pickering, Ontario is Bayly Street. It's likely few citizens of those communities know the many reasons why.

Final Words

While visiting Grace Garner at her home outside London, she pulled a red-covered book out of her bookcase. "This book was written a long time ago, but a lot of what's in it still relates today," she said. "You should read it." It was from 1942.

"…for we are of two worlds, the Old and the New, one foot in each, knowing England, knowing America, joined to each by blood and battle, speech and song. We alone are the hinge between them, and upon us hangs more than we know."

—Bruce Hutchison, *The Unknown Country*

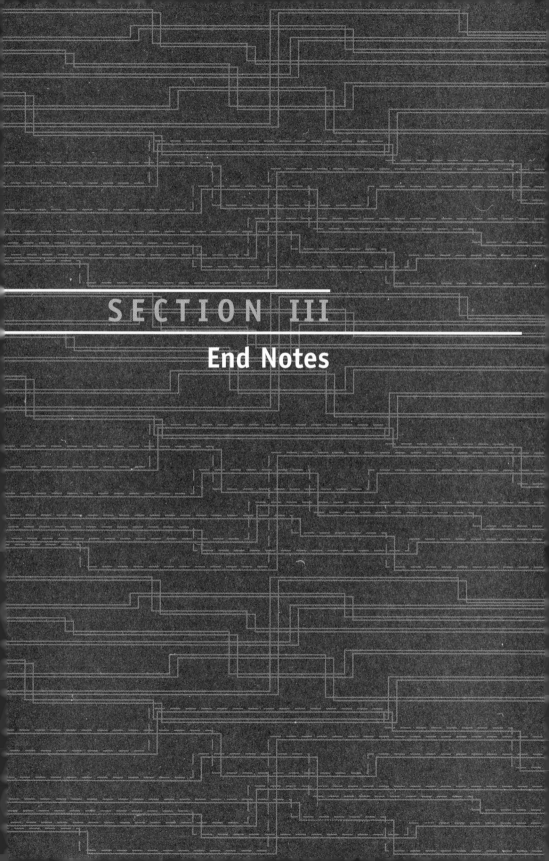

SECTION III

End Notes

Abbreviations

Abwehr	German Military Intelligence
AMCI	*A Man Called Intrepid*
BSC	British Security Coordination
CIA	US Central Intelligence Agency
COI	Coordinator of Information
FBI	Federal Bureau of Investigation
G-2	US Army Military Intelligence
GRU	Soviet Military Intelligence
MI5	British domestic security service, similar to FBI
MI6	Britain's foreign security service, similar to CIA
NKVD	Soviet Security Service, predecessor to KGB
OSS	Office of Strategic Services
OWI	Office of War Information
RCMP	Royal Canadian Mounted Police
SIS	British Secret Intelligence Service (MI6)
SOE	Special Operations Executive
Station M	False document factory in wartime Toronto
WSS	William S Stephenson

Camp X	BSC founded espionage and communications centre at Whitby-Oshawa, Ontario
ENIGMA	Portable German cipher machine
HYDRA	Communications radio centre established at Camp X
MAGIC	Intelligence derived from Japanese coding machine
ULTRA	Intelligence derived from decryption of German Enigma machine

Appendix A

The Windsor Letters

In 1987 a former MI5 officer broke his code of silence, and published a book dealing with his exploits with the service. The British government tried in vain to ban the book's publication. Peter Wright called his book *Spycatcher.*

When Wright was with section D-3, the known Soviet agent Anthony Blunt became his responsibility. Before he met Blunt, Wright had to attend a briefing with Michael Adeane, Private Secretary to the Queen at Buckingham Palace, as Blunt had been employed as the Queen's Surveyor of Pictures.

"The Queen," Adeane told him, "has been fully informed about Sir Anthony, and is quite content for him to be dealt with in any way that gets at the truth."

But Wright remembered there was one caveat. "From time to time," said Adeane, "you may find Blunt referring to an assignment he undertook on behalf of the Palace—a visit to Germany at the end of the war. Please do not pursue the matter. Strictly speaking it is not relevant to considerations of national security."

Wright says he spent hundreds of hours with Blunt but never learned about his secret mission to Germany. "But then," he concluded, "the Palace had several centuries to learn the difficult art of scandal burying. MI5 have only been in business since 1909!"[1]

Wright's statement in 1987 was one of the first confirmations from an MI5 source that Blunt spent the last months of his wartime service on a highly secret personal mission for the Royal Palace. The story that Blunt had been sent by King George VI after the war to recover incriminating letters between the former King (the Duke of Windsor) and Nazi leaders had been circulating for years. The Duke and his wife travelled to meet Hitler in October, 1937, and he was widely considered to be sympathetic to the Nazi cause. "Secret papers have disclosed his pro-Nazi perfidy which, of course, I was perfectly aware of at the time," Noel Coward recorded in his diary in 1962. "Poor dear, what a monumental ass he has always been."[2]

"Blunt was emissary for King George VI," the London *Sunday Times* reported on the front page, November 25, 1979, soon after Blunt was outed as a Soviet agent. According to the *Times*, Blunt travelled to Schloss Kronberg Hessen, a Hesse family castle near Frankfurt, with Owen Morshead, the then librarian of Windsor Castle. King George thought Prince Phillip of Hess was an intermediary, through the Duke of Kent, between the Duke of Windsor and Hitler, and the family kept the related papers in his palace, which was taken over by the American military. According to the paper, Blunt and Morshead met with members of the Hesse family after the war in a nearby village, and then proceeded to retrieve the archive, but the American officer in charge of the castle refused to release the documents to the them. However, the two persisted and covertly smuggled the papers into a truck, and off to Windsor castle. Blunt, a distant cousin of the Queen, was hired by the Royal family in 1945, and knighted in 1956. Morshead was knighted in 1958. Strangely, Blunt had been suspected of being a Soviet agent as early as 1951, and by 1964 he had confessed. The Soviet agent did quite well after confessing. (For example he fared much better than Dick Ellis, who lost his intelligence job at about the same time, soon after he tried to publicize the career of William Stephenson.) Not only was Blunt never prosecuted—he continued his position with the Palace. He wasn't stripped of his knighthood until 1979, when he was publicly exposed as a Soviet agent through the work of journalists.[3]

Blunt's escapades in Europe seem to be confirmed in the diary of Sir Alexander Cadogan. "King fussed about Duke of Windsor file in captured German documents. Promised to look into it," he wrote October 25, 1945.[4] Highly regarded British espionage historian Christopher Andrew also seems to think the story of Anthony Blunt carries a bit of establishment baggage. When questioned about Blunt, the name didn't immediately equate 'treason' or 'treachery', but White Hall and 'ancient secrets'.[5]

According to the *Times* story, sections of recovered Nazi files dealing with Windsor had a habit of disappearing. One part of the Berlin file dealing with Windsor was removed "by higher ups," and later returned. About 400 tons of documents were transferred to Britain and examined at Whadden Hall, near Bletchley. Donald Watt, later a professor at the London School of Economics, said sections of the Windsor file appeared to be missing and he doubted they had seen all the material. "Of course it is quite possible the Windsor material had been sifted before it reached Whadden Hall," Watt was quoted as saying. "The Royal Archivists have proper historians to advise them these days but at that time they were very secretive."[6]

The *Times* article also mentions the ubiquitous Hugh Trevor-Roper. He was unaware of the Windsor files in connection to Blunt, but he knew of the Soviet agent's trip. Blunt's assignment according to Trevor-Roper was to retrieve letters Queen Victoria sent to her daughter Vicky, who had married Frederick III of Prussia in 1858, and became the mother of Kaiser Wilhelm II.[7] Trevor-Roper's version of events was echoed in the official biography of the Duke eleven years later.[8] Edward's authorized biographer calls the Windsor file stories, "legend," "picturesque," and "fantasies." But, Philip Ziegler concludes, "Lack of evidence rarely inhibits the more venturesome biographers."[9]

How did the noted historian Trevor-Roper become an expert on the travels of Anthony Blunt? According to the journalist John Costello, Trevor-Roper told a Sunday *Times* reporter he simply ran into Blunt at MI5 St. James headquarters, while he was reporting to Guy Lidell on his mission.[10]

There is another version as to how Trevor-Roper became aware of Blunt's mission. According to the British writer Anthony Cave Brown, Trevor-Roper accompanied Blunt on one of his reconnaissance trips to the continent. He was apparently seconded in 1945 by Dick White to his counter-intelligence group at SHAEF, and his familiarity with captured German records enabled him to write *The Last Days of Hitler*. "There were rumours that actual correspondence between Windsor and Hitler was recovered by Professor Trevor-Roper and Anthony Blunt, the Queen's picture master, and that Kim Philby was the case officer for the operation."[11] Brown also maintains similar stories which assert that Philby's and Blunt's knowledge of the letters, their recovery, and their contents gave both men a degree of power over 'C,' the palace, and the British government, when it seemed they were about to be exposed. Brown seems to conclude the secrecy on the issue and possible treason was unavoidable. "If the entire matter of the Windsor letters appears medieval in its mystery, it must be remembered that no British government, Socialist or Conservative, would like to find itself required to provide evidence for a hanging charge against a royal prince who had once been King of England."[12]

Ironically if Trevor-Roper and Blunt were partners on a shadowy trip to Europe after the war, their fortunes went in completely opposite directions at the same time. In November 1979, Hugh Trevor-Roper was heralded into Britain's House of Lords—as Lord Dacre of Glanton. Days later, Prime Minister Margaret Thatcher announced in the House of Commons that the Queen's Surveyor of Pictures Sir Anthony Blunt was a Soviet agent. In December, 1979, Trevor-Roper was appointed master of Peterhouse at Cambridge, which freed him from his professorial duties at Oxford.[13]

'The Electrolux Man'

The Electrolux man was Swedish industrialist Axel Wenner Gren (1881-1961). He formed Electrolux in 1921 to manufacture vacuum cleaners. Shortly afterward he obtained plans, for $500,000, for the electric refrigerator. He was quite successful with these two business ventures. By 1938 he was one of the wealthiest men in the world, and he plied the world's waterways on his large yacht, Southern Cross. He had large land holdings around the world, including the Bahamas. The Southern Cross transported the Duke and Duchess of Windsor to the United States in December of 1940.

In 1935, Wenner Gren bought up a large part of Bofors Munitions from German interests, and he was known to have had close ties to Nazi Germany. "If there should happen to be a stalemate and a negotiated peace, I might be of great use. I have good standing in Germany," he was quoted as saying during the war. In 1941, he visited Rio de Janeiro as part of a Swedish-German consortium and attempted to buy up rich iron ore deposits in a rural state of Brazil.[14] This plan was thwarted through a move of the US Export-Import bank.

Shortly afterward he moved to Mexico, dealt in various investment enterprises and tried to interest his friend, the pro-Nazi General Maximino Camacho, the brother of the Mexican President, in a program of road building. He also became involved with a Mexican telephone company. He parked The Southern Cross in Mexico, gave it Mexican registry, and let the Mexican government use it. "If I took it out, people would say I was fuelling U-boats," he said.

In January 1941, Sumner Welles sent a confidential memo to the US State Department that said, "The most recent information I have regarding Mr. Wenner Gren indicated that he is in constant and close touch with the Duke of Windsor," and Wenner Gren was "anxious to participate in an American consortium planning the investment of a considerable amount of capital in Mexico."[15]

In January 1942 Wenner Gren was put onto a blacklist by the United States of people who were doing business with Nazi countries. A short time before this Chrysler Corporation obtained licenses for the famous Bofors anti-aircraft gun and began mass production.

In March 1941, about a dozen Mexicans, including Camacho, visited the Duke of Windsor in the Bahamas. The Mexicans were escorted to the Governor's mansion by multimillionaire Harry Oakes, a former prospector who made a fortune in Canada's gold industry. Oakes moved to the islands in 1935, and he was killed in July 1943, the victim of an unsolved murder.

Alfred de Marigny, Oake's son-in-law, who was charged and acquitted of murdering him, points out that the first indications of surreptitious dealings between Mexico, Oakes and Windsor came from "the famous British spy, H. Montgomery Hyde, who served on the staff of Sir William Stephenson."[16] Hyde was visiting the Duke to discuss the security of the Bahamas at the time. He theorized the Wenner Gren conference involved a scheme where the Nazis and others could launder foreign money through Mexican banks. This was "highly irregular for the Duke," Hyde says, as Mexico had recently broken off diplomatic relations with Britain and expropriated all British oil companies without offering compensation.[17]

Rudolf Hess

At the time of his arrival in Scotland Rudolf Hess was deputy leader of the Nazi Party. He took part in the Munich uprising in 1923, and shared imprisonment with Adolf Hitler. It has been reported that Hitler dictated *Mein Kampf* to Hess.

In May of 1941 Hess flew solo in a small plane to Britain on an mysterious peace mission. His arrival prompted Churchill's comment, "The maggot is in the apple." Hess asked to meet with the Duke Of Hamilton, but he was essentially kept under wraps, imprisoned, and eventually received a life sentence at Nuremberg in 1946. He died in 1987 of an apparent suicide, the only remaining prisoner of Spandau prison in Berlin.

About a month after Hess's flight, the Nazis attacked the Soviet Union. The entire quixotic sequence of events has inspired numerous conspiracy theorists. Hess's sortie also concerned many of the principals of the time.

Before visiting the Soviet Union, Lord Beaverbrook was one of the few who met with Hess following his imprisonment. When the Canadian-born British minister met with Stalin, the Soviet leader wondered what to make of Hess's flight. He asked Beaverbrook if Britain was going to make peace with Germany, as he considered Hess a possible line of communication. If the British were not dealing with the Nazis, he wondered, why wasn't Hess shot. Beaverbrook told him that Britain didn't shoot people without a trial. Stalin asked why Hess came to England and Beaverbrook said, "To persuade Britain to join Germany in making an attack on Russia."[18]

One of the chroniclers of Hess's career noted Hess's secret mission astonished the British, bewildered the Americans, horrified the Germans, and struck fear in the Russians. Apparently Washington was left in the dark. "Puzzled at the time by Churchill's silence, FDR remarked to an aide, 'I wonder what is *really* behind this story,' and continued to believe that there remained in Britain a small but potentially powerful minority who wanted peace conversations and were in fact having them."[19]

This may have been close to the truth. The disgraced former King Edward VIII and his wife Wallace Simpson dined twice at the home of Rudolf Hess during the thirties. According to Hess's son, Wolf-Rudiger Hess, they discussed the prospects of a "new world order" with Edward returned triumphantly to the British throne.[20]

Hess also appears in *Eclipse*, a book of fiction following the 'Intrepid' sagas by William Stevenson. One premise of the book is that Hess did not arrive in Britain alone. It also supposes that aerial photographs during the war revealed the Nazi extermination camps, but they were not bombed. One character in the novel concludes "the truth about Hess" was "that he negotiated with both the British and Soviets to let Hitler have his Jews."[21]

Edward VIII
Sun Tze's: The Use of Spies

Tu Mu enumerates the following classes as likely to do good service in this respect: *"Worthy men who have been degraded from office, criminals who have undergone punishment; also, favourite concubines who are greedy for gold, men who are aggrieved at being in subordinate positions, or who have been passed over in the distribution of posts, others who are anxious that their side should be defeated in order that they may have a chance of displaying their ability and talents, fickle turncoats who always want to have a foot in each boat. Officials of these several kinds,"* he continues, *"should be secretly approached and bound to one's interests by means of rich presents. In this way you will be able to find out the state of affairs in the enemy's country, ascertain the plans that are being formed against you, and moreover disturb the harmony and create a breach between the sovereign and his ministers."*

The love story of King Edward the VIII and Wallace Simpson, the twice-divorced American, is one of the most publicized relationships of the century. Less well documented is the former King and his partner's role leading up to and during the Second World War. The couple, in the words of one writer, have been misplaced by society, or history.[22]

The possibly treasonous activities of the former English king likely influenced William Stephenson's endeavours in the late 1930's. His 1940 'exile' from Europe, as Governor in the Bahamas, brought him directly under Stephenson's security umbrella.

Following the war the Duke penned his memoirs but they end with his abdication in 1936, and don't detail his activities afterward.

The Duchess of Windsor's tale is a bit more forthright and in subsequent years more and more information has emerged about the couple's later activities. Soon after resigning the British throne for the woman he loved, Edward and Wallis married at the French home of Charles Bedaux, a known Nazi sympathizer. Bedaux, who later committed suicide after being arrested as a Nazi collaborator, helped arrange a visit for the newlyweds with Adolf Hitler. The Royal couple met with Rudolf Hess and Hitler at Berchtesgaden. When Britain declared war on the Nazis the Windsors were relaxing by a pool in the south of France. According to the Duchess, a servant appeared to tell the Duke the British Ambassador was on the phone from Paris. The Duke then reported to his wife:

"...'Great Britain has just declared war on Germany, and I'm afraid in the end this may open the way for world communism.' Then there was a splash; he had dived into the pool."[23]

Later the Duke took a military posting on the continent and met with French and English troops in France and Belgium. His personal position was "delicate and difficult", the Duchess wrote, as he was a former monarch with a subordinate rank. Windsor visited the Belgian front and met his brother, the Duke of Gloucester there. When some British troops presented arms, Windsor took a salute meant for his higher-ranking brother. Windsor was later "coldly notified" that he violated military etiquette. This was particularly "galling" to him as he always had a gift for dealing with troops, his wife reported. Surprisingly, in the same paragraph, she equates their perceived status problems with the Second World War. The couple "had two wars to deal with— the big and still leisurely war, in which everyone was caught up, and the little cold war with the Palace, in which no quarter was given."

The 'leisurely war' eventually forced the Duchess to move south from Paris, to the coast near Spain. When she moved to Biarritz her hotel and room number were reported on German radio, which she describes in her book as an unchivalrous trick, "suggesting that Fifth Columnists were everywhere." This didn't deter her husband however, who gave her war updates from Paris. "David phoned every day. Through his guarded language I was made to realize that Paris was almost certainly doomed."[24]

The Duke left Paris and the couple ended up in Spain. In Madrid the couple were looked after by the British Ambassador Samuel Hoare. The well-known appeaser and friend of the Duke was not popular with the new Churchill government. The Under Secretary of the Foreign Office, Alexander Cadogan, reported in his diary for Sunday 12, May 1940, "S Hoare now to go to Madrid! I suppose they want him safely out of the country!" Hoare moved to the post of Spanish Ambassador in Madrid, and he arranged accommodation for the Windsors at the Ritz Hotel. "The slippery British Ambassador conveniently suspended all activities of the Secret Service in the Spanish capital for the duration of the Windsor's visit. They were thus free of surveillance."[25] The Windsors continued to meet with many pro-Nazi people at the Ritz. One Spanish General was full of information on German military might, Wallis wrote later. Another woman "completely disconcerted David and me by rendering the fascist salute."[26] British intelligence picked up information that the Windsors were to be kidnapped by the Nazis and reinstalled on the throne following the invasion of Britain. Churchill ordered the Royal duo to return to England, but the couple refused. The Prime Minister became increasingly agitated and pointed out in one cable, "Already there is a great deal of doubt as to the circumstances in which Your Royal Highness left Paris."[27] The Duke was serving in the military at the time, and in most democracies he would have been court-martialed for desertion.[28]

It was then decided that the Windsors could go to the Bahamas where he would become the Governor. The couple moved to Lisbon and prepared to leave the continent. On July 22, 1940, it was reported a secret message was sent to the German minister Joachim von Ribbentrop from London, saying the Duke was urging King George VI to appoint a new Pro-Hitler appeasement cabinet that would replace Churchill. Amongst those involved would be Lloyd George, Lord Halifax, Sir John Simon, and Sir Samuel Hoare.[29] There is also strong evidence that Windsor was more than an appeaser. In a July 11, 1940 cable to Berlin, the German Ambassador to Portugal, Oswald Baron von Hoyningen-Huene, wrote that, "The designation of the Duke as Governor of the Bahamas is intended to keep him far away from England, since his return would bring with it strong encouragement to English friends of peace, so that his arrest at the insistence of his opponents would certainly have to be expected. (The Duke) is convinced that if he had remained on the throne, war would have been avoided, and he characterizes himself as a firm supporter of a peaceful arrangement with Germany. The Duke believes that the continued severe bombings would make England ready for peace."[30] The author Charles Higham has pointed out that not long after the telegram was received in Berlin, some of the heaviest bombing of England began.[31]

Eventually the Windsors agreed to leave Europe, but the duo reportedly planned on going to the United States, not the Bahamas. On July 20,1940, the US Ambassador to Portugal, Herbert Pell, cabled Cordell Hull in Washington that the "Duke and Duchess of Windsor are indiscreet and outspoken against British government. Consider their presence in United States might be disturbing and confusing. They say that they intend remaining in the United States whether Churchill likes it or not, and desire apparently to make propaganda for peace." He suggested cancelling their visas.[32]

To compound the problem, Britain's Ambassador to the United States, Lord Lothian, was lobbying President Roosevelt to permit a visit from the Windsors. When the Royal couple finally arrived in the Bahamas, they wanted to head to the USA. Lord Lloyd sent a note to then Foreign Secretary Halifax that complained, "I have just got the Duke, as I thought, clamped down securely in the Bahamas for awhile, and now Lord Lothian is stirring up the waters again."[33] Lothian died suddenly not long afterward, in December, 1940. (He was a Christian Scientist and is said to have refused treatment that would have saved him.) Britain was without official representation in the United States at a pivotal point in its history.

In that same month, Wallis Windsor had a serious dental problem and arranged to travel to Florida for treatment. They sailed on Swedish industrialist Axel Wenner Gren's yacht, the Southern Cross. The couple were greeted by thousands of people in Miami. Following the death of Lothian, the Duke flew from Miami to meet with Roosevelt aboard Tuscaloosa, the presidential cruiser. He returned to Miami and sailed back toward the Bahamas, on the 17th of December.

Soon afterward the Duke met with another American, Fulton Oursler, the editor-in-chief of *Liberty*, a popular American weekly magazine. Oursler died in 1952, and a decade after his death, his son discovered he worked as a liaison between the FBI and agents in South America. Neither he nor others in his family knew anything about it. While going through his father's papers, Oursler Jr. discovered a seventeen page memo in one of his notebooks. The memorandum, dictated to a secretary at the time, described what he saw and heard at the end of December, 1940.

"There was a huge dichotomy between the public's perception, and what many British and American officials knew about Windsor," Fulton Oursler Jr. wrote later in *American Heritage* magazine. When the Windsors arrived in the Bahamas aboard the Southern Cross, December 19, 1940, Oursler was in Nassau waiting to interview him.[34]

In their meeting, the Duke amazed Oursler with his pro-Nazi sentiments. He said Hitler was the right and logical leader for the German people. "It would," the Duke told him, "be a tragic thing for the world if Hitler were overthrown."

After the interview Oursler was taken aside by an aide of the Duke's. A Captain Drury told Oursler to relay a message to the US president. "Tell Mr. Roosevelt that if he will make an offer of intervention for peace, that before anyone in England can oppose it, the Duke of Windsor will instantly issue a statement supporting it, and that will start a revolution in England and start peace."

Oursler and his family returned to the United States and he arranged to see Roosevelt himself, at the White House. On the morning of December 23, 1940 he met with Roosevelt in the Oval Office, but the editor was somewhat stunned that the President already seemed to know what he was about to say. Roosevelt told him, "Why, do you know that I am amazed to find some of greatest people in the British Empire, men of the so-called upper classes, men of the highest rank, secretly want to appease Hitler and stop the war?"

Roosevelt related to him a sequence of events following the abdication of Edward VIII. The Duke subsequently went to a castle in Austria and associated with German friends. Some people in Britain began to feel suspicious about it, Roosevelt said. When the war came, Windsor became a liaison officer between the British and French armies. He was present during the secret discussions of the Commanders-in-Chief of the two armies, and he was aware of everything that was going on. Periodically he would return to Paris for a few days.

"Now, I have nothing to prove what I am going to say, but I do know that there were nine shortwave wireless sets in Paris constantly sending information to the German troops, and no one has been able to decide how such accurate information could be sent over these stations," Roosevelt told the *Liberty* editor.

The President said it was suggested that the Duke go to the south of France to be with his wife. "... Finally he and his wife went to Madrid where they mingled with the wrong people."

The President dictated a letter to Oursler to send to the Duke's assistant Drury, which said, "everything is on a twenty-four hour basis and no one is able to read the future." Roosevelt also told the editor that in the thirties confidential documents were brought to the King daily from Downing street. The secret papers were found strewn around Fort Belvedere where Mrs. Simpson often socialized with "the Ribbentrop Set."

Oursler feared for his life with what he knew. Windsor's aide Drury told him if what he knew about the Duke became public, "the lid would be blown off the British Empire." The *Liberty* editor confided everything to Walter Karig, a journalist who often worked with him, "in case I should die too suddenly on the way home from Washington." When he started to talk to Karig, he found three chambermaids from the Willard Hotel were listening outside the door to their conversation.

Oursler's son considered publishing his father's memo for a 1963 biography, and he consulted Louis B Nichols, then third-in-command of the FBI. Nichols knew the entire story and hypothesized that British Intelligence must have known about the Windsors and their exploits. Nichols warned that even twenty years later the memo was still explosive, and it was never printed.

Oursler Sr. presumed at the time that certain agents must have kept tabs on the Duke and his household in the Bahamas, and the British Embassy must have passed on his information to Roosevelt. (He was perhaps forgetting the Ambassador had recently died, and embassy business was likely in slight state of turmoil.) There was, of course, one other unpublicized communications route between the Western hemisphere and the anti-Hitler forces in Europe— Bill Stephenson. The memo the *Liberty* editor dictated about the Duke on December 26, 1940, concluded as he stepped outside Roosevelt's White House office into the hall. He wrote:

"As I walked out I found a little man sitting in a chair just outside the door. I stopped and looked at him. He kept his head down so I could not see his face. Who was he? Only God and Franklin Roosevelt know."

Appendix B

General Reinhard Gehlen

General Reinhard Gehlen joined the German secret service in 1942 and was the chief of the section responsible for Eastern Europe on which the 'Organization Gehlen' was based. He established a network of saboteurs behind Russian lines, and at the end of the war Gehlen surrendered to the Americans. He is said to have made copies and hid all his files as he saw the end coming.

Gehlen's elaborate espionage organization interested the US, especially since the revelations of Igor Gouzenko alerted them to Soviet penetration of western democracies. The Americans funded his spy network until the government of West Germany took it over in 1955. He retired in 1968. Even decades after the war, his spy organization was regarded as "remarkable," and he accurately predicted the date of the Arab-Israeli Six Day War, and the Soviet invasion of Czechoslovakia in 1968.[35]

For years he refused to be photographed, and he was known as the man without a face. He changed his cars and identity frequently and carried a loaded gun. During the Cold War, reportedly there was a million-mark reward on his head from the eastern bloc.[36]

In his memoirs, Gehlen said that Martin Bormann, Hitler's top aide, was a Soviet agent and died in the Soviet Union in the late sixties. But he offered no proof.[37]

Gehlen wrote in *The Service* that during the Cold War the Soviets thought an important part was played "in the continuing struggle," by swaying opinion. Through "psycho-politics and *desinformatsiya*, or disinformation—a targeted stream of information designed to influence the recipient in a certain, predetermined manner," he wrote, one result the old Soviet Union tried to secure was "an indirect political gain from the penetration of the enemy mind."

"It was Marx who stated that an idea becomes a political force as soon as it penetrates the mind of the masses. If we accept the Communist theory of the absolute interdependence of all that happens, it follows that ... every political action carries within it the means of penetrating the mind: conversely, every mind-penetrating action both can and should lead to political consequences."[38]

In the West, according to Gehlen, Soviet psycho-political lobbying was done by 'influencers.' "In many cases the work of the influencers is not even punishable, it is this feature and their completely unsuspecting character, that makes it impossible even to estimate how many influencers there are, let alone pinpoint and neutralize them. In West Germany, it has not proved possible to identify more than a few isolated cases, and these influencers have been prevented from doing further harm.

"How welcome it must be for their Communist controllers to find that their own training and subtlety are actually aided by our guilelessness (which verges on downright rashness) and political ineptitude."[39] In his memoirs Gehlen quotes Sun-Tse's *Rules for Political and Psychological Subversion*, from about 500 BC, which he said still held true.

"There is no art higher than that of destroying the enemy's resistance without a fight on the battlefield. The direct tactic of war is necessary only on the battlefield, but only the indirect tactic of war can lead to a real and lasting victory.

"Subvert anything of value in the enemy's country. Implicate the emissaries of the major powers in criminal undertakings; undermine their position and destroy their reputation in other ways as well, and expose them to the public ridicule of their fellow citizens.

"Do not shun the aid of even the lowest and most despicable people. Disrupt the work of their government with every means that you can.

"Spread disunity and dispute among the citizens of the enemy's country. Turn the young against the old. Use every means to destroy their arms, their supplies, and the discipline of the enemies' forces. Debase old traditions and accepted gods. Be generous with promises and rewards to purchase intelligence and accomplices. Send out your agents in all directions. Do not skimp with money or with promises, for they yield a high return."[40]

Appendix C

On the Congressional

The early train, the Congressional, was popular at the time, Bayly said, as it left Washington about noon and got into New York around five in the afternoon. The other train was ten at night, and got in at four in the morning. On one trip in the private carriage Bayly sat beside an American in uniform and across from a businessman. The American had Signal Corps badges and crossed flags meaning US Army. "He asked me what my badges were, and I said, 'General List.' It means nothing. It's just anybody that doesn't belong anywhere else. Unidentified." As the trip continued, the uniformed passenger said, 'I'm not really a signaler. I'm making war movies for either instructional purposes, or propaganda purposes.' Then the businessman across the aisle took off his sun glasses, and said, 'Then you should know me. I'm Walt Disney.'"

"And it's Walt Disney," Bayly smiled. "We went into a dining car to have afternoon tea." During the course of their ride together Disney told Bayly he thought he was a Canadian as well. "He was born in Canada, the son of a Methodist minister in Goderich, I think. In any event it's on Lake Huron, and he left there at the age of three and his father had quit the church and became a contractor."

Years later Bayly played golf with Disney's lawyer and he knew nothing about any Canadian connection. "Disney told me this on the train, and I'm quite sure, because he described how his father had left Goderich, and why he was really a Canadian. I suspect they were in the country illegally. It wasn't hard to do in those days, but you didn't advertise you'd done it because immigration would throw you out if they felt they needed to. In those days they didn't toss you out, but if you weren't legally here they kept the information, so that if they wanted to throw you out for any reason they could. Now of course, because of the Mexican border and the difficulty there, they have tightened down on Canadians coming in." (A 1993 Disney biography by Marc Eliot implied that Disney was obsessed much of his life with not having a birth certificate to verify that he was born in Chicago in 1901. Reportedly he cut a deal with J Edgar Hoover to report on Hollywood Communists in exchange for Hoover's help proving his parentage.)

Bayly met many prominent people on the trains. Once, when he was transporting some courier papers, he rammed them into Eleanor Roosevelt in an aisle by mistake. "I tore out of my bedroom, just as a stout lady emerged from the outer bedroom and I hit her full on with the suitcase, and she was absolutely lovely about it; she said, 'I shouldn't have done that, sorry I backed out, it was unforgivable, my husband tells me I should never back out of a doorway.' This is Eleanor Roosevelt and I hit her full on with the suitcase... bang. I felt any lady who could be as nice about it as she was, must be exceptional." He met Watson Watt, the inventor of radar, on a train. At the Pentagon he bumped into the propaganda film producer whom he met while on the train with Disney. While there he also met a man looking for the cafeteria, so he showed him the way and had lunch with him. It was Darryl Zanuck.

Appendix D

Correspondence

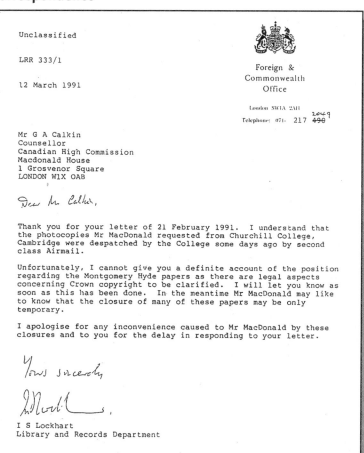

Unclassified

LRR 333/1

12 March 1991

Foreign &
Commonwealth
Office

London SW1A 2AH
Telephone: 071- 217 2049

Mr G A Calkin
Counsellor
Canadian High Commission
Macdonald House
1 Grosvenor Square
LONDON W1X OAB

Dear Mr Calkin,

Thank you for your letter of 21 February 1991. I understand that the photocopies Mr MacDonald requested from Churchill College, Cambridge were despatched by the College some days ago by second class Airmail.

Unfortunately, I cannot give you a definite account of the position regarding the Montgomery Hyde papers as there are legal aspects concerning Crown copyright to be clarified. I will let you know as soon as this has been done. In the meantime Mr MacDonald may like to know that the closure of many of these papers may be only temporary.

I apologise for any inconvenience caused to Mr MacDonald by these closures and to you for the delay in responding to your letter.

Yours sincerely,

I S Lockhart
Library and Records Department

Letter indicating that the Hyde files have been closed to the public

Epilogue

The end of any journey is a reflective period, and so too the completion of this book. It is difficult to conclude a book that encompasses so many separate threads. The course of research that began with biographic intentions became more of a compilation of information, that intruded and strayed. Discovery led to more questions. Although this author obviously has opinions on subjects raised, and the course of events, it would be presumptuous to point fingers or attempt answers. I have tried to step away from the material and will continue to do so here.

The bulk of this material was roughed together at the end of 1996. As this is being written, March 1998, somewhat negative stories about Bill Stephenson, based on previous books, still appear in British newspapers.[1] Some recent histories now refer to what the British were doing to sway the United States from neutrality.[2] I believe this research shows it was truly a multinational Allied effort with a lot of independence from London. Also, BSC's success could not be accomplished without the help and benevolence of many Americans such as Franklin Roosevelt, Robert Sherwood, Bill Donovan, and J Edgar Hoover.

When this research began, and it was discovered Stephenson's biographical information was incorrect, this writer questioned whether BSC ever existed, or was some sort of strange, exaggerated, propaganda balloon. It existed. Also, the rapid transition of Bill Stephenson, can opener salesman, to Bill Stephenson, 'brilliant scientist', seemed an impossible leap. On one trip to England, newspaper death listings of William Stephenson were checked with address indexes, to see whether he had died and someone else had assumed his identity. (This presented a rather unlikely scenario; a potential biographer trying to decide if his subject had actually died sixty years earlier than he thought). Eventually Stephenson's relatives, friends, various newspaper clippings, and pictures of him in England supplied by Margaret Jamieson of Winnipeg, proved it was the same person.

Winston Churchill titled his last book on the war *Triumph and Tragedy*. Perhaps an appropriate title for this volume would be 'Triumph and Anonymity.' British Security Coordination, and individuals such as Stephenson, Bayly, Turing and Welchman secretly accomplished much and then disappeared. They remained unknown. This was part of the profession, I was told. "We don't acknowledge anything." There are no bugles for spies. I think a more appropriate response is that of former SOE chief Colin Gubbins when he was told a book was being done on Stephenson, "honour where honour is done." It seems we have been poor caretakers of history when heroes of humanity's greatest tragedy are neglected and forgotten. Certainly these were lives of triumph that could be celebrated. Yet Bayly, the only one of the above people I met, seemed unaffected. It is easy to pass off anonymity, but when it looks you in the face, it can be a bit unsettling. (For example, Bayly didn't mention his role in the Allies' U-boats success until I raised the subject.)[3] Here truly was a man of accomplishment without ego. Perhaps he was what ancient Chinese texts describe as a 'man of calling,' and his career could be framed not by the *Art of War*, but a passage of the *I Ching*:

"If a man is free of vanity he is able to conceal his abilities and keep them from attracting attention too soon; thus he can mature undisturbed. If conditions demand it, he can also enter public life, but that too he does with restraint. The wise man gladly leaves fame to others. He does not seek to have credited to himself things that stand accomplished, but hopes to release active forces; that is, he completes his works in such a manner that they may bear fruit for the future."[4]

What of Bill Stephenson? The true 'Intrepid'? A definitive story of Stephenson is unlikely, but perhaps this book is at least a step in the right direction. Marion de Chastelain, when asked to sum up her war experience, stressed Bill Stephenson was the only person who could have accomplished what he did, when he did. Pat Bayly thought his former boss's greatest contribution was that he got along with people. With the help of many, anything was possible. In 1989, a California-based journalist lamented about the life and death of Stephenson. "Were it not for William Stephenson, there might not be a Western world today. And yet when he passed away, there was little tribute paid to him. Untold thousands, perhaps millions, owe their lives to Stephenson. He is a genuine hero in an age largely without heroes."

K L Billingsley's commentary fretted whether there were any 'Intrepids' left.[5] It's hard to imagine anything much more unlikely than the story of this unsuccessful can opener salesman, born to a family so poor he was given away. Today, would even Stephenson be able to rise from such a circumstance?

In retrospect, it seems for Stephenson WWI became somewhat of an equalizer. He left his insular preoccupations and he travelled. His medals and bravery in battle helped grant him, almost immediately, a certain status. WWII enhanced it. For a world hopefully without war, perhaps Stephenson himself had an appropriate vision:

"What seems poignantly evident to me is that humankind already has awesome enemies to engage—poverty, disease, and ignorance for example—and in such common cause there is reward and glory enough for all."[6]

---

1 The *Sunday Times*, London, March 1, 1998 in a book review referring to a new book by Nigel West

2 See Thomas Mahl, *Desperate Deception*, or Nicholas J. Cull, *Selling War*

3 The Bayly interview referred to was in November, 1991. Bradley F. Smith's, *The Ultra-Magic Deals* (1993) is the first instance I could find that verifies Bayly's account. It refers to, "Existing British channels," used to transmit ENIGMA material sent on, "high security cable routes ... used by BSC New York to carry German U boat ENIGMA intercepts." (p. 156) David Kahn's, *Seizing the Enigma* (1991) refers to 'keys' used by the British and Americans being exchanged, "through the office of British Security Coordination in Rockefeller Center, New York." (p. 239) Neither book footnotes this material. Neither book mentions Pat Bayly. Renowned American code expert Kahn, whose doctoral work with Hugh Trevor-Roper at Oxford resulted in his book, *Hitler's Spies* (1978), said he'd never heard of Bayly. (January 26, 1998 interview)

4 The *I Ching*, 'the Receptive,' Richard Wilhelm translation, Princeton University Press, 1950

5 *A Tale of a Man Called Intrepid*, February 1989 (undated), *Los Angeles Times*. (Billingsley was the California Correspondent for the *London Spectator*.)

6 Stevenson, *AMCI*, HBJ, 1976 foreword by WS Stephenson

Archives and Papers

- Cadogan, Alexander Diary. Churchill Archive Centre, Churchill College, Cambridge, England.

-Hyde, Harford Montgomery. Papers. Churchill Archive Centre, Churchill College, Cambridge, England (Hyde CCC)

- Stevenson, William. Papers. University of Regina Library (U of R). Regina, Saskatchewan.

- The National Archives and Record Administration in Washington, DC, (NARA)

- The William Donovan Papers in Carlisle, Pennsylvania, (Carlisle Papers)

- Sections of the top secret British Security Coordination history BSC: An Account of Secret Activities in the Western Hemisphere 1940-1945 were made available to me by a person who wished to remain anonymous.(BSC history)

* Cables indicated with capitalization.

** STEVERITE cable address of the author William Stevenson

Notes to Chapters and Appendices

Preface pg 10

1   When the British double agent Kim Philby was suspected of being a triple agent by Moscow, they demanded over and over, that he write out long detailed biographies of himself. It seems no one got a biography out of Stephenson. James Bamford's View From the KGB, *New York Times* January 29, 1995

2   He wrote, for example, that he knew the date of the 1967 Arab-Israeli War before it occurred. William Stevenson, About the Author, *90 Minutes at Entebbe*, 1976

3   Joseph P. Lash, *Roosevelt And Churchill* p. 140

4   *South* magazine, February 1991, no. 119, p. 78

5   Stephenson quoted in *CBC Times* September, 7-13 1968 issue

6   William Stevenson, *The Bormann Brotherhood* p. 21

7   Joseph Lelyveld, "Le Carre's Toughest Task," *New York Times*, March 16, 1986. The first novel not offered for clearance was his eleventh, *The Perfect Spy* in 1986

Introduction pg 16

1   *Manchester Guardian Weekly,* February, 1989

2   Stevenson, *A Man Called Intrepid* p. 4

3   Gislasson later said he was referring to a picture of Stephenson in a defunct Icelandic paper run by a relative. Subsequently another Stephenson picture was located, headlined *Islenzkur Flugmadur* - Icelandic Flyer

4   Unfortunately Derek Bedson died suddenly that week, so was unable to further discuss Stephenson

Chapter 1 Winnipeg pg 25

1 Lutheran funeral #427 First Lutheran Church Winnipeg, Death of, Funeral Service records

2 Heber previously interviewed a Mrs. Davies, who lived on Sutherland Street in Point Douglas, who knew the families, and was over a hundred years old when she died in 1986

3 In 1912, Thorarinn, Kristjan, and Gudmindur bought the general store in the Interlake town of Lundar, Manitoba. Because the brothers had different fathers, in the Icelandic tradition, they had different last names. They created a common surname, Breckman, after Klungubrekka, the Icelandic town they were from, and they named the Lundar store, "Breckman Brothers."

4 George Johnson interview, May 1989

5 *Winnipeg Free Press*, November 26, 1952

6 Alan Artibise, *Winnipeg An Illustrated History* p.55

7 Artibise, p. 104

8 James H Gray, *Red Lights on the Prairies* p. 68

9 Artibise, p. 105

10 IBID

11 *Manitoba Free Press*, November 12, 1910

12 *Winnipeg Telegram*, November 17, 18 1910

13 Artibise, p. 106

14 IBID

15 *Manitoba Free Press*, January 12, 1914

16 *Manitoba Free Press*, December 9, 1913

17 *Manitoba Free Press*, January 22, 1914

18 *Manitoba Free Press*, December 11, 1913

19 *Manitoba Free Press*, January 15, 1914

20 *Manitoba Free Press*, January 12, 13, 1914

Chapter 2 World War I pg 36

1 Attestation paper Canadian Overseas Expeditionary Force

2 It is not known why this is the case. Stephenson was perhaps concerned about being at least twenty to be sent overseas. One report in the Icelandic Manitoban paper, *Logberg Heimskringla* (March 10, 1989) indicates when he enlisted he was one year under age. A later newspaper story on his RAF flying exploits in the Icelandic Manitoban *Votgorold* May 14, 1918, has Stephenson's correct age, 21. Stephenson's relatives have record of his actual birth date. It is a strange anomaly

3 STEPHENSON TO STEVENSON, August 21 1975, U of R 83-7 801.1-1

4 *Manitoba Free Press*, September 9, 1919, also Hyde file photographs, Churchill College, Cambridge (CCC)

5 Stevenson, *AMCI*, p. 5, Anthony Cave Brown, *The Last Hero Wild Bill Donovan*, 1982 p. 32

6 Regiment records indicate it may have been later in 1917

7 Hyde, *The Quiet Canadian*, p. 7

8 Drew-Brook to Hyde, December 12, 1961, CCC, Hyde papers 1/5

9   *The Great Canadian Spy,* radio transcript U of R 1/5

10 INTREPID TO STEVERITE July 15, 1974, U of R, 83-7 801.1-1

11 *Gazette,* September 21, 1918, p. 11255 (107) 22/ 3/ 18 one, RFC communique No. 132, 83-7 box 9 Marteville, offensive patrol, 2 Vickers guns, Sopwith Camel No.B7502 305 PM 5000 feet March 24 1918 Sopwith Camel D6421 10:40 am, offensive patrol, 1000 feet 8-14 April 1918 Military Cross 2 Lt. William S. Stephenson (second lieutenant) p. 37 Royal Air Force 1918 Military Cross to 2nd Lt ... for conspicuous gallantry and devotion to duty. When flying low and observing an open staff car on a road, he attacked it with such success that later it was seen lying in the ditch upside down. During the same flight he caused a stampede amongst some enemy transport horses on a road. Previous to this he had destroyed a hostile scout and a two seater plane. His word has been of highest order and he has shown the greatest courage and energy in engaging every kind of target. (Gazette 22, June 1918, p. 7423) 3 /5/ 18 p.58 Lt W,. Stephenson, 73 sqn, in a general engagement between his patrol and a formation of EA. triplanes and scouts, singled out one EA scout and fired about 250 rounds into it. The EA went down and was followed a short distance by Lt Stephenson who watched it going down and eventually nose dive into Ploegsteert Wood. July 9 18 Sopwith Camel No. C8296, Moncheaux, 10500 feet one July 10 1918 Sopwith Camel C8296 one shot down, one out of control p.134 July 14, 1918 Enemy aircraft were also brought down during the period under review by 73 Lt W S Stephenson (one I suppose) p. 138 July 21 73 Lt W. S. Stephen- son July 21 shared Fokker triplane p. 143 22-28 July 1918 73 Lt W S Stephenson (3) July 22, 1918 Bazoches, 2, Fokker Triplane and biplane July 25 1918, Camel C8296, St. Thibaut, 10000 ft, Fokker biplane July 25 1918 same Camel, near Cohan, LVG two seater, (shared) p. 158 Honours and Awards DFC Lt WS Stephenson MC July 28, 1918, NW Fere-en-Tardenois, General Flying, at least one Fokker biplane Lieut Stephenson is missing after this engagement. Distinguished Flying Cross to Lt William Samuel Stephenson, MC "This officer has shown conspicuous gallantry and skill in attacking enemy troops and transports from low altitudes, causing heavy casualties. His reports have also contained valuable and accurate information. He had further proved himself to be a keen antagonist in the air having during recent operations accounted for six enemy aeroplanes."

12 Translation of extract from French paper *Avion* CCC Hyde 1/1

13 The *Avion* passage, and the fact that Stephenson was brought down by friendly fire demonstrates the difficulty assessing dog fight reports and 'kills' during the First War. (It is possible that when and if Stephenson said he shot down 26 aircraft, he was including Allied planes he'd shot down as well.)

14 Tommy Drew-Brook to Hyde, December 12, 1961 Hyde CCC 1/5

15 Hyde 1/6 CCC

16 *Winnipeg Tribune,* Canadian Press Wire story July 7, 1954

17 Hyde 1/6 CCC

18 Cited in *Manitoba Free Press,* August 28, 1923 (refers to recent article in leading London newspaper.)

Chapter 3 Britain pg 50

1   *Manitoba Free Press*, August 28, 1923 (For some reason this clipping is dated in the Hyde file at CCC as September 1924)
2   Current Biography 1940 Beaverbrook
3   Interview with Margaret Jamieson. Wilf Russell travelled to Winnipeg regularly to visit with the Jamieson family, as he had been engaged to her mother's deceased sister
4   *The Times* (London), January 1, 1926
5   Lion's Gate Bridge has become a venerable Vancouver landmark
6   Hyde, *The Quiet Canadian* p. 14. Hyde remembers Lord Londonderry, then Air Minister, bought one for his private use and Hyde frequently flew with him in it.
7   London Street indexes, 1934, Stephenson was #19, and Hambro #18 New Cavendish At some point the Cavendish street addresses were renumbered
8   *The Times*, May 4, 1936.
9   Thomas Troy, *Wild Bill and Intrepid* p. 166-68
10 *Times* (London) indexes, for June 20, 1927, indicates a story about someone named Stephenson, who spoke on a cinematographic film bill. I could not locate this in the paper
11 *The Financial Times* (London), July 7, 1939
12 *Daily Telegraph,* February 3, 1989
13 U of R 83-7 Box 9 801. 3-1 Frank Whittle died in 1996. His association is in *Daily Telegraph*, February 3, 1989 and other sources. Stephenson cabled to William Stevenson that he helped recruit BTH and GEC Labs to search for a high speed steel alloy that would remain hard even at red hot temperatures. (U of R 83-7 801.1-6). It is apparent from the correspondence that Stephenson knew Whittle, and the writer Stevenson met with Whittle during the writing of *A Man Called Intrepid*. Stephenson says in one cable, "Give my regards to Frank."
14 Letter William Stevenson to Lester B. Pearson, October 25, 1972 U of R 83-7 Box 9 801.7-2. Stephenson's or Churchill's attendance at a Fabian gathering could have been initiated through their mutual friend Beaverbrook, who's top *Evening Standard* columnist Arnold Bennett (1867-1931) was a well known Fabian. Beaverbrook was known for tolerating a wide spectrum of political views and Bennett accompanied him on a trip to Russia in 1929
15 Hyde, *The Quiet Canadian*, p. 15
16 Hyde, *Secret Intelligence Agent,* p. 80
17 Interview with Victor Bryant, January 1991
18 Anthony Cave Brown, *C*, p. 262
19 *The Times*, November 3, 1936
20 *The Times*, November 13, 1936
21 *The Times*, February 6, 1937
22 *The Times*, June 18, 1936
23 *The Times*, November 13, 1936
24 *Turning the Pages of History,* publication supplied by Earl's Court.
25 *The Globe and Mail*, May 20, 1982
26 Ellis in *A Man Called Intrepid,* CBC television documentary (1974 broadcast)

27 Interview with Dick Ellis *Tuesday Night,* Roll C Take 1, U of R
28 IBID
29 Stevenson, *A Man Called Intrepid* p. xxvii
30 Stevenson, *A Man Called Intrepid* p. 32
31 Hyde, *The Quiet Canadian* p. 14
32 Lord Londonderry's, *Ourselves and Germany* (1938)
33 Harold Nicolson, *Volume II, Diaries and Letters, The War Years 1939-1945* diaries p.458-459
34 FW Winterbotham, (1978) *The Nazi Connection* p. 133
35 Winterbotham, IBID
36 Robert Goralski, *World War II Almanac,* November 28, 1934 p. 30
37 Winterbotham, *The Nazi Connection* p. 157
38 Winterbotham, *The Nazi Connection* p. 158, 159
39 If England was sleeping, Kennedy's father Joe, the American Ambassador in England, was probably in a coma
40 John F Kennedy, *Why England Slept* p. 92-93.
41 Winterbotham, *The Nazi Connection* p. 163-164
42 Martin Gilbert, Richard Gott, *The Appeasers,* p. 28, citing Lord Londonderry, *Ourselves and Germany,* p. 97 February 21, 1936.)
43 Stephenson cable to STEVERITE November 2, 1975 U of R 83-7 801.1-6.
44 Interview with Dick Ellis, *Tuesday Night,* Roll C Take 1, U of R
45 Anthony Cave Brown, *'C' The Secret Life of Stewart Menzies,* p. 195
46 INTREPID to STEVERITE August 23, 1974 U of R 83-7 801.1-4
47 Brown, *C* p. 195
48 Hyde, *The Quiet Canadian* p. 20-24. There are numerous other references to this including an interview with Stephenson in the CBC television documentary, *A Man Called Intrepid* (1974)
49 *Tuesday Night,* Interview with Dick Ellis U of R Roll C Take One
50 INTREPID TO STEVERITE cable, September 12 1974, U of R, 83-7 801.1-1 (124)
51 Winston Churchill, *The Gathering Storm* p. 196-97
52 Robert Sherwood, *The White House Papers of Harry L. Hopkins* (1948) p. 151-152.
53 Beaverbrook to Churchill, December 13, 1940 Beaverbrook Archives (cited in Lovell p. 337)
54 Anthony Cave Brown, *C* p. 7
55 RG Grant, *MI5 MI6 Britains Security and Intelligence Services* p. 48, 49
56 Alvin Finkel and Clement Leibovitz, *The Chamberlain-Hitler Collusion* p. 286
57 An edited version of Cadogan's diary was published by David Dilks. The actual diary of Alexander Cadogan is at Churchill College, Cambridge. Cadogan, CCC

Chapter 4 British Security Coordination pg 69

1   Martin Gilbert, *Winston S Churchill* vol 6 p. 358
2   *Great Canadian Spy,* radio transcription U of R 83-7 Box 4 500. 1-7
3   Tunney to Thomas Troy (CIA) August 6, 1969 U of R 83-7 Box 9 801.9 Later Stephenson thanked Tunney for the role he played. "Sir William sent me a very charming letter thanking me for what I had done and telling me that I would be very proud to have

played the part of mediator, though I would expect no information about the affair. Sir William did refer to me in his book, *The Quiet Canadian* as having played the part I did, which was still of course secret."

4   Tunney to Stephenson, August 6, 1969 letter U of R 83-7 Box 9 801. 7-1
    In 1975, Troy completed a history of the CIA, produced in two volumes, "aimed at satisfying the need of the employees of the Central Intelligence Agency." It was classified SECRET. Later, in 1981, the work was reproduced as a single volume called *Donovan and the CIA: A History of the Establishment of the Central Intelligence Agency* - "released for leisurely reading outside the office." The history was reclassified, after it was reedited, and shorn of a total of about six pages. The Tunney references are not in the released text, although his letters appear in the sources. Tunney is mentioned in Troy's later book, *Wild Bill and Intrepid*. Numerous publications mention the Stephenson - Hoover meetings. None mention that British government officials were not to know about it

5   Hyde, *The Quiet Canadian* p. 26

6   Curt Gentry, *J Edgar Hoover the Man and his Secrets*, p. 265, citing an interview with Ernest Cuneo.

7   Letter from Ernest Cuneo to William Stephenson, December 15, 1975, U of R. 83-7 Box 10 801 10-4 Thomas Troy wrote that Cuneo didn't remember being the go-between at this early stage and a more likely conduit was Vincent Astor. Cuneo is quoted in Gentry's, *J Edgar Hoover the Man and the Secrets*, and didn't contradict the story

8   Cuneo wrote the introduction to a book by Winchell, *Winchell Exclusive* (1975)

9   STEPHENSON to STEVERITE December 20, 1975, U of R 83-7 801.1-6

10 Hyde, *The Quiet Canadian*, p. 26

11 Anthony Cave Brown, 'C' , p. 262

12 There has been some controversy about the date - that is the exact day of the week - of Beaverbrook's dinner outing decades ago, and incredibly, this has been used to question Stephenson's achievements, and whether he even knew Churchill or Beaverbrook. Following Stephenson's death, an article in *The Times* (London) by their Defence correspondent (*The Times* February 18, 1989) highlighted the concerns of an assortment of British "scholars," "historians" and "distinguished figures."
    "The meeting with Churchill at the centre of historian's arguments," read a subhead line. *"Stephenson chose the silliest of all dates (May 10, 1940) to claim his dinner session with Churchill. It was the one day everyone knew where Churchill was,"* Sir David Hunt commented in the story. The *Times* story also quotes from AJP Taylor's Beaverbrook biography, which says Churchill and Beaverbrook lunched and dined alone together on May 10, 1940 (The Taylor biography also says Beaverbrook's immediate task at the time was to advise Churchill on appointments, p.410). A cable from Stephenson to the writer Stevenson, October 25, 1973, years before *A Man Called Intrepid* was published, or there was any controversy, is the earliest mention of the meeting in available papers. In the cable, Stephenson says he can't recall the exact date of the Beaverbrook dinner, thirty-three years before, but it was probably May 12, 1940.(U of R 83-7 801.1-1) The centre of the historical argument seems a bit donut-like. The same article in the *Times* mentions intelligence files remain closed. The story contin-

ued, *"I've* (Hunt) *also spoken to Alan Taylor* (AJP Taylor, Beaverbrook biographer) *and there is no evidence Stephenson even knew Beaverbrook, let alone Churchill."* There was evidence in the files of H Montgomery Hyde, before they were closed by the British government. As cited earlier, in May of 1940, the month Stephenson was appointed to America, Churchill told his son "I shall drag the United States in." (Gilbert *Winston S Churchill* vol 6 p. 358) It is well documented that Churchill met, and knew William Donovan, Roosevelt's intelligence coordinator and the head of the OSS. It is rather ludicrous to suggest that Churchill would not know his own intelligence representative in the US. Apart from other references to the Stephenson and Churchill relationship in this book, Stephenson's working relationships with Franklin Roosevelt and Winston Churchill first became public in the 1950's. *The Quiet Canadian* mentions meetings between Churchill and Stephenson. The facts were never questioned by Churchill, who was still alive at the time. *The Sunday Times* of London, the sister paper of *The Times*, printed a syndicated version of *The Quiet Canadian* in 1962 , which told readers of Stephenson - Churchill association. It seems somewhat strange that *The Times* would later publish a story that questioned whether the relationship existed. If Churchill was still alive, it is unlikely such revisionism of history would have been allowed to occur

13 Hyde, *Secret Intelligence Agent* p. xv foreword, signed by Stephenson

14 INTREPID TO STEVERITE, March 19, 1974 83-7 801.1-3 Later discussing his relationship with Lothian and Roosevelt, Stephenson cabled:
"LOTHIAN CHRISTIAN SCIENTIST WAS DEATHLY ILL ME EVERY ONCE OF COOPERATION HIS HEALTH ALLOWED UNTIL HIS LAST DAYS WHEN I SITTING BY HIS BEDSIDE HOLDING HIS HAND IN FAREWELL BEING EN ROUTE URGENT VISIT LONDON STOP (December 1940) *HE DIED WHILST I WAS EN ROUTE AND MY MEETINGS THEREAFTER* (with Roosevelt) *STRICTLY DUO EXCEPT SON JAMES OCCASIONAL APPEARANCE AND LATER DONOVANS WHEN KNOX STIMSON AND HULL WERE ENLISTED BY DONOVAN TO IMPLEMENT FRANKLINS EDICTS OF ACQUIESCENCE TO URGENT AMERICAN MOVES OF STATESMANSHIP AND SELF INTEREST INTREPID*

15 Joseph Lash, *Roosevelt and Churchill* p. 140 Lash's book deals with correspondence between Roosevelt and Churchill and he does not specify the source. It is also in *A Man Called Intrepid.* A paraphrased revision of the passage appears in *The Quiet Canadian* p. 26-27

16 INTREPID TO STEVERITE May 16, 1974 U of R 83-7 801. 1-1

17 Cited in *Toronto Star* September 19, 1989 (Washington Post Syndicated story based on the 'BSC history' leaked to the paper by William Stevenson, and verified for authenticity by CIA historian Thomas Troy.)

Chapter 5 New York City pg 73

1 Hyde, *Secret Intelligence Agent,* foreword by Stephenson, p. xv

2 National Archives and Records Administration (NARA) RG59 702.4111/1608

3 Certificate of Admission in Troy's, *Wild Bill and Intrepid* p.35

4 Hyde, *The Quiet Canadian* p. 31-32

5 Ellis, *A Man Called Intrepid,* CBC TV Documetary, 1974

6 John Tracy, *Winnipeg Tribune,* Canadian Press Wire story July 7, 1954

7 *The Two Bills*, Bermuda Island Press, April 1968 U of R 83-7 Box 4 500. 1-7

8 Lash, *Roosevelt and Churchill*, p. 113, reporting comments of Harold Ickes.

9 Robert Goralski, *World War II Almanac* July 1, 1940 p. 125

10 Goralski, September 27, 1940 p. 133

11 quoted in *The World at War 1939-42*, documentary

12 Stephenson, dated May 1, 1982, in Foreword to *Donovan: America's Master Spy*, p. vii, Richard Dunlop, Rand McNally & Company 1982.

13 *The Two Bills*, Bermuda Island Press, April 1968 U of R, 83-7 Box 4 500. 1-7 Some of the Americans contacted at an early stage were Gene Tunney, Junius Morgan, Ernest Cuneo, Vincent Astor, Errett Cord, Henry Stimson, Frank Knox, Cordell Hull, Ben Cohen, Wendell Wilkie, and Edward Stettinius. Troy, *Wild Bill and Intrepid* p. 166-167 on meeting Donovan. "Stephenson was very fortunate in reestablishing contact with Donovan. He had known Donovan in the past, he had not any official connections with him, but knew him quite well. And it was through Donovan that he was able to meet people in high places in Washington ..." Dick Ellis in *Tuesday Night* documentary transcription. U of R Roll C Take 1

14 Anthony Cave Brown, *Wild Bill Donovan The Last Hero* p. 148

15 Donovan's *America's Master Spy*, Foreword (written by Stephenson), Dunlop p. viii.

16 Stephenson's The Early Days of OSS/COI, p. 4 cited in Troy, *Donovan and the CIA*, Hyde, *The Quiet Canadian* p. 36

17 Troy, *Donovan and the CIA* p. 55; The preface pages refer to the volume as the "product of official research," but not the official position of the Central Intelligence Agency

18 Morton to Colonel E I Jacob, September 18, 1941 Churchill Papers CCC, Box 145, Folder 463, item 2; also quoted in CIA paper entitled, " Studies in the history of intelligence, p. 109. printed in 1974. Cited in Lovell p. 339. Lovell infers the 'British officer' involved was Stephenson, as does Troy.

19 *The Great Canadian Spy*, Roll 3 of 4 83-7 box 4 500.1-7 p 3/1-2

20 Conyers Read's, "Pre-COI Period" transcript, OSS Records, Wash-Hist-Off-Op.23, cited in Troy page 146

21 Donovan's *America's Master Spy*, Foreword (written by Stephenson), Dunlop p. viii.

22 Pforzheimer Collection cited in Dunlop p. 206

23 Lee cited in Dunlop p. 210

24 "What was the best defense against air attack? Could the war be won by air power and blockade alone? Which types of ordnance were proving effective, and which types ineffective? How could intelligence operations be improved? What were the principal problems the British had in mobilizing economically for the war? The British were expanding their armed forces with the greatest possible speed and the United States would probably have to undertake a similar expansion; in what ways could we profit from the British experience?" extract from a biography of Donovan - NARA source unknown

25 "I note that Arthur Schlesinger makes it clear," Stephenson said later, that neither Churchill's "direct appeals, incidentally through me, nor the King's letter, moved FDR on the destroyers and it would tend to confirm that it was clearly only our clique including WJD, Stimson, Knox, Hull, Ben Cohen, Wendell and Stettinius and other

private and administrative citizens gathered with me to ease FDR into legal reasons and explanations that finally achieved the destroyers okay from FDR fearing a reluctant Congress to overcome and our group of lawyers found the way to the great advantage of the Allies and indeed the whole world." INTREPID TO STEVERITE, August 31, 1974 U of R83-7 801.1-1 Stephenson also said of the deal, *"DESTROYERS BASES DEAL HYDE PAGE 37 WORKED BY LEGAL FORMULA WITH DONOVAN AND LAWYER FRIENDS AND MINE INCLUDING SECRETLY WILKIE (*Wendell*) AFTER WINSTONS DIRECT AND PUBLIC APPEALS TO FDR HAD FAILED TO PRODUCE THIS VITAL LIFELINE PRODUCTION AS EARL M OF B SAID LATER TO YOU STOP* INTREPID TO STEVERITE July 15, 1974 U of R83-7 801.1-1

26 Stephenson in *The Two Bills*, transcript of an interview by Shaun Herron, Bermuda 1968, U of R 83-7 Box 4 500 1-7

27 *The Great Canadian Spy,* Roll 2 of 4 83-7 box 4 500.1-7 p. 2/8-9

28 Donovan's *America's Master Spy*, Foreword (written by Stephenson), Dunlop p. ix.

29 The BSC history, 'Procurement', p. 10, 11, 14, 17, 27, 334, 335, 352, 393-399.

30 *The Great Canadian Spy,* Roll 3 of 4 83-7 box 4 500.1-7 p. 3/1

31 *The Sunday Star* (Toronto), October 8, 1989, based on BSC history, and CIA study released in 1974

32 INTREPID TO STEVERITE, April 6, 1974, U of R83-7 801.1-3

33 Herb Rowland resume U of R 83-7 Box 9 801. 7-1 He was kept on after the war at the request of Britain's Foreign Office, employed by the Super Security Agency of British Foreign Office in Washington and was in continual liaison with the FBI and the CIA.

34 Stephenson was unsure he would live through the war and Hill's brother-in-law, Canadian lawyer Glenn McPherson, became executor of a new will.

35 *Canadians at War*, Reader Digest Volume 2 p. 512

36 IBID

37 Hyde, *The Quiet Canadian* p. 178, p.181

38 Stevenson mentions Tommy Drew-Brook, Charles Vining, Herb Rowland, Ernest Bavin. "I reduced the Canadian content simply because it shrinks within the larger picture...," Stevenson explained to R.S. Malone, the then editor-in-chief of the Toronto *Globe and Mail*. (June 4, 1974 letter) "You can see how the balance could come down rather heavily on US-UK aspects," continued the British-born journalist. "On the other hand Sir William is the central character and I have emphasized how vital his Canadian background was throughout BSC's history." 83-7 Box 9 801.4

39 Thomas Troy, *Donovan and the CIA,* 1981, p. 34

40 Tracy Canadian Press wire, OP CIT

41 *The Two Bills*, Bermuda Island Press April 1968 U of R 83-7 Box 4 500 1-7

42 cited in *Winnipeg Free Press*, September 23, 1989, *Washington Post* Syndicated, based on BSC history

43 cited in *The World at War* 1939-42 , 'On Our Way', producers Jeremy Isaacs, Peter Batty, Thames

44 cited in *Winnipeg Free Press,* September 23, 1989, *Washington Post* Syndicated

45 IBID

46 IBID

47 *Toronto Star*, September 19, 1989 *Washington Post* Syndicate story - citation from BSC history

48 Donald Downes, *The Scarlet Thread* , p.59-60

49 Donald Downes, *The Scarlet Thread* , p.60-61

50 In early April 1941, Brig. Gen. Sherman Miles, the Assistant Chief-of-Staff Intelligence wrote to the Chief-of-Staff warning of Donovan, "In great confidence ONI tells me that there is considerable reason to believe that there is a movement on foot, fostered by Col. Donovan, to establish a super agency controlling *all* intelligence. This would mean that such an agency, no doubt under Colonel Donovan, would collect, collate and possibility even evaluate all military intelligence which we now gather from foreign countries. From the point of view of the war department, such a move would appear very disadvantageous, if not calamitous." Memo, Miles to Marshall, April 8, 1941, Records of the Army staff, Army Intelligence Decimal File Record Group 319, File 310.11 , Washington National Records Centre, Suitland, Maryland, cited in Troy, *Donovan and the CIA* p. 42

51 William Donovan to Adjutant General War Department, through Joint Chiefs of Staff, Recommendation for Award of Distinguished Service Medal to William Stephenson, July 19 1944, attached to Memorandum for the President, from Donovan of same date.

52 *A Man Called Intrepid,* CBC television documentary, executive producer William Harcourt, 1974

53 Historical notes written by Dick Ellis (said to be given to Whitney Shepardson) undated CCC Hyde 1/12 Also Tuesday Night transcript Roll 3 U of R

54 June 19, 1944 William Donovan memorandum to Adjutant General War Department, through Joint Chiefs of Staff, with copy to Roosevelt, Donovan Papers, "OSS Reports to the White House 1942-1944," Carlisle, Penn

55 Stephenson, speaking in *A Man Called Intrepid,* CBC television documentary 1974

56 Noel Coward, *Future Indefinite* p. 271 p. 275

57 Ingall to Shaun Herron U of R 83-7 Box 9 801.7-2

58 William Donovan to Adjutant General War Department, through Joint Chiefs of Staff, Recommendation for Award of Distinguished Service Medal to William Stephenson, July 19 1944, attached to Memorandum for the President, from Donovan of same date

59 "Appointments and telephone calls, August 9, 1941- Sept 29, 1945," Donovan papers, cited in Troy, *Donovan and the CIA* p. 83

60 Cited in Dunlop p. 327 not footnoted - says message relayed by diplomatic pouch

61 Ian Fleming, "Memorandum to Colonel Donovan," June 27, 1941, OSS records, Wash-Dir-Op 125. Fleming sent copies to Admiral Godfrey and WS Stephenson. (Lovell and Troy) According to Ellis, "Fleming had nothing to do with it," and the main structure was established long before Fleming visited the US, *Tuesday Night* transcript Roll 4 p. 4 U of R

62 Historical notes written by Dick Ellis (said to be given to Whitney Shepardson) undated Hyde, CCC 1/12

63 Bradley F Smith, *The Ultra Magic Deals* p. 88 citing October 19, 1941 Lee to Washington, file 10/16/41, Box 247 Entry 59, R.G. 319, Suitland, NA

64 Historical notes written by Dick Ellis (said to be given to Whitney Shepardson) undated Hyde, CCC 1/12

65 *The Great Canadian Spy,* Roll 1 of 4 83-7 box 4 500.1-7 p. 1/9

66 *New York Times,* December 6, 1940, Dunlop p. 232

67 Nadya Gardner, Letter to WSS March 19, 1976 U of R 83-7 Box 11 801. 17-1 When she retired from she wrote a history of her cases which was to be deposited in the National Archives for use as a training manual in the event of future hostilities. She was told it would be available only on a direct Presidential order

68 Interview With Dick Ellis *Tuesday Night,* Roll 3 Page 1, U of R. According to *A Man Called Intrepid,* they were prepared in Toronto

69 *A Man Called Intrepid* - blurb, and other sources. This quote is also used in a summary of the career of William Stephenson, which was printed by the veterans of the OSS, indicating the veterans do not consider this quote, or the episode, as nonsense

70 Winston Churchill, *The Grand Alliance* p. 163

71 Winston Churchill, *The Grand Alliance,* p. 166-167

72 Letter from Acting Secretary of the Treasury, to Secretary of State 841.011B11, August 11, 1942

Chapter 6 London pg 91

1 Lovell, *Cast No Shadow* p. 330

2 Gubbins to Ellis, August 16, 1972 U. of R 83-7 Box 9 801.6

3 U of R 83-7 Box 10 801. 10-12

4 Gubbins, Foreword U of R 83-7 Box 10 801.10-9

5 Stephenson tells of another meeting with Churchill in a cable to the writer William Stevenson. Churchill was in bed reading reports at seven in the morning when Stephenson and Bill Donovan arrived. Churchill asked if they knew the French resistance leader Charles De Gaulle. Bill replied, "Oh yes. I have known him since his St. Cyr days. (De Gaulle graduated and taught at St. Cyr, a French military school). He is a very difficult and obstinate man with a Jean D'Arc complex. Requires tight hold on a short leash," Winston grunted, "Oh I suppose I have handled more difficult men in my time - garumph." At another time Churchill remarked, "Of all the heavy crosses I have had to bear the double-cross of Lorraine..." INTREPID TO STEVERITE August 29, 1974 U of R 83-7 801.4

6 Cuneo to Stephenson December 15, 1975 U of R 83-7 Box 10 801.10-4

7 In his letter to Stephenson, Cuneo says, "My war record is obscure, in the nature of things, and I should like a written document to indicate that, when my days are over...As the tontine works, you are the only high authority who is in a position to describe my services." IBID

8 *Maclean's,* December 1, 1952

9 Hand-written note Colin Gubbins to Dick Ellis, August 16, 1972, U of R 83-7 Box 9 801.6

10 Studio history provided by Shepparton Studios. The studio re-opened its film making business at the end of 1945 with six stages. One of their stages was a causality in the second of three air raids on the studios

11 Hyde to Harrington, June 15, 1942 CCC 3/22

12 Hyde, CCC 3/22

13 In September, 1942, Hyde met with the FBI Director to discuss the premature release of information regarding German agents in Trinidad who were sending wireless messages. Hoover thanked Dorothy Hyde for the instruction she gave to FBI, and said eight German saboteurs captured in July 42 broke down quickly. BSC was used to exchange information. Hoover was interested in preparations Axis nations were making for the use of bacteriological weapons, as the FBI had little information on the subject. There is a record of January 20, 1944, meeting between Hyde and Hoover as Hyde was leaving the US. Hyde CCC 3/30

14 Hyde, CCC 3/13

15 Herbert from Stephenson Hyde, CCC 3/13

16 The scope of North American security measures can be determined from this security executive paper marked Secret in Hyde's files:
(a) Port Security, (b) Alien's Policy, (c) Subversive Activities, (d) Anti-sabotage, (e) Control of Entry, (f) Colonial Security, (g) Security in South America
(1) Espionage, (2) Sabotage, (3) Subversive Activities, (4) Other Fifth Column Activities, (5) Aliens, (6) Control of Information and Communication, (7) Identity cards passes and permits, (8) Security of Special Localities, (9) Control of Entry Exit Travel Facilities, (10) Shipping Security, Hyde, CCC 3/13

17 U of R 83.7 801.1-3

18 Troy, *Donovan and the CIA*, p. 83

Chapter 7 Washington pg 97

1 STEPHENSON TO STEVENSON, April 18, 1974 U of R 83.7 801. 1-3

2 BSC history, p. 155

3 BSC history, p. 165

4 *INTREPID TO STEVERITE*, February 22, 1974 U of R 83-7 801.1-3

5 STEPHENSON TO 'BISON' Toronto, (Herb Rowland) October 15, 1973, U of R 83-7 Box 9 801.8, also p. 461 *Intrepid*

6 Outline U of R 83-7 box 9 801 .3-1

7 INTREPID TO STEVERITE December 30, 1975 U of R 83-7 801.1-6

8 INTREPID TO STEVERITE U of R 83-7 801.1-1 According to Stephenson, Tizard was at the Shoreham hotel when he received a phone call from the FBI about security of his possessions. Stephenson contacted Hoover who didn't know about it. Later the call was traced through Sam Foxworth to the German Embassy

9 *The Great Canadian Spy*, radio transcript, U of R 83-7 Box 4 500.1-7 Roll 2 of 4

10 British Embassy to Department of State January 21, 1941 NARA 841.0B11/185 Hoover is said to have thought of the name British Security Coordination

11 Hyde, CCC 3/23 October 30, 1942 (November 7, 1942 message)

12 February 6, 1941, letter from special agent Bannerman to Clark NARA 841.01B11/191

13 State Department copy of letter from British Embassy July 15, 1941 NARA 841.01 B11

14 Berle to Welles, Mar. 31, 1941 RG 59 State file 841.20211/23

15 FDRL February 5, 1942 Berle letter to Roosevelt

16 Berle diary, February 4, 1942

17 February 4, 1942 letter from Sherwood to Roosevelt

18 See 'Bill Ross Smith'
19 Biddle memorandum, February 26, 1942, Hyde Park New York
20 Berle diary March 5, 1942 NARA RG59, 841.20211/36
21 Berle diary March 10, 1942 NARA RG59 841.20211/36
22 David Ogilvy to WSS February 25, 1963 CCC Hyde 1/10
23 INTREPID TO STEVERITE April 6, 1974 U of R 83-7 801.1-3
24 A January 22, 1944 letter from Cox, US Assistant Solicitor General requested from BSC:
    (1) list of employees
    (2) supplemented with additional information
    (3) BSC will conduct and limit its activities
    -conduct no investigations of any kind without the written approval of the Director of the FBI
    - all information obtained about Western hemisphere should be transmitted to the FBI.
    - if transmitted to another US agency should be simultaneously sent to the FBI
    - BSC will maintain no arrangements with informants with or without compensation.
    - BSC will maintain liaison with the Combined Chiefs of Staff only through the British Joint Staff Mission.
    - BSC will maintain no liaison with the United States Civil Service.
    "While we are required under the Act to keep a record of the activities in which your organization may engage, we wish to do so without any unnecessary requirements or inconvenience to you and we shall be glad at any time to discuss with you question that may arise." Stephenson's response isn't recorded.
25 Hyde, *Secret Intelligence Agent* p. 232
26 letter Stone to Stephenson June 18, 1943 CCC Hyde 3/30
27 Tuesday Night transcript page 2 & 3 U of R Roll 8
28 Spruille Braden, *Diplomats and Demagogues* p. 247
29 Braden IBID. p. 252
30 Hyde, *Secret Intelligence Agent* p. 154-155 Hyde's later version admits the forgery
31 Braden, OP CIT p. 251
32 Cuneo cited in Desperate Deception, p. 14 CIA file
33 Sir Bede Clifford to Hyde July 5, 1963 CCC Hyde 1/11 (After reading Hyde's book Clifford thought the search may have had something to do with the smuggling of industrial diamonds p. 132 *Quiet Canadian*)
34 Letter Hoover to Stephenson March 30, 1945 CCC Hyde 1/1
35 Carlisle Papers, June 19, 1944, Memorandum for the President from Donovan recommendation for the award of Distinguished Service medal to Mr. William S Stephenson.

Chapter 8 The BSC History and the Last Case pg 110

1 BSC History Foreword by Stephenson
2 Interview with Grace Garner, London, February 1990
3 Interview with Tom Hill, March 10, 1993 (and subsequent Hill quotations)
4 Lovell, *Cast No Shadow* for MI6 classification p. 346
5 *Washington Post,* September 17, 1989
6 August 15, 1973 cable U of R 83-7 801 1-2

7   October 10, 1945, cited in *Spy Wars* p. 47

8   King diary cited in *Spy Wars* p. 56

9   INTREPID TO STEVERITE April 13, 1974, U of R 83-7 801.1-3

10 A history of the VENONA project released by the National Security Agency says Gouzenko's efforts had no bearing on the actual VENONA breakthroughs, but they "were important to Allied counterintelligence efforts."

11 INTREPID TO STEVERITE, December 20, 1975 U of R 83-7 801.1-6

12 John Sawatsky, *Gouzenko The Untold Story,* p. 122, 202

13 Peter Worthington, *Looking for Trouble* p. 431

14 U of R 83-7 Box 9 801. 3-2 January 9, 1976 letter to WSS

Chapter 9 Postwar pg 114

1   William Stephenson letter to the editor *Globe & Mail* following Malones death (undated in authors files)

2   *Maclean's,* December 1, 1952

3   *Evening Standard,* Londoners Diary, January 21, 1951

4   letter Smallwood to Stephenson, October 27, 1952 U of R 83-7 Box 9 801.7-3

5   April 2, 1976 letter, Rothschild to Stephenson, U of R 83-7 Box 9. 801. 9-1 (86)

6   *Time,* June 6, 1949

7   IBID

8   interview with Tom Hill, March, 1993

9   Caribbean Cement Co. Ltd. annual report, 1960 and WSS speech April 29 1961 in Hyde file

10 CARIBCEMCO will require twenty million for present expansion which I suppose I will have to fine (sic) for it, he cabled William Stevenson in 1973.Cable to Steverite August 15, 1973 U of R 83-7 801 1-2 According to Hill, some of the work was transferred to a company called Cement General which was changed to Canadian General.

11 Kingston *Daily Gleaner,* November 18, 1961

12 *Winnipeg Free Press,* December 23, 1954

13 Interview with Douglas Campbell, March 1989

14 January 11, 1974 MC Fulton, MD letter U of R 83-7 Box 10 801. 10-4

15 *Toronto Star,* May 27,1979

16 Dahl to Stephenson, June 28, 1972, U of R 83-7 Box 9 801. 7-1

17 letter Rothschild to Stephenson, May 25, 1976, U of R 83-7 box 9 801.9-1

18 Noel Coward, *The Noel Coward Diaries,* March 21, 1949 p. 125

19 Coward, *The Noel Coward Diaries,* November 12, 1956

20 Stevenson, *A Man Called Intrepid* p. 505

21 INTREPID TO STEVERITE March 14, 1975, U of R 83-7 801 1-5

22 Robert Collins, *Who He?* p. 179

23 INTREPID TO STEVERITE March 16, 1975 U of R 83-7 801.1-5

24 Thomas Troy, *Wild Bill and Intrepid* p.15

25 *Toronto Star,* May 27, 1979

26 INTREPID TO STEVERITE August 8, 1974 U of R83-7 801.1-4

27 *Winnipeg Free Press,* July 9, 1954 Canadian Press Wire

28 *Toronto Star,* May 27, 1979

29 October 25, 1972 U of R 83-7 Box 9 801.7-3

30 *Toronto Sun,* December 13, 1973, December 26, 1973 Worthington columns

31 INTREPID TO STEVERITE December 27, 1973, U of R 83-7 801.1-2

32 *Toronto Sun,* August 26, 1974

33 *Toronto Sun,* August 17, 1975

34 *Winnipeg Free Press,* July 8, 1980

35 Radio interview in possession of Stefansson family

36 Interview with Bina Ingimundson, June 1989

37 Interview with Irv Stefansson, June 1989

38 Interview with McKenzie Porter, March 10, 1991

39 Interview with David Young, April 1992

40 Interview with Dr. Phillip Hall, Winnipeg, March 1997

41 Interview with Derek Bedson, May 9, 1989

42 Interview with Irv Stefansson, May 1989

43 Carolyn Rickey, producer to WSS referring to April 20, 1977 broadcast, May 17, 1977 U of R 83-7 Box 11 801. 17-1

44 Well's (1866-1946) preoccupation with Utopian ideals - a belief that the millennium was coincident with the onward march of science - led to (his) scintillating dissertations. But, as he began to see that science could work for evil as well as good, his faith deserted him, and declined into pessimism." GB Shaw (1856-1950) often promoted the merits of individual virtue. "... Shavian morality of individual responsibility, self-discipline, heroic effort without thought of reward or atonement, and the utmost integrity." Chambers Dictionary

45 Quoted in *The Royal Gazette* (Bermuda), February 3, 1989

46 *Winnipeg Free Press,* February 3, 1989

Chapter 10 Out of the Shadows pg 130

1   Interview with McKenzie Porter, March 10, 1991

2   see *Maclean's,* December 1, 1952

3   *Logberg Heimskringla,* March 9, 1989

4   Napier Moore story on Cuneo, *Financial Post,* February 18, 1956

5   Noble information, August 25, 1975 cable INTREPID TO STEVERITE, U of R 83-7 801.1-6

6   Porter interview OP CIT

7   See Chapman Pincher's, *Their Trade is Treachery* (1981), Peter Wright's *Spycatcher* (1987)

8   WSS to Ellis, August 24, 1959, CCC Hyde 1/11

9   Porter interview OP CIT

10 letter August 23, 1962 CCC Hyde 1/6

11 interview with Bill Ross Smith, February 11, 1990

12 Tim Niftalli *Intrepid's Last Deception* Intelligence and National Security

13 Hyde, *Secret Intelligence Agent,* p. 119

14 *The Times* (London), August 12, 1989 Hyde had a dispute with the British authorities when he left his university position. The British Council "had an interest in his job in Pakistan," Hyde wrote to Stephenson in 1963. When Punjab University released him to pursue the Stephenson book it, "was not satisfactory," to the Council; they reneged on

helping Hyde with moving expenses from Asia. As a result Hyde took the Council to court. Hyde IBID.

15 *The Sunday Times,* October 21, 1962

16 *New York Times,* clipping undated p. 18 CCC Hyde 1/1

17 letter Ellis to Hyde 9-1 CCC Hyde 1/10

18 letter May 28, 1963 CCC Hyde 2/14

19 Mary Stephenson to Hyde CCC Hyde 1/9

20 letter to Stephenson July 30, 1963 CCC Hyde 1/11

21 Hyde CCC 1/5

22 *The Sunday Times* (London), October 21, 1962

23 letter to Hyde January 9. likely 1963, CCC Hyde 1/10

24 July 30, 1963 Hyde to Stephenson CCC Hyde 1/11

25 Hyde's file CCC, also Mary Lovell's *Cast No Shadow* p.376

26 Drew-Brook letter to Hyde December 12, 1961 CCC Hyde 1/5

27 Rosalyn Hyde interview February 1990

28 Cables addressed from INTREPID, March 13, 14,15,1963 CCC Hyde 1/11

29 IBID

30 Tim Naftalli, *Intrepid's Last Deception* p.96

31 August 24, 1959, letter Stephenson to Ellis, CCC Hyde file 1/11

32 *Winnipeg Tribune,* July 7, 1954 (CP wire story)

33 Ellis, *AMCI,* A Break in the Silence p. xxiv

34 Stevenson papers University of Regina October 20 1975 83-7 801.1-6. It seems Stephenson did not want the Ellis passage used.

35 *New York Times* Book Review, February 28, 1976 p.2.

36 cited in March 16, 1976 cable from Stephenson U of R 83-7 801. 1-7

37 Lovell, *Cast No Shadow* p. 376

38 Numerous books chronicle Philby's career see *Spyclopedia* p.358, 359 for Philby bibliography

39 Ducas interview 1990

40 Mahl, *Desperate Deception* p. xii

41 Mahl, *IBID.* p.xiii, citing L B Kirkpatricks review of Hyde's *Quiet Canadian* in Studies in Intelligence 7, the CIAs in-house journal, Summer 1963.

Chapter 11 *A Man Called Intrepid* pg 139

1 September 12, 1975 David Bruce to Julian Muller U of R 83-7 box 10 801.13

2 Gubbins to Ellis, August 16, 1972 U of R 83-7 Box 9 801.6

3 IBID

4 STEPHENSON TO STEVENSON, September 11, 1972 U of R 83-7 801 1-2

5 Chapman Pincher, *Their Trade Is Treachery,* p. 204

6 October 20, 1975 WSS cable to Stevenson U 0f R 83-7 801.1-6

7 Kildare Dobbs, book review, *A Man Called Intrepid* Globe and Mail, reprinted in *Winnipeg Free Press,* March 9, 1976

8 March 22, 1976 "I dropped reference to an association with you from the manuscript of *AMCI*...Kildare Dobbs may have picked something from the HBJ press release," explained Stevenson in a letter to the puzzled Stephenson. U of R 83-7 Box 9 801 3-2

9   About the Author, Stevenson, *Zanek!*

10 Stevenson, *90 Minutes at Entebbe*, About the Author

11 *New York Times*, February 18, 1976 U of R 83-7 Box 9 801.9

12 August 26, 1975 U of R 83-7 Box 9 801 3-2 p 2

13 August 26, 1975 U of R 83-7 Box 9 801. 3-2 p. 3

14 Stevenson to Stephenson, January 27, 1976 U of R, 83-7 Box 9 801. 3-2

15 For example: "...the fact is that I am still wading knee deep through *AMCI* material.
    But a quick run through it today has given me the sense at last that it is right. For
    example one copy editor suggested we should give more space to the Battle of Britain
    to explain why certain things were done - and I've finished what is really a brief
    insert, but what seems to me to be a moving summary of that Spitfire summer. It not
    only gives substance but puts that battle into new perspective - and a welcome
    counterbalance to these tales of the Mafia-CIA plots put out by the KGB
    Disinformation Bureau. July 24, 1974 p.6 letter Stevenson to WSS U of R "...we are
    faced with a task of psychological warfare fought on behalf of democracy, far more
    complex than anything experienced before. The Russians have learned from the Nazi
    mistakes. The communist subtleties are such that the masses are easily mislead..."
    "The situation within the media adds to the problem - not all newsmen by all means
    are willing dupes, but many have a social conscience and unwittingly advance
    Russia's long term interests by championing small causes that on the surface appear
    to have no communist inspiration or connection." Letter Stevenson to Stephenson
    83-7 Box 9 801.3-2 August 23, 1975 "I am satisfied the chief Russian objective is to
    subvert the media here, and in general to diminish the confidence between English
    speaking countries." August 23, 1975 letter to Stephenson 83-7 Box 9 801.3-2 U of R
    (In 1993 Oleg Kalugin, former head of foreign counter-intelligence for the KGB *did*
    say he publicized information of the RCMP's illegal activities in the 1970's to stir up
    trouble. "We always considered it our duty to fan discord among the allies of the
    United States, among the citizens and the structures of the government, among
    those who are our enemies at the time." Canadian Press wire based on CBC
    Fifth Estate interview, cited in *Winnipeg Free Press*, March 30, 1993)

16 August 25, 1975 letter to Stephenson, U of R 83-7 Box 9 801.3-2

17 interview with Ron Robbins May 19, 1992

18 letter to Malone June 4, 1974 U of R 83-7 box 9 801.4

19 Letter to Ogilvy August 9, 1974 U of R 83-7 Box 9 801.4

20 October 9, 1975 letter to Stephenson U of R 83-7 Box 9 801.3-2

21 STEPHENSON TO STEVENSON, October 20, 1975 U of R 83-7 801.1-6

22 Stevenson, *Zanek!*, The Reason Why p. vi

23 Stevenson, *A Man Called Intrepid* p. 481

24 There are references to Bohrs' departure from Europe in correspondence between
    Stevenson and Stephenson, and with SOE chief Colin Gubbins before the publication
    of *AMCI*. There are also, in the files of William Stevenson, copies of message sent to
    'Justitsraaden,' a Danish government department purporting to describe the location
    of microfilm hidden in a key with an "important message from the British govern-
    ment." (It seems that although Stephenson's sphere of influence was North America
    during the war, he was aware of some of the major clandestine activities on the

continent.) Stephenson says in a cable, that Bohr was "aboard one of the several fast subchasers I wangled from USN for SOE he then (sic) shipped to me and I handed him over to Admiral Strauss of the Manhattan Project." In the television documentary *A Man Called Intrepid*, Stephenson's recollection is similar. He says the 'torpedo boats' were usually used to ship ball bearings from Sweden, and, "they got him, flew into London, and put him on a ship to New York, where he was picked up and taken to the offices of the Manhattan project." Stephenson doesn't mention waiting for Bohr in a Scottish field. Gubbins wrote that Bohr was shipped out on a fishing boat to Sweden, and then onto the UK. He remembers Stephenson's subchasers were a "Godsend" and invaluable in shuttling agents ("How we and our Norwegian crews blessed 'little Bill'"), but from his letter to Stevenson, it seems he doesn't remember them in relation to transporting Bohr. Stephenson, in his correspondence with the writer, recalled the banker and former SOE chief Charles Hambro arranged, through a branch of his bank, to alert Bohr's son, "to ready and accompany Niels to boarding point off Copenhagen for trip to Scotland." In Stevenson's account Charles Hambro is not mentioned, and Stephenson tells, "a young officer who joined him," in Scotland, about the need to airlift out Bohr's son, as he was familiar with his father's work. July 30 (1972?) letter Gubbins to Stevenson U of R 83-7 Box 9 801.6

25 June 4, 1973 letter to Stephenson U of R 83-7 Box 9 801. 3-1
26 Stevenson to WSS U of R 83-7 Box 9 801.3-2 p. 2 July (1974?)
27 Sir David Hunt, *Times Literary Supplement*, May 28, 1976 review
28 David Ogilvy letter to author January 28, 1990
29 editor's note: author's passage deleted for legal reasons
30 letter Stevenson to WSS July 24 1974 U of R 83-7 box 9 801.3-2, p.6
31 letter Stevenson to WSS January 27,1976 U of R 83-7 Box 9 801. 3-2
32 letter Stevenson to WSS March 22, 1976 U of R 83-7 box 9 801. 3-2
33 letter to Stephenson August 25, 1975 U of R 83-7 Box 9 801.3-2
34 letter Stevenson to WSS March 16, 1976 U of R 83-7 box 9 801.3-2
35 WSS TO STEVENSON March 16, 1976 U of R 83-7 801. 1-7
36 Stevenson letter to WSS July 2, 1976 U of R 83-7 Box 11 801. 17-1
37 WSS TO STEVENSON August 21, 1975 U of R 83-7 801.1-1
38 Stevenson, *A Man Called Intrepid* p. 114, p. 310
39 ITT had numerous holdings in Germany, and Behn met with Hitler in 1933 with the assistance of the American Embassy in Berlin, as would be the normal course of events. By the end of the decade ITT had lost control of its operations in Nazi Germany, and Behn was not allowed even to visit the ITT's plants there. Currency controls were in effect, and there was no way of bringing funds out of Germany. Behn helped bring out scientists from occupied France in 1940, and their work helped Allied advances in radar and high frequency radio direction finding. ITT supplied radio and telephone equipment to allied forces, secured land lines, and later reorganized communications labs in France and Belgium to produce portable radio equipment. Behn was awarded the Medal of Merit by President Truman after the war, the highest honour the United States could give to a civilian. Behn was buried in Arlington National Cemetery in 1957 U of R 83-7 Box 11 801.17- 2

40 William Stevenson to Edward J Gerrity Jr, June 2, 1976 U of R 83-7 Box 11 801.17-2

41 Richard Deacon, *Spyclopedia* p. 229, and other sources

42 J C Masterman, *The Double-Cross System* p. 80

43 Nicolas J Cull, *Selling War* p. 186

44 Thomas Troy, 'The British Assault on J Edgar Hoover,' International Journal of Intelligence and Counterintelligence. Volume 3, No. 2 Summer 1989

45 INTREPID TO STEVERITE, November 16, 1974 U of R 83-7 801.1-4 Montagu was friendly with Stephenson. His wife Iris worked for BSC, February 2, 1975 Montagu to WSS U of R 83-7 Box 9 801.7-1

46 August 23, 1975 letter Stevenson to Stephenson U of R 83-7 Box 9 801.3-2

47 August 25, 1975 letter Stevenson to Stephenson U. of R 83-7 Box 9 801.3-2

48 Anthony Summers, *Official and Confidential The Secret Life of J Edgar Hoover* p. 128

49 Hyde, *The Atom Bomb Spies* p. xi

50 Robert Collins, *Who He?* p. 182

51 Gubbins to Stevenson February 6, 1976 U of R 83-7 Box 9 801.6

52 Mountbatten to WSS February 2, 1976 U of R 83-7 Box 11 801. 17-1 In early 1976, Stephenson cabled the author indicating he wanted this quote to be used on the book flap of future editions. It doesnt appear to have been used. Cable to Stevenson February 9, 1976 U of R 83-7 801.1-1

53 Gilbert Highet to Stephenson March 7, 1976 U of R 83-7 Box 9 801. 9-1

54 letter Bruce to Muller September 12, 1975 U of R 83-7 Box 10 801.13 U of R

55 *New York Times Book Review,* February 29, 1976 review

56 There was some controversy when Trevor-Roper was appointed Regius Professor of Modern history. Others on staff, such as the historian AJP Taylor, had an edge in published work. He was quite well known for written attacks on fellow historians, such as RH Tawney, Lawrence Stone, and Arnold Toynbee. He was particularly hard on Toynbee. Reviewing Toynbee's *A Study of History* Trevor-Roper wrote Toynbee was trying to establish himself as a prophet, and he compared him to Hitler. When Trevor-Roper was established as Regius Professor in 1957, the *Observer* reported that some were, "wondering about the influence on undergraduates of a man capable of writing a considered article with such elaborate violence and personal hatred." Politics were thought to be involved. The appointment was, "widely represented as an act of political partisanship by (former Prime Minister and publishing magnate) Harold Macmillan, and the appearance of jobbery was enhanced when Trevor-Roper organized the campaign for Mr. Macmillan's election to the Chancellorship of Oxford in 1960," John Grigg wrote in the *Guardian* in 1964. Trevor-Roper's, *The Last Days of Hitler* was published by Macmillan citations in Current Biography 1983, *The Guardian* January 23, 1964 In April 1983, Trevor-Roper's haughty reputation as a war expert put himself in the glare of publicity. The German magazine *Stern* acquired 60 volumes of diaries supposedly those of Adolf Hitler, that were written between 1932 and 1945. The London *Times* offered $400,000 for excerpts of the diaries and Trevor-Roper, who had been a director of Times Newspapers Ltd. since 1974, was sent to check their authenticity in the safe of a Zurich bank. On April 23, after a quick examination, Trevor-Roper announced that they were genuine. On May 6, 1983, it was proved by chemical tests that the diaries were forgeries

57 John Costello, *Mask of Treachery*, p. 381, Trevor-Roper, cited in *C*, Anthony Cave Brown, p. 229 Trevor-Roper acknowledged that he "knew of Philby's communist past,' before it was widely known. But it 'never occurred to me, at that time, to hold it against him,' because our superiors were lunatic in their anti-communism." That Trevor-Roper did not expose Philby, one writer concluded, owes as much to his own hostility to MI6 as an institution. He determined from his espionage career that the British services were flawed organizations. "When I looked coolly at the world in which I found myself, I thought that, if this was our intelligence system, we are doomed to defeat. Sometimes I encouraged myself by saying such an organization could not possibly survive, unchanged, the strain of war: it would have to be reformed. In fact I was wrong both times. We won the war and SIS at the end of it remained totally unreformed."

58 Peter Worthington, 'A Particular Canadian Trait' Ottawa Sun, March 5, 1989

59 *The New York Review of Books,* May 13, 1976 He says, for example, he remembers Stephenson as number 38000. Stephenson was 48000. "All SIS agents were known by their numbers and those in America had five figure numbers beginning with 3." He implies that this was where the author got the large estimated number, 30,000, of BSC employees

60 *Sunday Telegraph,* February 19, 1989, *Death of an Intrepid Fraud*

61 Hyde, *Secret Intelligence Agent,* 1982 foreword by Stephenson

62 *The New York Review of Books,* May 13, 1976

63 Heinz Hohne & Hermann Zolling, *The General was a Spy* (also called *Network*) 1971 p. xxxiii

64 David Stafford resume CCC Hyde 5/4

65 Stafford, *Camp X* p. 289

66 *The Sunday Star* (Toronto), October 8, 1989 and private information

67 *Saturday Night,* October 1990 Southam News Wire, *Winnipeg Tribune,* April 24, 1973

68 "miserable cockroaches" is in the Toronto *Sunday Sun,* April 10, 1988, "antisemitic" and, "Canadian-of-convenience" in *Toronto Sun* October, 1989, "Lies are their only ammunition."

69 Stafford article in *Saturday Night* 'The Defector' November 1984

70 *New Statesman,* March 26, 1976

71 *Times Literary Supplement,* May 28, 1976

72 *The Times* (London), February 18, 1989

73 *Toronto Sun,* July 17, 1981. The information refers to Coville's book *Winston Churchill and his Inner Circle*

74 Winston Churchill, *Their Finest Hour* p. 229

75 *The Times* (London), February 18, 1989

76 Richard Cleroux, *Official Secrets*(1990) p. 117

77 John Bryden, *Best Kept Secret* (1993) p. 335

78 Naftalli, *Intelligence and National Security* July 1983

79 *The Royal Gazette* (Bermuda), February 27, 1989

Chapter 12 BSC Recruits pg 163

1 cited in December 30, 1990 letter Patsy Sullivan to author.

Chapter 13 'Cynthia' and Marion pg 183

1 Deacon, *Spyclopedia* p. 17
2 Hyde *Secret Intelligence Agent*
3 It is possible the New York trips were before de Chastelain worked with her, as Cynthia is quoted as remembering New York meetings. "The routine never varied, I always stayed at the same hotel on Madison, awaited Marion or Mr. Howard. They debriefed me, gave me assignments and acted as paymasters. They were my only contacts."
4 Letter cited in Hyde's *Cynthia* p. 7
5 November 15, 1962 letter to Hyde CCC Hyde 2/7
6 John Colville, author and a Churchill secretary for a short time, wrote he didn't remember Churchill talking about Stephenson

Chapter 14 Bill Ross Smith pg 199

1 Kim Philby, *My Silent War*, p. 86
2 Richard Dunlop, *Behind Japanese Lines: With the OSS in Burma*, p. 84
3 Bill Ross Smith on the Ellis Affair

"Charles Howard Ellis known everywhere as Dick Ellis was accused first of all by Chapman Pincher, and following him by Nigel West, in various books. Chapman Pincher in *Their Trade Was Treachery* accused him for being a spy for the Germans and the Russians. Now, Chapman Pincher's source on this was undoubtedly Peter Wright, because Peter Wright tells virtually the same story in *Spycatcher*. Chapman Pincher published *Treachery* in 1980, five years after Ellis' death. And he tells the story of Ellis being sent to Paris by SIS in 1923 where he recruited as a subagent his brother-in-law Alexander Zolinsky, a White Russian, with considerable connections both in German and Russian intelligence. According to Pincher for the next 15 years Zolinsky had a high old time selling British secrets to Germany and Russia and vice-versa. This cumulated in, according to Pincher, the actual selling of the British order-of-battle to the Germans (sic). He was further accused, of giving the Germans the benefit of information the British had obtained by tapping into the hot line which Ribbontrop had installed in the German Embassy when he came there in about 1936.

"Now all of this is manifestly untrue because firstly Alexander Zolinsky did exist and was indeed Ellis' brother-in-law. But in 1923, when Pincher has him as a high-powered spy with connections throughout the hierarchies, he was in fact ten years of age. Secondly, Ellis never served in France at all. In the years 1923 to 1938 he was serving in the British consulate in Berlin, later in the British Chamber of Commerce in Vienna. In the years 35 to 38, I'd have to check the exact years, he served as an accredited correspondent to the League of Nations in Geneva ... where he was supplied with a nice flat and a chauffeured car. In fact, he didn't even join the service proper until 1938. The story therefore by Wright given to Pincher and taken up by the others is sheer fabrication. Thirdly, he could not have given the order-of-battle to the Germans for the same reason, and he could not have given the benefits of the Ribbontrop telephone line to them because it ceased to exist when Ribbontrop returned to Germany at the end of his Ambassadorship before 1938. Therefore, the subsequent statement that he had given this evidence up to the outbreak of war is chronologically false. Wright had also said he was a very senior SIS officer, having being in charge of SIS operations in the Far East before returning to England in about 1938 to take up as Chief of Western Hemisphere Intelligence. This is quite erroneous because he had just entered the Service proper in 1928, and he actually became Chief of Far East operations in Singapore after the war in 1946. He was never Chief of Western Hemisphere Intelligence. One could only assume, therefore, that Peter Wright made up these stories about a dead man in order to make a good story for his book and for the information which he sold to Pincher for his book, *Their Trade Was Treachery*. The story of Peter Wright is that he had worked for fifteen years for Navy Intelligence as a scientist, during which he came into contact with MI5 a lot. He told MI5 he wanted to join them. MI5 said they didn't poach on other services, but anytime he was free if he would like to talk to them again they would be pleased to speak to him. Some while later he left Naval intelligence and joined Marconi. Again in that capacity he came in contact with MI5. And after a couple of years with Marconi he proposed and was accepted as an employee of MI5. At that time he asked them to assume his fifteen years on Navy pension. They refused. When at the end of his service he again raised the question of fifteen years of navy pension, and named it; MI5 again refused, saying that they had hired him from Marconi and they had not had him transferred from the Navy to them, therefore they had no responsibility for his pension. He was very embittered about this and said that he would get even one day. He then left the country and went to Tasmania, where in due course had written about ten thousand words of a biography. Somewhere around 1978, Lord Rothschild invited him to come to England to write officially what Lord Rothschild had done for MI5 during Rothschild's service and afterward as a protection against any possibility he might be named under the general scandal following the Blunt affair. While he was in England as Rothschild's guest, he said to Rothschild he'd like to meet somebody who could write a book. Rothschild called Chapman Pincher and put them together. Wright and Pincher agreed to cooperate on this book, but it was decided to keep Wright's name right out of it and his financial part should be handled through a Swiss bank supposedly set up by Rothschild. His part of the royalties should be paid directly there, but his name would never appear. This is supposed to have netted Wright 30,000 pounds or more. He handed the ten thousand words to Chapman Pincher who used them as the basis of, *Their Trade Was Treachery*. Subsequently Wright wrote his own book called *Spycatcher*, and much of the same wording appears in it, particularly about the Ellis affair."

4 NARA RG 59 701.6511/1028
5 Hyde, *Cynthia* p. 117
6 NARA RG 59 701.6511/1037
7 *New York Times*, May 8, 1941
8 *New York Times*, May 8, 1941
9 BECK cable May 13, 1941 NARA RG59 701.6511/1050

Chapter 15 Betty Raymond pg 255
1 Hyde, *The Quiet Canadian* p. 79
2 Hyde, *Secret Intelligence Agent* p. 150

3   Hyde, *Secret Intelligence Agent* p. 154 Raymond was told the forged signature was checked by the FBI
4   *New York Times*, July 24, 1941
5   *New York Times*, July 24, 1941
6   *New York Herald Tribune*, July 30, 1941
7   Hyde, *Secret Intelligence Agent*, p. 160 Sumner Wells, *Seven Major Decisions* p. 101

Chapter 16 Astley and the Service pg 241

1   INTREPID TO MCEWEN Toronto, May 3, 1973 telegram U of R 83-7 Box 9 801.8
2   Astley, *The Inner Circle* p. 64
3   Astley, *The Inner Circle* p. 31
4   Brown, *Bodyguard of Lies* p. 687 citing Wingate interview
5   Duff Hart Davis, *Peter Fleming* p. 266
6   Astley, *The Inner Circle* p. 49-50
7   Anthony Cave Brown, *C* p. 606
8   Bell accompanied the Ambassador, Lord Inverchapel (Clark Kerr) to Washington in May 1946 as a special assistant. At the time, the First Secretary at the British Embassy was the infamous Donald Maclean, the Soviet double agent. In 1950 the Bells visited Maclean and his wife Melinda in Cairo in response to his "warm and repeated invitations." The Macleans lead a busy social life in Egypt, and even hosted a party for the Duke of Edinburgh. However, Donald Maclean had a reputation as a bit of drinker. On one occasion, he tried to strangle his wife at a party and was forcibly dragged off by fellow party-goers. Later, Maclean, in a drunken stupor, grabbed the loaded rifle of an Egyptian guard and threatened to smash his head. A Foreign Office colleague, Lees Mayall, tried to stop Maclean and in the ensuing struggle broke his leg.
One evening during the Bell's trip Maclean, the Head Of Chancery, went on a drunken binge with a reporter from the *Observer*, Philip Toynbee. The Bells received repeated phone calls to join him for a drink, but they declined, and Katie noticed Maclean sounded very angry that evening. During the night Maclean broke into the vacant apartment of an employee of the US Embassy in Cairo, drank her liquor, smashed her furniture, broke her bathtub in two and flushed her underwear down her toilet. Soon after, the US Ambassador to Egypt filed a formal complaint about the British representative of HMG. The FBI is also said to have inquired into Maclean's conduct. Maclean returned to England two days later, because, as one writer put it, "people began to talk." Maclean took some sick leave in Britain, but apparently faced no disciplinary action. In November of 1950 he was appointed head of the Foreign Office's American Department
9   Major General Carl Spaatz was the Commander-in-Chief of the United States Air Force in Europe during WWII. He was honored for heroism in WWI and between the wars he performed in the Army's Flying Circus. In 1929 Spaatz spent a world record 150 hours in the air, and was awarded the Distinguished Flying Cross.
In the summer of 1940, Spaatz was sent to England as a 'special military observer.' This was the same time as Bill Donovan's famous trip to Britain in which, according to INTREPID legend, the English were told to 'bear their hearts' by Bill Stephenson, and the red carpet was rolled out to convince Donovan and the Americans of Britain's

resolve to withstand the Nazi assault. At an airfield outside London, Spaatz signed his name and occupation in the guest book, 'Brigadier General Spaatz - Spy. (*Current Biography* 1942) According to John Gilbert Winant's book *Letters from Grosvenor Square,* in 1940 no man in the United States had a more accurate knowledge of the strength of the German air force than Spaatz. Winant also accompanied Donovan on the British trip to give President Roosevelt his opinion on the morale of the British civil population. Roosevelt was very conscious of the fact that supplies, munitions and equipment that had been dispatched to the continent were now in the hands of the Nazis, and he didn't want a similar fate for help - either public or private - sent to Britain. Winant wrote that American Army and Navy observers reported to Donovan that Britain did not have a hope. However, the then-Lieutenant Colonel Spaatz said he thought Britain would pull through. He talked to British pilots and flew their newest fighter planes. Spaatz thought the Germans could not beat the RAF, and the Nazis would not invade until they had air superiority. Donovan returned to the United States and recommended the transfer of destroyers to Britain and further assistance to the island

10 INTREPID TO STEVERITE July 15, 1974 U of R 83-7 801.1-1 There is a reference from Stephenson to one meeting with Ismay. "IT WAS LARGELY A RESULT BLACKETTS IMPASSIONED PLEA TO MYSELF THROUGH PUG ISMAY THAT TRIGGERED MY SPECIAL EXTRA PROCUREMENT OF HUNDRED LIBS FOR COASTAL COMMAND STOP"

11 Sir Edwin Leather, a Canadian, former Governor of Bermuda

12 The photo appears in *A Man Called Intrepid.* Many people assume the unidentified figure in the foreground is likely Brendon Bracken, Churchill's assistant. But the shadowy figure in a hat has also been identified as Stephenson. The famous *Times* Newspapers photo has also been reproduced at least twice (August 1965, July,1991) in *National Geographic.* A November, 1991 letter identifies the silhouette as Stephenson, without any editorial comments or corrections from the magazine

13 Her responsibilities grew to include being the organizational head of Britain's delega-tions to the Big Three conferences. "I was on the administrative side. You needed somebody setting it up. The trouble was, Ismay was a wise man and didn't believe in large staffs. The Cabinet Offices were very small, very hard-working, and very efficient. And the same went for the conferences. It always came to the cabinet office, because we were into the service, you see. You know all the services and the civil service were represented. We could set up a special conference organization in no time at all. A Brigadier, two Colonels, and four Captains, and six Lieutenants and a whole lot of ATS, and WACKs and who knows what. You see what I mean. Parkinson's law." A naval aide, paymaster Commander Morris Knott, helped with the organiza-tion in the beginning." I went to help him, and went to two or three conferences, and after he went out to sea, I did it myself. I became personal manager. You take anybody from the office You take one's self. It was very piece-meal but it worked... It was very big set up.

14 Astley, *The Inner Circle* p. 49

15 The telefilm was not Canadian but British according to the Internet Movie Database.

Chapter 17 Roald Dahl pg 252

1   The Cambridge Guide to Literature in English, 1988

2   Admiral Chester Nimitz actually became Commander-in-Chief of the US Pacific fleet December 17, 1941. He replaced Admiral Husband Kimmel who was relieved of his command pending the investigation into the Pearl Harbour attack. Although battle-ships Arizona, California, Oklahoma and West Virginia were sunk at Pearl Harbour and many other vessels were damaged, all the valuable aircraft carriers were at sea

3   Montgomery Hyde's papers seem to indicate although Stephenson set the wheels in motion for the first book, he didn't pay to have it written about the organization. Montgomery Hyde's papers show that once the book came out, Stephenson suppressed attempts to publicize *The Quiet Canadian,* and refused to permit the selling of film rights

4   In various files I could find only records of two speeches

5   Dahl, in *A Man Called Intrepid*, CBC television documentary (1974 broadcast)

6   *The Price of Vision*, The Diary of Henry A Wallace 1942-1946 p. 385, 492

7   Stevenson to Ogilvy August 9, 1974, U of R 83-7 Box 9 801.4

8   Hyde Papers CCC 3/21 February 21, 1942 memo VW to WSS

9   After the war Churchill was often a guest of the rich and famous, and many were not former friends or associates. This irritated his wife, and on occasion she refused to accompany him

10 Ian Fleming regarded Stephenson as a hero. In 1962 Fleming wrote, "In this era of the anti-hero when anyone on a pedestal is assaulted, unfashionably and obstinately I have my heroes ... high up on my list is one of the great secret agents of the last war... 'Little Bill' was awarded the Presidential Medal for Merit, and I think is the first non-American ever to receive this highest honour for a civilian. But it was surely, 'the Quiet Canadian's' supreme reward as David Bruce ... records, that when Sir Winston Churchill recommended Bill Stephenson for a knighthood he should have minuted to King George VI 'This one is dear to my heart.' It seems other and far greater men than I also have their heroes." *The Sunday Times*, October 21, 1962

11 It is unlikely Stephenson would try and deceive Dahl about personal contact with Roosevelt when Dahl knew the president and, in theory, could verify if Stephenson was lying. In discussions with other BSC staff and through various documents, it is obvious Stephenson knew Roosevelt

12 George Gallup was labeled America's foremost soothsayer, and an oracle during the 1930's. In 1935 he set up the American Institute of Public Opinion at Princeton, which did numerous research surveys, and soon afterward he started a similar British Centre. His new techniques flourished. By 1940 there were some objections to the possible political influence of his polls, and he was called, "the most discussed man in the advertising world." Ogilvy's knowledge of Gallup's polling methods were utilized to an extent by the psychological warfare departments of the allies. Following the war, advertising became Ogilvy's full-time career

13 In a biography of Dahl, Jeremy Treglown says he could find no evidence Dahl had achieved the rank of Wing Commander. However the diaries of former US Vice President Henry Wallace refer to his acquaintance with Flight Commander Dahl in 1944, and later Wing Commander Dahl in 1945. The writer Treglown, who inter-

viewed some former members of BSC for his book, said Stephenson had a thousand or more regular informants. (Treglown later refers to Dahls's work with the BSC history being compiled in Oshinawa (sic), Ontario.) Jeremy Treglown, *Roald Dahl: A Biography* p. 67, 68

14 April 2, 1976 Pepper to Stephenson U of R 83-7 Box 11 801.17-1
15 Letter from David Ogilvy to author January 28, 1990
16 Letter from David Ogilvy to author April 1, 1992

Chapter 18 Grace Garner pg 267

1 *Canadians at War* p. 516
2 *The Times* February 18, 1989
3 John Keats, from *Ode to a Nightingale*
> Thou was not born for death, immortal Bird!
> No hungry generations tread thee down;
> The voice I hear this passing night was heard
> In ancient days by emperor and clown:
> Perhaps the self-same song that found a path
> Through the sad heart of Ruth, when, sick for home,
> She stood in tears amid the alien corn;
> The same that oft-times hath
> Charm'd magic casements, opening on the foam
> Of perilous seas, in faery lands forlorn

4 Anthony Cave Brown, *Bodyguard of Lies* p. 317
5 The codeword for the deception for COSSAC's first operation was actually Cockade, according to Cave Brown. Torch was the code name of the invasion of Africa
6 Double Agent Dusko Popov was given an intelligence survey regarding Pearl Harbour by the Germans before December 7, 1941, which he relayed to the Allies.
7 The book *implies* the organization had something to do with the assassination. It refers to mock-ups at Camp X, and assassination discussions at BSC, but it also refers to 'Icicle,' "the Czech parachute assassins," "Baker Street instructor." William Stevenson, *A Man Called Intrepid* p.382 The only reference this writer could find in available papers is a short reference from Stephenson who wrote, "quietly flowed the Don since last heard of Heydrich. "June 23, 1974 CABLE TO STEVENSON U of R 83-7 801. 1-3. Harry Smith, who was at Camp X during the life of the training Camp said, "Let's say we went through a lot of schemes with people, that could have been applied to that. But whether anything was ever used? I don't know if the people who were involved with the Heydrich assassination were ever at the camp, but it was the sort of thing that you put students through all the time."
8 John Pearson, *Ian Fleming*. An account of the Kennedy meeting also appears in *Ian Fleming,* by Andrew Lycette (p.367-68) According to Lycette, the next day Allen Dulles, the then-head of the CIA, asked to talk to Fleming
9 The Soviet Union was invaded in 1941
10 June 6, 1973 letter William Stevenson to Julian Muller U of R 83-7 Box 10 801.10-10
11 *The Gouzenko Transcripts* Robert Bothwell and J L Granastein 1981
12 U of R 83-7 Box 10 801. 10-12 (no date)

13 July 24,1974 letter to Stephenson U of R 83-7 box 9 801. 3-2

14 RSHA IV

1 (a) Marxism, enemy broadcasting, enemy propaganda, partisms, Russian prisoners-of-war.

1 (b) Reaction, monarchism, pacifism, liberism, rumours undermining moral, defeatism.

2 Sabotage, radio jamming, parachutists, commandos.

3 (a) Counter-intelligence, careless talk

(b) Economics, foreign exchange

(c) Frontier Controls

4 (a) Catholicism, Protestantism, Freemasonry

(b) Jews

5 (a) Anti-social behavior, shirking

(b) Party affairs, press

6 (a) Card Index, personal dossiers, information

(b) Protective custody, concentration camps. p. 92- 93

15 Edward Crankshaw, *GESTAPO*, Putnam, London, 1956 p. 94 "For the purpose of general supervision and repression, the Gestapo modelled itself closely on the Soviet Secret Police. Himmler had at his command an extremely able police officer, Heinrich Mueller who became known as Gestapo Mueller, a close and devoted friend of Soviet methods. Mueller was impressed by the efficiency of the internal spy system which had been perfected by the Soviet government, the effect which, ideally, was to isolate the individual by making it impossible for anybody to trust anybody else. He set to reproduce this system in Germany by more economical means."

16 Jacques Delarue, *The Gestapo* p.393

17 Journal of Contemporary History, Story by Robert Stephan. October 1987, Volume 22 #4, According to a Soviet history of the Special Departments, there were several suggestions at a meeting with Stalin of names for the new organization. One of the suggestions was Smernesh or 'Smert nemetskim Shipionam' (Death to German spies). Stalin replied: 'And why as a matter of fact should we only be speaking only of German spies? Aren't other intelligence services working against our country? Let's call it 'Smert Shipionam.' Hence the nickname 'Death to Spies' was given to the GUKR-NKD."

Chapter 19 Benjamin de Forest Bayly pg 307

1 For Stephenson's roll see Troy's *Wild Bill and Intrepid*. As for a history of the NSA, former historian for the CIA, Troy wrote, "re: an Official NSA history, the answer is No. In fact there is no official history of any American intelligence service." Troy to author November 1, 1994. Very little information about the top secret Canadian Communications Security Establishment, or the American National Security Agency has ever been widely released. The existence of the CSE was only acknowledged publicly by the government in 1983. The history of Canada's communications code-breaking dates back to an organization called the Examination Unit, which was start-ed before WWII. The creative force in the organization regarded as a 'hired gun' was renown American code-breaker Herbert Yardley. According to Canadian-based acade-

mic Wesley Wark a series of documents related to the Examination Unit were released by the Canadian government in 1984, only after there was a federal law suit launched by an anonymous respondent 'X.' (In an article in *JCH*, Wark says the court documents were provided to him by David Stafford. *Journal of Contemporary History*, Vol. 22, #4, 1987) Later, in what almost seems to be a chapter from John Le Carré's *The Night Manager*, Wark wrote the anonymous respondent 'X' turned out to be a night desk person at a hotel in Kingston, Ontario. The *Globe and Mail*, February 5, 1994

2   Winston Churchill, *Their Finest Hour* p. 381

3   Stafford, *Camp X* p. 159 citing November 19, 1941 letter Gambier Parry to Stephenson, letter in Hyde papers at CCC. This document was censored by the British government during the author's numerous visits to CCC

4   Friedman was born in Russia. The Friedman family emigrated to America in 1892 and settled in Pittsburgh. After first enrolling in Agriculture College, Friedman attended Cornell University (Science). In 1915, Friedman was hired by Riverbank laboratories in Geneva, Illinois as a geneticist. The owner of Riverbank, George Fabyan, also dabbled in language and cryptography, and he was attempting to prove the works of William Shakespeare were actually written by Francis Bacon. Friedman, and his soon-to-be wife Elizabeth, moved on to the study of ciphers at Riverbank. Cryptographers try to decipher communication which is in either code or cipher. Codes are letters or numbers that substitute for a whole word or a phrase. The weakness of codes is that with repetition, they can't be used for long, and be considered safe. As a result, new code books have to be devised and distributed. Ciphers are more difficult to crack, as every letter of a word is replaced with a different letter or numeral. In 1920 Friedman published, *The Index of Coincidence and Its Applications in Cryptography*, which helped elevate the study from theory, into a science of statistics. All codebreakers begin with a letter frequency count. In English, the most commonly used letters are E, T, A, O, N, I, and the least used are J, K, X, Q, Z. Eventually, if individual characters of an intercepted message are charted and graphed, certain peaks and valleys usually occur which may indicate particular letters, and lead to breaking. Contact analysis, or the common placing of letters, and other linguistic characteristics are also used. In English, for example, 'TH' is a common pairing. 'S' is often beside a consonant, 'R' is usually with vowels, and so on. Friedman moved this study of linguistic quirks into the realm of mathematics. In the late 1930's, using his theories, Friedman and his team attacked the Japanese diplomatic machine cipher, code named Purple. Simply by analysing intercepted messages, Friedman and his team were able to construct a machine which could consistently solve the foreign puzzles. The decrypts were appropriately called 'Magic'. Remarkably the Japanese machine that created the ciphered messages was never seen or recovered. For years, Friedman's accomplishments were shrouded in secrecy, and only after his death have his contributions to the covert world of communications breaking, and the importance of that success on the battlefield, been more fully recognized. Fifty years later, the cipher-breaking machine the Friedman team constructed to break the Japanese code, is still under guard in a secret warehouse in Maryland

5   *Tuesday Night,* Dahl Interview U of R Roll 1 page 5

6 David Stafford, *Camp X* p. 163 Gorden Welchman, *The Hut Six Story* p. 172 Welchman also says the transmission could be adjusted for atmosperic conditions

7 Gordon Welchman, *The Hut Six Story* p.174-175

8 December 4, 1974 U of R 83-7 801 .1-4 Bayly didn't remember 'Watson of IBM'

9 The debriefing of Igor Gouzenko, the former cipher clerk, identified a number of Soviet undercover agents in Canada, the United States, and Britain. One was Kay Willsher, an employee of the Ottawa High Commission, who's cover name was 'Elli.' However Gouzenko said there was another 'Elli' who worked in either MI5 or 'five of MI,' (section 5 of MI6) who had something Russian in his background. Gouzenko always felt the British never followed up on his findings. There has been some question about why the Soviets would have had two people with the same code name, or a feminine name for a male agent. Some writers have guessed 'Elli' could have been Roger Hollis, a former British MI5 head. Others thought it could be Dick Ellis, because of the similarity of their names

10 Curt Gentry's, *J Edgar Hoover: The Man and His Secrets*, p. 265 Hoover wasn't known for getting along with non-Americans. According to William Sullivan, who worked for him, the FBI head "didn't like the British, didn't care for the French, hated the Dutch, and couldn't stand the Australians." There seems to be no reference of what he thought of Canadians

11 Bayly's Buick had a licence plate that was untraceable to police. An identification search would come up simply 'classified.' On one occasion he was chewed out on Parliament Hill, as a convenient parking space he frequently used belonged to the Prime Minister

12 It is difficult to ascertain the exact date or which U-boat this was. It is possible it could be U-505 which was captured by the Americans, June 4, 1944, and towed into Bermuda, U-744 boarded by the HMCS Chilliwack, March 6, 1944, or one of the U-boats that disappeared and was not seen again. The Queen Mary's greatest defense against torpedoes was speed, and the ship was not allowed to stop. October 2, 1942, the ship hit the HMS Curacoa, cutting it in two, killing over 300 sailors. The ship's bow was eventually repaired in Boston, and moored in New York. Stephenson could have been using the need-to-know to avoid the truth

13 It was Manchester

14 Cited in *Camp X* p. 278

NOTE: Key to Cover cipher A175SW 48000 737007 58WW2 3945SS U33VZ:
Alpha /175 Syndicate Street, Winnipeg / WSS agent number / 73rd Squadron / WWI Military number / World War II / 1939-45 / SS / U-boat 33/Victory / Omega

Notes to Appendices

1 Peter Wright, *Spycatcher* p. 275-276

2 Noel Coward, *Noel Coward Diaries* December 31, 1962 p. 520

3 Andrew Boyle, *Climate of Treason*

4 The Diary of Sir Alexander Cadogan, 1945 CCC

5 Christopher Andrew, University of Manitoba, MPR UMSU, November 1991. Andrew is considered by *The Times* of London to be, "Britain's leading unofficial historian of intelligence." He has co-written a couple of books with Oleg

Gordievsky who, according to the British, worked for them as a penetration agent inside the KGB since 1974. Andrew was asked the following question on a speaking tour: "Anthony Blunt confessed in the 1960's yet nothing happened to him until a journalist found out that he had confessed. He didn't lose his knighthood until his confession became public knowledge. What does this say about the SIS cleansing itself, and how many more do they still have hidden?"

"Well none is the answer to the last question. But I'll come back to that in a minute, don't forget he was in MI5, he wasn't in SIS. I hope that it is reasonably clear that I don't think that White Hall's attitude to ancient secrets is anything other than ludicrous. It's something I've said so many times, in so many places, that you must forgive me, if I have forgotten to repeat it today. So nothing I say today will seek to, I hope will give the impression that I think that the British Government is anything more than stupid in the way that it keeps so many ancient secrets. But so far as nonprosecuting Blunt is concerned, I suggest that they may have had a rather good point. The reason is this. Security services all around the world, SIS included are very shy in admitting one straight foward fact, which is, that it is diabolically difficult to get the conviction for espionage. If we look at the cases which happened after WWI, they vitually all involve, and that includes the British convictions of Alan May and the Fuchs people, those who were fooled into making confessions"

6   *The Sunday Times*, Colin Simpson, David Leitch, and Phillip Knightley, November 25, 1975

7   Philip Ziegler, *King Edward VIII* p. 550 Zielger says Blunt and Morshead also travelled to the Netherlands to pick-up relics of the Kaiser

8   Philip Ziegler, *King Edward VIII* p. 52

9   Ziegler IBID

10 John Costello, *Mask of Treachery*, 1988 p.406

11 Anthony Cave Brown, *C*, 1967 p. 683 This information has also been referred to by the journalist Peter Worthington, *Ottawa Sun*, March 5, 1989

12 Brown IBID

13 *The Times* (London) December 20, 1979

14 *Current Biography* 1942, Also *Cambridge Biographical Encyclopedia* 1994

15 Alfred de Marigny, *A Conspiracy of Crowns* p. 298

16 Alfred de Marigny, *A Conspiracy of Crowns*, p. 298 Referrring to Hyde's 1982's *Secret Intelligence Agent*

17 Hyde, *Secret Intelligence Agent* p. 117

18 AJP Taylor, *Beaverbrook* p. 485 Taylor states: "It is often said that Hess came to Great Britain in order to enlist British support against Russia. When he came the German attack on Russia had not started, and it is unlikely that Hess was informed of Hitler's plans. He simply wanted to end the war between Great Britain and Germany." It is likely Hess knew of Hitler's designs on the Soviet Union. Plans for Hitler's attack on the Soviet Union, Barbarossa, were issued in December 1940. Hess arrived in May 1941

19 Anthony Cave Brown, *C* p. 349 Douglas Hamilton cited

20 Reuters wire story, November 13, 1995

21 *Eclipse*, Stevenson p. 352

22 Alfred de Marigny, *A Conspiracy of Crowns*, p. 298

23 The Duchess of Windsor, *The Heart has Its Reasons* p. 325

24 The Duchess of Windsor, *The Heart has Its Reasons* p. 335-336

25 The Duchess of Windsor, *The Heart has Its Reasons* p. 338

26 Charles Higham, *The Duchess of Windsor* p. 279

27 The Duchess of Windsor, *The Heart has its Reasons* p. 346

28 cited in Higham p. 280

29 cited in *The Traitor King*, (documentary) A & E December 1996, broadcast

30 cited in Higham p. 289

31 Martin Gilbert and Richard Gott, *The Appeasers* p. 324

32 Higham p. 385

33 Higham p. 288

34 Lloyd to Halifax, Higham p. 305 September 28, 1940

35 *American Heritage*, December 1991

36 Charles Whiting, *Gehlen: Germany's Master Spy*

37 *The Service: The Memoires of General Reinhard Gehlen* p. 70 On September 1, 1945 The Toronto *Globe and Mail* reported that the Soviet-controlled Berlin radio had announced that Martin Bormann, Hitler's Chief Deputy in the Nazi Party was, "in Allied hands."

38 *The Service: The Memoires of General Reinhard Gehlen* p. 299-300

39 IBID p. 330-331

40 Quoted in *Encyclopedie Français*, 1959, and Gehlen's memoires, p. 331

Bibliography

Alcorn, Robert Hayden. *No Bugles For Spies: Tales of the OSS*. New York: Van Rees Press, 1962

Allen, Peter. *The Crown and the Swastika*. London: Robert Hale Ltd, 1983

Andrew, Christopher. *For the President's Eye's Only: Secret Intelligence and the American Presidency from Washington to Bush*. New York: Harper Collins, 1995

Artibise, Alan. *Winnipeg: An Illustrated History*. Toronto: James Lorimer & Company 1977.

Astley, Joan Bright. *The Inner Circle: A View of War at the Top*. Boston: Little, Brown and Company, 1971.

_____. *The Inner Circle: A View of War at the Top*. London: Hutchinson & Co. Ltd., 1971.

Astley, Joan Bright and Wilkinson Peter. *Gubbins and SOE*. London: Leo Cooper, 1993.

Aarons, Mark and Loftus, John. *Ratlines*. London: Mandarin Paperbacks, 1980.

Barnet, Sylvan, Berman, Morton and Burto, William. *Nine Modern Classics*. Boston: Little, Brown and Company., 1973.

Beesly, Patrick. *Very Special Intelligence*. London: Sphere Books Ltd., 1977.

Bloch, Michael. *Operation Willi*. Toronto: Random House, 1984.

_____. *Wallis and Edward: Letters 1931-1937*. New York: Summit Books, 1986.

_____. *The Duke of Windsor's War*. New York: Coward McCann & Geoghegan, 1983 Boldt, Gerhard. *Hitler's Last Days*. London: Sphere Books Ltd., 1947.

Bothwell, Robert, and Granatstein, JL ed., *The Gouzenko Transcripts*. Ottawa: Deneau Publishers, 1982

Boyle, Andrew. *The Climate of Treason*. London: Coronet Books, 1979.

Braden, Spruille *Diplomats and Demagogues*. New Rochelle NY: Arlington House, 1971.

Brinkley, David. *Washington goes to War*. New York: Ballantine Books, 1988.

Brody, Iles. *Gone with the Windsors*. Toronto: The John C. Winston Company, 1953.

Brown, Anthony Cave. *Bodyguard of Lies*. New York: Harper & Row Publishers, 1975.

_____. *C: The Secret Life of Sir Stewart Graham Menzies*. New York: Macmillan Publishing Company, 1987.

_____. *The Secret War Report of the OSS*. New York: Berkeley Publishing Corporation, 1976.

_____. *Wild Bill Donovan: The Last Hero*. New York: Times Books, 1982

Bryan III, J and Murphy, Charles JV. *The Windsor Story*. New York: William Morrow & Company, Inc.,1979.

Bryce, Ivar. *You Only Live Once: Memories of Ian Fleming*. London: Weidenfeld & Nicolson, 1984.

Bryden, John. *Best-Kept Secret*. Toronto: Lester Publishing Ltd., 1993.

Casey, William. *The Secret War Against Hitler*. Washington: Regnery Gateway, 1988.

Chambers Biographical Dictionary, Edinburgh: W&R Chambers Ltd., 1984.

Chisholm, Anne, & Davie Michael, *Beaverbrook A Life*. London: Hutchinson, 1992.

Churchill, Winston S. *The Gathering Storm*. Boston: Houghton Mifflin Company, 1948.

_____. *Their Finest Hour*. Boston: Houghton Mifflin Company, 1949.

_____. *The Hinge of Fate*. Boston: Houghton Mifflin Company, 1950.

_____. *The Grand Alliance*. Boston: Houghton Mifflin Company, 1950.

_____. *Closing the Ring*. Boston: Houghton Mifflin Company, 1951.

_____. *Triumph and Tragedy*. Boston: Houghton Mifflin Company, 1953.

Cleroux, Richard. *Official Secrets: The Inside Story of the Canadian Security Intelligence Service*. Toronto: M&S Paperbacks, 1990.

Collins, Robert. *Who He?* Vancouver: Greystone Books, 1993.

Colvin, Ian. *Chief of Intelligence*. London: Victor Gollancz Ltd., 1951.

Costello, John. *Mask of Treachery*. New York: Warner Books edition, 1990.

_____. *Ten Days to Destiny*. New York: Morrow, 1991.

Coville John, *Winston Churchill and His Inner Circle*. New York: Wyndam, 1981

Coward, Noel. *Future Indefinite*. New York: Doubleday, 1954

Cull, Nicholas John. *Selling War The British Propaganda Campaign Against American Neutrality in World War II*. New York: Oxford University Press, 1995.

Deacon, Richard. *Spyclopaedia*. London: Futura Publications, 1987.

_____ , and West, Nigel. *SPY!* London: British Broadcasting Corporation, 1980.

Delarue, Jacques. *The Gestapo: A History of Horror.* New York: Dell Publishing Co. Inc.,1964.

De Marigny, Alfred. *A Conspiracy of Crowns.* New York: Crown Publishers, 1990.

Donaldson, Frances. *Edward VIII.* Philadelphia and New York: J.B. Lippincott Company, 1974.

Downes, Donald. *The Scarlet Thread.* Verschoyle, 1953

Dunlop, Richard. *Donovan: America's Master Spy.* Foreword by William Stephenson, New York: Rand McNally & Co., 1982.

Farago, Ladislas. *The Game of the Foxes.* New York: David McKay Company, Inc., 1971.

Farago, Ladislas. *Aftermath.* Simon and Schuster, New York, 1974.

_____. *Burn after Reading: The Espionage History of World War II.* Pinnacle Books, New York City, 1961.

_____. *Burn after Reading.* Macfadden Books, New York, 1961.

_____. *Spymaster.* Paperback Library Inc., New York, 1954.

Finklel, Alvin and Leibovitz, Clement *The Chamberlain-Hitler Collusion.* Halifax: James Lorimer & Company (Merlin Press, UK), 1997.

Fleming, Ian. *From Russia With Love.* London: Gildrose Productions, 1957.

Fromm, Erich. *Escape from Freedom.* New York: Holt, Rinehart and Winston, Inc., 1941.

Gehlen, Reinhard. *The Service.* New York: Popular Press, 1972.

Gentry, Curt. *J Edgar Hoover The Man and the Secrets.* New York: WW Norton & Company, 1991.

Gilbert, Martin, and Gott, Richard. *The Appeasers.* London: Weidenfeld & Nicolson, 1963.

Goldston, Robert. *The Road Between the Wars: 1918-1941,* New York: Fawcett Crest, 1978.

Goralski, Robert. *World War II Almanac: 1931-1945.* New York: GP Putnam's Sons, 1981.

Gouzenko, Igor. *This Was My Choice.* Toronto: JM Dent, 1948

Government of Canada Veterans Affairs, *Uncommon Courage.* Minister of Supply and Services Canada, Ottawa, 1985.

Granatstein, JL & Stafford, David. *Spy Wars.* Toronto: Key Porter Books Ltd., 1990.

Granatstein, JL & Bothwell, Robert, *The Gouzenko Transcripts.* Ottawa: Deneau Publishers, 1982

Grant RG *MI5 MI6 Britain's Security and Intelligence Services.* London: Bison Books 1989

Gray, James H, *Red Lights on the Prairies.* Toronto: Macmillan, 1971.

Greene, Graham, & Greene, Hugh. *The Spy's Bedside Book: An Anthology.* London: R Hart Davis, 1957.

Halter, Jon C *Top Secret Projects of World War II.* New York: Julian Messner, 1978.

Higham, Charles. *The Duchess of Windsor: The Secret Life.* New York: McGraw-Hill Book Company, 1988.

Hilton, Stanley E. *Hitler's Secret War in South America. 1939-1945*, New York: Ballantine Books, 1981.

Hinsley, FH. et al. *British Intelligence in the Second World War*. Vols 1-5. HMSO, 1979-1990.

_____, and Stripp, Alan, ed. *Codebreakers The Inside Story of Bletchley Park*. New York: Oxford University Press, 1993.

Hodges, Andrew. *Alan Turing: The Enigma*, London: Vintage, 1983.

Hohne, Heinz and Zolling, Herman. *The General was a Spy: The Truth about General Gehlen and his Spy Ring*. London: Pan Books Ltd., 1971.

Hyde, Harford Montgomery. *The Quiet Canadian*. London: Hamish Hamilton, 1962.

_____. *Room 3603*. Toronto: Farrar, Straus-Giroux,1962.

_____. *Cynthia*. New York: Ballantine Books, 1965

_____. *The Atom Bomb Spies*. London: Hamish Hamilton, 1980.

_____. *Secret Intelligence Agent*. foreword by William Stephenson. New York: St. Martin's, 1983.

Hutchison, Bruce. *The Unknown Country*. Toronto: Longmans, Green & Company, 1942.

Irving, David. *Churchill's War*. Avon Books, New York, 1987.

_____. *Hess: The Missing Years 1941-1945*. Grafton Books, London, 1987.

Jones, RV *Most Secret War*. Hamish Hamilton Ltd., Great Britain, 1978.

Kahn David. *The Codebreakers*. New York: MacMillan, 1967 (Signet 1973)

_____. *Hitler's Spies: The Extraordinary Story Of German Military Intelligence*. London: Arrow Books, 1978.

_____. *Seizing the Enigma*. Boston: Houghton Mifflin, 1991

Keegan, John. *The Battle for History: Refighting World War Two*. Toronto: Vintage Books 1995

Kennedy, John F. *Why England Slept*. New York: Dolphin Books, 1961.

Lash, Joseph P. *Roosevelt and Churchill*. New York: Norton, 1976.

Lovell, Mary S. *Cast No Shadow: The Life of American Spy Who changed the Course of World War II* . New York: Pantheon, 1992.

Lycett, Andrew. *Ian Fleming*. London: Weidenfeld & Nicolson, 1995.

Mahl, Thomas E. *Desperate Deception: British Covert Operations in the United States*. 1939-44, Brassey's Washington, London, 1998

Masterman, JC *The Double-Cross System in the War of 1939 to 1945*. New Haven and London: Yale University Press.

Neal, Patricia. *As I Am*. London: Arrow edition, 1989.

Nicolson, Harold. *The War Years: Volume II of Diaries and Letters*. New York: Atheneum, 1967.

Ogilvy, David. *Blood Brains and Beer*. London: Hamish Hamilton, 1978.

Payne, Graham, Morley, Sheridan ed. *The Noel Coward Diaries*. London: Weidenfeld & Nicolson, 1982.

Pearson, John. *The Life of Ian Fleming*. New York: McGraw Hill, 1966.

Philby, Kim (Harold Adrian Russell) *My Silent War*. London: MacGibbon 1968, Grafton 1989

Pincher, Chapman. *Their Trade is Treachery*. London: Sidgewick and
  Jackson, 1981.
_____. *Too Secret Too Long*. New York: St. Martin's Press, 1984.
Popov, Dusko. *Spy Counterspy*. Greenwich Conn.: Fawcett Crest 1974
Reader's Digest Association, *The Canadians at War. 1939/45*.
  Volume 1 & 2, Montreal: Reader's Digest Association, 1969.
Rusbridger James, and Nave Eric. *Betrayal at Pearl Harbor*. New York:
  Simon & Shuster
Sklar, Dusty. *The Nazis and the Occult*. New York: Dorset Press 1977
Sherwood Robert, *Roosevelt and Hopkins*. New York: Harper & Bros., 1948.
Sigmundsson Elva. *Icelandic Settlers in North America*. Winnipeg:
  Queenston House Publishing, 1981
Speer Albert, *Inside the Third Reich*. New York: Macmillan. 1970.
Smith, Bradley F. *The Shadow Warriors: OSS and the Origins of the CIA*.
  New York: Basic Books, 1983.
_____. *The Ultra - Magic Deals*. Novato: Presido Press, 1993
Stafford, David. *Camp X*. Toronto: Lester & Orpen Dennys Limited, 1986.
_____. *The Silent Game* .Toronto: Lester & Orpen Dennys Limited, 1988.
_____. *Churchill and Secret Service*. Toronto: Stoddart, 1997.
Stevenson, William. *The Bormann Brotherhood*. New York: Bantam 1974 edition.
_____. *A Man Called Intrepid*. New York: Harcourt Brace Jovanovich, 1976
_____. *Intrepid's Last Case*. New York: Villard Books, 1983.
_____. *Eclipse*. New York: Doubleday & Company, 1986.
Summers, Anthony. *Official and Confidential: The Secret Life of J. Edgar Hoover*.
  New York: GP Putnam's Sons, 1993.
Sawatsky John. *Gouzenko The Untold Story*. Toronto: MacMillan of Canada 1984
Sweet-Escott, Bickham. *Baker Street Irregulars*. Methuen 1965
Taylor, AJP. *Beaverbrook*. New York: Simon and Shuster 1972
Treglown, Jeremy. *Roald Dahl: A Biography*. London: Faber and Faber, 1994.
Troy, Thomas F. *Donovan and the C.I.A.* New York: University Press of
  America, 1981.
_____. *Wild Bill and Intrepid*. New Haven: Yale University Press 1996.
Wallace, Henry A. *The Diary of Henry A Wallace 1942-1946*
  The Price of Vision. Boston: Houghton Mifflin, 1973.
Welchman, Gordon. *The Hut Six Story*. New York: McGraw-Hill, 1982.
West, Nigel. *GCHQ*. London: Weidenfeld & Nicolson, 1986.
_____. *Unreliable Witness*. London: Weidenfeld & Nicolson, 1986.
_____. *MI5: The True Story of the Most Secret Counterespionage Organization in the
World*. New York: Stein and Day, 1982.
_____.ed *The Faber Book of Treachery*. London: Faber & Faber, 1995.
Whiting, Charles, *Gehlen: Germany's Master Spy*. New York:
  Ballantine Books, 1972
Winant, John Gilbert. *Letter From Grosvenor Square*. Boston: Houghton
  Mifflin, 1947.

Windsor, The Duchess of, *The Heart Has Its Reasons*. New York:
Award Books, 1956 (1974 edition)

Windsor, The Duke of, *A King's Story: The Memoirs of the Duke of Windsor*.
New York: GP Putnam, 1951.

Winterbotham, FW. *The Ultra Secret*. London: Weidenfeld & Nicolson, 1974.

_____. *The Nazi Connection* New York: Dell, 1978.

Worthington, Peter. *Looking for Trouble*. Toronto: Key Porter, 1984.

Wright, Peter. *Spycatcher: The Candid Autobiography of a Senior Intelligence Officer*.
New York: Viking, 1987.

Ziegler, Philip. *King Edward VIII: The Official Biography*. London: Collins, 1990.

Selected Articles and Reviews

Collins, Robert. "Master of Intrigue." Champion of Liberty, *Reader's Digest*
December, 1984.

Cavendish Anthony. "Inside Intelligence." *Granta 24* Summer 1988.

Evans, Michael. "The Enigma of a man they call Intrepid" *The Times*
February 18, 1989.

'Mandrake' "Death of an Intrepid Fraud." *The Sunday Telegraph*
February 12, 1989.

Fleming, Ian "Intrepid Silhouette of a Secret Agent." *The Sunday Times*
October 21, 1962.

Le Carre, John. "England's Spy in America." *New York Times Book Review*,
February 29, 1976.

Naftali, Timothy J. "Intrepid's Last Deception: Documenting the Career of
Sir William Stephenson." *Intelligence and National Security* 8 (July 1993): 72-92.

Oursler, Fulton Jr. " Secret Treason: The Shocking Truth about the
Duke of Windsor," *American Heritage*, Volume 42, Number 8, December, 1991.

Porter, McKenzie. "The Biggest Private Eye of All." *Maclean's Magazine*,
December 1, 1952.

Stafford, David. "A Myth Called Intrepid." *Saturday Night* October, 1989.

Saturday Night. Letters. "The Case For Intrepid." October, 1990.

Trevor- Roper, HR. "Superagent." *New York Review of Books* 13, May, 1976.

Troy, Thomas F. "The British Attack on J Edgar Hoover: The Tricycle Case,"
International Journal of Intelligence and CounterIntelligence, Intel Publishing
Group Volume 3, No. 2

Acknowledgements

This work was completed with the assistance of many people such as: Irv Stefansson, Mary Jane Stefansson, Kris Stefansson, Steena Stefansson, Ragnar Gislasson, Margaret Rimmer, Norma Feller, Joan Morrison, Brad Stephenson, Kay Germaine, Elly Heber, Margaret Jamieson, the late Derek Bedson, Joy (Bedson) Grant, Gerald Stephenson, the late George Johnson, the late Douglas Campbell.

Former members of British Security Co-ordination: Molly Phair, Georgie McCance, Ruth Ferguson, the late Marjorie Ferguson, Patsy Sullivan, Mary Taylor, Enid Bence, the late Bill Ross Smith, the late Roald Dahl, the late Pat Bayly, the late Tom Hill, Kathleen Taylor Cockburn, Walter Bell, Betty Raymond, Dolores Hogg, Charmaine Manchee, Helen Wooley, Janet FitzGerald, Gwen Rollaston, the late Nancy Thompson, Dorothy Evanson, Jean Peacock, Marion de Chastelain, and David Ogilvy. Grace Garner's help was invaluable.

Also to: the late Harry Smith, Eric Adams, Norm Delahunty, Hugh Whitney Morrison, Eddie Chow, George Carothers, Thomas F Troy, Mary S Lovell, Anthony Cave Brown, Mark Jaffe, Ron Robbins, Monica Jensen-Stevenson, Andrew Lycett, Peter Worthington, Peter Chapman, McKenzie Porter, Rosalyn Hyde, Joan Bright Astley, Pauline McGibbon, Churchill College (Cambridge), Elizabeth Bennett, Patricia Ackerman, Sheila Claire, University of Regina, Shelley Sweeney, Selina Coward, First Luthern Church (Winnipeg), Gregg Calkin at the Canadian High Commission London, Cross and Cockade, Dr. Rodney Hunter, David Young, Dr Phil Hall, Ken Reddig, James Hutchison, Vaughan Baird, Tom Finkelstein.

Many people from many places provided assistance with such things as transcribing hours of interview tapes, indexing, introducing me to various books, and helping with transportation and overseas research. From Australia: Jane Brockhouse. From Germany: Karen Kosmider, Andreas Hertz. From Switzerland: Nicole Ramseier. From the United States: Renee Johnson, James Bell. From Malaysia: Daljit Singh. From Great Britain: Sarah Betts, Garry Norris, Jule & Kate, Gail Thompson. A special thanks to Mike McNabb in London for his hospitality and assistance. Ross Green, Bruce & Gwen Roberts, Lance Barber, Rick Jost, Tim Dirks, Bill Lawrence. Peter Willms, Peter Hees, Bruce Benson, Kim Wright, David Becket, Marcus Wolfe, and Rod Brecht.

A trip grant was provided by the Manitoba Arts Council. The excerpt From Russia With Love is reprinted by permission of Glidrose Publications Ltd.

In 1994, an Intrepid Society, founded by Winnipegger Syd Davy, was formed to remember the life and work of William Stephenson. In 1997, a Winnipeg library was named after Stephenson. A large statue is being completed by renowned sculptor Leo Mol for display somewhere in Winnipeg.

To my publisher, Tim Lawson and editor, Allan Safarik for their faith in this project and for their effort in getting it into print and to Neil Sawatsky for his inspired design.

And finally, I would like to thank my immediate family, Joan and especially Claire, without whose help this book would not have been possible.

Bill Macdonald
Winnipeg, 1998

Photo credits

Front cover - Insert of William Stephenson,
Maclean's magazine (Cover photo-illustration, N J Sawatsky)
Back cover - (Stephenson group) Margaret Jamieson
Frontispiece - Rockefeller Center, Thomas Airways, NYC

Photos in text:
Bill Macdonald; p. 28, p.187, p. 224, p. 235
Brad Stephenson; p. 36, 37
Churchill Archive Centre, CCC, England; p. 182
NSA, Cryptologic Museum; p. 311
George C Marshall Research Library, Lexington, VA; p. 316
Allan Safarik; p. 432

Photographs, first insert:
Norma Feller; plate 1
Family; plates 2, 3
Norma Feller; plate 4
Margaret Jamieson; plates 6, 7
Allan Safarik; plates 8, 9, 10
Bill Macdonald; plate 11
Margaret Jamieson; plates 12, 13, 14
Wide World Photo; plate 16
Margaret Jamieson; plate 17
Imperial War Museum; plate 18

Photographs, second insert:
Thomas Troy; plates 2, 3
George C Marshall Research Library,
    Lexington, VA; plates 4, 5
Robert Stuart, Camp X Museum; plates 6, 7
Franklin Delano Roosevelt Library; plate 8
Mary Lovell; plate 9
Robert Stuart, Camp X Museum; plate 10
Bill Macdonald; plate 11
Molly Phair (McClelland); plates 12, 13, 14
The late Benjamin de Forest Bayly; plate 15
George C Marshall Research Library,
    Lexington, VA; plate 16
Robert Stuart, Camp X Museum; plate 17
Bill Macdonald; plate 18 (and insert at top)
National Portrait Gallery, London; plate 19
Acme Photo; plate 20
VL Baird; plate 21
Tim Lawson; plates 22, 23

Index

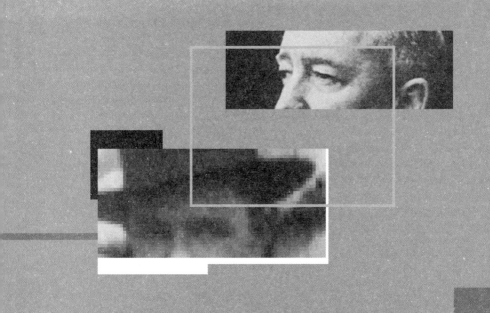

BRITISH SECURITY CO-ORDI

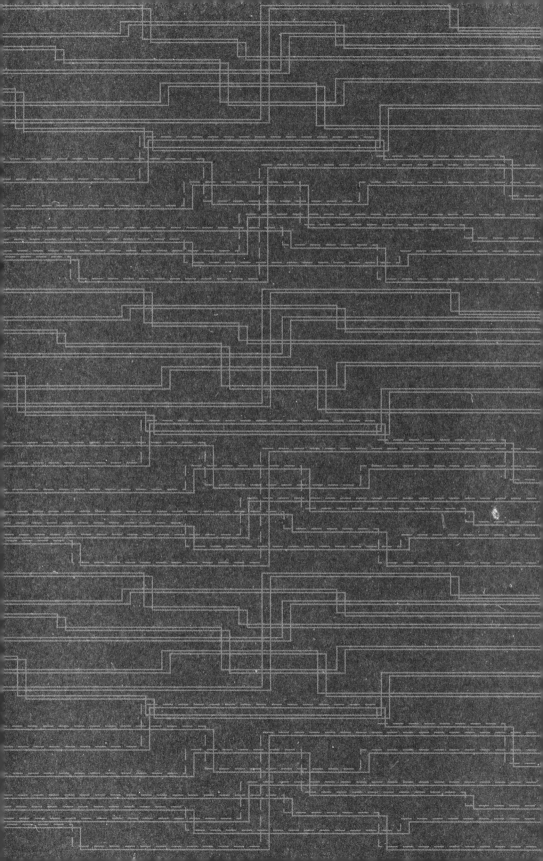

BORN AND RAISED IN WINNIPEG, Bill Macdonald completed his Bachelor of Arts at the University of Manitoba and returned there later for a teaching degree. After teaching for three years in northern Manitoba he travelled around the world for a year, after which he decided to go into journalism. Still bitten by the travel bug, he took over the management of Hostelling International's Winnipeg tourist facility. While working full time, he completed the Creative Communications journalism program at Red River Community College.

After graduation Macdonald free-lanced for Winnipeg publications. Among other assignments he returned to the north for a few weeks to cover the Helen Betty Osborne murder trial in The Pas, Manitoba for Canadian Press, the *Winnipeg Sun,* and the town's newspaper, the *Opasquia Times.* Later Macdonald moved to radio, doing free-lance work for the CBC in Winnipeg and on occasion, he worked as an assistant producer for the morning show. Macdonald has remained involved in the travel business, founding (1991) and operating a seasonal tourist facility—-Guest House International in Winnipeg.

Macdonald, who has become an acknowledged authority on William Stephenson, has been contacted by a number of international authors, and approached for information and quoted by the former staff historian of the Central Intelligence Agency, Thomas Troy for his new history on the agency, *Wild Bill and Intrepid.*